312-9

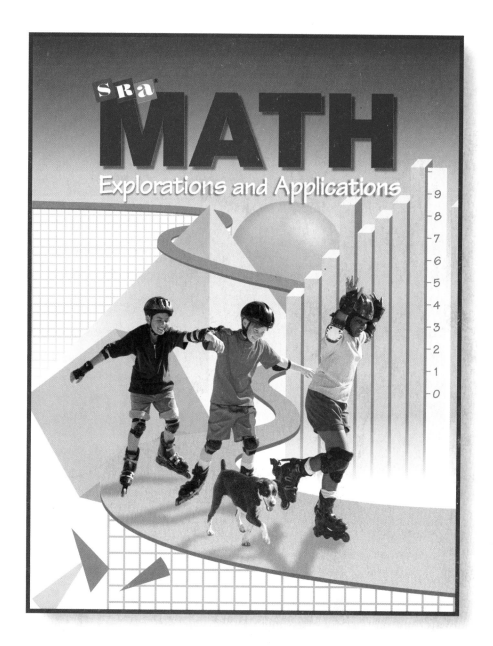

MATH
Explorations and Applications

Stephen S. Willoughby
Carl Bereiter
Peter Hilton
Joseph H. Rubinstein
Coauthor of Thinking Story® selections **Marlene Scardamalia**

SRA McGraw-Hill

Columbus, Ohio

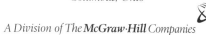

A Division of The McGraw-Hill Companies

SRA/McGraw-Hill

A Division of The **McGraw·Hill** *Companies*

Printed in the United States of America.

Send all inquiries to:
SRA/McGraw-Hill
250 Old Wilson Bridge Road, Suite 310
Worthington, OH 43085

ISBN 0-02-687855-0

2 3 4 5 6 7 8 9 VHP 02 01 00 99 98 97

Contents

■ Application ● Preteaching ▲ Revisiting

Contents

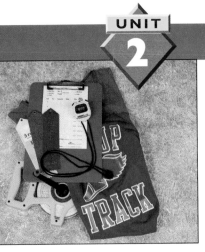

UNIT 2 — Multiplication and Division — 98

UNIT 3 — Algebra Readiness and Geometry — 174

■ Application   ● Preteaching   ▲ Revisiting

Contents

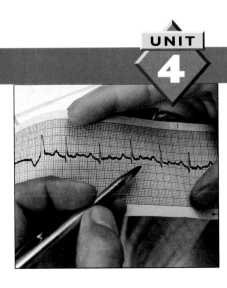

UNIT 4   Multidigit Multiplication   266

■ Application   ● Preteaching   ▲ Revisiting

Contents

UNIT 5 Division   354

■ Application   ● Preteaching   ▲ Revisiting

Contents

UNIT 6 — Fractions and Decimals   430

■ Application   ● Preteaching   ▲ Revisiting

Contents

Resources

■ Application   ● Preteaching   ▲ Revisiting

Dear Student,

You'll find a lot of things in this *Math Explorations and Applications* book. You'll find stories with Mr. Muddle, Ferdie, Portia, Manolita, Marcus, and their friends, whom you may remember from earlier years.

You'll find games that will give you a chance to practice and put to use many of the skills you will be learning.

You'll find stories and examples that will show you how mathematics can help you solve problems and cut down on your work.

You'll be reading and talking about many of the pages with your class. That's because mathematics is something people often learn together and do together.

Of course, this book isn't all fun and games. Learning should be enjoyable, but it also takes time and effort. Most of all, it takes thinking.

We hope you enjoy this book. We hope you learn a lot. And we hope you think a lot.

The Authors of *Math Explorations and Applications*

UNIT 1

Addition and Subtraction

UNDERSTANDING NUMBER

- place value

- perimeter

- reading maps

- fractions

- decimals

SCHOOL TO WORK CONNECTION

Chefs use math . . .

The ingredients for most recipes are measured in fractional amounts like $\frac{1}{2}$ cup or $\frac{1}{4}$ teaspoon. When a chef doubles a recipe, he or she must know how to add fractions. To cut a recipe in half, the chef subtracts fractions. A chef must also determine cooking or baking time and temperature.

3

ACT IT OUT

Estimating

A Basket of Apples

The Cortland Apple Orchard gave Jeremy a crate of apples for his school. Help him estimate how many apples there are in the crate. You may want to act out the students taking apples to help solve the problem.

1. Write down your best estimate of how many apples there are in the crate.

◆ How did you make your estimate?

◆ Do you think you have a good chance of being exactly right?

Jeremy's friends helped him carry away the apples.

2 Ten children took ten apples each. How many apples did they take?

There were still lots of apples left.

◆ Now do you know exactly how many apples there were all together?

3 Make a second estimate of how many apples there were.

Then ten more children came. They each took ten apples. Then the crate looked like this.

4 So far, 20 children have taken ten apples each. How many apples is that?

5 Make a third estimate of how many apples there were.

◆ **LESSON 1** Estimating

More children came and took apples.

6 So far, 30 children have taken ten apples each. How many apples have they taken?

◆ How many apples do you think are left?

7 Make a fourth estimate of how many apples there were.

All 30 children came back. They each took another ten apples.

8 Counting both times the children took some apples, how many apples did each child take?

9 How many apples have the 30 children taken all together?

10 Make a fifth estimate of how many apples there were.

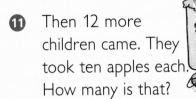

11 Then 12 more children came. They took ten apples each. How many is that?

12 How many apples have been taken all together?

13 How many apples are left?

14 How many apples were there all together?

◆ Is this an estimate, or are you certain?

◆ What was your first estimate about how many apples there were?

◆ What was your second estimate? What was your third estimate?

◆ What was your fourth estimate? What was your fifth estimate?

◆ Did your estimates get closer?

In your Math Journal explain how you made your estimates.

Place Value

Place value lets us read and write numbers of any size using only ten digits. In this lesson you'll explore place value by thinking about groups of tacks.

The Eversharp Company makes and sells tacks. The tacks are packaged like this:

		Number of Tacks	
		one	1
There are ten tacks on a **strip.**		ten	10
There are ten strips on a **card.**		one hundred	100
There are ten cards in a **box.**		one thousand	1,000
There are ten boxes in a **case.**		ten thousand	10,000
There are ten cases in a **shipping carton.**		one hundred thousand	100,000

	Number of Tacks	
There are ten shipping cartons in a **vanload.**	one million	1,000,000
There are ten vanloads in a **truckload.**	ten million	10,000,000

Write the number of tacks. The first one has been done for you. Watch your numbering.

1. 2 shipping cartons and 2 boxes **202,000**

2. 4 cases and 8 cards

3. 3 truckloads and 6 cases

4. 4 shipping cartons, 3 boxes, and 1 strip

5. 6 vanloads, 7 cases, and 10 cards

6. 8 shipping cartons and 4 strips

7. 11 cases, 8 cards, and 12 strips

8. 1 truckload, 2 boxes, and 8 strips

9. 3 truckloads, 3 vanloads, and 9 cards

10. 11 cases and 11 strips

11. 1 truckload and 1 box

12. 3 shipping cartons and 1 case

13. 2 cards and 1 strip

14. 4 vanloads and 2 cases

15. 8 truckloads and 2 cases

◆ How would you say each number?
(For problem 1, you would say
"two hundred two thousand.")

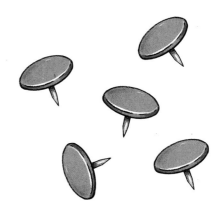

◆ **LESSON 2 Place Value**

GEOGRAPHY CONNECTION

As of mid-1995, the population of Myanmar (formerly Burma) was estimated to be 45,103,809. This lesson will show you how to read that number, and other numbers, by using place value.

MILLIONS			THOUSANDS					
Hundreds	Tens	Ones	Hundreds	Tens	Ones	Hundreds	Tens	Ones
	4	5	1	0	3	8	0	9

Forty-five million, one hundred three thousand, eight hundred nine

The 4 stands for 4 ten millions.	40,000,000
The 5 stands for 5 millions.	5,000,000
The 1 stands for 1 hundred thousand.	100,000
The 0 stands for 0 ten thousands.	0
The 3 stands for 3 thousands.	3,000
The 8 stands for 8 hundreds.	800
The 0 stands for 0 tens.	0
The 9 stands for 9 ones.	9

Write the numbers in standard form. The first one has been done for you.

16 700 + 30 + 5   **735**

17 9 + 100 + 2000

18 50 + 5

19 900,000 + 6,000 + 500

20 600 + 20 + 7

21 500,000 + 6 + 7,000

22 1000 + 400 + 8

23 40 + 9 + 90,000

24 400,000 + 50 + 7

25 80,000,000 + 300,000 + 9,000 + 200

26 9000 + 10 + 1

27 20 + 700 + 800,000

28 10,000 + 4,000 + 400

29 7,000,000 + 300,000 + 60,000 + 900

30 8000 + 10

31 50,000,000 + 30,000

GAME

Roll a Number Game

Players:	Two or more
Materials:	One 0–5 cube (red)
Object:	To make the greatest three-digit number
Math Focus:	Place value and mathematical reasoning

RULES

1. Draw lines for a three-digit number on your paper, like this:

   _____   _____   _____

2. The first player rolls the cube three times.

3. Each time the cube is rolled, write that number in one of the three blanks you made. After all three rolls, you will have made a three-digit number.

4. The player who makes the greatest three-digit number is the winner of the round.

SAMPLE GAME

Number Rolled:	Amy's Number:	Jack's Number:	Ellen's Number:
First roll **3**	3 _ _	_ _ 3	_ 3 _
Second roll **1**	3 _ 1	_ 1 3	_ 3 1
Third roll **5**	3 5 1	5 1 3	5 3 1

Ellen won this round.

OTHER WAYS TO PLAY THIS GAME

1. The least three-digit number wins.

2. Make a four-digit number. (Roll the cube four times.)

3. The greatest even number wins.

4. Use a 5–10 cube (blue). If a 10 is rolled, roll that cube again.

LESSON
3

Numerical Sequence

Sometimes it's useful to count up. Sometimes it's useful to count down.

Count up. Write the missing numbers.

1 7, 8, 9, 10, 11, ■, ■, ■, ■, ■, ■, ■, 19

2 194, 195, 196, ■, ■, ■, ■, ■, ■, ■, 204

3 2987, 2988, 2989, ■, ■, ■, ■, ■, ■, ■, ■, 2998

4 5098, 5099, ■, ■, ■, 5103

5 36,571; 36,572; ■; ■; ■; ■; ■; ■; ■; ■; 36,581

Count down. Write the missing numbers.

6 15, 14, 13, ■, ■, ■, ■, ■, ■, ■, ■, 4

7 64, 63, 62, ■, ■, ■, ■, ■, ■, ■, ■, 53

8 334, 333, 332, ■, ■, ■, ■, ■, ■, 325

9 805, 804, 803, ■, ■, ■, ■, ■, ■, 796

10 8403, 8402, 8401, ■, ■, ■, ■, ■, 8395

Count up or down. Write the missing numbers.

11 13,207; 13,208; 13,209; ■; ■; ■; ■; 13,214

12 9996; 9997; 9998; ■; ■; ■; ■; 10,003

13 38,004; 38,003; 38,002; ■; ■; ■; 37,998

14 146,236; 146,235; 146,234; ■; ■; ■; ■; 146,229

15 999,997; 999,998; ■; ■; ■; ■; 1,000,003

12 • Addition and Subtraction

GAME

Order Game

Players:	Two
Materials:	Two 0–5 cubes (red), two 5–10 cubes (blue)
Object:	To be the first to fill in all the boxes
Math Focus:	Place value and mathematical reasoning

RULES

1. Make a game form like the one shown.

2. Roll any three cubes. If you roll a 10, roll that cube again.

3. Combine any two numbers rolled to make a two-digit number. Write your first number in the START box on your game form.

4. On each turn, choose three cubes to roll. Make a two-digit number greater than the last number you made and write it in the next box.

5. If you cannot make a greater two-digit number, or if you choose not to, you lose your turn.

6. The first player to fill in all the boxes on his or her game form is the winner.

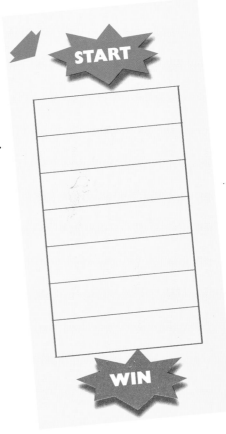

ANOTHER WAY TO PLAY THIS GAME

Roll four cubes and make three-digit numbers.

MATH JOURNAL

In your Math Journal explain your strategy for playing this game.

Greatest and Least Numbers

Because of place value, the same digits can stand for different numbers. For example, a 7 and a 4 can make 74 or 47. In this lesson you'll use the same digits to make greater and lesser numbers.

You can make different numbers using the digits 5, 2, and 8.

The greatest number you can make is 852.

The least number you can make is 258.

Use a computer or other means to copy and complete the chart.

	Use These Digits	Greatest Number	Least Number
1	4, 7, 1	■	■
2	6, 5	■	■
3	3, 9	■	■
4	6, 7, 1	■	■
5	8, 3, 3	■	■
6	1, 9, 9	■	■
7	6, 9, 1, 2	■	■
8	7, 5, 7, 5	■	■
9	1, 6, 2, 2, 4	■	■
10	4, 3, 3, 6, 6	■	■

You can make six different numbers using the digits 1, 2, and 3. Here are the six numbers in order from greatest to least:

321   312   231   213   132   123

Write six different numbers in order from greatest to least.

11 Use the digits 4, 5, and 6.   **12** Use the digits 2, 6, and 8.

COOPERATIVE LEARNING

GAME

Roll a 15 Game

Players:	Two
Materials:	Two 0–5 cubes (red), two 5–10 cubes (blue)
Object:	To get the sum closer to 15
Math Focus:	Addition, subtraction, and mathematical reasoning

RULES

1. Roll the cubes one at a time.

2. Add the numbers as you roll. The sum of all the cubes you roll should be as close to 15 as possible.

3. You may stop after two, three, or four rolls.

4. The player with the sum closer to 15 wins the round.

If you rolled:	The sum would be:
7 and 1 and 4 and 7	19
8 and 5	13
4 and 4 and 8	16
9 and 3 and 3	15
5 and 10	15

ANOTHER WAY TO PLAY THIS GAME

Start at 20 and subtract the numbers rolled. Try to get as close to 5 as possible.

MATH JOURNAL

In your Math Journal describe your strategy for playing this game.

LESSON 5

Practicing Addition

Keep in shape by practicing your number facts for addition.

SELF ASSESSMENT

Are You Shiny or Rusty?

Very shiny   46 or more right
Shiny   41–45 right
A bit rusty   36–40 right
Rusty   Fewer than 36 right

The letter *n* stands for an unknown number. To solve for *n*, figure out the number that belongs where the *n* is.

Add to solve for *n*.

1 $5 + 3 = n$ 2 $9 + 9 = n$ 3 $4 + 1 = n$

4 $n = 6 + 2$ 5 $6 + 4 = n$ 6 $n = 6 + 6$

7 $7 + 1 = n$ 8 $n = 4 + 6$ 9 $10 + 9 = n$

10 $1 + 7 = n$ 11 $8 + 8 = n$ 12 $0 + 8 = n$

13 $n = 5 + 5$ 14 $1 + 9 = n$ 15 $n = 5 + 7$

16 $10 + 10 = n$ 17 $8 + 4 = n$ 18 $4 + 7 = n$

19 $8 + 7 = n$ 20 $7 + 7 = n$ 21 $n = 0 + 0$

22 $6 + 5 = n$ 23 $6 + 7 = n$ 24 $3 + 9 = n$

25 $9 + 2 = n$ 26 $9 + 5 = n$ 27 $3 + 8 = n$

Add.

28	6	29	7	30	2	31	3	32	2	33	1	34	4
	+ 5		+ 9		+ 2		+ 7		+ 8		+ 9		+ 8

35	3	36	0	37	8	38	6	39	7	40	4	41	1
	5		6		3		6		8		4		3
	+ 2		+ 9		+ 9		+ 6		+ 3		+ 4		+ 4

Add to solve for _n_.

42 $5 + 3 + 3 + 3 + 4 = n$ 43 $7 + 1 + 3 + 4 + 3 = n$

44 $4 + 4 + 4 + 4 + 4 = n$ 45 $3 + 3 + 3 + 2 + 2 = n$

46 $n = 1 + 2 + 3 + 4 + 5$ 47 $n = 5 + 4 + 3 + 2 + 1$

48 $n = 3 + 3 + 3 + 3 + 3$ 49 $n = 1 + 5 + 2 + 4 + 3$

Solve.

50 Connie and her brother Dan each have two cats. Their cousin Jim has three cats. How many cats do they have all together?

51 Mary had nine CDs, then she received one CD for her birthday. How many CDs does Mary have now?

About 3000 tons of dusty material from space falls on Earth every day.

◆ **LESSON 5** Practicing Addition

Muddle at Bat

Part 1

Mr. Muddle was looking for a job again. At last he was hired by a baseball team, the Lakeside Dips. The first day Mr. Muddle came to work wearing a catcher's mask and a fielder's glove. "I'm ready to play any position," he said.

"Position?" grumbled the manager. "We didn't hire you to play ball. We hired you to be a tester."

"What's that?"

"You will test balls, bats, gloves, and so on. We want to know which ones we should buy. For a start, test these three kinds of bats. Find out which kind is best."

Mr. Muddle had been watching TV. He had seen that when people want to find out which things are best, they often ask doctors. So Mr. Muddle took the three bats to all the doctors in town. He asked each doctor which bat he or she thought was best.

When he was finished, Mr. Muddle went back to the manager. This was his report: "Three doctors told me they thought the Slugger bat was best. One doctor said the Arrow looked best. Two said they liked the Champ. The other 54 doctors either said they didn't know anything about baseball bats or said they didn't want to be bothered."

"What does that tell you?" the manager asked.

"It tells me the Slugger bat is best, of course," Mr. Muddle said.

The manager snorted. "It tells *me* nine out of ten doctors would rather not be asked," he said.

. . . to be continued

Work in groups. Discuss your answers and how you figured them out. Then compare your answers with those of other groups.

1 Do you agree with Mr. Muddle that his test shows the Slugger bat is best? Why or why not?

2 What are some good qualities to test a bat for? List as many as you can think of.

3 Why do you think the manager said that nine out of ten doctors would rather not be asked about bats?

Practicing Subtraction

Keep in shape by practicing your number facts for subtraction.

SELF ASSESSMENT

Are You Shiny or Rusty?

Very shiny	64 or more right
Shiny	59–63 right
A bit rusty	54–58 right
Rusty	Fewer than 54 right

Subtract to solve for *n*.

1 $5 - 3 = n$
2 $10 - 5 = n$
3 $13 - 6 = n$

4 $8 - 3 = n$
5 $n = 9 - 7$
6 $15 - 6 = n$

7 $12 - 7 = n$
8 $16 - 8 = n$
9 $n = 17 - 8$

10 $18 - 9 = n$
11 $n = 16 - 9$
12 $13 - 9 = n$

13 $6 - 1 = n$
14 $20 - 10 = n$
15 $n = 14 - 6$

16 $n = 12 - 6$
17 $14 - 5 = n$
18 $14 - 7 = n$

19 $15 - 6 = n$
20 $6 - 5 = n$
21 $n = 12 - 9$

22 $9 - 9 = n$
23 $7 - 7 = n$
24 $13 - 7 = n$

25 $9 - 0 = n$
26 $n = 13 - 8$
27 $9 - 8 = n$

28 $14 - 2 = n$
29 $11 - 8 = n$
30 $6 - 3 = n$

31 $n = 18 - 10$
32 $n = 11 - 8$
33 $8 - 0 = n$

34 $13 - 5 = n$
35 $15 - 7 = n$
36 $4 - 3 = n$

Subtract.

③⑦ 10   ③⑧ 6   ③⑨ 12   ④⓪ 18   ④① 20   ④② 15
  − 5   − 5   − 7   − 9   − 10   − 2

④③ 13   ④④ 16   ④⑤ 12   ④⑥ 8   ④⑦ 10   ④⑧ 4
  − 7   − 5   − 9   − 8   − 8   − 2

④⑨ 6   ⑤⓪ 14   ⑤① 19   ⑤② 4   ⑤③ 17   ⑤④ 8
  − 5   − 7   − 10   − 3   − 8   − 7

⑤⑤ 7   ⑤⑥ 9   ⑤⑦ 16   ⑤⑧ 17   ⑤⑨ 10   ⑥⓪ 16
  − 4   − 5   − 7   − 9   − 2   − 8

⑥① 17   ⑥② 10   ⑥③ 8   ⑥④ 4   ⑥⑤ 6   ⑥⑥ 2
  − 4   − 1   − 0   − 3   − 2   − 2

Solve.

⑥⑦ Ann had ten marbles. She gave six of them to her friend Wendy. How many marbles does Ann have left?

⑥⑧ Tom received eight presents for his birthday. He unwrapped three of them at his party. How many presents does Tom still have to unwrap?

⑥⑨ The bicycle shop had 12 new mountain bikes to sell. On Saturday eight of them were sold. How many mountain bikes are left?

Skin is the body's largest organ. An average adult human is covered by 14 to 18 square feet of skin, which weighs about 6 pounds.

LESSON 7

Adding and Subtracting

Try to solve addition and subtraction facts as fast as you can.

SELF ASSESSMENT

Are You Shiny or Rusty?

Very shiny 30 or more right

Shiny 25–29 right

A bit rusty 20–24 right

Rusty Fewer than 20 right

Add or subtract to solve for *n*. Watch the signs.

1. $6 + 9 = n$
2. $0 + 0 = n$
3. $14 - 8 = n$
4. $12 - 7 = n$
5. $14 - 5 = n$
6. $n = 7 + 5$
7. $19 - 10 = n$
8. $n = 10 + 10$
9. $3 + 3 = n$
10. $6 - 6 = n$
11. $n = 14 - 9$
12. $2 + 10 = n$
13. $6 + 6 = n$
14. $n = 15 - 7$
15. $7 + 3 = n$
16. $16 - 8 = n$
17. $n = 9 + 5$
18. $n = 13 - 8$
19. $7 + 7 = n$
20. $5 + 5 = n$
21. $1 + 1 = n$
22. $n = 2 + 8$
23. $13 - 5 = n$
24. $15 - 8 = n$
25. $n = 15 - 5$
26. $17 - 10 = n$
27. $4 + 8 = n$
28. $8 + 7 = n$
29. $6 + 7 = n$
30. $16 - 9 = n$

Add or subtract.

31. $\begin{array}{r} 8 \\ + 5 \\ \hline \end{array}$
32. $\begin{array}{r} 2 \\ + 2 \\ \hline \end{array}$
33. $\begin{array}{r} 15 \\ - 9 \\ \hline \end{array}$
34. $\begin{array}{r} 9 \\ + 9 \\ \hline \end{array}$
35. $\begin{array}{r} 10 \\ + 5 \\ \hline \end{array}$

You can use your addition and subtraction skills to figure out distances on a map.

Study the map. Then answer the questions.

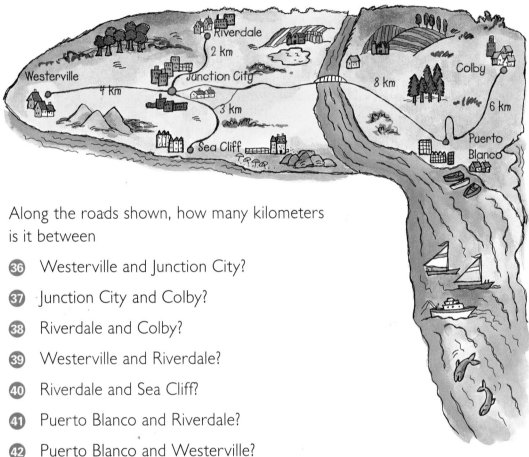

Along the roads shown, how many kilometers is it between

36 Westerville and Junction City?

37 Junction City and Colby?

38 Riverdale and Colby?

39 Westerville and Riverdale?

40 Riverdale and Sea Cliff?

41 Puerto Blanco and Riverdale?

42 Puerto Blanco and Westerville?

43 Sea Cliff and Colby?

44 Westerville and Sea Cliff?

45 Westerville and Colby?

46 From Westerville, is it a shorter trip to Puerto Blanco or to Sea Cliff? How much shorter?

47 From Colby, is it a longer trip to Sea Cliff or to Riverdale? How much longer?

48 Which is farther, Junction City to Sea Cliff or Junction City to Riverdale? How much farther?

49 If you drove from Westerville to Sea Cliff to Riverdale, how many kilometers would you drive in all?

LESSON 8

Practicing Addition and Subtraction

ALGEBRA READINESS

Suppose you put a number into this function machine. The machine will add 5 to it. We say that the function rule for this machine is +5.

in +5 out

If you put 3 into the machine, 8 will come out.

If you put 5 into the machine, 10 will come out.

Use a computer or other means to draw and complete this chart for a +5 function machine.

+5

In	Out
3	8
5	10
7	▪
9	▪
11	▪
13	▪

Use a computer or other means to draw and complete each chart. Watch the function rule.

① -5

In	Out
10	5
12	7
14	9
16	
18	
20	

② +2

In	Out
0	2
1	
2	
3	
4	
5	

③ -3

In	Out
4	
7	
10	
13	
16	
19	

④ +10

In	Out
40	
50	
60	
70	
80	
90	

⑤ +9

In	Out
1	
2	
3	
4	
5	
6	

⑥ -4

In	Out
14	
12	
10	
8	
6	
4	

⑦ -10

In	Out
60	
50	
40	
30	
20	
10	

⑧ +7

In	Out
2	
3	
5	
6	
8	
9	

⑨ -6

In	Out
19	
17	
15	
13	
11	
9	

◆ **LESSON 8   Practicing Addition and Subtraction**

In solving problems like these, you may find it helpful to draw pictures or act out the stories. All prices include sales tax.

Lydia has $18. Josh has $13.

10 Does Lydia have enough money to buy a checkers set, a calculator, and a bicycle horn?

11 Suppose Josh buys a checkers set and pays for it with a $10 bill. How much change should he get?

12 Lydia has already spent $5 today. If she buys a bicycle horn, how much will she have spent today?

13 Suppose Lydia buys a checkers set and a calculator. How much money will she have left?

14 Suppose Josh owes his mother $5 and wants to give it to her today. Would he be able to give it to her if he buys

   a. only the bicycle horn?

   b. only the checkers set?

   c. only two checkers sets?

Use the information on page 26 to help you answer these questions.

15 Suppose Lydia decides to buy a calculator.

    a. How much money will she have left?

    b. If she then wants to buy a basketball, will she have enough money?

16 Suppose the store owner puts the basketballs on sale for $9. How much has the price been lowered?

17 Suppose Josh buys a calculator and a softball. Will he be on time for the 3:00 softball game?

$3.00

$5.00

$10.00

$13.00

18 Suppose Lydia buys a basketball and Josh buys a checkers set and a can of tennis balls.

    a. Who spent more money?

    b. How much more?

    c. Can Josh now buy a bicycle horn?

    d. Can Lydia now buy a softball and a can of tennis balls?

To figure the temperature (in degrees Fahrenheit), count the number of times a cricket chirps in 15 seconds and add 37.

LESSON 9

Missing Addends

Jeremy's class is doing the "Numbers on the Back" activity.

$$4 + n = 9$$

What number does Jeremy have on his back?

ALGEBRA READINESS

In each case, write the number that Jeremy has on his back. The first one has been done for you.

	Brittany has:	The sum is:	Jeremy has:
1	9	14	5
2	6	16	■
3	2	8	■
4	7	14	■
5	7	16	■
6	10	11	■
7	3	9	■
8	0	6	■
9	7	15	■
10	8	8	■

In each problem below, think of the *n* as a number on your back that you can't see. You can see the other number on a partner's back and the class has told you the sum or difference. If they told you the difference, they also told you whose number was greater.

Solve for *n*.

11 $n + 5 = 7$ 12 $15 - n = 10$ 13 $2 + n = 10$

14 $2 + n = 7$ 15 $15 - n = 9$ 16 $n + 6 = 15$

17 $10 - n = 6$ 18 $15 - n = 8$ 19 $10 + n = 20$

20 $10 - n = 4$ 21 $0 + n = 9$ 22 $n + 6 = 14$

23 $n - 10 = 6$ 24 $3 + n = 13$ 25 $2 + n = 12$

26 $7 + n = 10$ 27 $3 + n = 12$ 28 $6 + n = 18$

29 $8 + n = 10$ 30 $n + 4 = 13$ 31 $0 + n = 8$

32 $9 + n = 10$ 33 $n + 5 = 13$ 34 $9 + n = 12$

35 $10 + n = 10$ 36 $n + 6 = 13$ 37 $2 + n = 12$

38 $8 + n = 17$ 39 $9 + n = 18$ 40 $4 + n = 15$

Does the missing-term sentence help you solve the problem? Solve for *n*.

41 Abigail has seven horse figures. She would like to have ten horse figures. How many more horse figures does she need?
$$7 + n = 10$$

42 Sam plans to take a 10-mile bicycle trip. He has already ridden 4 miles. How far does he still have to go?
$$4 + n = 10$$

43 Kumar had 12 crayons. He lost some. He still has eight crayons. How many did he lose?
$$12 - n = 8$$

44 Wendy is reading a story that starts on page 1 and ends on page 12. She just finished reading page 8. How many more pages does she have to read?
$$8 + n = 12$$

◆ **LESSON 9   Missing Addends**

Solve.

45 Barbara's family lives 15 kilometers from Sandy Hook Beach. They left home to drive to Sandy Hook Beach. They have already driven 8 kilometers. How much farther is it to the beach?

46 Brenda sells hot dogs at the game. She began with $8 in her pocket. Now she has $17. How much money has she taken in so far?

47 Ricardo's cat had a litter of kittens. He has found homes for two of them. He needs to find homes for the other four. How many kittens were in the litter?

48 Isaac wants to buy a video that costs $16. He has earned $7. How much more money does he need?

49 Yesterday Mina bought a bag of marbles. She lost nine playing with Tran. Now she has only nine marbles. How many were in the bag?

The squid has the largest eyes of any animal yet discovered. Its eyes are the size of dinner plates.

Solve these problems.

50. Andy has four cents. He wants nine cents for milk money. How much more money does he need?

51. Jiro gave away two bananas. He has six left. How many bananas did he start with?

52. Last night Trina had five apples, but she ate some. How many does she have now?

53. After his birthday, Karim had 12 model rockets. He broke some and now has nine rockets left. How many rockets did he break?

54. During band Quentin broke three clarinet reeds. Now he has four reeds. How many reeds did he have at the beginning of band?

55. After school Paco ate three cookies from the plate. Now there are five left. How many cookies were on the plate when Paco came home from school?

56. Olga has to do ten math problems. She has done six problems. How many problems are left to do?

57. Every week Ines runs 14 kilometers. She has run 10 kilometers so far this week. How many more kilometers does she need to run this week?

58. Yesterday Vera had five baseball cards, then she won some more. How many does she have now?

59. Chloe picked nine baskets of strawberries. She needs 20 baskets to make some jam. How many more baskets must she pick?

LESSON 10

Perimeter

The **perimeter** of a figure is the distance around it. To find the perimeter of this square, add 3 + 3 + 3 + 3.

The perimeter is 12 centimeters.

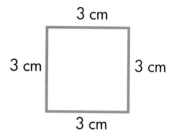

3 cm

3 cm   3 cm

3 cm

Find the perimeter.

1

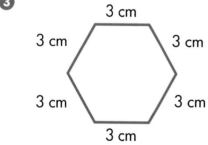

3 cm

2 cm   2 cm

3 cm

2

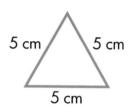

5 cm   5 cm

5 cm

3

3 cm

3 cm   3 cm

3 cm   3 cm

3 cm

4

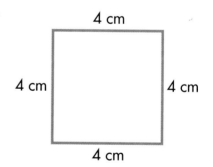

4 cm

4 cm   4 cm

4 cm

5

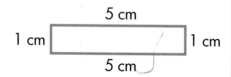

5 cm

1 cm   1 cm

5 cm

6

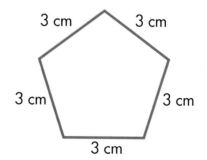

3 cm   3 cm

3 cm   3 cm

3 cm

Solve these problems. Drawing diagrams might help.

7 Central Park is shaped like a rectangle. The length of one side of the park is 300 yards. A second side is 150 yards. If Troy runs around the perimeter of the park, how far will he run?

8 One side of Seward Park, which is square-shaped, measures 235 yards. What length of fencing is needed to completely fence in the park?

9 In an equilateral triangle, all three sides are equal. The perimeter of a garden shaped like an equilateral triangle is 24 feet. What is the length of each of the sides?

10 In an isosceles triangle, two sides are equal. The perimeter of an isosceles triangle is 30 inches. One of its sides is 12 inches. What are the lengths of the other sides?

11 On a baseball field, all of the bases lie at the corners of a square. The distance between first and second base is 90 feet.

   a. How far is it around the bases?

   b. About how far does a player run if he or she hits a triple?

12 Go to the library to find out the dimensions of a football field.

   a. What is the length of the field?

   b. What is the width of the field?

   c. What is the perimeter of the field?

13 Each side of a square measures 5 centimeters. What is its perimeter?

◆ **LESSON 10 Perimeter**

Muddle at Bat

Part 2

You may want to refer to the first part of the Thinking Story, on pages 18–19.

The manager's face turned red with anger. "I don't care what doctors say about a bat. I want to know how well a bat does what it's supposed to do. How well does it swing? How far can it hit a ball? How strong is it?"

Mr. Muddle first set out to test the bats for hitting. He asked the pitcher to throw to him as he tested the bats. Mr. Muddle swung at ten pitches with the Slugger bat. He missed every time. Then he changed to the Arrow bat. He kept missing with it, too. On the 24th pitch, he managed to hit a ball. The ball went hopping back to the pitcher.

"Nice hit, Mr. Muddle," said the pitcher. "Just ten times farther and you'd have had a home run."

Finally Mr. Muddle tried the Champ bat. He made 17 swings and misses. By then the pitcher was tired of throwing to him and quit. Mr. Muddle reported to the manager. "I'm proud to say that the Arrow bat is far better than any other for getting hits."

. . . to be continued

Work in groups. Discuss your answers and how you figured them out. Then compare your answers with those of other groups.

1. Why did Mr. Muddle say the Arrow bat is best? What do you think?

2. What are some reasons why Mr. Muddle might have hit the ball with the Arrow bat and not with the others?

3. What would be a better way to find out which bat is best for getting hits?

4. For a home run the ball would have to go about 120 meters. If the pitcher is right, how far did Mr. Muddle hit the ball?

LESSON
11

Using Maps and Charts

You can often tell when answers are wrong, even without calculating the solution.

GEOGRAPHY
CONNECTION

Estimate the driving distances, in kilometers, between the following United States cities. For each pair of cities four distances are given in kilometers, but only one is correct. Select the correct distance.

1 New York City to Washington, D.C.

    a. 1974   **b.** 375   **c.** 1050   **d.** 35

2 New York City to Atlanta

    a. 503   **b.** 3475   **c.** 1020   **d.** 1353

3 Los Angeles to Miami

    a. 4323   **b.** 6219   **c.** 3219   **d.** 649

4 Denver to New York City

    a. 1594   **b.** 2849   **c.** 4129   **d.** 739

5 Chicago to Dallas

    a. 1475   **b.** 2138   **c.** 931   **d.** 4321

6 Chicago to Denver

    a. 976   **b.** 1201   **c.** 3011   **d.** 1603

7 Cleveland to Seattle

    a. 4975   **b.** 3232   **c.** 3778   **d.** 2178

Study the chart. Then answer the questions for the cities listed in the table.

Population Change in Five U.S. Cities

City	1970 Population	1980 Population	1990 Population
Anchorage, Alaska	48,081	174,431	226,338
Cleveland, Ohio	750,879	573,822	505,616
Dallas, Texas	844,401	904,599	1,007,618
New York City, New York	7,895,563	7,071,639	7,322,564
Phoenix, Arizona	584,303	789,704	983,403

8 Name the city or cities that had a smaller population in 1990 than in 1970.

9 Name the city or cities that had a greater population in 1990 than in 1970.

10 Name the city with the greatest population in 1970. In 1980. In 1990.

11 How many people lived in Dallas in 1980? Do you think your answer is exactly right?

12 Which city showed the greatest gain in population when you compare 1970 and 1990?

13 Which city showed the greatest loss in population when you compare 1970 and 1990?

14 Did any city lose in population between 1970 and 1980 and gain in population between 1980 and 1990? If so, which city or cities?

Use information in the chart to make up two more problems. Write them in your Math Journal.

LESSON 12

Multidigit Addition

HEALTH CONNECTION

Sean orders a slice of pepperoni pizza and a garden salad with dressing. The salad has 225 calories. The pizza has 389 calories. Add to find the total number of calories in Sean's meal.

Add: 225 + 389 = ?

Here's how:

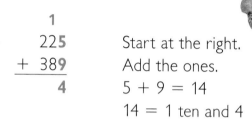

```
  1
  225
+ 389
    4
```
Start at the right.
Add the ones.
5 + 9 = 14
14 = 1 ten and 4

```
 11
  225
+ 389
   14
```
Add the tens.
1 + 2 + 8 = 11
There are 11 tens.
11 tens = 1 hundred and 1 ten

```
 11
  225
+ 389
  614
```
Add the hundreds.
1 + 2 + 3 = 6
There are 6 hundreds.
Sean's meal has 614 calories.

Remember: Start at the right. Use the same rules in every column.

Here are more examples:

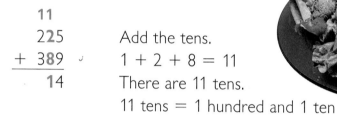

```
 11  11
 2 3 , 4 7 5
+ 4 8 , 6 3 9
 7 2 , 1 1 4
```

```
   1   1
   4 9 0 7
+    6 8 5
   5 5 9 2
```

Add. Use shortcuts when you can.

1   35
    + 42

2   92
    + 30

3   25
    + 25

4   75
    + 75

5   63
    + 72

6   125
    + 237

7   499
    + 499

8   562
    + 31

9   602
    + 718

10   100
    + 95

11   500
    + 499

12   5712
    + 6314

13   15,576
    + 37,659

14   89,341
    + 10,659

15   4315
    + 2690

16   1395
    + 7239

17   29,324
    + 65,591

18   323,759,902
    + 474,621,326

19   35
    63
    + 75

20   19
    25
    36
    + 143

21   31
    25
    324
    + 567

22   25
    25
    25
    + 25

23   565
    394
    237
    + 465

24   600
    + 900

25   2374
    + 1042

26   464
    + 280

27   621
    + 289

28   297
    + 30

◆ LESSON 12 Multidigit Addition

Without using pencil and paper, you can often tell whether an answer could be right.

Jensen's TV Store

ITEM	COST	
M2117		
Television	$375	62
Tax	26	29
Total	$638	52

In each problem, two of the answers don't make sense, and one is correct. Choose each correct answer. Discuss your methods for finding the answers. Which methods worked best?

29. $49 + 49 = $ ▪ **a.** 98 **b.** 198 **c.** 518

30. $84 + 120 = $ ▪ **a.** 204 **b.** 34 **c.** 974

31. $36 + 71 = $ ▪ **a.** 67 **b.** 107 **c.** 227

32. $125 + 237 = $ ▪ **a.** 1762 **b.** 222 **c.** 362

33. $275 + 129 = $ ▪ **a.** 104 **b.** 404 **c.** 804

34. $27 + 54 = $ ▪ **a.** 81 **b.** 31 **c.** 171

35. $48 + 71 = $ ▪ **a.** 199 **b.** 319 **c.** 119

36. $472 + 376 = $ ▪ **a.** 1028 **b.** 628 **c.** 848

37. $359 + 982 = $ ▪ **a.** 1041 **b.** 1341 **c.** 941

38. $412 + 562 = $ ▪ **a.** 974 **b.** 1274 **c.** 774

39. $73 + 793 = $ ▪ **a.** 766 **b.** 1066 **c.** 866

40. $1475 + 325 = $ ▪ **a.** 800 **b.** 1800 **c.** 2800

41. $1379 + 1682 = $ ▪ **a.** 4061 **b.** 2061 **c.** 3061

42. $2257 + 1279 = $ ▪ **a.** 3536 **b.** 536 **c.** 5536

43. $4778 + 173 = $ ▪ **a.** 951 **b.** 4951 **c.** 4751

44. $7253 + 347 = $ ▪ **a.** 10,600 **b.** 7000 **c.** 7600

GAME

Don't Go Over 1000 Game

Players:	**Two or more**
Materials:	**Two 0–5 cubes (red), two 5–10 cubes (blue)**
Object:	**To get the sum closest to, but not over, 1000**
Math Focus:	**Place value, multidigit addition, and mathematical reasoning**

RULES

1. Roll all four cubes. If you roll a 10, roll that cube again.

2. Combine three of the numbers rolled to make a three-digit number.

3. Roll all four cubes again. Make a second three-digit number and add it to your first number.

4. You may stop after your second roll, or you may make another three-digit number and add it to your previous sum.

5. The player whose sum is closest to, but not over, 1000 is the winner.

SAMPLE GAME

Megan rolled: Megan wrote:

5	4	3	6

643

3	6	7	2

+ 327

970

Megan stopped.

Rosalie rolled: Rosalie wrote:

0	5	9	1

519

3	7	7	1

+ 137

656

8	2	3	9

+ 329

985

Rosalie was the winner.

MATH JOURNAL

If you played this game again, would you play it the same way? Explain why or why not in your Math Journal.

Multidigit Subtraction

Trini sold 594 tickets for the spring music festival. She sold 378 adult tickets. The rest were children's tickets. How many children's tickets did Trini sell? You can subtract to find the difference.

Subtract: 594 − 378 = ?

594 − 378	Start at the right. Subtract the ones. You can't subtract 8 from 4.
5̶9̶4̶ − 378	Regroup the 9 tens and 4.
8 14 5̶9̶4̶ − 378	9 tens and 4 = 8 tens and 14
8 14 5̶9̶4̶ − 378 6	Subtract the ones. 14 − 8 = 6
8 14 5̶9̶4̶ − 378 16	Subtract the tens. 8 − 7 = 1 There is 1 ten.
8 14 5̶9̶4̶ − 378 216	Subtract the hundreds. 5 − 3 = 2 There are 2 hundreds. Trini sold 216 children's tickets.

$$\begin{array}{r} 905 \\ - 466 \\ \hline \end{array}$$

What do you do in a case like this?
There are no tens to regroup.

$$\begin{array}{r} 8915 \\ \cancel{905} \\ - 466 \\ \hline \end{array}$$

9 hundreds is the same as 90 tens.
Regroup 90 tens and 5.
90 tens and 5 = 89 tens and 15

$$\begin{array}{r} 8915 \\ \cancel{905} \\ - 466 \\ \hline 439 \end{array}$$

Now subtract.

Subtract. Use shortcuts when you can.

1. $35 - 23$
2. $65 - 29$
3. $47 - 40$
4. $47 - 39$
5. $93 - 87$

6. $\begin{array}{r} 425 \\ - 425 \\ \hline \end{array}$
7. $\begin{array}{r} 691 \\ - 25 \\ \hline \end{array}$
8. $\begin{array}{r} 201 \\ - 187 \\ \hline \end{array}$
9. $\begin{array}{r} 905 \\ - 377 \\ \hline \end{array}$
10. $\begin{array}{r} 391 \\ - 280 \\ \hline \end{array}$

11. $\begin{array}{r} 276 \\ - 137 \\ \hline \end{array}$
12. $\begin{array}{r} 672 \\ - 314 \\ \hline \end{array}$
13. $\begin{array}{r} 6542 \\ - 3000 \\ \hline \end{array}$
14. $\begin{array}{r} 1000 \\ - 3 \\ \hline \end{array}$
15. $\begin{array}{r} 349{,}619{,}721 \\ - 218{,}700{,}399 \\ \hline \end{array}$

Add or subtract. Use shortcuts when you can.

16. $\begin{array}{r} 871 \\ - 645 \\ \hline \end{array}$
17. $\begin{array}{r} 700 \\ - 200 \\ \hline \end{array}$
18. $\begin{array}{r} 901 \\ + 675 \\ \hline \end{array}$
19. $\begin{array}{r} 279 \\ + 813 \\ \hline \end{array}$

20. $\begin{array}{r} 700 \\ + 200 \\ \hline \end{array}$
21. $\begin{array}{r} 700 \\ - 199 \\ \hline \end{array}$
22. $\begin{array}{r} 307 \\ - 295 \\ \hline \end{array}$
23. $\begin{array}{r} 492 \\ - 374 \\ \hline \end{array}$

24. $\begin{array}{r} 770 \\ + 199 \\ \hline \end{array}$
25. $\begin{array}{r} 700 \\ - 201 \\ \hline \end{array}$
26. $\begin{array}{r} 496 \\ - 496 \\ \hline \end{array}$
27. $\begin{array}{r} 285 \\ + 139 \\ \hline \end{array}$

◆ **LESSON 13 Multidigit Subtraction**

Answer the following questions.

28 On school days Boris needs at least 20 minutes to eat breakfast, three minutes to brush his teeth, 15 minutes to get dressed, and seven minutes to gather all of the materials he needs. What's the least amount of time it takes Boris to get ready for school?

29 At the beginning of the school year, Park Elementary had 311 students. During the year, 14 students moved away and 12 new students entered the school. How many students were there at the end of the school year?

30 In 1900 the population of Park City was about 27,800. By 1950 the population was about 36,200. By about how much did the population increase?

31 Damon and his friends went bowling. In his first game Damon had a score of 131. Halfway through his second game he had a score of 89. How many more points did he need in the second game to beat his previous score?

32 Ronda wants to use her babysitting money to pay for a new bicycle. She kept track of the money she earned for four weeks. She earned $15 the first week, $25 the second week, $20 the third week, and $27 the fourth week. How much more money does she need to make in order to buy a bicycle that costs $120?

33 Abraham Lincoln was born on February 12, 1809. He became president on March 4, 1861. How old was he when he became president?

If the average adult human's blood vessels were attached end-to-end, they would form a tube more than 60,000 miles (97,000 km) long.

Roll a Problem Game

Players: Two or more
Materials: One 0–5 cube (red)
Object: To get the greatest sum
Math Focus: Multidigit arithmetic, place value, and mathematical reasoning

RULES

1. Use blanks to outline an addition problem on your paper, like this:

$$\begin{array}{r} \underline{\quad}\ \underline{\quad} \\ +\ \underline{\quad}\ \underline{\quad} \\ \hline \underline{\qquad\qquad} \end{array}$$

2. The first player rolls the cube four times.

3. Each time the cube is rolled, write that number in one of the blanks in your outline.

4. When all the blanks have been filled in, find the sum of the two two-digit numbers.

5. The player with the greatest sum is the winner.

OTHER WAYS TO PLAY THIS GAME

1. Try to get the least sum.

2. Add two three-digit numbers.

3. Add three two-digit numbers.

4. Use a 5–10 cube. If a 10 is rolled, roll again.

5. Subtract. Try to get the least difference, 0 or greater.

In your Math Journal explain how you played this game.

LESSON 14

Multidigit Addition and Subtraction

Add or subtract.

1 22
  + 31

2 63
  − 41

3 36
  − 21

4 67
  + 22

5 93
  − 36

6 27
  + 49

7 48
  + 35

8 82
  − 57

9 67
  + 74

10 77
  − 68

11 34
  − 19

12 83
  + 28

13 368
  + 121

14 529
  + 310

15 476
  − 287

16 687
  − 321

17 568
  − 37

18 329
  + 692

19 474
  + 289

20 274
  + 189

21 6725
  + 1235

22 7925
  + 2136

23 2748
  − 1692

24 1897
  − 769

25 28,133
  − 14,960

Solve.

26 Clara and Tomás ran for school president. Clara got 743 votes. Tomás got 916 votes.

a. Who won?

b. By how many votes?

c. How many students attend the school?

d. How many people voted?

FANTASTIC FACT

It would take a car traveling 100 miles per hour more than 29 million years to reach Earth's nearest star, Proxima Centauri.

SCIENCE CONNECTION

Planet	Average Distance from Sun (in millions of miles)	Diameter (in miles)
Mercury	36	3,031
Venus	67	7,519
Earth	93	7,927
Mars	141	4,221
Jupiter	383	88,734
Saturn	887	74,977
Uranus	1,783	32,000
Neptune	2,794	30,450
Pluto	3,666	1,430

Answer the following questions based on the table.

27 How much greater is the diameter of Earth than the diameter of Mars?

28 What is the difference between the average distance from the sun to Neptune and to Earth?

29 Jupiter's greatest distance from the sun is 124 million miles greater than its average distance. What is Jupiter's greatest distance from the sun?

30 Which two planets have the least difference in diameter? What is the difference between their diameters?

31 Which two planets have the greatest difference in diameter? What is the difference between their diameters?

32 Suppose Earth and Venus are both at their average distances from the sun. What is the closest they could be to each other? What is the farthest they could be from each other?

◆ **LESSON 14 Multidigit Addition and Subtraction**

**THINKING
STORY**

Muddle at Bat

Part 3

*You may want to refer to previous parts of this Thinking
Story, on pages 18–19 and 34–35.*

"Y ou should use one of our regular players," said
the manager. "After all, we don't care how good
a bat is for you. We want to know how good it is
for them."

Mr. Muddle asked Sandy Hare, leading batter for the Dips,
to try the bats. First Sandy batted for a while with the
Slugger bat. He had 19 hits with it. Then he batted for a
while with the Arrow bat and got 20 hits. When he used the
Champ bat, he had only 11 hits.

"I am happy to say that I was right," Mr. Muddle told the
manager. "The Arrow bat is by far the best for getting hits."

. . . to be continued

Work in groups. Discuss your answers and how you figured them out. Then compare your answers with those of other groups.

1 Do you agree with Mr. Muddle that the Arrow bat was by far the best? Why or why not?

2 What are some reasons why Sandy Hare might have gotten more hits with the Arrow bat?

3 How would you change the test to make it more fair?

Mid-Unit Review

Write the numbers in standard form.

1 $800 + 70 + 4$

2 $90,000,000 + 7 + 5000$

3 $1000 + 30 + 2$

4 $10,000 + 400 + 5$

5 $30,000 + 2000 + 700 + 50 + 1$

6 $5,000,000 + 200,000 + 10,000 + 300$

7 $3 + 80 + 200 + 600,000 + 9,000,000$

Count up or down. Write the missing numbers.

8 397, 398, 399, ■, ■, ■, ■, 404

9 903, 902, 901, ■, ■, ■, ■, ■, 895

10 8,000,104; 8,000,103; 8,000,102; ■; ■; ■; ■; 8,000,097

Write the greatest number and the least number.

11 Use the digits 5, 3, and 8.   **12** Use the digits 6, 8, 2, and 1.

Write six different numbers in order from greatest to least.

13 Use the digits 2, 8, and 9.   **14** Use the digits 1, 4, and 7.

Add or subtract to solve for *n*.

15 $7 + 4 = n$ **16** $17 - 9 = n$ **17** $15 - 8 = n$

18 $4 + 9 = n$ **19** $8 + 8 = n$ **20** $13 - 6 = n$

21 $6 + 9 = n$ **22** $8 - 6 = n$ **23** $n = 14 - 8$

24 $n = 8 + 6$ **25** $n = 4 + 9$ **26** $n = 15 - 9$

27 $n + 8 = 17$ **28** $13 = n + 6$ **29** $7 + n = 14$

30 $15 = 9 + n$ **31** $12 = 5 + n$ **32** $8 + n = 16$

Use a computer or other means to copy and complete each chart. Watch the function rule.

33 −6

In	Out
26	■
18	■
16	■
12	■
7	■

34 +8

In	Out
0	■
2	■
5	■
10	■
22	■

Solve these problems.

35 Reba had $13. She bought a belt for $7. How much money does she have left?

36 David had $15. He bought an artist's pad for $6 and a paint set for $7. Can he afford to buy a $3 paintbrush?

37 Bike horns usually cost $10. They are on sale for $7. How much money would Emma save by buying a horn at the sale price?

Find the perimeter.

38
6 cm
2 cm [   ] 2 cm
6 cm

39
8 cm
3 cm
6 cm

In each problem, two of the answers don't make sense, and one is correct. Choose the correct answers.

40 49 + 39 =   **a.** 88   **b.** 188   **c.** 718

41 1375 + 225 =   **a.** 600   **b.** 1600   **c.** 2600

42 793 − 627 =   **a.** 166   **b.** 1420   **c.** 400

43 1614 − 876 =   **a.** 1207   **b.** 175   **c.** 738

44 66 + 104 =   **a.** 170   **b.** 17   **c.** 1700

45 2350 − 2245 =   **a.** 50   **b.** 105   **c.** 507

LESSON 15

Applying Addition and Subtraction

Answer these questions.

Amalia needs 55¢ for mailing a letter. She has these stamps:

1. Can Amalia make exactly 55¢ in postage stamps?

2. Which stamps make exactly 55¢?

3. How many postage stamps will Amalia have left?

4. What will be the total value of the stamps she has left?

These three children are collecting baseball cards. Lia has 742 cards, Peter has 643, and A. J. has 392.

5. How many more cards does A. J. need to have as many as Lia?

6. How many more cards does Peter need to have as many as Lia?

7. Suppose Peter gives A. J. 343 cards. Will A. J. then have as many cards as Lia?

8. Suppose Lia gives A. J. 200 cards. Will A. J. then have as many as Lia?

9. **Challenge:** How many cards would Lia have to give to A. J. for the two of them to have the same number?

REAL-WORLD CONNECTION

Sasha made a chart to help her find the least expensive supermarket. First she decided which items she wanted. Can you complete the bottom line of Sasha's chart?

Item	Price		
	Super-Duper Supermarket	**Hi-Value Supermarket**	**Best-Buy Supermarket**
1 dozen eggs (Grade AA large)	$1.09	$1.05	$1.15
1 quart of apple juice (Top-Core brand)	$1.25	$1.37	$1.29
2 pounds of potatoes	$ 0.88	$ 0.96	$ 0.80
Total	■	■	■

10 Which supermarket is least expensive for the three items listed?

11 Which supermarket is most expensive?

12 For each supermarket, write the total amount in cents.

13 Sasha met Mr. Tanaka, who was going shopping. "I have to buy bread, butter, apples, and peanut butter, " said Mr. Tanaka. "Do you know which supermarket will be least expensive?" he asked. Does Sasha know the answer to Mr. Tanaka's question? Why or why not?

◆ Go comparison shopping. Use a computer or pencil and paper to make a chart like the one above. Write the names of the stores you will go to and the items you will check prices for. Then fill in your chart with the prices you find.

Using Relation Signs

Do you remember what these signs mean?

Here are some examples:

25 < 30 means 25 **is less than** 30.

10 > 7 means 10 **is greater than** 7.

4 + 9 = 13 means 4 plus 9 **is equal to** 13.

Copy each statement and replace ● with <, >, or = to make each statement true.

1. 27 ● 19
2. 11 ● 77 + 66
3. 39 ● 52 + 49

4. 36 ● 18
5. 79 ● 77 + 10
6. 8 + 9 ● 8 − 2

7. 19 ● 79
8. 16 ● 21 + 3
9. 18 − 9 ● 18 + 3

10. 4 + 3 ● 3 + 4
11. 56 ● 40 + 20
12. 33 − 6 ● 33 − 7

13. 9 ● 19 + 10
14. 39 ● 29 + 29
15. 49 + 3 ● 49 + 5

16. 100 ● 73 + 10
17. 63 ● 33 + 23
18. 77 − 16 ● 74 − 16

19. 84 ● 73 − 10
20. 55 ● 55 − 13
21. 20 − 15 ● 25 − 10

Solve.

22. Mr. Bannerji has $100. Does he have enough money to pay for

    a. a jacket and a tie?

    b. a pair of pants and a sweater?

    c. a sweater and three ties?

Inequality Game

Players:	**Two**
Materials:	**Two 0–5 cubes (red), two 5–10 cubes (blue)**
Object:	**To fill in an inequality statement correctly**
Math Focus:	**Identifying inequalities and mathematical reasoning**

GAME

RULES

1. Make one of these game forms on a sheet of paper:

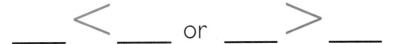

_____ < _____ or _____ > _____

2. Roll all four cubes, make two two-digit numbers, and write their sum on either side of the inequality sign. If you roll a 10, roll that cube again.

3. The other player rolls all four cubes, makes two two-digit numbers, and writes his or her sum in the remaining space.

4. If the inequality statement is true, the other player wins. If the inequality statement is false, you win.

5. Players take turns being first.

MATH JOURNAL

If you played this game again, how would you play it? Would you use the same strategy? Explain your strategy in your Math Journal.

◆ **LESSON 16** Using Relation Signs

THINKING STORY

Muddle at Bat

Part 4

You may want to refer to previous parts of this Thinking Story, on pages 18–19, 34–35, and 48–49.

M r. Muddle thought of a better way to test baseball bats. He tested how well the bats worked in real games. For the next two weeks, Sandy Hare always used the Arrow bat when he played. Al Button, the second-best batter on the team, always used the Slugger bat. And Speck Tackle, a pinch hitter, used the Champ bat. Mr. Muddle went to every game. He kept a record of what happened.

Sandy Hare batted 40 times and got 15 hits with the Arrow bat. Al Button, with his Slugger, batted 41 times and got 12 hits. Speck Tackle, using the Champ bat, batted eight times and got five hits.

. . . to be continued

Work in groups. Discuss your answers and how you figured them out. Then compare your answers with those of other groups.

1 Who do you think did the best hitting? Why?

2 Does this test tell you which bat is best for getting hits? Explain.

Addition and Subtraction with Hidden Digits

ALGEBRA READINESS

Paint has been spilled on these two pages. One answer is correct in each case. Decide which answer is correct, then discuss methods for solving these problems.

Example: 23
             + 4[paint]

    a. 51

    b. 61

    c. 71

The sum must be at least 63. It could be as much as 72. So the correct answer must be **c**, 71.

1   68
     + 2[paint]

    a. 86
    b. 96
    c. 106

2   204
     + 7[paint]

    a. 99
    b. 279
    c. 949

3   53[paint]
     + 330

    a. 259
    b. 863
    c. 1059

4   2[paint]5
     + 3[paint]

    a. 83
    b. 492
    c. 613

5   456
     + 31[paint]

    a. 143
    b. 769
    c. 283

6   670[paint]
     + [paint]

    a. 6532
    b. 7413
    c. 9705

7   87[paint]
     − 3[paint]

    a. 51
    b. 64
    c. 92

8   82[paint]
     − 3[paint]

    a. 46
    b. 56
    c. 66

9　100
　　− 7

a. 15
b. 25
c. 35

10　74
　− 283

a. 406
b. 582
c. 462

11　8
　− 3 5

a. 482
b. 607
c. 758

12　30
　−

a. 206
b. 317
c. 402

13　812
　− 368

a. 4
b. 5
c. 6

14　7904
　− 6

a. 1250
b. 725
c. 76

15　3406
　− 759

a. 757
b. 747
c. 647

16　207
　+ 6

a. 367
b. 269
c. 142

17　875
　− 10

a. 771
b. 975
c. 676

18　65
　− 4

a. 13
b. 23
c. 103

19　273
　+1 5

a. 329
b. 128
c. 398

20　46
　+21

a. 690
b. 258
c. 675

The highest mountains on the moon, the lunar Appennines, reach more than 24,600 feet.

LESSON 18 Approximation: Applications

SOCIAL STUDIES CONNECTION

Sometimes you don't need an exact answer. Select the best answer for each problem. You don't have to do the calculations.

1 George Washington was born in 1732. About how many years ago was that?
   a. About 270   **b.** About 170   **c.** About 570

2 The zipper was invented in 1891. About how many years ago was that?
   a. About 50   **b.** About 150   **c.** About 100

3 Christopher Columbus reached America in 1492. About how many years ago was that?
   a. About 500   **b.** About 250   **c.** About 100

4 The American Declaration of Independence was signed in 1776. About how many years ago was that?
   a. About 100   **b.** About 200   **c.** About 300

5 According to the 1990 census, the population of Houston, Texas, was 1,630,553 and the population of Chicago, Illinois, was 2,783,726. About how many more people lived in Chicago than in Houston?
   a. About 115,000   **b.** About 1,150,000   **c.** About 11,500,000

6 In 1994, 66,435,252 passengers flew into or out of Chicago's O'Hare Airport. That same year 54,090,579 passengers flew into or out of Atlanta's Hartsfield Airport. About how many more passengers flew into or out of O'Hare than Hartsfield?

a. 12,300,000   **b.** 1,230,000   **c.** 123,000

7 In 1996 the United States minted $69,858,000 worth of 50-cent pieces (half-dollars). About how many coins is that?

a. 140,000,000   **b.** 13,970,000   **c.** 5,000,000

8 In 1995 the number of kilometers of railroad track in Canada was 56,000; in Mexico it was 19,573. About how many more kilometers of track did Canada have than Mexico?

a. 3640   **b.** 36,400   **c.** 364

9 The air distance between Boston, Massachusetts, and Seattle, Washington, is 4016 kilometers. The air distance between Boston and Los Angeles, California, is 3131 kilometers. Boston is about how much farther away from Seattle than it is from Los Angeles?

a. 90 kilometers   **b.** 710 kilometers   **c.** 900 kilometers

◆ **LESSON 18** Approximation: Applications

THINKING STORY

Muddle at Bat

Part 5

You may want to refer to previous parts of this Thinking Story, on pages 18–19, 34–35, 48–49, and 56–57.

One day when Al Button was batting, his Slugger bat broke. "That proves Slugger bats are no good," he said. "Let's use Arrow bats."

The manager said, "Not so fast. I want a better test." He told Mr. Muddle to take ten of each kind of bat and test how strong they were.

Mr. Muddle carried all the bats off in a wagon. He kept going until he found a big rock. Then he took each bat and hit it against the rock. Not one of the bats broke. "All of the bats are strong," Mr. Muddle told the manager.

"Give them a harder test," said the manager.

Mr. Muddle went back and found a bigger rock. He hit each bat against the rock. Again, none of them broke.

"Give them a harder test yet," said the manager.

Mr. Muddle went out again with his wagon full of bats. On the street he stopped to watch a crew tearing down a building. The workers had a crane that swung a huge steel ball back and forth. When the steel ball hit a wall, the wall crashed down. Mr. Muddle put all the bats on the ground. He asked the workers, "Would you try to break these bats with your steel ball?"

"Are you sure you want us to do that?" asked one of the workers.

"Yes," said Mr. Muddle. "I'm giving the bats a test."

The steel ball came crashing down on the bats. Pieces of wood flew into the air.

Later Mr. Muddle reported to the manager. "The bats are all alike. They all passed the easy tests and they all failed the hard test."

. . . to be continued

Work in groups. Discuss your answers and how you figured them out. Then compare your answers with those of other groups.

❶ How many bats did Mr. Muddle test?

❷ Why should he have to test so many bats? Why not one of each kind?

❸ Was the second test harder than the first? Explain.

❹ Is Mr. Muddle right that the bats are all alike? If some are stronger, how could you find out?

LESSON 19

Introduction to the Calculator

Calculators are useful machines. They can do all sorts of calculations very quickly. However, they only do what somebody tells them to do. Sometimes the calculator may not do what you think it will. You should explore any calculator you plan to use to see if it does what you expect.

The display is the rectangular window that communicates information to you. Once the calculator is turned on you should see "0." on the display. Experiment with the calculator.

Solve the following problems both with your calculator and in your head. Does the calculator get the right answers?

1. $2 + 2 = ?$

2. $10 + 10 = ?$

3. $2 \times 3 = ?$

4. $8 \div 2 = ?$

5. $100 + 100 = ?$

6. $5 \times 5 = ?$

7. $50 \times 50 = ?$

8. $500 \times 500 = ?$

9. $5000 \times 5000 = ?$

10. $50{,}000 \times 50{,}000 = ?$

11. $500{,}000 \times 500{,}000 = ?$

Did the calculator get the right answer for every problem? Did it do anything strange? What did the answers to questions 10 and 11 look like? Calculator displays have only a small space to show the digits of their answers. Most can show only eight or ten digits.

When a calculator tries to show more digits than it can, it may give an error message (maybe an "E" or some other symbol on the display). Directions for your calculator should tell you what it will do and what to do next. Sometimes the calculator will "lock" and stop working until you do something, like press the ON/C key.

12 Using the memory key, find the sum of 5 × 6, 4 × 7, and 3 × 8. Press the CLEAR key between each problem.

Some calculators have a constant function built in so that if you do a problem like 4 + 4 = and then press the = key again it will show 12. Press the = key a third time and it will show 16, and so on. For others you have to press a special key to use the constant feature. See if you can figure out how your calculator does this.

13 Clear the calculator and press 50 – 5 =. Does the display show 45? Continue subtracting 5 repeatedly. What numbers do you get? What happens after you reach 0? What is the number that came right after 0 in this sequence? Is there a negative symbol on the calculator?

14 Continue subtracting 5. Look at the number line below. Does the calculator show the numbers you'd expect it to show?

```
←——+——+——+——+——+——+——+——+——+——+——+——+——+——+——+——→
  –30 –25 –20 –15 –10 –5   0   5  10  15  20  25  30  35  40
```

15 If you started at 20 and continually subtracted 4, what are the first three numbers you would expect to appear after 0? Try this on your calculator and see if you get the same numbers.

Try different operations with your calculator to find out more about how it works. Write about your findings in your Math Journal.

Salt water is, on the average, 3.3 to 3.7% salt. If the salt in all the oceans were combined, it would form a solid mass of salt the size of Africa.

◆ LESSON 19 Introduction to the Calculator

Add and subtract with and without your calculator. See if you get the same answer both ways. Watch your numbering.

16. 2 − 1 − 1 − 1 − 1

17. 20 − 10 − 10 − 10 − 10

18. 10 − 80

19. 80 − 10

20. 8 − 10

21. 100 − 80

22. −2 + 5

23. −20 + 50

24. 1 − 5

25. 10 − 50

26. 100 − 50

27. 6 − 6

28. 8 − 8

29. 80 − 80

Add and subtract without using your calculator. Then use your calculator to see whether you get the same answer.

30. 783 + 97

31. 880 − 97

32. 783 − 80

33. 703 + 80

34. 7 + 5

35. 70 + 50

36. 700 + 500

37. 7000 + 5000

38. 17 − 8

39. 170 − 80

40. 1700 − 800

41. 7 − 7

42. 7 − 8

43. 70 − 80

44. 700 − 800

45. 49 + 501

46. 48 + 52

47. 480 + 520

48. 626 + 24

49. 509 + 20

50. 529 − 20

51. 600 − 298

52. 6000 − 2980

53. 3 − 6

54. 30 − 60

55. 60 − 30

Figure out how to change the first display to the second display. Try to use no more than one step. Watch your numbering.

56	0.	72.	**57**	−8.	10.
58	783.	83.	**59**	70.	−20.
60	46.	346.	**61**	51.	1000.
62	2000.	2010.	**63**	297.	800.
64	2000.	1998.	**65**	408.	478.
66	457.	407.	**67**	−5.	7.
68	7000.	5000.	**69**	90.	−40.
70	1600.	900.	**71**	3333.	3030.
72	1600.	1900.	**73**	2345.	1234.
74	900.	0.	**75**	830.	1100.
76	401.	40.	**77**	30.	70.
78	539.	509.	**79**	700.	300.
80	49.	650.	**81**	−70.	30.

Solve these problems.

82 Winter Elementary School has 400 students. Packard Elementary School has 600 students. How many students do the two schools have all together?

83 The temperature outside was −20°F in the morning. By late afternoon the temperature was 10°F. By how much did the temperature rise?

84 The Cook family's cat had six kittens. Two of the kittens were adopted by neighbors, and the Cooks decided to keep three kittens. How many kittens still need to be adopted?

It takes the planet Pluto 247 Earth years to complete an orbit of the sun.

LESSON 20

Estimating with Fractions

Fractions are often used to describe parts of a whole.

Answer these questions.

1 About how full is the fuel tank?

    a. $\frac{1}{2}$ full **b.** $\frac{1}{3}$ full **c.** $\frac{3}{4}$ full

2 About how much of the pie is left?

    a. $\frac{1}{6}$ **b.** $\frac{1}{16}$ **c.** $\frac{1}{3}$

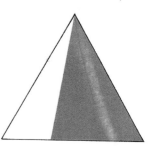

3 About how full is the glass?

    a. $\frac{1}{4}$ full **b.** $\frac{1}{2}$ full **c.** $\frac{2}{3}$ full

4 About how much of the triangle is colored?

    a. $\frac{1}{2}$ **b.** $\frac{2}{3}$ **c.** $\frac{3}{4}$

5 About how much of the bookshelf is empty?

    a. $\frac{1}{8}$ **b.** $\frac{1}{3}$ **c.** $\frac{1}{2}$

6 The length of the short stick is about what fraction of the length of the long stick?

    a. $\frac{1}{8}$ **b.** $\frac{1}{4}$ **c.** $\frac{1}{3}$

Which statements do not make sense? Write your reasons.

7 In Diana's class, $\frac{1}{2}$ of the students are girls, and $\frac{2}{3}$ are boys.

8 In Masani's class, $\frac{1}{2}$ of the students are boys, and $\frac{3}{4}$ of the students are wearing sneakers.

9 Eric tossed a coin 12 times. $\frac{1}{2}$ of the tosses turned up heads. $\frac{1}{4}$ of the tosses turned up tails.

10 Jordan is using a recipe that makes three servings. Only two people will be eating, so Jordan makes $\frac{2}{3}$ of the amount given for each ingredient.

11 There are ten fireplace logs in a bundle. If five logs are burned, $\frac{1}{2}$ of the bundle is left.

12 In $\frac{1}{2}$ of an hour, Dan, Rachel, and Leon planted a small flower garden. If they started at 9:00 A.M., they must have worked until 10:30 A.M.

13 The bottom half of this bottle holds more juice than the top half.

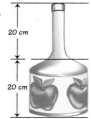

20 cm

20 cm

14 A spinner has six parts of the same size.

a. $\frac{1}{2}$ of the area of the spinner is red.

b. If you spin the spinner many times, you would land on red about $\frac{1}{2}$ of the time.

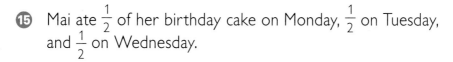

15 Mai ate $\frac{1}{2}$ of her birthday cake on Monday, $\frac{1}{2}$ on Tuesday, and $\frac{1}{2}$ on Wednesday.

LESSON 21

Fractions and Money

You can use the United States' money system to understand fractions.

dollar

one dollar = 100 cents
1 dollar = 100¢

half-dollar

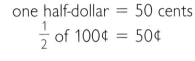

one half-dollar = 50 cents
$\frac{1}{2}$ of 100¢ = 50¢

quarter

one quarter dollar = 25 cents
$\frac{1}{4}$ of 100¢ = 25 cents

dime

one tenth dollar = 10 cents
$\frac{1}{10}$ of 100¢ = 10 cents

Write the amount as a fraction of a dollar. Then write how many cents. The first one has been done for you.

	Coins	Fraction of a Dollar	Cents
1		$\frac{2}{4}$	50¢
2		■	■
3		■	■
4		■	■
5		■	■

◆ How many quarters are in one dollar?

◆ How many quarters are in one half-dollar?

◆ How many dimes are in one dollar?

◆ How many dimes are in one half-dollar?

◆ Which would you rather have, ten dimes or four quarters?

Solve.

6 Dr. Kumi is driving to a town 100 kilometers from her home. She has 40 kilometers left to go. Is she halfway there yet?

7 A bicycle that usually sells for $100 is on sale for $72. Is that more than $\frac{1}{4}$ off the regular price?

8 In a class of 16 students, $\frac{3}{4}$ of the students are girls. Are there more boys than girls in the class?

9 Last night DeAnna read the first 27 pages of a 120-page book. Has she read a third of the book yet?

10 Eddie is baking muffins. The recipe calls for 800 grams of flour and two eggs. Because Eddie has only one egg, he can make only $\frac{1}{2}$ the recipe. How much flour will he use?

11 Maureen cut her pie into eight equal slices. Seven slices were eaten. Is more than $\frac{1}{4}$ of the pie left?

12 The gas tank on Mr. Lee's car holds 84 liters. He just put in 64 liters of gas to fill the tank. About how full was the tank before filling?

a. About $\frac{1}{4}$ full   **b.** About $\frac{1}{2}$ full   **c.** About $\frac{3}{4}$ full

13 Tim is saving money to buy a kite that costs $20.00. He has saved $9.57. Has he saved $\frac{1}{2}$ the cost of the kite yet?

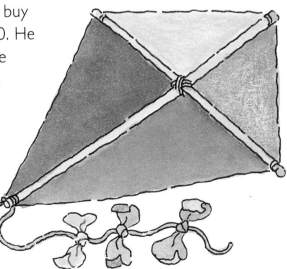

LESSON 22

Decimals and Money

Another way to understand money is to use decimals.

1 dollar = $1.00

50¢ = $0.50

Write the amount shown in cents, then in dollars and cents. The first one has been done for you.

#		cents	dollars
1		35¢	$0.35
2		▪	▪
3		▪	▪
4		▪	▪
5		▪	▪
6		▪	▪
7		▪	▪

25¢ = $0.25   10¢ = $0.10   5¢ = $0.05   1¢ = $0.01

Write the amount in dollars and cents.

8 10 cents = ▪   **9** 1 dollar and 2 dimes = ▪

10 2 dimes = ▪   **11** 3 dollars and 4 dimes = ▪

12 4 dimes and 7 cents = ▪   **13** 6 dollars and 3 cents = ▪

14 8 dimes and 6 cents = ▪   **15** 1 dollar, 3 dimes, and 6 cents = ▪

16 8 cents = ▪   **17** 3 dollars, 6 dimes, and 2 cents = ▪

18 5 dollars and 5 cents = ▪   **19** 2 dollars, 2 dimes, and 2 cents = ▪

20 6 dimes and 6 cents = ▪   **21** 5 cents = ▪

22 1 dollar and 1 cent = ▪   **23** 1 dollar, 1 dime, and 1 cent = ▪

Copy each statement. Replace ● with <, >, or = to make the statement true.

24 $4.00 ● $3.48   **25** $9.43 ● $19.43

26 $6.00 ● $5.98   **27** $11.11 ● $1.11

28 $3.28 ● $3.28   **29** $96 ● $96.00

30 $2.80 ● $0.28   **31** $0.04 ● $4.04

32 $0.97 ● $97   **33** $38.95 ● $40

34 $21.31 ● $35.57   **35** $18.95 ● $18.95

36 $17.99 ● $18.00   **37** $20.00 ● $20.01

38 $4.75 ● $3.88   **39** $19.00 ● $20.99

◆ LESSON 22 Decimals and Money

Suppose you work the cash register of a store. You want to give change with the fewest coins. Which coins would you use?

40 A pen costs 57 cents. A customer gives you three quarters.

41 A pencil costs 34 cents. A customer gives you four dimes.

42 A pad costs 80 cents. A customer gives you one dollar.

43 A calculator costs $4.32. A customer gives you a five-dollar bill.

44 An eraser costs 63 cents. A customer gives you three quarters.

45 A notebook costs $2.69. A customer gives you three dollars.

46 A box of envelopes costs $1.25. A customer gives you one dollar and one half-dollar.

Which of the following are possible? For those that are possible, list the coins. For those that are not possible, write *not possible*.

47 Make 57 cents with five coins. **48** Make 23 cents with four coins.

49 Make 57 cents with four coins. **50** Make 20 cents with three coins.

51 Make 89 cents with ten coins. **52** Make 61 cents with three coins.

53 Make 51 cents with four coins. **54** Make 51 cents with five coins.

An astronaut in a space suit weighs 300 pounds on Earth but only 50 pounds on the moon.

Money Roll Game

Players:	Two
Materials:	One 0–5 cube (red), one 5–10 cube (blue)
Object:	To make a number for the greater amount of money
Math Focus:	Place value, decimal and money notation, and mathematical reasoning

RULES

1. Use blanks, a decimal point, and a dollar sign to outline an amount of money on your paper, like this:

   $ \$ \underline{} \ \underline{} \ . \ \underline{} \ \underline{} $

2. Players take turns rolling either cube.

3. Each time a cube is rolled, both players write that number in one of the blanks in their outlines. If you roll a 10, roll that cube again.

4. The player who makes the number for the greater amount of money is the winner.

SAMPLE GAME

Number rolled:	Peggy wrote:	Katie wrote:
3	$ \$ \underline{}\ \underline{} . \mathbf{3}\ \underline{} $	$ \$ \underline{}\ \underline{} . \underline{}\ \mathbf{3} $
7	$ \$ \underline{}\ \underline{} . 3\ \mathbf{7} $	$ \$ \underline{}\ \mathbf{7} . \underline{}\ 3 $
8	$ \$ \mathbf{8}\ \underline{} . 3\ 7 $	$ \$ \underline{}\ 7 . \mathbf{8}\ 3 $
6	$ \$ 8\ \mathbf{6} . 3\ 7 $	$ \$ \mathbf{6}\ 7 . 8\ 3 $

Peggy was the winner.

OTHER WAYS TO PLAY THIS GAME

1. Use only a 0–5 cube or a 5–10 cube.

2. Use ten pieces of paper numbered 0–9 instead of cubes.

Adding and Subtracting Money

Rosa had $1.29. Then she was given a $5 bill for her birthday. When she told Dan, he said, "I can tell you how much money you have all together." Then he added like this: "You had $1.29, and the 5 more you got makes $1.34 in all."

"That can't be," said Rosa. "You should be more careful when you add numbers with decimal points."

◆ Why doesn't Dan's answer make sense?

Then Rosa added like this:

$$\begin{array}{r} \$1.29 \\ +\ 5.00 \\ \hline \$6.29 \end{array}$$

"I guess that answer makes more sense," said Dan. "But you wrote zeros after the 5."

"That's right, " said Rosa. "But whether I write $5 or $5.00, it's still five dollars."

In each problem, two of the answers are clearly wrong and one is correct. Choose each correct answer.

1 $2.98 + $4.00   **a.** $3.02   **b.** $6.98   **c.** $3.38

2 $3.05 − $1.50   **a.** $1.55   **b.** $2.90   **c.** $4.55

3 $6.75 + $1.25   **a.** $7.00   **b.** $6.90   **c.** $8.00

4 $0.50 + $0.47   **a.** $9.70   **b.** $97.00   **c.** $0.97

5 $0.37 − $0.12   **a.** $25.00   **b.** $0.25   **c.** $0.49

6 $3.98 + $0.45   **a.** $4.43   **b.** $3.43   **c.** $4.75

When you add numbers, like 475 and 137, you line
them up like this:

$$475$$
$$+\ 137$$

You add ones to ones, tens to tens,
and so on.

When you add amounts of money, like $4.75 and $1.37,
you line up the decimal points.

$$\$4.75$$
$$+\ \ \ 1.37$$

You add cents to cents, dimes to
dimes, dollars to dollars, and so on.

When you subtract numbers, like 178 from 342, you line them
up like this:

$$342$$
$$-\ 178$$

You subtract ones from ones,
tens from tens, and so on.

When you subtract amounts of money, like $1.78 from $3.42,
you line up the decimal points.

$$\$3.42$$
$$-\ \ \ 1.78$$

You subtract cents from cents,
dimes from dimes, dollars from
dollars, and so on.

Here are two examples to help you.

A. $65.47 + $39.80
Remember to line up the
decimal points:

$$\$65.47$$
$$+\ \ \ \ 39.80$$
$$\overline{\$105.27}$$

B. $14.98 + $17
You can write $17 as $17.00 to
help you line up the decimal points:

$$\$14.98$$
$$+\ \ \ \ 17.00$$
$$\overline{\$31.98}$$

Add or subtract. Use shortcuts when you can.

7 $15 + $3.98

8 $5.98 + $3.15

9 $5.37 + $43

10 $0.25 + $0.75

11 $2.00 − $1.25

12 $6.35 − $1.27

13 $19.99 − $9.99

14 $11.99 − $0.49

15 $13.98 − $1.39

16 $20.00 + $31.98

17 $16.99 − $2.49

18 $12.60 − $10.62

19 $14.65 + $2.55

20 $2.10 + $6.08

21 $10.50 − $2.25

◆ LESSON 23 Adding and Subtracting Money

The **balance** in a bank account is how much money you have in the bank. When you take out money, it's called a **withdrawal.** When you put in money, it's called a **deposit.**

Alicia had $62.93 in her bank account. She made a withdrawal of $18.50. What is her balance now?

$62.93 —old balance
− 18.50 —withdrawal
$44.43 —new balance

Damon had $146.50 in his bank account. Then he made a deposit of $25.95. What is his balance now?

$146.50 —old balance
+ 25.95 —deposit
$172.45 —new balance

Liam, Hector, Kizzie, Gloria, Jeb, and Ben also have bank accounts. This chart shows the deposits and withdrawals they made this week. Write the new balance for each person.

		Old Balance	Deposit	Withdrawal	New Balance
22	Liam	$32.50	$6.50	—	▪
23	Hector	$75.00	—	$20.00	▪
24	Kizzie	$65.98	$11.75	—	▪
25	Gloria	$82.76	$18.07	—	▪
26	Jeb	$107.98	—	$25.25	▪
27	Ben	$40.75	—	$5.00	▪

28 After Ben withdrew $5.00 from his account, as shown in the chart, he made the following withdrawal and deposits. What was his final balance?

Deposit $15.25
Deposit $12.94
Withdrawal $10.00

Solve these problems.

29 Mark has $4.23. He wants to buy a book that costs $7.50 plus 38 cents tax. How much more money does he need?

30 Sara had $7.48. She bought some things at the store. When she came home she had $5.76. How much did she spend at the store?

31 Maggie's total bill at the supermarket was $25.87. She gave the clerk three ten-dollar bills. How much change should she get?

32 Max wants a CD that costs about $14.00 including tax. He has already saved $9.25. About how much more must he save?

33 Tickets to the museum cost $6.00 for adults and $2.50 for children.

   a. On Saturday Mr. and Mrs. Brown took their two children to the museum. Mrs. Brown gave the clerk $20.00. How much change should she get?

   b. On Tuesdays tickets to the museum are half price. How much would the Browns have saved if they had gone to the museum on Tuesday?

34 Estimate. About how much money do these foods cost? After you make your estimate, check the prices in a newspaper advertisement or at a supermarket.

1 gallon of milk

1 quart of orange juice

1 dozen large eggs

2 pounds of apples

1 loaf of bread

1 box of your favorite cereal

5 pounds of sugar

LESSON 24

Using Addition and Subtraction

SANDWICHES

Hamburger (100 grams) _____ 75¢

Super Burger (200 grams) _____ $1.50

Turkey Sandwich _____ 90¢

Cheese Sandwich _____ 55¢

SALADS

Potato Salad _____ 55¢

Lettuce and Tomato _____ 30¢

Bean Salad _____ 40¢

Cole Slaw _____ 25¢

DRINKS

Milk _____ 20¢

Juice _____ 25¢

DESSERTS

Pie _____ 65¢

Gelatin _____ 40¢

Ice Cream _____ 50¢

All prices include tax

Donna wants to eat something different for lunch each school day. But she can spend only $2.50 or less on lunch. She wants to buy at least one sandwich, one salad, one dessert, and one drink each day.

Donna has made a chart so that she can plan her lunches for the week. She knows what she will buy on Monday, and she has selected a sandwich for Tuesday.

Help Donna plan her menu for the rest of the week. Use a computer or other means to copy and complete the chart.

Day	Sandwich	Salad	Dessert	Drink	Total Price
Monday	Hamburger 75¢	Potato salad 55¢	Pie 65¢	Milk 20¢	$2.15
❶ Tuesday	Super Burger $1.50	▪	▪	▪	▪
❷ Wednesday	▪	▪	▪	▪	▪
❸ Thursday	▪	▪	▪	▪	▪
❹ Friday	▪	▪	▪	▪	▪

Answer the following questions based on the cafeteria menu. Assume Donna still can spend only $2.50 and always orders one sandwich, one salad, one dessert, and one drink.

5 How much is the least expensive lunch Donna can have?

6 Which menu items can Donna not have on the same day as she has a Super Burger?

7 What is the most expensive lunch possible with only one drink and one food from each category?

8 How many different combinations of one sandwich and one salad could a student order?

9 Roger is allergic to milk, milk products, and tomatoes, and he does not like hamburgers. Would Roger be able to have a different lunch every day, Monday through Friday?

10 Why might a 200-gram Super Burger cost less than twice as much as a 100-gram hamburger?

Add or subtract.

11
$$\begin{array}{r} 483 \\ + \ 169 \\ \hline \end{array}$$

12
$$\begin{array}{r} 295 \\ + \ 184 \\ \hline \end{array}$$

13
$$\begin{array}{r} 1492 \\ - \ 1285 \\ \hline \end{array}$$

14
$$\begin{array}{r} 291 \\ - \ 105 \\ \hline \end{array}$$

15
$$\begin{array}{r} 764 \\ + \ 892 \\ \hline \end{array}$$

16
$$\begin{array}{r} 2476 \\ + \ 9321 \\ \hline \end{array}$$

17
$$\begin{array}{r} 8921 \\ - \ 6430 \\ \hline \end{array}$$

18
$$\begin{array}{r} 1847 \\ + \ 3433 \\ \hline \end{array}$$

19
$$\begin{array}{r} 279 \\ - \ 108 \\ \hline \end{array}$$

20
$$\begin{array}{r} 1000 \\ + \ 899 \\ \hline \end{array}$$

21
$$\begin{array}{r} 64{,}258 \\ - \ 21{,}796 \\ \hline \end{array}$$

22
$$\begin{array}{r} 74{,}185 \\ - \ 23{,}431 \\ \hline \end{array}$$

23
$$\begin{array}{r} 649 \\ + \ 291 \\ \hline \end{array}$$

24
$$\begin{array}{r} 2701 \\ - \ 905 \\ \hline \end{array}$$

25
$$\begin{array}{r} 3842 \\ - \ 1650 \\ \hline \end{array}$$

It takes five seconds for the sound of thunder to travel 1 mile.

◆ **LESSON 24 Using Addition and Subtraction**

THINKING STORY

Muddle at Bat

Part 6

You may wish to refer to previous parts of this Thinking Story, on pages 18–19, 34–35, 48–49, 56–57, and 62–63.

"Since you can't tell what kind of bat is best," said the manager, "we'll buy the cheapest ones. Find out what the best deal is for buying 20 new bats."

This is what Mr. Muddle found out:

◆ Slugger bats cost $25 each.

◆ Arrow bats cost $30 each, but if you buy four, you get one extra bat free.

◆ Champ bats are two for $55, but if you buy a dozen or more you get a $75 discount. That is, you get $75 back.

Mr. Muddle told his friend Marcus, "I get all mixed up trying to figure out how much 20 bats will cost." Marcus helped him. It was hard work, but together they were able to find the cheapest way to buy 20 bats.

. . . the end

Work in groups. Discuss your answers and how you figured them out. Then compare your answers with those of other groups.

❶ How much will 20 Sluggers cost? 20 Arrows? 20 Champs?

❷ What kind of bat is cheapest if you buy 20 of them?

❸ You may be surprised to know that Mr. Muddle bought 20 bats for $450. Can you figure out how he did that?

Making Inferences

Planet	Average Distance from the Sun (in millions of kilometers)
Mercury	58
Venus	108
Earth	299
Mars	456
Jupiter	778
Saturn	1429
Uranus	2863
Neptune	4491
Pluto	5879

Use the table to choose the best answer.

1 How far is Earth from the sun?
a. 58 million km **b.** 299 million km **c.** 778 million km

2 Which of these planets is usually farthest from the sun?
a. Mars **b.** Earth **c.** Pluto

3 About how much farther from the sun is Pluto than Uranus?
a. 1000 million km **b.** 3000 million km **c.** 5000 million km

4 About how much farther from the sun is Jupiter than Earth?
a. 500 million km **b.** 700 million km **c.** 900 million km

5 About how much farther from the sun is Pluto than Mercury?
a. 1 million km **b.** 10 million km **c.** 5800 million km

6 About how much farther from the sun is Uranus than Saturn?
a. 1400 million km **b.** 2800 million km **c.** 4200 million km

7 About how much farther from the sun is Jupiter than Mars?
a. 100 million km **b.** 200 million km **c.** 300 million km

Lynn completed a survey about the birthdays of all the students at Evers School. She recorded the results on a chart. But she lost about half of the chart when her dog chewed it up. Study what is left of Lynn's chart.

Month	Number of Student Birthdays
January	15
February	18
March	13
April	20
May	17
June	16

Give exact answers to these questions.

8 How many students have birthdays in
  a. February?   **b.** June?

9 Name a month in which exactly 17 students have birthdays.

10 How many more students have birthdays in February than in January?

11 How many students have birthdays during the first three months of the year?

Make good estimates about the answers to these questions.

12 About how many students have birthdays in
  a. August?   **b.** September?

13 About how many students have birthdays during the second half of the year?

14 About how many students do you think there are in Evers School?

Use a computer or other means to make a similar chart for your school or class. See how well you can estimate the number of birthdays in the whole year from the number in the first half of the year (January through June).

Make up some problems that can be answered from the chart. Write them in your Math Journal. Ask a friend to answer them.

LESSON
26

Unit 1 Review

Count up or down. Write the missing numbers.

Lesson 3

1 47, 48, 49, ▓, ▓, ▓, ▓, ▓, 55

2 5494, 5493, 5492, ▓, ▓, ▓, ▓, 5487

3 666, 667, 668, ▓, ▓, ▓, ▓, ▓, 674

4 26,549; 26,548; 26,547; ▓; ▓; ▓; ▓; 26,542

Add or subtract to solve for n.

Lessons 5–7

5 $17 - 7 = n$ **6** $n = 6 + 8$ **7** $15 - 6 = n$

8 $8 + 9 = n$ **9** $n = 7 + 9$ **10** $14 - 8 = n$

11 $12 - 6 = n$ **12** $n = 5 + 8$ **13** $7 + 7 = n$

Solve for n.

Lessons 8, 9

14 $8 + n = 12$ **15** $14 = n + 5$ **16** $5 + n = 10$

17 $n - 7 = 10$ **18** $9 = 17 - n$ **19** $n - 10 = 6$

20 $n + 6 = 18$ **21** $15 = n + 8$ **22** $18 = 9 + n$

Add or subtract.

Lessons 12–15

23 $87 - 46$ **24** $49 + 73$ **25** $492 + 764$ **26** $231 - 108$

27 $792 + 83$ **28** $201 - 49$ **29** $643 + 27$ **30** $896 - 498$

31 $2741 + 893$ **32** $205 - 106$ **33** $4812 + 689$ **34** $2974 - 105$

35
$$\begin{array}{r} 63,587,304 \\ -\ 24,069,253 \end{array}$$

36
$$\begin{array}{r} 30,942,176 \\ +\ 58,417,926 \end{array}$$

37
$$\begin{array}{r} 27 \\ 62 \\ +\ 48 \\ \hline \end{array}$$

38
$$\begin{array}{r} 95 \\ 106 \\ +\ 247 \\ \hline \end{array}$$

39
$$\begin{array}{r} 8921 \\ -\ 4639 \end{array}$$

40
$$\begin{array}{r} 4761 \\ +\ 2984 \end{array}$$

41
$$\begin{array}{r} 743 \\ -\ 646 \end{array}$$

42
$$\begin{array}{r} 29,873 \\ -\ 21,791 \end{array}$$

Replace ● with <, >, or =.

Lessons 16, 22

43. $4.75 ● $3.89

44. $5.62 ● $5.62

45. $2.75 ● $2.57

46. $21.31 ● $36.57

47. $18.99 ● $25.47

48. $17.99 ● $18.00

49. $25.44 ● $16.43

50. $28.00 ● $32.50

51. $2.98 ● $2.98

Add or subtract.

Lesson 23

52. $3.50 + $4.61

53. $8.03 − $3.99

54. $2.49 + $6.98

55. $5.00 − $3.21

56. $9.68 + $17.97

57. $8.43 − $2.73

58. $16.43 + $10.41

59. $18.41 − $2.90

60. $10.00 − $5.50

Find the perimeter.

Lesson 10

61.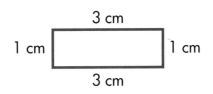

62.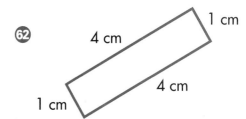

63.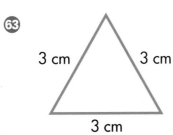

64.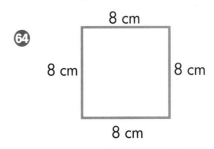

Study the chart. Then give exact answers to these questions.

Lesson 11

65. How many boys ride to school?

66. How many students ride the bus?

67. How many more girls ride to school than walk?

68. How many students ride to school in a car?

69. How many more boys than girls ride in cars?

How We Go to School		
	Boys	Girls
Walk	32	45
Bus	57	43
Car	23	18

◆ **LESSON 26 Unit 1 Review**

Distances from New York, New York

City	Distance (in kilometers)
Alexandria, Egypt	8,034
Bombay, India	13,175
Colón, Panama	3,178
Istanbul, Turkey	8,064
Lisbon, Portugal	4,717
Paris, France	4,830
St. John's, Newfoundland	1,740
Shanghai, China	14,643

Use the table to choose the best answer.

Lessons 11, 14, 18, 25

70 About how much farther is it from Lisbon to New York than from Lisbon to St. John's?

   a. About 1,500 km
   b. About 3,000 km
   c. Not enough information

71 About how much farther is it from New York to Istanbul than from New York to Paris?

   a. About 1,500 km
   b. About 3,000 km
   c. About 5,000 km

72 About how far is it from Alexandria to New York to Shanghai?

   a. About 16,000 km
   b. About 8,000 km
   c. About 22,500 km

73 About how far is it from Bombay to New York to Colón?

   a. About 14,500 km
   b. About 16,000 km
   c. About 18,000 km

Lesson 20 **74** About how full is the gas tank?

    a. Completely full

    b. $\frac{3}{4}$ full

    c. $\frac{1}{2}$ full

75 About how full is the pitcher?

    a. $\frac{3}{4}$

    b. $\frac{1}{3}$

    c. $\frac{1}{2}$

76 About what fraction of the spinner is red?

    a. About $\frac{1}{3}$

    b. About $\frac{1}{2}$

    c. About $\frac{2}{3}$

Solve these problems.

77 The car Ms. Simon wants to buy costs about $9000. She has saved about $4500. About how much more money does she need?

Lessons 13, 15, 21

78 Yesterday Sabina bought a bicycle for $98. Today she bought a basket for it for $13. Jane bought the same kind of bicycle with a basket for $109. Who paid less for her bicycle and basket?

79 Ahmed is 11 years old. He is four years older than his brother and six years older than his sister. How old is his brother?

80 Dwayne ran around the track 17 times in one direction and six times in the other direction. How many times did he run around the track?

LESSON 27

Unit 1 Practice

Add or subtract.

Lessons 5–9

① $5 + 8 = n$ ② $n = 4 + 4$ ③ $18 - 8 = n$ ④ $n = 8 + 8$

⑤ $n = 5 + 8$ ⑥ $17 - 8 = n$ ⑦ $n = 12 - 10$ ⑧ $8 - 8 = n$

⑨ $n = 7 + 9$ ⑩ $n = 14 - 6$ ⑪ $8 + 3 = n$ ⑫ $n = 16 - 9$

⑬ $2 + 8 = n$ ⑭ $n = 12 - 9$ ⑮ $14 - 9 = n$ ⑯ $n = 16 - 10$

ALGEBRA READINESS

Solve for *n*. Watch the signs.

Lessons 5–9

⑰ $8 + n = 13$ ⑱ $6 + n = 15$ ⑲ $10 = 13 - n$ ⑳ $14 - n = 6$

㉑ $15 = 8 + n$ ㉒ $n - 5 = 10$ ㉓ $10 = 17 - n$ ㉔ $14 = n + 9$

㉕ $4 + n = 8$ ㉖ $4 = n - 9$ ㉗ $8 + n = 14$ ㉘ $10 = n - 8$

㉙ $12 = 6 + n$ ㉚ $9 = 18 - n$ ㉛ $8 + n = 8$ ㉜ $10 = n - 7$

Lesson 5 **Add.**

㉝	㉞	㉟	㊱	㊲	㊳
7	6	5	3	1	2
9	8	4	5	3	3
6	3	6	8	5	5
+ 5	+ 2	+ 3	+ 1	+ 7	+ 7

㊴	㊵	㊶	㊷	㊸	㊹
5	8	5	3	7	9
+ 6	+ 9	+ 9	+ 9	+ 6	+ 2

Lesson 5 **Add. Solve for *n*.**

㊺ $5 + 7 + 3 = n$ ㊻ $9 + 7 + 3 = n$ ㊼ $6 + 7 + 5 = n$

㊽ $8 + 6 + 4 = n$ ㊾ $8 + 3 + 7 + 4 = n$ ㊿ $3 + 2 + 9 + 4 = n$

(51) $3 + 5 + 2 = n$ (52) $5 + 9 + 8 + 1 = n$ (53) $7 + 4 + 7 + 3 = n$

(54) $2 + 7 + 4 = n$ (55) $4 + 2 + 8 + 1 = n$ (56) $6 + 2 + 1 + 4 = n$

(57) $8 + 1 + 2 = n$ (58) $5 + 4 + 3 + 1 = n$ (59) $7 + 3 + 2 + 4 = n$

Lesson 12 **Add.**

60. 56
    + 97

61. 83
    + 46

62. 186
    + 39

63. 39
    + 208

64. 346
    + 287

65. 470
    + 208

66. 3408
    + 2697

67. 210
    + 25

68. 789
    + 300

69. 3461
    + 2879

Lesson 13 **Subtract.**

70. 793
    − 200

71. 92
    − 67

72. 607
    − 289

73. 573
    − 381

74. 491
    − 268

75. 60
    − 37

76. 589
    − 280

77. 260
    − 173

78. 3508
    − 809

79. 6379
    − 370

Lessons 14, 15 **Add or subtract. Watch the signs.**

80. 593
    + 248

81. 28
    + 7

82. 43,572
    − 1,281

83. 53,408,761
    + 721,508

84. 3,472,694
    + 5,309,721

85. 61,204
    − 34,561

86. 793
    + 291

87. 804,721
    − 712,438

Find the missing digit.

ALGEBRA READINESS

88. 407
    − 229
    1■8

89. 602
    − 345
    25■

90. 321
    − 285
    ■6

91. 775
    − 391
    3■4

92. 274
    − 106
    16■

Lesson 17

93. 437
    − 328
    1■9

94. 581
    − 437
    14■

95. 862
    − 392
    4■0

96. 349
    − 178
    1■1

97. 943
    − 271
    6■2

◆ **LESSON 27**   Unit 1 Practice

Add or subtract. Watch the signs.

Lesson 23

98 $2.30
  + 5.40

99 $6.81
  + 7.93

100 $3.75
  + 4.25

101 $5.25
  − 3.75

102 $18.75
  + 14.50

103 $4.73
  − 3.98

104 $18.75
  − 14.50

105 $6.00
  − 1.75

Replace ● in each statement with <, >, or =.

Lessons 16, 22

106 $6.38 ● $4.98   **107** $5.05 ● $5.05   **108** $3.76 ● $4.00

109 $5.11 ● $5.51   **110** $7.00 ● $6.97   **111** $4.00 ● $4

112 $5.05 ● $5.50   **113** $8.95 ● $8.59   **114** $23.70 ● $2.37

115 $2.39 ● $2.93   **116** $7.53 ● $7.00   **117** $9.00 ● $9

Solve.

118 After school Miguel, Billy, and Tracy ate six of the twelve brownies Billy's father had baked. About what fraction of the brownies did they eat?

Lesson 20

a. About $\frac{1}{4}$ **b.** About $\frac{1}{2}$ **c.** About $\frac{3}{4}$

119 The United Fund drive in Seneca has a goal of $50,000. So far, $30,000 has been raised. About what fraction of the goal has been raised so far?

a. About $\frac{1}{5}$ **b.** About $\frac{2}{5}$ **c.** About $\frac{3}{5}$

120 Kim put all her comic books in a stack. So did Paco. The height of Kim's stack is about what fraction of the height of Paco's stack?

a. About $\frac{1}{3}$ **b.** About $\frac{1}{2}$

c. About $\frac{1}{8}$

KIM   PACO

Lesson 21 Write each amount as a fraction of a dollar. Then write it as cents. The first one has been done for you.

	Coins	Fraction of a Dollar	Cents
121		$\frac{3}{4}$	75¢
122		■	■
123		■	■
124		■	■

Solve these problems.

125 Franklin wants to swim 20 laps in the pool. If he swims 11, has he swum more than $\frac{1}{2}$ of them?

Lessons 13, 15, 21

126 Hannah has walked six blocks from her house toward her aunt's house. There are 13 blocks between their houses. About what part of the distance has she walked?
  a. About $\frac{1}{4}$ **b.** About $\frac{3}{4}$ **c.** About $\frac{1}{2}$

127 There are 1000 meters in a kilometer. How many meters are there in 2 kilometers?

128 There are 1000 grams in a kilogram. How many grams are there in 2 kilograms?

129 Juan weighs 47 kilograms. His father weighs 76 kilograms. What is the difference in their weights?

130 Jess bought a car for $12,000. He withdrew $7345 from his savings account to pay for it. How much money does Jess still owe for the car?

Unit Test

Count up or down. Write the missing numbers.

1 526, 525, 524, ▇, ▇, ▇, ▇, ▇, 518

2 207, 208, 209, ▇, ▇, ▇, ▇, 214

3 85, 84, 83, ▇, ▇, ▇, ▇, ▇, ▇, 76

Add or subtract to solve for *n*. Watch the signs.

4 $n = 8 + 9$ **5** $17 - 9 = n$ **6** $10 = 19 - n$

7 $n = 13 - 6$ **8** $n = 8 + 6$ **9** $6 + n = 13$

10 $6 + 9 = n$ **11** $11 - 2 = n$ **12** $n - 14 = 3$

13 $7 + 8 = n$ **14** $n = 16 - 9$ **15** $5 + n = 18$

16 $n = 8 - 3$ **17** $n = 9 + 5$ **18** $14 - 5 = n$

19 $5 + 9 = n$ **20** $3 + 9 = n$ **21** $17 = n + 5$

Add or subtract.

22 45
+ 38

23 927
− 359

24 271
+ 899

25 4789
+ 2228

26 4789
− 2228

27 12,021
− 2,867

28 36
49
+ 82

29 329
472
+ 605

30 405
328
+ 82

31 839
642
+ 100

Replace ● with <, >, or =.

32 $6.58 ● $3.27   **33** $11.22 ● $13.08   **34** $6.39 ● $6.93

35 $5.05 ● $5.05   **36** $14.00 ● $14   **37** $2.55 ● $2.45

Add or subtract.

38 $7.05 − $6.88   **39** $6.00 − $2.50   **40** $5.95 − $2.90

41 $86. 41 + $3.98   **42** $122.67 + $8.05   **43** $80.00 + $4.93

Find the perimeter.

44 1 cm [rectangle] 5 cm / 5 cm / 1 cm

45 2 cm [triangle] 2 cm / 2 cm

46 1 cm [rectangle] 2 cm / 2 cm / 1 cm

Solve.

47 About how much of the rectangle is colored?

a. $\frac{1}{4}$ **b.** $\frac{1}{2}$ **c.** $\frac{7}{8}$

48 About how full is the glass?

a. $\frac{1}{2}$ **b.** $\frac{2}{3}$ **c.** $\frac{1}{4}$

49 About how full is the gas tank?

a. $\frac{1}{4}$ **b.** $\frac{1}{2}$ **c.** $\frac{3}{4}$

Solve these problems.

50 The talking movie was invented in 1927. The telephone was invented 51 years earlier. In what year was that?

51 There were 12 people who finished a 10,000-meter race. Charlene finished third. How many people finished behind her?

52 Mark weighs 37 kilograms. Two years ago he weighed 31 kilograms. How much weight did he gain in those two years?

53 Chicago, Illinois, is about 460 kilometers from St. Louis, Missouri. About how far is a round trip between these cities?

Theodore Roosevelt was born in 1858. Franklin Roosevelt was born in 1882.

54 Who was older in 1890?

55 How old was Franklin Roosevelt in 1890?

HOW MANY BOOKS ARE IN THE SCHOOL LIBRARY?

Six students in Mrs. Yonteff's fourth-grade class had a contest. Each student estimated the number of books in the school library. Their first estimates were made without visiting the library. Their second estimates were made after visiting the library for five minutes. That was too short a time to count the books. They recorded their estimates to determine who won the contest.

Here's how they recorded their estimates.

NAME	FIRST ESTIMATE	SECOND ESTIMATE
Mark	152,345	4750
Sara	23,456	5675
Wendy	1265	3896
Todd	5000	5500
Nancy	47,568	3987
Ahmad	10,450	8934

When the contest was over, the class asked Mr. Culyer, the librarian, how many books were in the library. He said that according to his records, the library had more than 4650 books. Most of the time about 200 library books are checked out.

1 Whose estimate was the highest before visiting the library?

2 Whose estimate was the lowest before visiting the library?

3 Whose estimate changed the most after visiting the library? By how much?

4 Whose estimate changed the least after visiting the library?

5 Who do you think made the most accurate estimates? Write your reasons.

Have Your Own Contest

Estimate how many books are in your school library.

Decide how to make the contest fair.

◆ Does your school have enough books in the library? How can you find out? If more books are needed, what can you do to help?

UNIT
2

Multiplication and Division

OPERATIONS

- angles

- adding and subtracting time

- measurement

- algebra readiness

- common multiples

SCHOOL TO WORK CONNECTION

Athletes use math . . .

Coaches use addition, subtraction, multiplication, and division to calculate athletes' average times or distances. Runners must calculate their fastest times for a variety of distances. Pole vaulters and discus throwers also use their knowledge about angles and speed to achieve good distances and heights.

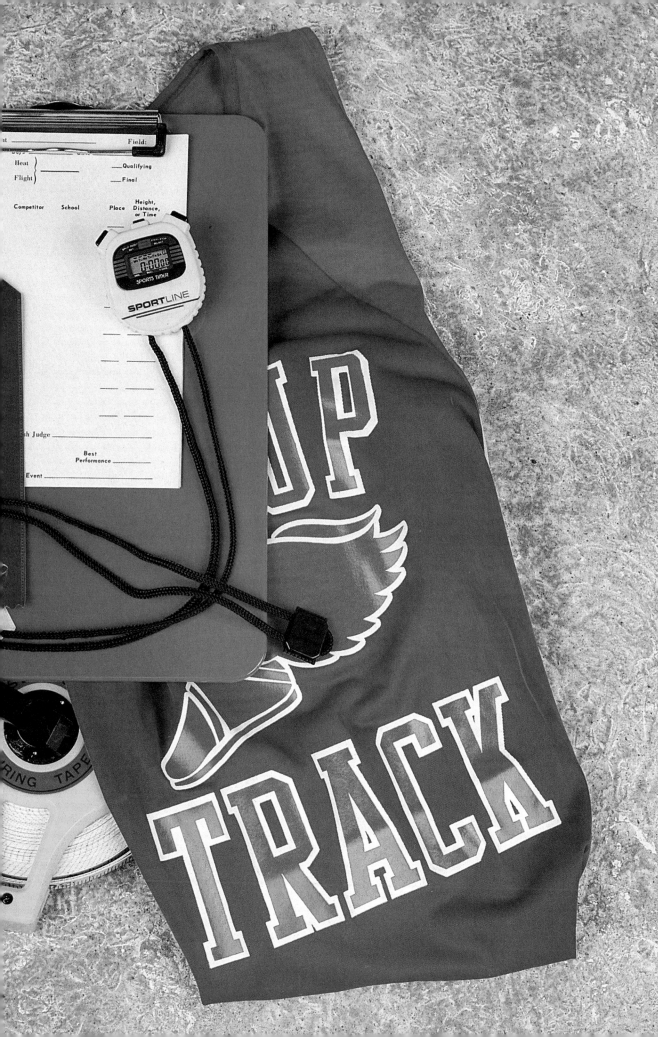

Multiplying by 0, 1, 2, and 10

George knows his birthday is exactly eight weeks from today. He wants to know how many days that is. He starts counting on the calendar, "1, 2, 3, 4, 5, 6, 7, 8, 9, . . ."

"I know a better way," Sharon says. "Add 7 and 7 and 7, and so on until you've added eight 7s."

$$7 + 7 + 7 + 7 + 7 + 7 + 7 + 7 = ?$$

◆ Do you know a quicker way?

◆ Do you remember what 8×7 is?

SEPTEMBER						
SUNDAY	MONDAY	TUESDAY	WEDNESDAY	THURSDAY	FRIDAY	SATURDAY
	1	2	3	4	5	6
7	8	9	10	11	12	13
14	15	16	17	18	19	20
21	22	23	24	25	26	27
28	29	30				

Solve these problems.

There are seven days in a week.

1. How many days are there in eight weeks? $8 \times 7 = n$

2. How many days are there in seven weeks? $7 \times 7 = n$

3. How many days are there in six weeks? $6 \times 7 = n$

4. How many days are there in five weeks? $5 \times 7 = n$

5. How many days are there in nine weeks? $9 \times 7 = n$

Remember, to find the area of a rectangle, multiply the length by the width.

What is the area of the rectangle?

Area = 3 × 5 square centimeters

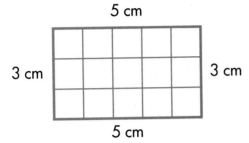

Let's turn the rectangle on its side.

Area = 5 × 3 square centimeters

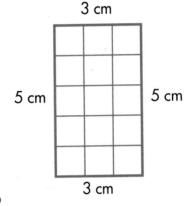

◆ Did the area of the rectangle change?

◆ Does 3 × 5 = 5 × 3?

◆ What is 3 × 5?

◆ What is 5 × 3?

Rule: **The order in which two numbers are multiplied makes no difference to the answer.**

Multiply. Compare the problems in each pair.

6 $2 \times 5 = n$
$5 \times 2 = n$

7 $1 \times 8 = n$
$8 \times 1 = n$

8 $10 \times 4 = n$
$4 \times 10 = n$

9 $5 \times 5 = n$
$5 \times 5 = n$

10 $9 \times 0 = n$
$0 \times 9 = n$

11 $3 \times 4 = n$
$4 \times 3 = n$

12 $3 \times 9 = n$
$9 \times 3 = n$

13 $5 \times 8 = n$
$8 \times 5 = n$

14 $6 \times 9 = n$
$9 \times 6 = n$

15 $7 \times 9 = n$
$9 \times 7 = n$

16 $6 \times 4 = n$
$4 \times 6 = n$

17 $4 \times 8 = n$
$8 \times 4 = n$

18 $2 \times 4 = n$
$4 \times 2 = n$

19 $3 \times 5 = n$
$5 \times 3 = n$

20 $9 \times 1 = n$
$1 \times 9 = n$

21 $4 \times 2 = n$
$2 \times 4 = n$

◆ LESSON 28 Multiplying by 0, 1, 2, and 10

Solve these problems.

There are seven days in a week.

22 How many days are there in two weeks?
$2 \times 7 = n$

23 How many days are there in one week?
$1 \times 7 = n$

24 How many days are there in zero weeks?
$0 \times 7 = n$

25 How many days are there in ten weeks?
$10 \times 7 = n$

There are five fingers on a hand.

26 How many fingers are there on two hands?
$2 \times 5 = n$

27 How many fingers are there on one hand?
$1 \times 5 = n$

28 How many fingers are there on zero hands?
$0 \times 5 = n$

29 How many fingers are there on ten hands?
$10 \times 5 = n$

In your Math Journal state a rule and give an example for:

◆ **Multiplying by 2.**

◆ **Multiplying by 1.**

◆ **Multiplying by 0.**

◆ **Multiplying by 10.**

Multiply. Watch your numbering.

30 $6 \times 10 = n$ **32** $9 \times 10 = n$ **34** $7 \times 10 = n$

31 $10 \times 6 = n$ **33** $10 \times 9 = n$ **35** $10 \times 7 = n$

Multiply to solve for _n_.

(36) $0 \times 5 = n$ (37) $4 \times 10 = n$ (38) $6 \times 2 = n$

(39) $5 \times 0 = n$ (40) $2 \times 9 = n$ (41) $10 \times 2 = n$

(42) $8 \times 1 = n$ (43) $9 \times 2 = n$ (44) $1 \times 9 = n$

(45) $1 \times 8 = n$ (46) $1 \times 10 = n$ (47) $7 \times 0 = n$

(48) $2 \times 7 = n$ (49) $10 \times 0 = n$ (50) $0 \times 8 = n$

(51) $2 \times 10 = n$ (52) $5 \times 10 = n$ (53) $8 \times 10 = n$

(54) $10 \times 4 = n$ (55) $2 \times 8 = n$ (56) $7 \times 2 = n$

Multiply.

(57) $\begin{array}{r} 7 \\ \times\ 1 \\ \hline \end{array}$ (58) $\begin{array}{r} 6 \\ \times\ 2 \\ \hline \end{array}$ (59) $\begin{array}{r} 7 \\ \times\ 10 \\ \hline \end{array}$ (60) $\begin{array}{r} 10 \\ \times\ 8 \\ \hline \end{array}$ (61) $\begin{array}{r} 4 \\ \times\ 10 \\ \hline \end{array}$

(62) $\begin{array}{r} 10 \\ \times\ 2 \\ \hline \end{array}$ (63) $\begin{array}{r} 8 \\ \times\ 0 \\ \hline \end{array}$ (64) $\begin{array}{r} 5 \\ \times\ 2 \\ \hline \end{array}$ (65) $\begin{array}{r} 2 \\ \times\ 8 \\ \hline \end{array}$ (66) $\begin{array}{r} 2 \\ \times\ 7 \\ \hline \end{array}$

(67) $\begin{array}{r} 1 \\ \times\ 8 \\ \hline \end{array}$ (68) $\begin{array}{r} 0 \\ \times\ 1 \\ \hline \end{array}$ (69) $\begin{array}{r} 2 \\ \times\ 10 \\ \hline \end{array}$ (70) $\begin{array}{r} 2 \\ \times\ 9 \\ \hline \end{array}$ (71) $\begin{array}{r} 10 \\ \times\ 5 \\ \hline \end{array}$

(72) $\begin{array}{r} 4 \\ \times\ 1 \\ \hline \end{array}$ (73) $\begin{array}{r} 9 \\ \times\ 1 \\ \hline \end{array}$ (74) $\begin{array}{r} 7 \\ \times\ 2 \\ \hline \end{array}$ (75) $\begin{array}{r} 10 \\ \times\ 0 \\ \hline \end{array}$ (76) $\begin{array}{r} 8 \\ \times\ 2 \\ \hline \end{array}$

For many people, two of the hardest multiplication facts to remember are $7 \times 8 = 56$ and $7 \times 6 = 42$. Try to remember them!

(77) $\begin{array}{r} 8 \\ \times\ 7 \\ \hline \end{array}$ (78) $\begin{array}{r} 7 \\ \times\ 6 \\ \hline \end{array}$ (79) $\begin{array}{r} 7 \\ \times\ 8 \\ \hline \end{array}$ (80) $\begin{array}{r} 6 \\ \times\ 7 \\ \hline \end{array}$

Multiplying by 5 and 9

$7 \times 8 = ?$

The multiplication table is a short way to list the multiplication facts. To find 7×8, look in the row marked 7 and the column marked 8.

◆ What number do you find there?

◆ Did you expect to find that number?

Use the table to find these facts.

1 $8 \times 7 = n$

2 $7 \times 6 = n$

3 $7 \times 7 = n$

4 $8 \times 8 = n$

Compare the columns marked 5 and 10 on the multiplication table.

◆ What is 4×10?
   What is 4×5?

◆ What is 6×10?
   What is 6×5?

◆ What is 8×10?   What is 8×5?

x	0	1	2	3	4	5	6	7	8	9	10
0	0	0	0	0	0	0	0	0	0	0	0
1	0	1	2	3	4	5	6	7	8	9	10
2	0	2	4	6	8	10	12	14	16	18	20
3	0	3	6	9	12	15	18	21	24	27	30
4	0	4	8	12	16	20	24	28	32	36	40
5	0	5	10	15	20	25	30	35	40	45	50
6	0	6	12	18	24	30	36	42	48	54	60
7	0	7	14	21	28	35	42	49	56	63	70
8	0	8	16	24	32	40	48	56	64	72	80
9	0	9	18	27	36	45	54	63	72	81	90
10	0	10	20	30	40	50	60	70	80	90	100

x	0	1	2	3	4	5	6	7	8	9	10
0	0	0	0	0	0	0	0	0	0	0	0
1	0	1	2	3	4	5	6	7	8	9	10
2	0	2	4	6	8	10	12	14	16	18	20
3	0	3	6	9	12	15	18	21	24	27	30
4	0	4	8	12	16	20	24	28	32	36	40
5	0	5	10	15	20	25	30	35	40	45	50
6	0	6	12	18	24	30	36	42	48	54	60
7	0	7	14	21	28	35	42	49	56	63	70
8	0	8	16	24	32	40	48	56	64	72	80
9	0	9	18	27	36	45	54	63	72	81	90
10	0	10	20	30	40	50	60	70	80	90	100

To multiply 8×10, you can write 8 with a 0 after it. To multiply 8×5, you can write $\frac{1}{2}$ of 8 (which is 4) with a 0 after it. This is because 5 is $\frac{1}{2}$ of 10.

Try to solve these problems without looking at the multiplication table.

5 $2 \times 5 = n$ **6** $4 \times 5 = n$ **7** $6 \times 5 = n$ **8** $8 \times 5 = n$

9 $10 \times 5 = n$ **10** $5 \times 6 = n$ **11** $5 \times 8 = n$ **12** $5 \times 10 = n$

To solve 7×5 isn't so easy. But here's a way: You know that 6×5 is 30. Now add one more 5 to make 7×5. That's 30 and 5 more, which is 35.

Try to solve these problems without looking at the multiplication table.

⑬ $3 \times 5 = n$ ⑭ $5 \times 5 = n$ ⑮ $7 \times 5 = n$ ⑯ $9 \times 5 = n$

⑰ $5 \times 7 = n$ ⑱ $5 \times 1 = n$ ⑲ $5 \times 9 = n$ ⑳ $5 \times 3 = n$

On the multiplication table, compare the 9 and 10 columns.

◆ What is 7×10?   What is 7×9?

   Is it $70 - 7$?

◆ What is 8×10?   What is 8×9?

   Is it $80 - 8$?

To find 7×9, you can find 7×10 and then subtract 7.

To find 8×9, you can find 8×10 and then subtract 8.

◆ What can you do to find 6×9?

×	0	1	2	3	4	5	6	7	8	9	10
0	0	0	0	0	0	0	0	0	0	0	0
1	0	1	2	3	4	5	6	7	8	9	10
2	0	2	4	6	8	10	12	14	16	18	20
3	0	3	6	9	12	15	18	21	24	27	30
4	0	4	8	12	16	20	24	28	32	36	40
5	0	5	10	15	20	25	30	35	40	45	50
6	0	6	12	18	24	30	36	42	48	54	60
7	0	7	14	21	28	35	42	49	56	63	70
8	0	8	16	24	32	40	48	56	64	72	80
9	0	9	18	27	36	45	54	63	72	81	90
10	0	10	20	30	40	50	60	70	80	90	100

Now try these. Solve for _n_.

㉑ $9 \times 8 = n$ ㉒ $9 \times 7 = n$ ㉓ $7 \times 9 = n$ ㉔ $5 \times 9 = n$

㉕ $4 \times 9 = n$ ㉖ $9 \times 9 = n$ ㉗ $9 \times 6 = n$ ㉘ $3 \times 9 = n$

㉙ $9 \times 2 = n$ ㉚ $6 \times 9 = n$ ㉛ $8 \times 9 = n$ ㉜ $9 \times 1 = n$

◆ What happens when you add the digits in the answer to 9×8?

$9 \times 8 = 72$

$7 + 2 = 9$ The sum of the digits is 9.

㉝ Add the digits in each answer for problems 21 through 32.

LESSON 30

Reviewing Multiplication Facts

You may be surprised to find out how many of the multiplication facts you already know.

◆ Use a computer or other means to draw and complete this multiplication table.

How many multiplication facts do you know?

◆ Do you know the 0, 1, 2, and 10 multiplication facts? If you do, cross off the 0, 1, 2, and 10 columns and the 0, 1, 2, and 10 rows.

◆ Do you know the 5 and 9 multiplication facts? If you do, cross off the 5 and 9 rows and columns.

×	0	1	2	3	4	5	6	7	8	9	10
0	0	0									
1		1									
2		2	4	6		10	12	14			
3				9	12	15		21			
4								28	32		
5									40		
6								42	48		
7								49			
8							48	56			
9							54				
10							60	70			

If you do not know these multiplication facts, practice them!

Do you remember these? Solve for n.

❶ $7 \times 8 = n$ ❷ $8 \times 7 = n$ ❸ $6 \times 7 = n$ ❹ $7 \times 6 = n$

There are 121 facts listed in the multiplication table.

◆ How many do you know?

◆ How many are left to learn?

Help a classmate learn the multiplication facts. Ask each other several multiplication facts. You may use the multiplication table to help you.

Keep in shape by practicing your multiplication facts.

SELF ASSESSMENT

Are You Shiny or Rusty?

Very shiny	37 or more right
Shiny	32–36 right
A bit rusty	27–31 right
Rusty	Fewer than 27 right

Multiply to solve for n.

5 $5 \times 8 = n$ **6** $0 \times 8 = n$ **7** $5 \times 4 = n$ **8** $1 \times 5 = n$

9 $4 \times 9 = n$ **10** $1 \times 8 = n$ **11** $7 \times 5 = n$ **12** $5 \times 3 = n$

13 $7 \times 8 = n$ **14** $2 \times 8 = n$ **15** $2 \times 5 = n$ **16** $5 \times 9 = n$

17 $6 \times 7 = n$ **18** $7 \times 2 = n$ **19** $9 \times 5 = n$ **20** $9 \times 2 = n$

21 $10 \times 6 = n$ **22** $2 \times 9 = n$ **23** $0 \times 9 = n$ **24** $9 \times 3 = n$

25 $7 \times 0 = n$ **26** $8 \times 7 = n$ **27** $9 \times 9 = n$ **28** $9 \times 4 = n$

29 $8 \times 9 = n$ **30** $7 \times 6 = n$ **31** $3 \times 9 = n$ **32** $9 \times 8 = n$

33 $6 \times 9 = n$ **34** $5 \times 6 = n$ **35** $2 \times 2 = n$ **36** $10 \times 7 = n$

Multiply.

37 $\begin{array}{r} 9 \\ \times\ 6 \\ \hline \end{array}$ **38** $\begin{array}{r} 9 \\ \times\ 7 \\ \hline \end{array}$ **39** $\begin{array}{r} 2 \\ \times\ 6 \\ \hline \end{array}$ **40** $\begin{array}{r} 5 \\ \times\ 2 \\ \hline \end{array}$ **41** $\begin{array}{r} 2 \\ \times\ 0 \\ \hline \end{array}$

42 $\begin{array}{r} 5 \\ \times\ 7 \\ \hline \end{array}$ **43** $\begin{array}{r} 5 \\ \times\ 10 \\ \hline \end{array}$ **44** $\begin{array}{r} 10 \\ \times\ 5 \\ \hline \end{array}$ **45** $\begin{array}{r} 0 \\ \times\ 10 \\ \hline \end{array}$ **46** $\begin{array}{r} 5 \\ \times\ 6 \\ \hline \end{array}$

LESSON 31

Using Multiplication: Area of a Square

A **right angle** looks like this:

These are right angles: These are not right angles:

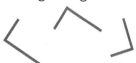

◆ Can you find some right angles in your classroom?

◆ Can you find some angles in your classroom that are not right angles?

A triangle that has a right angle is called a **right triangle.**

These are right triangles: These are not right triangles:

SOCIAL STUDIES CONNECTION

The ancient Greeks found something very interesting about right triangles. They found it by looking at squares on the sides of the triangles. Look at this triangle and the three squares. See if you find anything interesting.

Remember, to find the area of a square, multiply the length of a side by itself.
$A = side \times side$

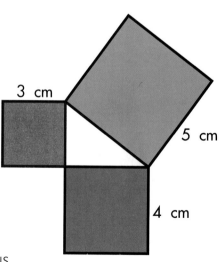

3 cm

5 cm

4 cm

Solve these problems.

1 What is the area of the red square?

2 What is the area of the blue square?

3 What is the area of the red square plus the area of the blue square?

4 What is the area of the green square?

Each small box is 1 square centimeter.

◆ Does the triangle have a right angle?

◆ What is the area of the red square?

◆ What is the area of the blue square?

◆ What is the area of the green square? (Hint: Count the square centimeters. Pair the half squares to make whole squares.)

◆ What is the area of the red square plus the area of the blue square?

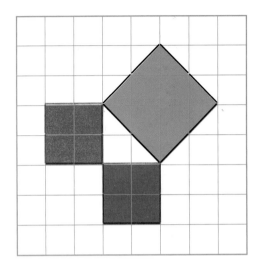

Using graph paper, try this experiment yourself. Complete the chart.

Length of Side	Area of Square
1 cm	■
2 cm	■
3 cm	■
4 cm	■
5 cm	■
6 cm	■
7 cm	■
8 cm	■
9 cm	■
10 cm	■

(5) (6) (7) (8) (9) (10) (11) (12) (13) (14)

Multiplying by 3, 4, 6, and 8

Add the Products Game

COOPERATIVE LEARNING

Players:	Two or more
Materials:	Two 0–5 cubes
Object:	To score a total of 50 or more
Math Focus:	Multiplication and addition

RULES

1. Take turns rolling both cubes.

2. On each turn, find the product of the two numbers you roll.

3. Add the product to your last score.

If your score was:	And you rolled:	Your new score would be:
12	3 2	18
36	4 0	36
25	5 1	30

4. The first player whose score totals 50 or more is the winner.

OTHER WAYS TO PLAY THIS GAME

1. Use one 0–5 cube and one 5–10 cube. Try to score a total of 150 or more.

2. Use two 5–10 cubes. Try to score a total of 450 or more.

You can use the multiplication facts you know to figure out many other facts.

Multiples of 3 can be found by counting by 3s from a product you know.

Example: $3 \times 7 = n$ Let's say you know that $2 \times 7 = 14$.

Then $3 \times 7 = 14 + 7 = 21$.

Multiples of 6 can be found by doubling multiples of 3, because 6 is twice 3.

Example: $6 \times 7 = n$ Let's say you know that $3 \times 7 = 21$.

Then 6×7 is twice 3×7.

So $6 \times 7 = 21 + 21 = 42$.

Multiples of 4 can be found by doubling multiples of 2.

Example: $4 \times 7 = n$ Let's say you know that $2 \times 7 = 14$.

Then 4×7 is twice 2×7.

So $4 \times 7 = 14 + 14 = 28$.

Multiples of 8 can be found by doubling multiples of 4.

Example: $8 \times 9 = n$ Let's say you know that $4 \times 9 = 36$.

Then 8×9 is twice 4×9.

So $8 \times 9 = 36 + 36 = 72$.

Multiply. Solve for *n*.

1. $4 \times 3 = n$
2. $4 \times 6 = n$
3. $6 \times 4 = n$
4. $8 \times 4 = n$
5. $3 \times 6 = n$
6. $6 \times 6 = n$
7. $9 \times 4 = n$
8. $6 \times 8 = n$
9. $7 \times 3 = n$
10. $7 \times 6 = n$
11. $8 \times 7 = n$
12. $9 \times 8 = n$
13. $8 \times 3 = n$
14. $8 \times 6 = n$
15. $4 \times 7 = n$
16. $8 \times 0 = n$
17. $9 \times 3 = n$
18. $9 \times 6 = n$
19. $4 \times 5 = n$
20. $5 \times 8 = n$
21. $3 \times 9 = n$
22. $5 \times 6 = n$
23. $8 \times 8 = n$
24. $10 \times 8 = n$

Multiplication Facts

You have now reviewed all of the multiplication facts. Try to solve the problems quickly while still getting the right answers.

SELF ASSESSMENT

Are You Shiny or Rusty?

Very shiny	**70 or more right**
Shiny	**65–69 right**
A bit rusty	**60–64 right**
Rusty	**Fewer than 60 right**

Multiply to solve for *n*.

1. $5 \times 3 = n$
2. $n = 4 \times 3$
3. $8 \times 5 = n$
4. $n = 4 \times 5$
5. $3 \times 1 = n$
6. $n = 7 \times 0$
7. $8 \times 2 = n$
8. $n = 2 \times 8$
9. $3 \times 7 = n$
10. $5 \times 10 = n$
11. $7 \times 8 = n$
12. $5 \times 7 = n$
13. $n = 2 \times 7$
14. $5 \times 0 = n$
15. $n = 3 \times 6$
16. $7 \times 1 = n$
17. $n = 6 \times 5$
18. $10 \times 1 = n$
19. $0 \times 8 = n$
20. $4 \times 6 = n$
21. $7 \times 6 = n$
22. $n = 2 \times 5$
23. $6 \times 7 = n$
24. $n = 6 \times 10$
25. $4 \times 4 = n$
26. $n = 9 \times 2$
27. $9 \times 5 = n$
28. $10 \times 7 = n$
29. $1 \times 8 = n$
30. $8 \times 8 = n$
31. $3 \times 4 = n$
32. $n = 2 \times 7$
33. $6 \times 4 = n$
34. $7 \times 3 = n$
35. $n = 9 \times 3$
36. $n = 10 \times 2$

Multiply.

37 5 × 5	**38** 9 × 8	**39** 7 × 8	**40** 9 × 6	**41** 9 × 9	**42** 5 × 1
43 8 × 9	**44** 5 × 9	**45** 6 × 7	**46** 7 × 7	**47** 6 × 6	**48** 3 × 8
49 6 × 8	**50** 5 × 4	**51** 7 × 8	**52** 3 × 8	**53** 6 × 4	**54** 10 × 1

55 6 × 1	**56** 0 × 6	**57** 9 × 7	**58** 6 × 9
59 3 × 3	**60** 9 × 4	**61** 3 × 9	**62** 7 × 6
63 5 × 6	**64** 2 × 7	**65** 6 × 8	**66** 2 × 0
67 7 × 5	**68** 4 × 7	**69** 8 × 3	**70** 3 × 9
71 5 × 8	**72** 5 × 3	**73** 8 × 4	**74** 3 × 1

Solve.

75 Tom gets five baseball cards in every pack of gum that he buys. How many cards will he get in three packs?

On your paper, draw a ring around the problems that took you a long time and the ones you got wrong. Make flash cards for these facts and practice them.

In your Math Journal make a list of real-life examples of when you use multiplication.

◆ **LESSON 33** **Multiplication Facts**

Money Matters

Part 1

Portia and Marcus had the idea of starting a club. Manolita, Ferdie, and Willy joined it. They needed a clubhouse. Mr. Breezy said they could use a shed in his backyard, but they would have to get a new door for it.

"How much will a door cost?" Portia asked.

"You should be able to get a used door for about $10," said Mr. Breezy.

Where would they get $10? "Let's put on a show," said Ferdie. "We'll make people pay money to see it."

Everyone thought that was a good idea. The children found funny clothes to wear. They made a stage by laying an old door on top of some boxes. They cut up pieces of paper and made ten $1 tickets.

Ten people came to the show. Portia sang. Marcus told jokes. Manolita did magic tricks. Ferdie danced. And Willy sold tickets. Everyone liked the show. When it was over, the children rushed to Willy's ticket booth.

"I sold every ticket," Willy said proudly.

"How much money do we have?" the others asked.

"Ten cents," said Willy.

"Just a minute," said Marcus. "We made ten $1 tickets. You said you sold all of them."

"That's right," said Willy. "I sold them for a penny apiece. Here's the money."

"A penny apiece!" they all shouted. "Tickets were supposed to be a dollar apiece!"

"Nobody told me that," Willy said. "I charged what I thought they were worth. I didn't think a little piece of paper was worth a dollar. I figured each ticket cost us about a penny. So that's what I charged."

The children all sat down sadly on their stage. "Now we'll never get a door," Ferdie moaned.

"Yes, we will," said Marcus.

Work in groups. Discuss your answers and how you figured them out. Then compare your answers with those of other groups.

1 How much money would the children have made if Willy had sold all the tickets for the amount planned?

2 Perhaps they wouldn't have made any money at all if Willy had asked as much as he was supposed to for the tickets. How could that be?

3 Do you agree with Willy that it wouldn't be fair to sell tickets for a dollar when they cost only about a penny to make? Why or why not?

4 How could Marcus be so sure they will get a door?

LESSON 34

Using Multiplication

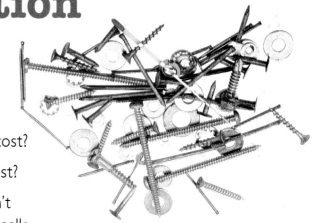

Elena works in a hardware store.
Washers cost 2¢ each.

Answer these questions.

1 How much do seven washers cost?

2 How much do nine washers cost?

3 Elena made a chart so she won't
have to multiply each time she sells
washers. Her chart looks like this:

×2

Washer Chart										
Number of washers	1	2	3	4	5	6	7	8	9	10
Amount (in cents)	2	4								

Use a computer or other means to draw the chart.

4 Nails also cost 2¢ each. Elena decides to
make a nail chart. What will it look like?
Do you think she should make the chart?

5 Small springs cost 7¢ each. Make a chart
for springs like Elena's chart for washers.

6 Lag bolts cost 7¢ each. Either make a
chart for lag bolts or write what you
could use instead.

7 Sets of hooks and eyes cost 9¢ each.
Make a hook-and-eye chart.

8 Make a chart for sandpaper that costs
10¢ a sheet.

Jiro works at a shop that sells stickers. Most stickers cost 20¢, 30¢, 40¢, and so on up to $1.00. On Saturday the store is having a half-price sale, so Jiro decided to make a half-price chart.

Use a computer or other means to draw and complete Jiro's chart. Use play money to help if you need it.

Sticker Chart									
Price (in cents)	20	30	40	50	60	70	80	90	100
Half-Price (in cents)	10			25					

Use Jiro's chart to answer the following questions.

9 On half-price day,

    a. How much would you pay for one sticker regularly priced at 40¢ each?

    b. How much would you pay for two stickers regularly priced at 40¢ each?

    c. How much would you pay for one sticker that usually costs 50¢ each?

    d. How much would you pay for two stickers that usually cost 50¢ each?

10 How much would you pay for both a 20¢ sticker and a 40¢ sticker at the regular price?

11 How much would you pay for a 20¢ sticker and a 40¢ sticker at half-price?

12 How much would you save all together on the stickers in question 11 at the half-price sale?

13 How much would you pay all together for three 30¢-stickers and two 60¢-stickers at the regular price? At half price?

◆ **LESSON 34** Using Multiplication

Use a computer or other means to draw and complete the charts. Complete them by finding what numbers the machines will send out.

⑭ **×5**

In	Out
1	5
2	■
3	■
4	■
5	■

⑮ **×3**

In	Out
8	■
7	■
6	■
5	■
4	■

⑯ **×7**

In	Out
0	■
2	■
4	■
6	■
8	■

⑰ **×2**

In	Out
0	■
2	■
4	■
6	■
8	■

⑱ **×6**

In	Out
8	■
7	■
6	■
5	■
4	■

⑲ **×8**

In	Out
8	■
4	■
2	■
1	■
0	■

⑳ **×4**

In	Out
0	■
2	■
4	■
6	■
8	■

㉑ **×10**

In	Out
3	■
9	■
6	■
4	■
2	■

㉒ **×9**

In	Out
9	■
8	■
7	■
6	■
5	■

Remember, to find the area of a rectangle, multiply the length by the width. $A = l \times w$

What is the area of each rectangle?

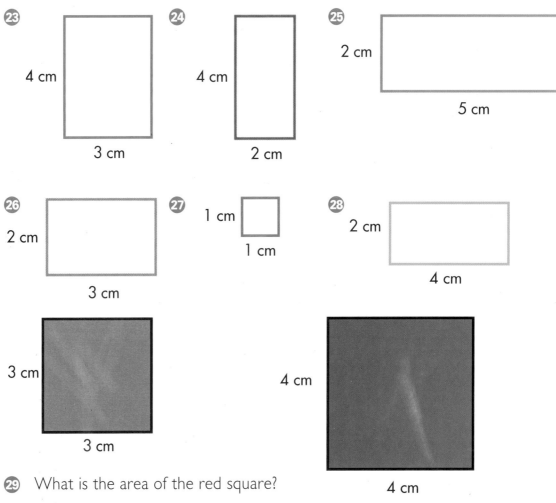

23 4 cm × 3 cm

24 4 cm × 2 cm

25 2 cm × 5 cm

26 2 cm × 3 cm

27 1 cm × 1 cm

28 2 cm × 4 cm

29 What is the area of the red square?

3 cm × 3 cm

30 What is the area of the blue square?

4 cm × 4 cm

Each side of the green square is between 3 and 4 centimeters long.

31 Can the area of the green square be less than 9 square centimeters?

32 Can the area of the green square be more than 16 square centimeters?

Trace the green square. Compare its area with the areas of the red and blue squares.

Calculating Elapsed Time

PHYSICAL EDUCATION CONNECTION

How long is a basketball game?

National Basketball Association (NBA) rules call for the following times.

Regulation Time

◆ The four quarters are each 12 minutes long.

◆ The break between the first and second quarters is $1\frac{1}{2}$ minutes.

◆ The half-time break is ten minutes.

◆ The break between the third and fourth quarters is $1\frac{1}{2}$ minutes.

◆ Time-outs can be called for various reasons.

Overtime

◆ If a game is tied, an overtime period of five minutes is allowed. The five-minute overtime periods continue until there is a winner.

Answer these questions.

How long will a basketball game last if

1 There are no time-outs and no overtime?

2 There are eight minutes of time-outs and two overtime periods?

3 There are 17 minutes of time-outs and no overtime?

Not all whales sing, but humpback whales are known for their beautiful songs. Humpbacks can sing for half an hour at a time and can be heard underwater for hundreds of miles.

Times for high school basketball games are different.

◆ The four quarters are each eight minutes long.

◆ There is a one-minute break between the first and second quarters and between the third and fourth quarters.

◆ There is a ten-minute halftime break between the second and third quarters.

◆ There are three-minute overtime periods.

◆ Time-outs can be called for various reasons.

Answer these questions.

How long will a high school basketball game last if

4 There are no time-outs and no overtime?

5 There are three overtime periods and ten minutes of time-outs?

6 There are 21 minutes of time-outs and no overtime?

Linton High School wants to schedule two basketball games for the same evening. There will be a girls' game and a boys' game. Suppose there are two overtime periods, 23 minutes of time-outs per game, and a 30-minute break between games.

7 What time will the second game end if the first game starts at 7 P.M.?

8 Suppose the principal wants the second game to end by 9 P.M. About what time should the first game start? Explain your reasoning.

In your Math Journal write a paragraph describing real-life situations in which calculating elapsed time is important.

◆ **LESSON 35** Calculating Elapsed Time

Solve these problems. Simplify each answer. You may use a calculator.

⑨ 1 week 4 days + 3 weeks 6 days = ▨

⑩ 13 weeks 5 days + 12 weeks 4 days = ▨

⑪ 2 hours 50 minutes + 3 hours 40 minutes = ▨

⑫ 2 weeks 5 days − 1 week 4 days = ▨

⑬ 5 weeks 2 days − 2 weeks 5 days = ▨

⑭ 3 days 12 hours + 2 days 14 hours = ▨

⑮ 3 weeks 5 days 13 hours 47 minutes + 5 weeks 8 days 21 hours 7 minutes = ▨

⑯ 23 weeks 6 days 9 hours 32 minutes + 17 weeks 5 days 12 hours 48 minutes = ▨

⑰ 23 weeks 6 days 9 hours 32 minutes − 17 weeks 5 days 12 hours 48 minutes = ▨

⑱ 16 weeks 4 days 8 hours − 11 weeks 5 days 7 hours 31 minutes = ▨

⑲ 4 days 40 minutes − 2 hours 35 minutes = ▨

⑳ 6 days 17 hours + 1 week 7 hours = ▨

Halley's Comet was first observed 2200 years ago.

Add or subtract. Use a calculator if you wish.

21. 5 + 2 + 2 + 2

22. 11 − 2 − 2 − 2

23. 1091 + 3 + 3 + 3

24. 2000 − 3 − 3 − 3

25. 5 − 2 − 2 − 2

26. −1 − 2 − 2 − 2

27. −7 + 2 + 2 + 2

28. −1 + 2 + 2 + 2

29. 50 − 60

30. 300 − 500

31. −20 + 90

32. −500 − 100

33. −80 + 30

34. 6 − 3 − 3 − 3

35. 400 − 900

36. −80 − 20

37. 10 − 20 − 20

38. 10 − 20 − 20 − 20

39. −4 − 2 − 2 − 2 − 2

40. −3 + 3 + 3 + 3

41. −8 − 4 − 7 − 2 − 0

42. −4 + 9 − 6 + 2 − 2

43. 110 − 40 − 60 + 2

44. −18 + 12 − 7 − 4 + 2

Solve the following problems.

45. Christine has two weeks and one day of school until summer vacation. Her cousin Jenny, who lives in Florida, has one week and two days left until vacation. How many days will Jenny be out of school while Christine is in school?

46. It took Russ three days and 14 hours to finish the cross country race. It took Gary 2 days and 19 hours to finish. How many hours faster was Gary?

47. Jean's family took a trip to the beach. They drove for one hour and 40 minutes. Angie's family went to the mountains. They drove for two hours and 35 minutes. How much longer was Angie's trip?

LESSON
36

Choosing Appropriate Customary Units

There are 12 inches in 1 foot.
There are 3 feet in 1 yard.
There are 1760 yards, or 5280 feet, in 1 mile.

Remember:

There are 16 ounces in 1 pound.
There are 2000 pounds in 1 ton.

Remember:

There are 8 fluid ounces in 1 cup.
There are 2 cups in 1 pint.
There are 2 pints in 1 quart.
There are 4 quarts in 1 gallon.

For each problem the measure in one of the statements makes more sense than the other. Choose the one that makes more sense. It may be hard to decide which one makes more sense. If you think that both make sense, explain why.

1. I'm going to buy **64 fluid ounces** or **2 quarts** of milk.

2. Hakim is about **$1\frac{3}{4}$ yards** or **5 feet, 3 inches** tall.

3. I want to buy **10 pounds** or **160 ounces** of potatoes.

4. The package contains **4 ounces** or **$\frac{1}{4}$ pound** of jellybeans.

5. The library is about **2 miles** or **3520 yards** from the hospital.

6. The truck weighs about **8000 pounds** or **4 tons**.

7. The bottle of perfume holds about **2 ounces** or **$\frac{1}{8}$ pint**.

8. Allie's desk at school is about **3 feet** or **1 yard** wide.

9. The car's gasoline tank holds about **13 gallons** or **52 quarts** of gas.

10. I need **4 quarts** or **1 gallon** of apple juice.

11. The classroom is about **40 feet** or **480 inches** long.

12. The box contains **$15\frac{1}{2}$ ounces** or **almost a pound** of cereal.

13. The barrel holds **54 gallons** or **216 quarts** of oil.

14. The step is about **11 inches** or **1 foot** high.

15. My older brother weighs about **160 pounds** or **2560 ounces**.

First estimate. Then measure to check.

◆ Name three places that are about 1 mile from your school.

◆ Find three items that come in 1-pint packages.

◆ Name three items that might weigh about 1 pound.

◆ Name three items that come in packages of 1 cup.

LESSON **37**

Choosing Appropriate Metric Units

People in most other countries and some businesses in this country use the metric system of measures. One way to remember the relationships among units in the metric system is to think about the system of money we use. This chart shows the relationships.

Units of Length	Units of Weight	Units of Volume	United States Currency	Number in Basic Unit
millimeter	milligram	milliliter	mill	1000
centimeter	centigram	centiliter	cent	100
decimeter	decigram	deciliter	dime	10
meter*	gram	liter*	dollar*	1
dekameter	dekagram	dekaliter	10 dollars	0.1
hectometer	hectogram	hectoliter	100 dollars	0.01
kilometer	kilogram*	kiloliter	1000 dollars	0.001

The chart shows that just as there are 100 cents in 1 dollar, there are 100 centimeters in 1 meter. An asterisk marks the basic units.

Use the chart to answer these questions.

❶ How many cents are in $1?

❷ How many centimeters are in 1 meter?

❸ How many dollars are in $1000?

❹ How many grams are in 1 kilogram?

❺ How many milliliters are in 1 liter?

❻ How many mills are in $1?

126 • Multiplication and Division

Prepare three questions that can be answered by studying the chart. Exchange questions with a friend. Can you answer all the questions with the chart in front of you? Can you do it without the chart?

Use a dictionary to help answer these questions.

7 What does the prefix *milli-* mean?

8 What does the prefix *centi-* mean?

9 What does the prefix *kilo-* mean?

10 Define the following words. How does each word relate to the metric system?
   a. millisecond
   b. century
   c. kilowatt

Visit a supermarket or study supermarket advertisements in the newspaper.

11 List five products that are labeled in metric units of volume.

12 List five products that are labeled in metric units of weight.

First estimate. Then measure to check.

◆ Find three items that measure 1 centimeter.

◆ Find three items that weigh about 1 gram.

◆ Find three items that are measured in liters.

◆ Find three items that are measured in kilograms.

Discuss the reasons why some products are packaged in whole units, such as 1 kilogram or 1 liter, while other products are packaged in an unusual number of units, such as 452 grams or 240 milliliters.

Practice with Linear Measurement

Although it's good to know about patterns in the metric system, you don't have to be able to measure in all of those units. Several units in the chart on page 126 are in common use. Those units are also described below.

Length

Centimeter: An unsharpened pencil is about 19 centimeters long.
Meter: Most classroom doors are about 1 meter wide.
Kilometer: You can walk 1 kilometer in about 12 minutes.

Weight

Gram: A United States nickel weighs about 5 grams.
Kilogram: This book weighs about 1.4 kilograms.

Volume

Liter: Four average-sized glasses hold about 1 liter.
Milliliter: A raindrop is about 1 milliliter of water.

Choose the measure that makes more sense. It may be hard to decide which measure makes more sense. If you think that both make sense, explain why.

1 Yesterday I ran about **3 kilometers** or **3000 centimeters**.

2 The box contains **500 grams** or **5000 milligrams** of cereal.

3 The glass holds $\frac{1}{5}$ **liter** or **200 milliliters** of juice.

4 A square garden measures about **4 meters** or **400 centimeters** on each side.

5 I bought **0.457 kilograms** or **457 grams** of potatoes.

SCIENCE CONNECTION

Build a rubber band scale like the one in the picture. Perform the following experiment.

6 Measure the length of the rubber band.

7 Place one or two marbles or other weights in the paper cup. Measure the length of the rubber band again.

8 Add another weight. Measure the length of the rubber band. Keep adding weights, one or two at a time. Measure the rubber band after each addition.

9 How does the weight of the objects affect the length of the rubber band?

10 Keep your results in a chart like the one shown.

Number of Marbles	Length of Rubber Band

Now find something that you think weighs more than two marbles, but less than the most marbles you used.

How many marble units does that object weigh?

What other objects can you weigh with your scale?

Try to make a scale that will weigh heavier objects.

Can you modify your scale so you can weigh objects in standard units?

Area: Upper and Lower Bounds

Amir is thinking of a rectangle. He says, "It is at least 4 centimeters long, but no more than 5 centimeters long. It is at least 1 centimeter wide, but no more than 2 centimeters wide."

Amir can't be thinking of this rectangle, because it is less than 4 cm long.

He can't be thinking of this rectangle, because it is more than 2 cm wide.

He might be thinking of this rectangle.

Which of these rectangles could be the one Amir is thinking of?

Write *yes* or *no* for each one. Use a centimeter ruler to measure. Watch your numbering.

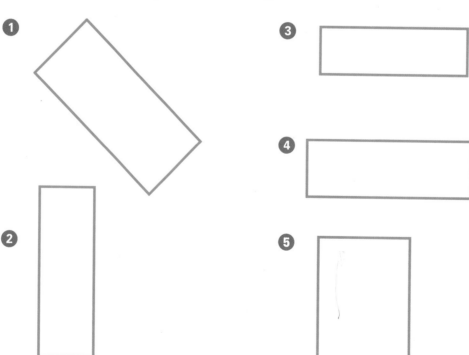

Solve these problems.

Onawa and Simon had an argument about whose garden was bigger. They decided to measure. Onawa's garden is at least 9 meters long, but no more than 10 meters long. It is at least 6 meters wide, but no more than 7 meters wide.

6 Draw a picture of the smallest garden Onawa might have.

7 What is the smallest area Onawa's garden could be?

8 Draw a picture of the largest garden Onawa might have.

9 What is the largest area Onawa's garden could be?

Simon's garden is at least 8 meters long, but no more than 9 meters long. It is at least 7 meters wide, but no more than 8 meters wide.

10 Draw a picture of the smallest garden Simon might have.

11 What is the smallest area Simon's garden could be?

12 Draw a picture of the largest garden Simon might have.

13 What is the largest area Simon's garden could be?

14 Can you tell whose garden has the greater area, Onawa's or Simon's?

Complete this chart about other people's gardens.

Garden Owner	Length (meters)		Width (meters)		Area (square meters)	
	At Least	No More Than	At Least	No More Than	At Least	No More Than
15 Anita	9	10	4	5	36	▪
16 Larry	7	8	7	8	▪	▪
17 Celia	8	9	5	6	▪	▪
18 Jesse	6	7	5	6	▪	▪

LESSON 40 Multiplication Practice

These pages will give you a chance to check how well you are doing in remembering multiplication facts quickly.

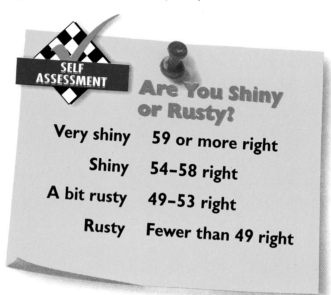

SELF ASSESSMENT

Are You Shiny or Rusty?

Very shiny	**59 or more right**
Shiny	**54–58 right**
A bit rusty	**49–53 right**
Rusty	**Fewer than 49 right**

Multiply to solve for _n_.

1. $6 \times 10 = n$
2. $6 \times 6 = n$
3. $8 \times 7 = n$
4. $4 \times 3 = n$
5. $2 \times 7 = n$
6. $2 \times 4 = n$
7. $6 \times 0 = n$
8. $4 \times 6 = n$
9. $7 \times 1 = n$
10. $3 \times 5 = n$
11. $10 \times 10 = n$
12. $3 \times 9 = n$
13. $6 \times 9 = n$
14. $6 \times 8 = n$
15. $3 \times 3 = n$
16. $2 \times 2 = n$
17. $7 \times 7 = n$
18. $8 \times 9 = n$
19. $5 \times 7 = n$
20. $2 \times 8 = n$
21. $9 \times 9 = n$
22. $3 \times 6 = n$
23. $5 \times 2 = n$
24. $0 \times 3 = n$
25. $9 \times 8 = n$
26. $7 \times 6 = n$
27. $5 \times 9 = n$
28. $5 \times 6 = n$
29. $7 \times 9 = n$
30. $9 \times 2 = n$
31. $2 \times 4 = n$
32. $6 \times 9 = n$
33. $10 \times 0 = n$
34. $8 \times 1 = n$
35. $9 \times 3 = n$
36. $7 \times 3 = n$

Multiply.

③⑦ 5 ×0	③⑧ 4 ×4	③⑨ 2 ×3	④⓪ 4 ×2	④① 1 ×8
④② 6 ×7	④③ 10 ×2	④④ 7 ×8	④⑤ 0 ×9	④⑥ 9 ×7
④⑦ 8 ×6	④⑧ 2 ×6	④⑨ 8 ×8	⑤⓪ 7 ×5	⑤① 5 ×8
⑤② 4 ×9	⑤③ 5 ×5	⑤④ 6 ×5	⑤⑤ 3 ×7	⑤⑥ 5 ×4
⑤⑦ 6 ×9	⑤⑧ 7 ×4	⑤⑨ 2 ×9	⑥⓪ 10 ×0	⑥① 3 ×8

Solve.

⑥② Jim bought two pencil erasers. Each eraser cost 7¢. How much money did Jim spend on erasers?

⑥③ What is the area of a square garden that measures 8 feet on each side?

⑥④ Gretchen bought three packs of markers. Each pack contained eight markers. How many markers did she buy all together?

◆ **LESSON 40** Multiplication Practice

Money Matters

Part 2

Mr. Mudancia wondered why there were $1 bills, $2 bills, $5 bills, and $10 bills, but not $3, $4, $6, $7, $8, and $9 bills. "I think I could change that a little," he said.

The next day he went to a bookstore to buy a book that cost $6. "Here's a $6 bill," he said to the clerk.

"Something is wrong with this bill," said the clerk. "It's thicker and stiffer than it should be. It says $5 on one side and $1 on the other. This is a fake bill! Police! Police!"

"Calm down," said Mr. Mudancia. "You wanted $6 and I gave you $6. I don't know what you're so worried about. By the way, I think I'll take this magazine, too. How much is it?"

"It's $1."

"Then give me back my $6 bill and I'll give you $7," said Mr. Mudancia.

The clerk was glad to give Mr. Mudancia back his $6 bill. But the clerk was not glad when Mr. Mudancia said, "Here's a $7 bill instead."

"This bill is worse then the other one," said the clerk. "It's even thicker and stiffer. And it still says $5 on one side and $1 on the other side. You can't tell me this makes $7!"

"Not everything shows," said Mr. Mudancia.

Work in groups. Discuss your answers and how you figured them out. Then compare your answers with those of other groups.

1 How did Mr. Mudancia make his $6 bill?

2 Why was his $6 bill thinner than his $7 bill?

3 **Challenge:** What are five different ways that Mr. Mudancia could make a $20 bill?

4 **Detective question:** How could Mr. Mudancia make a $7 bill that was no thicker than the $6 bill he made?

5 Do you think it would be a good idea to have $3, $4, $6, $7, $8, and $9 bills in addition to the bills we already have? Why or why not? What about $99 bills?

Mid-Unit Review

Multiply to solve for *n*.

① $6 \times 0 = n$ **②** $4 \times 6 = n$ **③** $0 \times 3 = n$

④ $1 \times 8 = n$ **⑤** $5 \times 5 = n$ **⑥** $4 \times 4 = n$

⑦ $6 \times 9 = n$ **⑧** $3 \times 5 = n$ **⑨** $4 \times 8 = n$

⑩ $7 \times 2 = n$ **⑪** $3 \times 7 = n$ **⑫** $8 \times 5 = n$

Solve.

⑬ How many fingers are there on four hands?

⑭ How many days are there in ten weeks?

⑮ How many feet are there on six dogs?

Multiply.

⑯ 7×8 **⑰** 7×6 **⑱** 8×9

⑲ 9×6 **⑳** 7×9 **㉑** 2×6

㉒ 8×8 **㉓** 6×3 **㉔** 7×7

Complete the chart.

	Length of Side	Area of Square
㉕	2 cm	▪
㉖	4 cm	▪
㉗	6 cm	▪
㉘	8 cm	▪
㉙	10 cm	▪

Which is the right triangle?

㉚

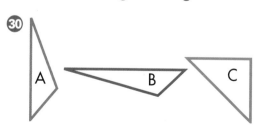

㉛

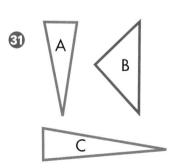

What is the area of each rectangle?

32

4 cm

3 cm

33

5 cm

1 cm

Copy and complete the price chart.

Buttons at 7¢ Each

Number of buttons	1	2	3	4	5	6	7	8	9	10
34 Price (in cents)	7									

Choose the measure that makes more sense.

35 The classroom is about **35 feet** or **30 yards** wide.

36 A can of soda holds about **30 liters** or **355 milliliters**.

37 A nickel weighs about **5 grams** or **5 milligrams**.

38 A loaf of bread weighs about **10 ounces** or **1 pound**.

Copy and complete the function charts.

39 ×9

In	Out
0	
3	
4	
7	
8	
9	

40 ×4

In	Out
10	
8	
6	
3	
1	
0	

LESSON 41

Finding Missing Factors

ALGEBRA READINESS

Taneesha's class is doing the "Missing Factor" activity.

$$3 \times n = 15$$

What number does Taneesha have on her back?

In each case, write the number that Taneesha has on her back.

	Pak Has This Number	The Product Is	Taneesha Has This Number
1	3	24	8
2	6	18	▪
3	9	45	▪
4	5	50	▪
5	4	36	▪
6	7	49	▪
7	2	18	▪
8	10	10	▪
9	1	8	▪
10	0	0	▪

Look at problem 10 again. Can you tell which number Taneesha has? What numbers might she have?

Solve the following problems.

11. A machine at Dough-Boyz Donuts cuts holes in the middle of nine doughnuts every minute. How many minutes will it take the machine to cut holes in 90 doughnuts?

$n \times 9 = 90$

12. Jorge made eight trips around the park on his bike. He rode a total of 24 kilometers. How long is each trip around the park?

$8 \times n = 24$

13. Gina earns $5 each time she mows her aunt's lawn. How many times will she have to mow the lawn to earn the $35 she needs for a new tennis racquet?

$n \times 5 = 35$

14. Grant had $15 when he went to the ball game. He had $6 when he got home. How much did he spend?

$15 - n = 6$

15. Each day, Katy listens to her radio for four hours. A battery will power the radio for about 36 hours of listening. About how many days can Katy listen to her radio before the battery goes dead?

$4 \times n = 36$

16. Jared baked 24 cookies. He takes three cookies in his lunch every day. For how many days will he have cookies in his lunch?

$3 \times n = 24$

17. Tim works 15 hours a week at the pizza shop. If he works the same amount of time each of three days during the week, how many hours must he work each day?

$3 \times n = 15$

◆ **LESSON 41 Finding Missing Factors**

Solve.

18 Each day, Craig knits 10 centimeters on the scarf he's making. He wants the scarf to be 1 meter (100 centimeters) long. How many days will it take Craig to make his scarf?

19 Every day, Tanya uses four slices of bread for her lunch sandwiches. A loaf of bread has 28 slices. How many days can Tanya make sandwiches from one loaf of bread?

20 Marcia is inviting 28 friends to her birthday party.

a. She has four days to write all the invitations. If she writes six invitations each day, will she finish in time?

b. If she writes seven each day, will she finish in time?

c. If she writes eight each day, will she finish in time?

Solve for n.

21 $9 \times n = 27$

22 $n \times 10 = 60$

23 $6 \times n = 30$

24 $3 \times n = 0$

25 $72 = 9 \times n$

26 $n \times 6 = 54$

27 $20 = n \times 10$

28 $48 = 8 \times n$

29 $7 \times n = 42$

30 $6 \times n = 48$

31 $n \times 8 = 72$

32 $3 \times n = 27$

33 $32 = n \times 8$

34 $5 \times n = 35$

35 $45 = n \times 5$

36 $5 \times n = 25$

37 $6 \times n = 36$

38 $81 = n \times 9$

39 $14 = n \times 2$

40 $n \times 8 = 32$

41 $64 = n \times 8$

140 • Multiplication and Division

Solve.

42 Raulito has $87 in his bank account. He wants to deposit enough money to bring his balance to exactly $100. How much money should he deposit?

43 Manuel has already driven 87 miles of a 100-mile trip. How many more miles must he drive?

44 Juanita needs 100 coupons to collect a prize. She already has 87 coupons. How many more coupons does she need?

Do you notice anything about the first three problems on this page? Notice that the mathematics in these problems is the same, only the situations are different.

 **Work in groups. Make up other problems that are similar to problems 42, 43, and 44.**

Solve these problems.

45 Richard needs 45 hats for a party. Hats come five to a package. How many packages of hats does he need?

46 Ed had $150 in his bank account. He wrote a check, but he forgot to write down the amount. He called the bank and found out that he has $126 in his account. For what amount was the check written?

47 Mary wrote a check for $24. That brought the balance in her checking account to $126. What was her balance before she wrote the check?

48 John had a balance of $250 in his checking account. He wrote one check for $20. Then he wrote another check, but he forgot to record the amount. How much money is in his bank account now?

49 Nina's class just finished Lesson 38 in their geography book. The book has 112 lessons. How many more lessons must the class complete to finish the book?

Multiplication and Division

Multiplication and division are related. When you solved missing-term problems that involved multiplication, you were getting ready for division.

Use multiplication facts to solve these division problems.

❶ Keith earns $4 each hour at his job. Today he earned $20. How many hours did he work today?

❷ María has to work only two hours to earn $20. How much does she earn each hour?

❸ Eight children want to share 24 cookies equally. How many cookies should each child get?

❹ When the Crickets and the Ravens play football, they can score only by getting touchdowns and kicking extra points. Frankie is the extra-point kicker for the Crickets team. She never misses, so each time they get a touchdown, the Crickets get 7 points. As of halftime, they had scored 42 points. How many touchdowns did they get?

❺ Paul kicks extra points for the Ravens football team. He had a bad day and missed every kick, so each touchdown earned only 6 points. How many touchdowns did the Ravens need to score 42 points?

❻ In the game between the Crickets and the Ravens, the final score was 56 to 54.

    a. Which team won?

    b. How many touchdowns did the winning team score?

    c. How many touchdowns did the losing team score?

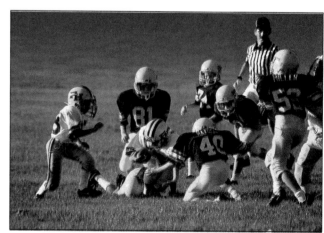

Division undoes multiplication, just as subtraction undoes addition.

◆ $8 + 6 = 14$, so $14 - 6 = ?$ ◆ $8 \times 6 = 48$, so $48 \div 6 = ?$

◆ $56 = 7 \times 8$, so $56 \div 8 = ?$ ◆ $49 = 7 \times 7$, so $? = 49 \div 7$

Divide. Solve for n.

7 $10 \div 10 = n$ **8** $72 \div 9 = n$ **9** $63 \div 7 = n$

10 $20 \div 5 = n$ **11** $35 \div 7 = n$ **12** $n = 56 \div 8$

13 $n = 5 \div 1$ **14** $72 \div 8 = n$ **15** $64 \div 8 = n$

16 $n = 14 \div 7$ **17** $60 \div 6 = n$ **18** $80 \div 10 = n$

19 $42 \div 7 = n$ **20** $n = 30 \div 5$ **21** $n = 100 \div 10$

22 $40 \div 8 = n$ **23** $45 \div 9 = n$ **24** $81 \div 9 = n$

25 $16 \div 2 = n$ **26** $n = 30 \div 10$ **27** $64 \div 8 = n$

You know that the $\div$ sign means "divided by."

Another way to show division is to use this symbol: $\overline{)}$.

Example: $7\overline{)56}$

This means that we are going to divide 56 by 7. Write the answer as shown:

$$7\overline{)56}^{\,8}$$

Divide.

28 $5\overline{)50}$ **29** $7\overline{)63}$ **30** $10\overline{)90}$ **31** $5\overline{)30}$ **32** $8\overline{)16}$

33 $3\overline{)21}$ **34** $5\overline{)40}$ **35** $1\overline{)2}$ **36** $5\overline{)25}$ **37** $3\overline{)6}$

38 $9\overline{)18}$ **39** $7\overline{)42}$ **40** $6\overline{)54}$ **41** $4\overline{)28}$ **42** $9\overline{)81}$

Keeping Sharp

Keep in shape by practicing adding, subtracting, multiplying, and dividing. Pay attention to the signs.

ALGEBRA READINESS

Add or subtract. Solve for *n*.

1 $8 + 7 = n$ **2** $12 = 3 + n$ **3** $10 = 20 - n$

4 $16 - 7 = n$ **5** $14 = 7 + n$ **6** $18 - n = 9$

7 $10 - 10 = n$ **8** $n = 12 - 7$ **9** $16 - 0 = n$

10 $9 + 8 = n$ **11** $8 = n + 3$ **12** $10 + n = 18$

13 $4 + n = 7$ **14** $6 + 4 = n$ **15** $17 - n = 10$

16 $18 = n + 9$ **17** $3 + n = 15$ **18** $12 = 10 + n$

19 $n - 6 = 2$ **20** $17 - 8 = n$ **21** $5 - 5 = n$

Add or subtract. Use shortcuts when you can.

22
```
  25
+ 37
```

23
```
  92
- 35
```

24
```
  671
- 234
```

25
```
  1000
-  500
```

26
```
  76
+ 28
```

27
```
  197
+ 803
```

28
```
  8216
- 3216
```

29
```
  1711
- 1699
```

30
```
  7345
-   28
```

31
```
  250
+ 150
```

32
```
  800
- 750
```

33
```
  800
- 799
```

34
```
  25
  25
  25
+ 25
```

35
```
  10
  17
+  3
```

36
```
  15
  17
  18
+  2
```

37
```
   2
   9
  11
+ 10
```

Multiply or divide. Solve for *n*.

38. $9 \times 4 = n$
39. $28 \div 4 = n$
40. $9 \div n = 3$

41. $64 \div 8 = n$
42. $27 \div 3 = n$
43. $42 = n \times 7$

44. $8 \times 7 = n$
45. $10 \times 9 = n$
46. $36 = 4 \times n$

47. $18 \div 9 = n$
48. $8 \times n = 56$
49. $100 = n \times 10$

50. $81 \div 9 = n$
51. $n \times 8 = 32$
52. $24 \div n = 6$

53. $63 \div n = 9$
54. $n \times 8 = 40$
55. $24 \div n = 4$

56. $5 = 45 \div n$
57. $9 \times n = 63$
58. $n \times 3 = 21$

59. $42 \div 6 = n$
60. $9 \times n = 90$
61. $54 \div n = 9$

62. $25 \div 5 = n$
63. $18 \div 6 = n$
64. $27 \div n = 3$

65. $10 \times n = 40$
66. $8 \times n = 0$
67. $n = 4 \times 9$

68. $14 \div n = 7$
69. $7 \times n = 21$
70. $10 = 5 \times n$

71. $54 = 9 \times n$
72. $32 = 8 \times n$
73. $56 = n \times 8$

74. $14 = 2 \times n$
75. $20 = n \times 4$
76. $8 \times 2 = n$

Solve these problems.

77. Tad paid 72¢ for eight erasers at the school bookstore. How much did each eraser cost?

78. Myers Office Store charges 10¢ per page for copies. Mary needs to copy five pages of her report, and she has 40¢. Does she have enough money to copy her whole report?

79. David paid 80¢ for two writing tablets. How much did each tablet cost?

◆ **LESSON 43 Keeping Sharp**

Money Matters

Part 3

Marcus, Portia, Willy, and Ferdie were all collecting coins. One day they got together to see who had the most money.

Marcus had a stack of quarters that was 4 centimeters high.

Willy had a stack of dimes. It was about as high as Marcus's stack.

Portia had a stack of nickels. Her stack was about twice as high as Marcus's stack.

Ferdie had a stack of pennies. His stack was four times as high as Marcus's stack.

Ferdie was excited. "I have the most because my stack is the highest."

"I have the most because quarters are worth the most," said Marcus.

"I have the most because dimes are so thin," said Willy. "If you count my dimes and Marcus's quarters, you'll find that I have more coins than he does."

Portia said, "I think I have the most. Don't forget that my stack is very high and I have nickels."

Work in groups. Discuss your answers and how you figured them out. Then compare your answers with those of other groups.

1 Copy and complete the bar graph to show the heights of the four stacks of money.

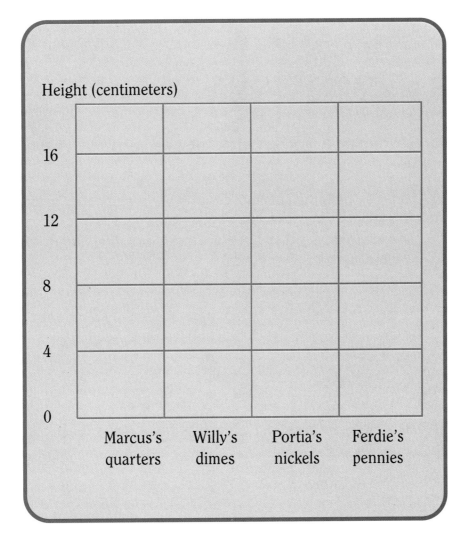

2 **Super detective questions:** Who has the greatest amount of money? The second greatest amount of money? The third greatest amount? Who has the least amount?

Division with Remainders

Sasha, Tina, Nikia, and Liza hunted for treasure on the beach. When they found valuable things, they sold them. Sometimes they found money. At the end of each week they divided all their money equally.

Use play money to act out what they did. Answer these questions.

1 The first week, the girls found some shells and coral. They sold these for $27. They also found $5 in cash.

   a. How much money did they get all together?

   b. How much money should each girl get?

2 The second week, they found more shells and an old coin. They sold these for $31. They also found $5 in cash.

   a. How much money did they get all together?

   b. How much money should each of them get?

3 The third week, they found some driftwood and three old bottles. They sold these for $23. They also found $7 in cash.

   a. How much money did they get all together?

   b. How much money should each of them get?

There are several good answers to the last question. Each person can get $7, leaving $2. They can put the $2 in the fund for next week. Or they can divide it equally. Each person would get an extra 50 cents. Or they could spend the $2 on something they all could use, such as a water bottle or beach bag.

Seven children want to divide 56 cents equally. How much will each child get?

$$\frac{8}{7)\overline{56}}$$

Seven children want to divide 57 cents equally. How much will each child get?

$$7)\overline{57}$$

After each child gets 8 cents, there is still 1 cent left over. Sometimes we wish to divide a whole number of things equally but cannot do so without something left over, or remaining. We can write:

$$\frac{8\ R1}{7)\overline{57}}$$

When we read this answer, we say, "8 remainder 1."

Six children want to divide 40 cents equally. How much will each child get? How much will be left over?

$$\frac{6\ R4}{6)\overline{40}}$$

$6 \times 6 = 36 \qquad 40 - 36 = 4$

Each child gets 6 cents, and there are 4 cents remaining.

Divide. Watch for remainders.

4. $8)\overline{48}$ 5. $8)\overline{51}$ 6. $9)\overline{54}$ 7. $9)\overline{58}$ 8. $5)\overline{37}$

9. $7)\overline{43}$ 10. $3)\overline{26}$ 11. $10)\overline{46}$ 12. $3)\overline{29}$ 13. $6)\overline{36}$

14. $5)\overline{47}$ 15. $4)\overline{38}$ 16. $6)\overline{63}$ 17. $8)\overline{34}$ 18. $10)\overline{85}$

19. $2)\overline{15}$ 20. $9)\overline{47}$ 21. $5)\overline{45}$ 22. $7)\overline{54}$ 23. $4)\overline{26}$

LESSON 45

Division Review

Remember to think about the multiplication facts you know to help you divide.

Divide. Watch for remainders.

① 4)30　② 7)29　③ 8)43　④ 5)38　⑤ 4)36

⑥ 6)20　⑦ 5)22　⑧ 2)15　⑨ 9)73　⑩ 10)26

⑪ 4)19　⑫ 8)39　⑬ 5)17　⑭ 5)25　⑮ 6)50

⑯ 9)56　⑰ 7)56　⑱ 3)16　⑲ 2)12　⑳ 1)8

㉑ 5)28　㉒ 6)34　㉓ 10)41　㉔ 8)12　㉕ 7)51

㉖ 2)19　㉗ 9)17　㉘ 6)55　㉙ 7)42　㉚ 3)23

Solve these problems.

Mr. Zalesky has a lot of pennies to give away. He tells his neighbors that he will give nine cents to each child who comes to his house on Saturday morning, until he runs out of pennies.

㉛ Suppose Mr. Zalesky has 78 cents.

    a. How many children will get nine cents?

    b. How many cents will be left?

㉜ Suppose Mr. Zalesky has 83 cents.

    a. How many children will get nine cents?

    b. How many cents will be left?

㉝ Suppose he has 63 cents.

    a. How many children will get nine cents?

    b. How many cents will be left?

Solve these problems.

Ed needs 46 noisemakers for a party. At Paul's Party Store noisemakers come five to a box. A box costs $2.00.

34 How many boxes must Ed buy?

35 If Ed buys nine boxes, how many noisemakers will he have?

36 Will he have enough noisemakers?

37 If Ed buys ten boxes, will he have enough noisemakers?

38 How many will he have?

39 How much money will Ed spend?

COOPERATIVE LEARNING

Work in cooperative groups for these problems. Be sure to explain how you get your answers.

At Party Palace Ed can buy the same kind of noisemakers in packages of ten to a box. Each box costs $3.00.

40 How many boxes must Ed buy?

41 How much money will he have to spend?

42 At which store should Ed buy the noisemakers?

43 How much money would Ed save at the less expensive store?

A baseball game has nine innings. The Sluggers were behind 12 to 5 at the end of the sixth inning.

44 How many more runs do the Sluggers need to win the game if the other team doesn't score again?

45 About how many runs per inning is that?

Suppose the Sluggers got one run in the seventh inning and the other team scored two runs.

46 Now how many more runs do the Sluggers need to win?

47 About how many runs per inning is that?

◆ **LESSON 45   Division Review**

Money Matters

Part 4

Mr. Muddle is very honest, but sometimes he forgets to pay for things. One day he had $3.00 when he went out shopping. He bought a carton of eggs, some nails, and a mousetrap. When he got home, he had $1.60 left.

"I think I forgot to pay someone," he said. "Let's see. The eggs were marked $1.40. The mousetrap was marked 80¢. And the bag of nails was marked 60¢."

Mr. Muddle told Loretta the Letter Carrier about his problem. She said, "If you forgot to pay for something, then it must be the eggs."

"I'm amazed that you can tell what I forgot, just by looking at the eggs," said Mr. Muddle. But he took Loretta's word for it and went to pay the grocer $1.40.

"What's this for?" asked the grocer. "I know that you paid for those eggs. I remember I talked to you in the checkout line."

"This is very confusing," said Mr. Muddle. As he walked along the street, he counted his money again.

"What's the matter, Mr. Muddle?" asked a woman. She was watching him from the door of her hardware shop. "Are you worrying about the $1.40 you owe me?"

Work in groups. Discuss your answers and how you figured them out. Then compare your answers with those of other groups.

① If Mr. Muddle had paid for everything, how much money would he have left?

② Why would Loretta the Letter Carrier think Mr. Muddle had forgotten to pay for the eggs? Why didn't she guess the nails or the mousetrap?

③ How could Mr. Muddle owe the woman at the hardware shop $1.40?

④ Why did Loretta give Mr. Muddle the wrong answer to his problem?

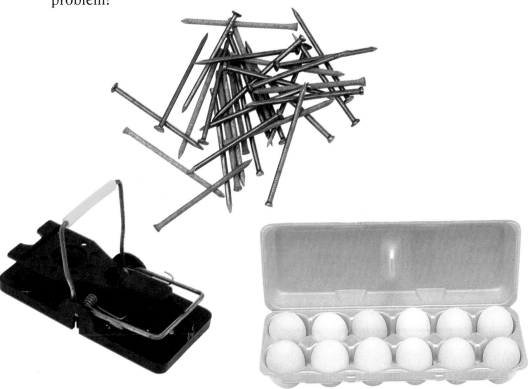

Common Multiples

In the multiplication fact 3 × 6 = 18, 3 and 6 are **factors** of 18. Factors are numbers you multiply to get the **product**.

A **multiple** of a number is some whole number multiplied by that number. Multiples of 3 are 3, 6, 9, 12, 15, 18, and so on. Multiples of 6 are 6, 12, 18, 24, 30, and so on.

You can call 18 a **common multiple** of 3 and 6 because it is a multiple of both numbers.

You can use a table to find multiples and common multiples. Here are parts of tables with multiples of 2 and of 5:

	×0	×1	×2	×3	×4	×5
Multiples of 2	0	2	4	6	8	10

	×0	×1	×2	×3	×4	×5
Multiples of 5	0	5	10	15	20	25

Look for a common multiple of 2 and 5. Do you see it? You can extend the tables to find other common multiples. Use a calculator to help you.

COOPERATIVE LEARNING **Work with a partner to find the first three common multiples of each pair of numbers. Watch your numbering.**

1 3 and 7   **2** 5 and 9   **3** 5 and 4

4 2 and 3   **5** 9 and 8   **6** 8 and 5

7 6 and 10   **8** 2 and 8   **9** 9 and 12

10 5 and 10   **11** 6 and 9   **12** 8 and 12

Answer the following questions.

13 What seems to be true of the first common multiple of each of the pairs listed in exercises 1–6? What seems to be true of the second common multiple of all of the pairs?

14 In what way are the first common multiples for exercises 7–12 different from those for exercises 1–6?

15 Look at exercises 1–6. We call a number that divides exactly into another number a **factor** of that number. Is there any whole number greater than 1 that divides evenly into both

a. 3 and 7?	**b.** 5 and 9?
c. 5 and 4?	**d.** 2 and 3?
e. 9 and 8?	**f.** 8 and 5?

16 Look at exercises 7–12. What is the largest whole number that divides evenly into both 6 and 10? [Notice that $(6 \times 10) \div 2 = 30$.] What is the largest whole number that divides evenly into both

a. 2 and 8?	**b.** 9 and 12?
c. 5 and 10?	**d.** 6 and 9?
e. 8 and 12?	

17 Try to find an interesting pattern for exercises 7–12.

18 Think of other pairs of numbers. Predict what their first common multiple will be. Work with a partner to check your prediction.

To match the acceleration of an attacking rattlesnake, you would have to drive a car from 0 miles per hour to 60 miles per hour in half a second.

ACT IT OUT

Parentheses

A Medical Problem

Act out and discuss this story.

Brenda and her friends like to visit Celine, the dog trainer.

"May we help feed your dogs?" the children asked.

"Yes," said Celine. "But first I have to mix some medicine in their food. All the dogs have sore throats from barking so much. You can help me figure out how much medicine to mix in. How much is $4 \times 3 + 2$?"

"It's 14," said Brenda, Jamal, and Cindy.

"It's 20," said Elise and Aaron.

The children argued about which answer was right, but they couldn't decide. Finally Cindy said, "Why don't you tell us the whole problem?"

"It doesn't seem like a very hard problem," Celine said. "I have to give four spoonfuls of medicine to each dog. I have three black dogs and two brown dogs. That is $4 \times 3 + 2$, right?"

"Now we know what the right answer is," they all said.

◆ How could Brenda, Jamal, and Cindy have gotten the answer 14?

◆ How could Elise and Aaron have gotten 20?

◆ Which is the right answer to Celine's problem? Why?

◆ Can you think of a way to ask the question about the numbers 4, 3, and 2 so that people would know which way to answer it?

Here is a way to write the problem that means add 3 and 2, then multiply by 4:

$$4 \times (3 + 2)$$

Here is a way to write the problem that means multiply 4×3, then add 2:

$$(4 \times 3) + 2$$

Rule: Do the operations inside the parentheses first.

$4 \times (3 + 2) = 4 \times 5 = 20$

$(4 \times 3) + 2 = 12 + 2 = 14$

$6 + (5 \times 2) = 6 + 10 = 16$

$(6 - 3) \times 6 + 1 = 3 \times 6 + 1 = 18 + 1 = 19$

$(6 + 5) + (3 - 2) + (7 + 9) + (8 + 2) =$
$11 + 1 + 16 + 10 = 38$

$(4 \times 7) + (4 \times 3) = 28 + 12 = 40$

$(8 + 4) + 5 = 12 + 5 = 17$

$18 \div (6 + 3) = 18 \div 9 = 2$

$4 \times (4 - 0) = 4 \times 4 = 16$

◆ LESSON 47 Parentheses

We do operations inside the parentheses first.

Examples:

a. $40 \div (5 + 3) = 40 \div 8 = 5$ b. $(40 \div 5) + 3 = 8 + 3 = 11$

c. $12 - (8 - 3) = 12 - 5 = 7$ d. $(12 - 8) - 3 = 4 - 3 = 1$

e. $7 \times (5 + 4) = 7 \times 9 = 63$ f. $(7 \times 5) + 4 = 35 + 4 = 39$

g. $32 \div (8 \div 2) = 32 \div 4 = 8$ h. $(32 \div 8) \div 2 = 4 \div 2 = 2$

Solve for n. Watch the parentheses. Watch the signs.

1. $24 \div (6 \div 2) = n$ 2. $(24 \div 6) \div 2 = n$

3. $28 - (8 \div 4) = n$ 4. $(28 - 8) \div 4 = n$

5. $7 \times (4 + 6) = n$ 6. $(7 \times 4) + 6 = n$

7. $16 + (7 + 5) = n$ 8. $(16 + 7) + 5 = n$

9. $16 - (7 - 5) = n$ 10. $(16 - 7) - 5 = n$

11. $(2 \times 3) \times 3 = n$ 12. $2 \times (3 \times 3) = n$

13. $(18 \div 6) \div 3 = n$ 14. $18 \div (6 \div 3) = n$

15. $(25 - 12) - (20 - 7) = n$ 16. $4 \times (6 - 6) = n$

For each problem below, see how many different answers you can get by putting parentheses in different places. The first two have been done for you.

17. $5 + 4 \times 3 = n$ 18. $2 \times 10 \div 2 = n$

$(5 + 4) \times 3 = 27$ $(2 \times 10) \div 2 = 10$

$5 + (4 \times 3) = 17$ $2 \times (10 \div 2) = 10$

There are two answers.   **There is one answer.**

19. $17 - 10 + 1 = n$ 20. $2 \times 3 + 4 = n$ 21. $4 \times 6 \div 3 = n$

22. $16 + 3 \times 2 = n$ 23. $16 \div 4 \times 2 = n$ 24. $16 - 4 \times 2 = n$

25. $2 \times 3 \times 4 = n$ 26. $12 - 2 \times 6 = n$ 27. $12 - 2 \times 3 = n$

28. $8 + 12 \div 2 = n$ 29. $18 \div 6 \times 3 = n$ 30. $8 \times 3 \div 3 = n$

Using parentheses always makes it clear which operation to do first. However, some long math problems use lots of parentheses. So, people sometimes use other methods to solve them.

The rule used by many people is to simply do the operations from left to right.

$$3 + 7 \times 6 - 5 + 4 = 10 \times 6 - 5 + 4 = 60 - 5 + 4 = 55 + 4 = 59$$

A second rule that is sometimes used is to do all of the multiplications and divisions first, and then do the additions and subtractions.

$$3 + 7 \times 6 - 5 + 4 = 3 + 42 - 5 + 4 = 45 - 1 = 44$$

A third possible rule would be to do all of the additions and subtractions first, and then do the multiplications and divisions.

$$3 + 7 \times 6 - 5 + 4 = 10 \times 5 = 50$$

Try the problem above with several different people and with several different calculators.

Are the answers different? Which method was used?

Use a calculator if necessary to solve the following problems using each of the three rules. You might discover that two or three of your answers are the same. Sometimes none of your answers will match. Try to predict which answers will be the same before doing the problems (it may save you some work).

Solve.

31 $8 + 7 \times 6 - 4 = ?$

32 $20 - 3 \times 4 + 6 + 2 \times 8 = ?$

33 $2 \times 3 \times 4 + 8 = ?$

34 $2 \times 3 \times 4 + 8 \times 5 = ?$

35 $2 + 3 + 4 \times 8 = ?$

36 $2 + 3 + 4 \times 8 + 2 = ?$

37 $3 \times 4 + 7 = ?$

38 $3 + 4 \times 7 = ?$

39 $2 \times 3 \times 4 \times 5 = ?$

40 $2 + 3 + 4 + 5 = ?$

41 $2 \times 3 + 4 \times 5 = ?$

42 $2 + 3 \times 4 + 5 = ?$

43 $2 \times 3 \times 4 + 5 = ?$

44 $2 + 3 + 4 \times 5 = ?$

LESSON
48

Applying Math

In this lesson you can apply the skills you've learned to solve different kinds of problems. Use any problem-solving methods that work for you.

Solve.

1. Mike received $24.75 on his birthday. Three days later he got a birthday card with $5 in it. How much money did Mike receive all together for his birthday?

2. The Circle K Ranch is 5 kilometers wide. What is the area of the ranch?

3. Melissa has 35 customers on her paper route. She began her route with 35 papers and now has ten left. How many more papers does she have to deliver?

4. Jeff has a room shaped like a rectangle. It is 4 meters long and 3 meters wide. What is the area of the floor in Jeff's room?

5. Last spring the ecology club planted 108 tree seedlings. Of those, 19 seedlings didn't survive the winter. How many trees made it through the winter?

6. Leilani can ride 1 kilometer on her bike in about four minutes. About how long will it take her to ride to Echo Lake, a distance of 8 kilometers?

7. Paul has 249 stamps in his stamp collection. Jack has 157 stamps. How many stamps do the boys have all together?

8. Billy's rectangular tree house is 4 feet long and 2 feet wide. What is the perimeter of the tree house?

9 In 1980 the population of the state of Arizona was 2,716,546. In 1990 the population was 3,665,228. About how many people moved to or were born in Arizona between 1980 and 1990?

10 Dan has $17.93 and his brother has $14.59. They want to buy their mother a birthday gift. Do they have enough money to buy a sweater that costs $33.00?

11 Leroy wants to put new carpeting in his room. He measured the floor and found that it is a square with sides 4 meters long. He can buy a rectangular piece of carpet that is 8 meters long and 3 meters wide. If he cut up the carpet, would he have enough to cover his floor completely?

12 The balance in Anya's bank account was $217.86. She withdrew $74.98 to buy in-line skates. What is the balance in her account now?

13 Mr. Chang bought eight cans of juice for a party. Each can serves seven people. How many people can he serve with the juice he bought?

14 Amanda has invited 26 people to a party. She wants to give each person a party hat. Hats come in packages of ten. How many packages does she need to buy?

15 Manuel saved $27 to spend on video games while on vacation. He wants to spend the same amount each of the three weeks of his vacation. How much should he spend each week?

◆ LESSON 48 Applying Math

Read each problem carefully. Think about which operations to use.

Solve.

16 The Nila family and the Lee family walked to the science museum. The Nilas bought four tickets. The Lees bought five tickets. Tickets cost $3 each. How much did the two families spend all together?

17 The Freeman family drove to the science museum. They bought five tickets. Parking costs $4. Tickets cost $3 each. How much did the Freemans spend in all?

18 The science museum raised the price of tickets to $4, but also offers a new group plan. A group of up to ten people can buy one group ticket for $5, plus $3 for each person in the group.

a. How much would a group of four people pay using the group plan? Would they save money compared to buying their tickets separately?

b. How much would a group of five people pay using the group plan? Would they save money compared to buying their tickets separately?

c. How much would a group of ten people pay using the group plan? Would they save money compared to buying their tickets separately?

19 Mr. and Mrs. Kuhn and their two children ate lunch in the Cosmic Cafeteria at the science museum. They shared a $3 jumbo order of Far-Out French Fries, and each person ordered a Martian Meatball Platter for $5. How much did they spend on lunch all together?

Neptune's largest moon, Triton, is thought to be one of the coldest bodies in the solar system, with a surface temperature of about −455°C.

GAME

Cubo Game

Players:	Two or more
Materials:	Two 0–5 cubes, two 5–10 cubes
Object:	To score as close to 21 as possible
Math Focus:	Mental math with all four operations

RULES

1. Roll all four cubes on each turn.

2. Use any combination of the four operations (addition, subtraction, multiplication, and division) on the numbers rolled. Use the number on each cube only once. If two cubes have the same number, you must use both.

If you rolled:	You could make these numbers:	By doing these operations, for example:
3	19	$6 - 3 = 3$; $3 \times 6 = 18$; $18 + 1 = 19$
6	23	$3 \times 6 = 18$; $18 + 6 = 24$; $24 - 1 = 23$
6	21	$6 - 1 = 5$; $5 \times 3 = 15$; $15 + 6 = 21$
1	21	$6 - 3 = 3$; $6 + 1 = 7$; $3 \times 7 = 21$

3. The player who scores 21 or closest to it is the winner of the round.

ANOTHER WAY TO PLAY THIS GAME

Make the goal a number other than 21.

MATH JOURNAL

In your Math Journal explain your strategy for playing this game.

ASSESSMENT

Unit 2 Review

Lessons 28–30, 32

Multiply.

1. 9×6 2. 8×7 3. 7×5 4. 9×3

5. 3×6 6. 5×8 7. 9×8 8. 4×5

Lesson 44

Divide. Watch for remainders.

9. $9)\overline{18}$ 10. $6)\overline{59}$ 11. $4)\overline{36}$ 12. $7)\overline{21}$ 13. $9)\overline{63}$

14. $7)\overline{56}$ 15. $4)\overline{37}$ 16. $3)\overline{26}$ 17. $4)\overline{32}$ 18. $10)\overline{51}$

19. $2)\overline{10}$ 20. $9)\overline{27}$ 21. $7)\overline{49}$ 22. $3)\overline{15}$ 23. $6)\overline{19}$

Lesson 43

Add or subtract to solve.

24. $\begin{array}{r} 7 \\ + 5 \\ \hline \end{array}$ 25. $\begin{array}{r} 12 \\ - 9 \\ \hline \end{array}$ 26. $\begin{array}{r} 6 \\ + 3 \\ \hline \end{array}$ 27. $\begin{array}{r} 6 \\ - 3 \\ \hline \end{array}$ 28. $\begin{array}{r} 8 \\ - 5 \\ \hline \end{array}$

29. $\begin{array}{r} 15 \\ - 5 \\ \hline \end{array}$ 30. $\begin{array}{r} 8 \\ + 7 \\ \hline \end{array}$ 31. $\begin{array}{r} 7 \\ + 6 \\ \hline \end{array}$ 32. $\begin{array}{r} 9 \\ - 5 \\ \hline \end{array}$ 33. $\begin{array}{r} 3 \\ + 7 \\ \hline \end{array}$

Solve for *n*. Watch the signs.

34. $n - 4 = 12$ 35. $n = 36 + 25$ 36. $9 \times n = 27$

37. $n = 14 - 13$ 38. $7 + n = 23$ 39. $32 = n \times 8$

Lesson 41

Add or subtract.

Lesson 43

40. $\begin{array}{r} 73 \\ + 96 \\ \hline \end{array}$ 41. $\begin{array}{r} 97 \\ - 38 \\ \hline \end{array}$ 42. $\begin{array}{r} 24 \\ + 56 \\ \hline \end{array}$ 43. $\begin{array}{r} 89 \\ + 46 \\ \hline \end{array}$

44. $\begin{array}{r} 605 \\ - 416 \\ \hline \end{array}$ 45. $\begin{array}{r} 860 \\ + 320 \\ \hline \end{array}$ 46. $\begin{array}{r} 197 \\ - 45 \\ \hline \end{array}$ 47. $\begin{array}{r} 4973 \\ - 2984 \\ \hline \end{array}$

164 • Multiplication and Division

**Lessons
28, 34,
41, 44,
45, 48**

Solve these problems.

48 Erica bought eight pencils. They cost 9¢ each. She gave the storekeeper 75¢. How much change should she get?

49 The Conlan family had a rectangular swimming pool built.

   a. What would the area of the pool be if it was 8 meters long and 6 meters wide?

   b. Is the area of this pool larger or smaller than the area of a pool that is 7 meters long and 7 meters wide?

50 About what is the length of a string that is made by tying two 9-meter strings together?

51 A kite string is about 65 meters long. Another string that is about 75 meters long is tied to it. About how long is the combined string?

52 William paid 48¢ for six carrots. How much did each carrot cost?

53 Mrs. Sandina knows that the area of her rectangular rug is between 50 and 60 square meters and that the length of the rug is 9 meters. She also knows that the width of the rug is a whole number of meters. What is the width?

54 Teresa has 47 stickers to give to five children.

   a. How many stickers will each child get?

   b. How many stickers will be left over?

55 Vance has 47 pears. He wants to give an equal number of pears to each of four children. But he also wants to keep at least ten pears for himself.

   a. How many should he give to each child?

   b. How many should he keep for himself?

LESSON
50

Unit 2 Practice

Solve for *n*.

Lessons 28–30, 32, 41

1 $2 \times 10 = n$ **2** $4 \times n = 28$ **3** $6 \times 8 = n$

4 $n = 8 \times 9$ **5** $5 \times 9 = n$ **6** $n = 5 \times 5$

7 $5 \times 9 = n$ **8** $64 = 8 \times n$ **9** $1 \times n = 7$

10 $n \times 7 = 35$ **11** $9 \times n = 54$ **12** $6 \times 5 = n$

13 $24 = 4 \times n$ **14** $80 = n \times 10$ **15** $3 \times n = 18$

Solve for *n*. Watch the parentheses. Watch the signs.

Lesson 47

16 $4 \times (3 + 5) = n$ **17** $17 - (9 - 5) = n$

18 $n = (3 \times 5) + (3 \times 4)$ **19** $n = (4 + 8) - 3$

20 $6 + (5 \times 2) = n$ **21** $6 \times (8 - 5) = n$

22 $(17 - 9) - 5 = n$ **23** $8 \times (2 + 7) = n$

24 $n = 4 \times (3 - 1)$ **25** $n = 5 + (3 \times 4)$

Solve for *n*. Watch the signs.

Lesson 41

26 $n = 24 - 8$ **27** $n \div 3 = 7$ **28** $n \times 7 = 63$

29 $7 \times n = 56$ **30** $56 - n = 18$ **31** $n = 82 - 39$

32 $8 + 3 = n$ **33** $15 + 6 = n$ **34** $n + 18 = 97$

Divide to solve for *n*.

Lesson 42

35 $15 \div 3 = n$ **36** $n = 35 \div 7$ **37** $24 \div 8 = n$

38 $n = 27 \div 9$ **39** $n = 72 \div 9$ **40** $n = 54 \div 9$

41 $30 \div 10 = n$ **42** $49 \div 7 = n$ **43** $42 \div 6 = n$

Divide. Watch for remainders.

Lesson 44

44 $7\overline{)49}$ **45** $7\overline{)39}$ **46** $8\overline{)72}$ **47** $5\overline{)40}$ **48** $6\overline{)18}$

49 $7\overline{)50}$ **50** $5\overline{)36}$ **51** $6\overline{)24}$ **52** $3\overline{)24}$ **53** $8\overline{)68}$

Solve. Watch the signs.

Lesson 43

54.
$$89 \atop + 17$$

55.
$$64 \atop - 23$$

56.
$$19 \atop + 85$$

57.
$$2379 \atop + 1893$$

58.
$$6497 \atop - 2999$$

Solve these problems.

Lessons 31, 41, 42, 44, 45

59. Andrew bought three pencils for 9¢ each at the department store. How much did they cost all together?

60. Julia sells apples at a fruit stand. Today she sold seven apples for 8¢ each. How much money did she take in?

61. Jenny needs ten hair ribbons to match each of her outfits. If there are four ribbons in a pack, how many packs must Jenny buy?

62. Oko wants to buy two erasers that cost 35¢ each. How much change should he get for three quarters?

Niran wants to buy 35 marbles. They come in bags of ten.

63. How many bags should he buy?

64. How many extra marbles will he have?

A cotton shirt costs $22. Ties cost $8.

65. How much do two cotton shirts cost?

66. How much do two shirts and four ties cost?

Patricia's patio is square. It measures 6 meters on each side.

67. What is the area of the patio?

68. What is the perimeter of the patio?

There are three rows of bunkbeds in Mr. Garvey's cabin. Each row has nine bunkbeds.

69. How many bunkbeds are there in the cabin?

70. If each bunkbed has a top bed and a bottom bed, how many people can sleep in the cabin?

◆ **LESSON 50** Unit 2 Practice

Use the information in these charts to make up questions. Exchange questions with a friend and solve them.

For example:

◆ Which stadium has the most seats?

◆ In which stadium is it easiest to hit a home run? Why?

◆ How many more seats are there in Cinergy Field than in Wrigley Field?

American League Stadiums

Team	Stadium	Home-Run Distances (feet)			Seating Capacity
		Left Field	Center Field	Right Field	
Baltimore Orioles	Oriole Park at Camden Yards	333	400	318	48,262
Boston Red Sox	Fenway Park	310	390	302	34,218
California Angels	Anaheim Stadium	333	404	333	64,593
Chicago White Sox	New Comiskey Park	347	400	347	44,321
Cleveland Indians	Jacobs Field	325	405	325	43,345
Detroit Tigers	Tiger Stadium	340	440	325	52,416
Kansas City Royals	Kauffman Stadium	320	410	320	40,625
Milwaukee Brewers	Milwaukee County Stadium	315	402	315	53,192
Minnesota Twins	Hubert H. Humphrey Metrodome	343	408	327	55,883
New York Yankees	Yankee Stadium	318	408	314	57,545
Oakland A's	Oakland-Alameda County Coliseum	330	400	330	48,219
Seattle Mariners	Kingdome	331	405	312	59,166
Texas Rangers	Ballpark at Arlington	334	400	325	49,178
Toronto Blue Jays	Sky Dome	328	400	328	50,516

National League Stadiums

Team	Stadium	Home-Run Distances (feet)			Seating Capacity
		Left Field	Center Field	Right Field	
Atlanta Braves	Turner Field	335	400	330	49,831
Chicago Cubs	Wrigley Field	355	400	353	38,765
Cincinnati Reds	Cinergy Field	330	404	330	52,952
Colorado Rockies	Coors Field	347	415	350	50,200
Florida Marlins	Pro Player Stadium	330	404	385	47,662
Houston Astros	Astrodome	325	400	325	54,816
Los Angeles Dodgers	Dodger Stadium	330	395	330	56,000
Montreal Expos	Le Stade Olympique/Olympic Stadium	325	404	325	43,739
New York Mets	Shea Stadium	338	410	338	55,601
Philadelphia Phillies	Veterans Stadium	330	408	330	62,382
Pittsburgh Pirates	Three Rivers Stadium	335	400	335	47,971
St. Louis Cardinals	Busch Memorial Stadium	330	402	330	57,672
San Diego Padres	Jack Murphy Stadium	327	405	330	59,022
San Francisco Giants	3 Com Park	335	400	328	63,000

Unit Test

Multiply.

① 9 × 9 **②** 6 × 5 **③** 0 × 9 **④** 8 × 9

⑤ 8 × 0 **⑥** 7 × 3 **⑦** 9 × 3 **⑧** 7 × 5

Divide. Don't forget remainders.

⑨ 5)‾40 **⑩** 7)‾42 **⑪** 2)‾15 **⑫** 6)‾24 **⑬** 9)‾38

⑭ 5)‾38 **⑮** 6)‾39 **⑯** 8)‾65 **⑰** 4)‾32 **⑱** 8)‾17

Solve for *n*.

⑲ $24 \div (6 \div 2) = n$ **⑳** $4 \times (6 - 6) = n$

㉑ $(16 - 7) - 5 = n$ **㉒** $(18 \div 6) \div 3 = n$

㉓ $2 \times (3 \times 3) = n$ **㉔** $(16 + 7) + 5 = n$

㉕ $(7 \times 4) + 6 = n$ **㉖** $(7 \times 5) + 4 = n$

Solve for *n*. Watch the signs.

㉗ $16 \div 4 = n$ **㉘** $8 \times 7 = n$ **㉙** $42 \div 7 = n$

㉚ $n \times 7 = 28$ **㉛** $n \times 8 = 24$ **㉜** $13 + 28 = n$

㉝ $n = 49 \div 7$ **㉞** $42 - n = 6$ **㉟** $18 + n = 20$

㊱ $3 \times n = 27$ **㊲** $n + 8 = 17$ **㊳** $81 \div n = 9$

Solve. Watch the signs.

㊴   54   **㊵**   83   **㊶**   207   **㊷**   118   **㊸**   297
    − 36   + 17   − 68   + 125   − 199

㊹   39   **㊺**   465   **㊻**   7300   **㊼**   4802   **㊽**   34,621
    + 38   − 190   − 480   + 2169   − 29,291

Find the area.

49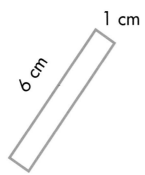

1 cm

6 cm

50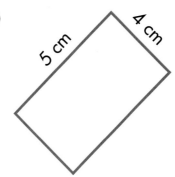

5 cm

4 cm

51

2 cm

52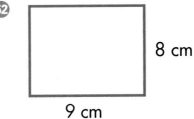

8 cm

9 cm

Solve.

53 There are 12 eggs in a carton. How many eggs are in seven cartons?

54 The refund on a soda bottle is 5¢. How many bottles did Jim return to the grocery store if he received 60¢?

55 Team caps cost $6 each. How much do four team caps cost?

56 Jill has 20 sweatshirts. She can fit five in each box. How many boxes will she need?

57 Renato planted nine seeds. Three of them sprouted. How many didn't sprout?

58 The top of Adiva's table is 2 meters wide and 3 meters long. What is the area of the tabletop?

59 Kareem needs 30 hamburger buns for a picnic. They come in packages of eight. How many packages should he buy?

60 Katherine's classroom has five groups of desks. Each group has six desks. How many desks are there in the classroom?

Exploring the Multiplication Table

A multiplication table has more in it than just factors and products. It also has patterns.

	0	1	2	3	4	5	6	7	8	9	10
0	0	0	0	0	0	0	0	0	0	0	0
1	0	1	2	3	4	5	6	7	8	9	10
2	0	2	4	6	8	10	12	14	16	18	20
3	0	3	6	9	12	15	18	21	24	27	30
4	0	4	8	12	16	20	24	28	32	36	40
5	0	5	10	15	20	25	30	35	40	45	50
6	0	6	12	18	24	30	36	42	48	54	60
7	0	7	14	21	28	35	42	49	56	63	70
8	0	8	16	24	32	40	48	56	64	72	80
9	0	9	18	27	36	45	54	63	72	81	90
10	0	10	20	30	40	50	60	70	80	90	100

**Use the multiplication table to find these patterns.
Then write the patterns and extend them.**

0, 2, 4, 6, 8, 10, ____, ____, ____, ____, 20

6, 12, 18, ____, 30, 36, ____, 48, 54, 60

0, 1, 4, 9, 16, ____, 36, ____, ____, 81, 100

0, 2, 6, 12, 20, ____, 42, ____, 72, 90

**Find other patterns in your multiplication table.
Explain your patterns to a friend.**

Now look at this part of your multiplication table.

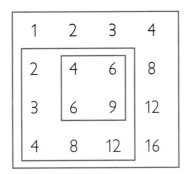

1 How much is 4 × 9? How much is 6 × 6?

2 How much is 4 × 6? How much is 2 × 12?

3 How much is 4 × 4? How much is 1 × 16?

Do these patterns work for all squares in the multiplication table?

Challenge: Without adding all of the numbers, can you find the sum of all of the numbers in the multiplication table?

First hint: What is the sum of these numbers?

1 + 2 + 3 + 4 + 5 + 6 + 7 + 8 + 9 + 10

Second hint: What is the sum of these numbers? You don't have to add them to find the sum.

2 + 4 + 6 + 8 + 10 + 12 + 14 + 16 + 18 + 20

Third hint: What is the sum of these numbers? You don't have to add them to find the sum.

10 + 20 + 30 + 40 + 50 + 60 + 70 + 80 + 90 + 100

If you need more hints, ask your teacher or work with a friend.

Algebra Readiness and Geometry

SPATIAL SENSE

- graphing ordered pairs
- graphing functions
- points, lines, rays, and angles
- congruence, similarity, and symmetry
- rotation, reflection, and translation

SCHOOL TO WORK CONNECTION

Pilots use math . . .

An air traffic controller and a pilot use ordered pairs to find and identify exact locations. Instruments in the cockpit use angles to indicate the position of the plane at take-off, in the air, and at landings. Other instruments show the plane's speed and its height above the ground.

Coordinate Grids

Graph City is laid out with numbered streets running north and south, and numbered avenues running east and west.

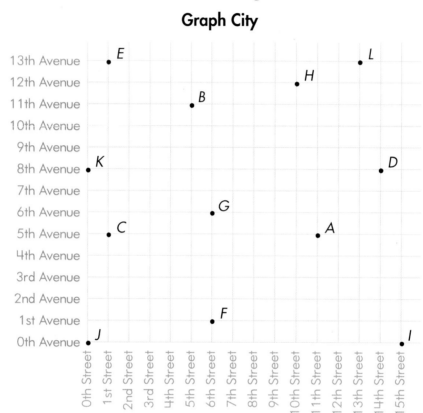

Look at the map of Graph City.

If you went to the corner of 11th Street and 5th Avenue, where would you be? The point is labeled A.

◆ Where is point B?

◆ Suppose a friend in Graph City asked you to meet her at the corner of 11th and 5th. Where would you go?

◆ If your friend didn't go to the same place you went, where do you think she might be?

◆ What would you do about it?

Suppose the people of Graph City agree to always give the street name first and the avenue name second. Answer these questions.

1 Where is the corner of 11th and 5th?

2 Where is the corner of 5th and 11th?

3 How many blocks would you have to walk to get from 11th and 5th to 5th and 11th? (Do not cut across blocks.)

4 Is there more than one way to get from 11th and 5th to 5th and 11th by walking only 12 blocks? See how many ways you can find.

5 Suppose you don't cut across blocks and you don't walk in a wrong direction on purpose.

   a. Do all ways of getting from 11th and 5th to 5th and 11th require walking exactly 12 blocks?

   b. What must you do to make the path longer?

6 How many blocks would you have to walk to get from 8th and 8th to 8th and 8th?

7 How many blocks would you have to walk to get from 4th and 7th to 6th and 3rd?

Give the location of these points on the map of Graph City. Always give the street name first and the avenue name second. The first one has been done for you.

8 A 11th and 5th   **9** E   **10** I

11 B   **12** F   **13** J

14 C   **15** G   **16** K

17 D   **18** H   **19** L

The footprints left on the moon by the *Apollo* astronauts will last about 10 million years.

ALGEBRA
READINESS

Coordinates

Places on a graph can be located quickly by pairs of numbers called coordinates. In this lesson you'll learn how to find and name coordinates of locations in Graph City.

You may remember that the people in Graph City say "11th and 5th" as a short way to say "the corner of 11th Street and 5th Avenue."

Here's an even shorter way: (11, 5)

You can use this way for the graph on page 179. For example, to tell where point *B* is, you can write (3, 8).

◆   How would you tell where point *E* is?

The two numbers that tell the location of a point on a graph are called the **coordinates** of that point.

The coordinates of point *B* are (3, 8).
The coordinates of point *E* are (13, 2).

The "sideways" coordinate is given first. The "up-and-down" coordinate is given second.

Answer these questions.

① What are the coordinates of point *D*?

② What are the coordinates of point *M*?

③ What are the coordinates of point *A*?

④ What are the coordinates of point *X*?

⑤ What are the coordinates of point *Z*?

Solve these riddles by writing the correct letter for each of the coordinates. Use the graph on page 179.

⑥   What did the acorn say when it grew up?

(0, 5), (13, 2), (1, 2), (8, 3), (13, 2), (0, 12), (10, 7), (8, 12)

or

(0, 5), (13, 2), (13, 2)   (7, 10), (8, 3)   (6, 6)

(0, 12), (10, 7), (13, 2), (13, 2)

7 Which president of the United States would you have gone to if your clothes needed mending?

(0, 12), (6, 6), (8, 12), (11, 12), (1, 2), (10, 7)

8 Which two presidents of the United States had the same names as cars?

(2, 1), (1, 2), (10, 7), (14, 10) and

(11, 12), (7, 10), (13, 5), (5, 13), (1, 2), (11, 12), (13, 5)

9 What kind of sand is found at the bottom of the Pacific Ocean?

(5, 2), (13, 2), (0, 12)   (3, 10), (6, 6), (13, 5), (14, 10)

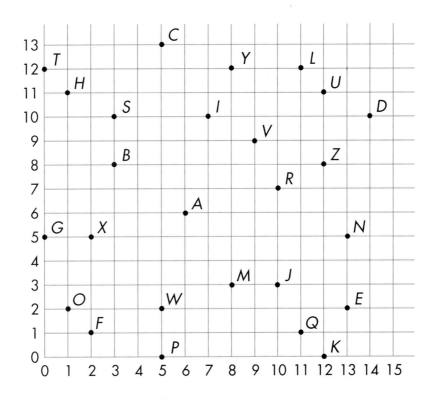

Make up your own riddles or questions and write them in your Math Journal. Ask a friend to solve them.

LESSON
53

Determining Function Rules

You've worked with function machines with known rules. In this lesson you'll review how to figure out unknown function rules.

This function machine does something to numbers that are put into it. If you put in a 7, a 12 will come out. We will write that like this:

7 —(?)→ 12

Arrows can be curved or straight. They can go in any direction, but they must point from the number going in to the number coming out.

If we put in 10, 15 will come out.

10 —(?)→ 15

This set of arrow operations shows what happens when we put in 0, 4, 9, and 25.

0 —(?)→ 5

4 —(?)→ 9

9 —(?)→ 14

25 —(?)→ 30

◆ What do you think will come out if you put in 100?

◆ What do you think the function machine is doing?

The function rule for this machine is **add 5.** We will write the **add 5** function like this:

Find a function rule for each set of arrow operations.

1
3 — ? → 10
6 — ? → 13
8 — ? → 15
1 — ? → 8

2
3 — ? → 6
4 — ? → 8
5 — ? → 10
1 — ? → 2

3
4 — ? → 12
5 — ? → 15
7 — ? → 21
0 — ? → 0

4
8 — ? → 6
5 — ? → 3
2 — ? → 0
3 — ? → 1

5
10 — ? → 5
20 — ? → 15
5 — ? → 0
6 — ? → 1

6
8 — ? → 4
4 — ? → 2
2 — ? → 1
0 — ? → 0

7
9 — ? → 3
12 — ? → 4
30 — ? → 10
3 — ? → 1

8
5 — ? → 5
8 — ? → 8
126 — ? → 126
3 — ? → 3

9
3 — ? → 27
5 — ? → 45
1 — ? → 9
8 — ? → 72

◆ **LESSON 53 Determining Function Rules**

Suppose you put 4 into a function machine and 20 comes out.
What is the function rule?

◆ Could the function rule be ×5?

◆ If the function rule
was ×5 and 6 went
into the machine,
what would come out?

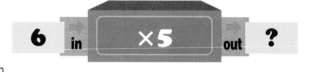

Let's see what happens when 5 goes into the function machine.

◆ With this information do you think the function rule could
be ×5?

◆ Can you find a function rule that works with both examples?
What is that rule?

When you try to figure out function rules, it is important to use
at least two examples and be sure that the rule fits both of them.

For each of the following, write two possible function rules.

⑩ 4 —(?)→ 8   ⑪ 30 —(?)→ 15

⑫ 10 —(?)→ 20   ⑬ 125 —(?)→ 500

⑭ 3 —(?)→ 21   ⑮ 50 —(?)→ 10

⑯ 15 —(?)→ 30   ⑰ 1 —(?)→ 1

Challenge: Can you find three rules for problem 17?

The rule for a certain function machine is +4. If you put the number 7 into the machine, what number will come out?

Here's another way to ask the same question:

 7 —(+4)→ y   What is y?

In each case, tell what y is.

18 7 —(+4)→ y   19 5 —(+0)→ y

20 8 —(+4)→ y   21 5 —(−0)→ y

22 16 —(+4)→ y   23 5 —(×1)→ y

24 7 —(×4)→ y   25 5 —(÷1)→ y

26 y ←(×4)— 8   27 y ←(×0)— 5

28 6 —(×4)→ y   29 7 —(×8)→ y

30 16 —(−4)→ y   31 27 —(+8)→ y

32 y ←(−4)— 12   33 53 —(−12)→ y

34 16 —(÷4)→ y   35 y ←(×0)— 7

36 8 —(÷4)→ y   37 41 —(×0)→ y

38 20 —(÷5)→ y   39 8 —(×2)→ y

40 43 —(−8)→ y   41 y ←(+7)— 17

Inverse Functions

If you know the function rule and the number coming out of a function machine, you can find out the number put into the machine.

For example, if the rule is $\times 10$ and 30 comes out, you know that 3 went in. That's because $3 \times 10 = 30$.

The rule for a certain function machine is $+4$. If the number that comes out is 10, what number was put into the machine?

Here's another way to ask the same question:

x —(+4)→ 10   What is x?

In each case, tell what x is.

1 x —(+4)→ 10

2 x —(−4)→ 4

3 x —(+4)→ 15

4 x —(÷2)→ 1

5 x —(+4)→ 20

6 x —(÷2)→ 5

7 x —(−4)→ 10

8 x —(÷2)→ 6

9 x —(−4)→ 15

10 x —(÷2)→ 10

11 x —(−4)→ 20

12 x —(÷2)→ 9

13 x —(×2)→ 14

14 x —(+9)→ 14

15 x —(×2)→ 20

16 x —(−9)→ 14

17 x —(×2)→ 2

18 x —(×2)→ 0

19 x —(×5)→ 10

20 x —(÷3)→ 3

21 x —(−8)→ 4

22 x —(+7)→ 12

Look at these function machines.

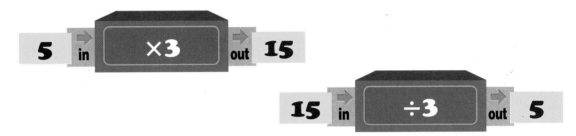

If you put 5 into the first machine, you get out 15. The second machine does the opposite. If you put in 15, you get out 5.

Because these machines do opposite things, we say that

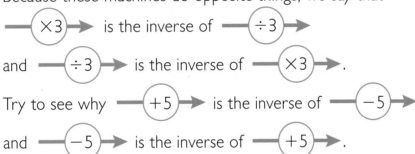

Write the inverse arrow operation.

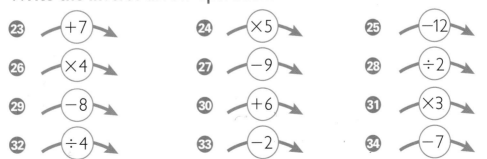

35 Suppose a function machine followed this rule:

What number could you put in to get out 21?

◆ **LESSON 54** Inverse Functions

Inverse arrow operations can help you find what number went into a machine.

Example: x ———($\times 6$)➔ 18   What is x?

Use the inverse arrow operations.

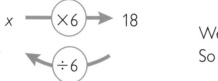

We know that $18 \div 6 = 3$.
So the value of x is 3.

Use inverse arrow operations, if they help you, to find the value of x.

36 x ———(+7)➔ 8   **37** x ———(+86)➔ 100

38 x ———(+17)➔ 19   **39** x ———($\times 2$)➔ 100

40 x ———(−3)➔ 10   **41** x ———($\div 10$)➔ 4

42 x ———($\times 5$)➔ 25   **43** x ———($\times 8$)➔ 8

44 x ———($\times 10$)➔ 90   **45** x ———($\times 10$)➔ 100

46 x ———($\div 4$)➔ 8   **47** x ———(+99)➔ 100

48 x ———(−15)➔ 0   **49** x ———(+0)➔ 0

50 x ———($\times 0$)➔ 0   **51** x ———(−8)➔ 11

52 x ———($\div 7$)➔ 2   **53** x ———($\times 5$)➔ 35

Can x have more than one value? Can you solve problem 50?

Find *x* or *y*.

54 3 —(×4)→ *y*   **55** *x* —(+7)→ 13

56 *x* —(+6)→ 13   **57** *x* —(+14)→ 20

58 5 —(−3)→ *y*   **59** 21 —(÷7)→ *y*

60 *x* —(÷3)→ 7   **61** 19 —(+2)→ *y*

62 12 —(÷6)→ *y*   **63** 17 —(+3)→ *y*

64 *x* —(÷5)→ 3   **65** 18 —(÷3)→ *y*

66 *x* —(−12)→ 3   **67** 1 —(×0)→ *y*

68 5 —(+10)→ *y*   **69** 14 —(−7)→ *y*

70 5 —(×3)→ *y*   **71** *x* —(+8)→ 12

72 *x* —(×1)→ 15   **73** *x* —(÷5)→ 4

Find a function rule for each set of arrow operations.

74 2 —(?)→ 4   4 —(?)→ 6   6 —(?)→ 8

75 8 —(?)→ 2   12 —(?)→ 3   20 —(?)→ 5

76 6 —(?)→ 12   3 —(?)→ 9   15 —(?)→ 21

77 12 —(?)→ 4   15 —(?)→ 7   9 —(?)→ 1

78 4 —(?)→ 28   2 —(?)→ 14   10 —(?)→ 70

79 10 —(?)→ 5   14 —(?)→ 7   6 —(?)→ 3

80 10 —(?)→ 13   4 —(?)→ 7   0 —(?)→ 3

81 0 —(?)→ 5   3 —(?)→ 8   9 —(?)→ 14

LESSON
55

Ordered Pairs

Look at this function machine.

It works according to this rule: x —(+5)→ y

7 in   **+5**   out **12**

If you put in 7, then 12 comes out.

Let's write that pair of numbers like this: (7, 12)

The first number in the pair (7) is the one that went in. The second number in the pair (12) is the one that came out.

A pair of numbers written this way, (7, 12), is called an **ordered pair.** We call it that because the order is important to show which number is which.

We can list other ordered pairs for the +5 function machine.

If we put in 3, then 8 comes out: (3, 8)

If we put in 9, then 14 comes out: (9, 14)

And so on.

In this way, we can say that a function machine produces ordered pairs of numbers.

Copy each list of ordered pairs, but replace the *x* or *y* with the correct number.

❶ x —(+5)→ y (7, 12), (12, y), (15, y), (0, y), (x, 7)

❷ x —(÷4)→ y (8, 2), (x, 4), (x, 3), (x, 7), (x, 9)

❸ x —(−3)→ y (9, 6), (7, y), (x, 7), (12, y), (x, 1)

❹ x —(+8)→ y (5, 13), (4, y), (x, 11), (x, 15), (6, y)

❺ x —(×5)→ y (1, 5), (3, y), (x, 10), (0, y), (8, y)

6 x —(−9)→ y   (11, y), (20, y), (25, y), (x, 0), (x, 8), (x, 9)

7 x —(×3)→ y   (2, y), (4, y), (8, y), (10, y), (x, 6), (x, 15)

8 x —(÷2)→ y   (6, y), (18, y), (12, y), (6, y), (x, 7), (x, 1)

9 x —(×0)→ y   (7, y), (12, y), (50, y), (2589, y), (x, 0)

◆ Suppose problem 9 included the ordered pair (x, 7). What would your answer be?

Here's a secret code to help you solve the riddles below.

A	B	C	D	E	F	G	H	I	J	K	L	M
26	25	24	23	22	21	20	19	18	17	16	15	14

N	O	P	Q	R	S	T	U	V	W	X	Y	Z
13	12	11	10	9	8	7	6	5	4	3	2	1

Use function rules to help solve the riddles. Find the value of x or y in each ordered pair. Then use the code to find what letter each value stands for.

10 What's a noisy group of people?

Use this function rule: x —(+3)→ y

(23, y)   (12, y), (x, 15), (3, y), (20, y)   (21, y), (6, y), (9, y), (x, 7), (x, 26)

11 What's another name for a police chief?

Use this function rule: x —(−5)→ y

(31, y)   (12, y), (17, y), (x, 6)   (x, 19), (x, 7), (16, y)

Sound travels about five times faster through water than through air.

◆ **LESSON 55** Ordered Pairs

THINKING STORY

The Lost Island of Addonia

Part 1

After their ship sank, Ferdie, Portia, Manolita, and Marcus spent three days on a raft. Then their raft drifted to the shore of a green island. A woman and a little girl came down to meet them.

"Welcome to Addonia," said the woman.

"Thank you," said Portia. "How far is it to the nearest library? I haven't had anything to read for three days."

"The library is 10 kilometers from here," said the girl.

"That's right," said the woman. "It's 43 kilometers from here."

"Wait a minute," said Marcus. "Something's crazy here." An old man was sitting on a rock near them. Marcus asked him, "Who is telling the truth about how far the library is?"

"They both are," said the old man. "The library is exactly 86 kilometers from here." When he saw how puzzled the children looked, the old man smiled.

"I guess you don't know how we do things here in Addonia," he said. "We have a secret way of saying numbers. It protects us from spies. But you children don't look like spies. I'll tell you the secret. Whenever we say a number, we always add our age to it."

"You mean," said Manolita, "that if it was 2 o'clock, I'd have to say it was 11 o'clock, because I'm nine years old?"

"That's right," said the old man. "And I would say it's 85 o'clock."

. . . to be continued

Work in groups. Discuss your answers and how you figured them out. Then compare your answers with those of other groups.

1 If you wanted to talk about six things in Addonia, what number would you say instead?

2 If a ten-year-old wanted 10 cents, what would he or she have to ask for?

3 A 12-year-old in Addonia said, "There are 17 people in my family." How many are there really?

4 **Detective question:** How old is the old man?

5 **Super detective question:** How far is it to the library?

LESSON
56

Function Rules and Ordered Pairs

In this lesson you will do more work with function rules.

Find the values of *x* in the ordered pairs.

① $x \xrightarrow{+5} y$ ⠀⠀⠀⠀ (x, 5), (x, 7), (x, 15), (x, 205), (x, 73)

② $x \xrightarrow{-5} y$ ⠀⠀⠀⠀ (x, 5), (x, 25), (x, 30), (x, 35), (x, 45)

③ $x \xrightarrow{\div 8} y$ ⠀⠀⠀⠀ (x, 1), (x, 3), (x, 8), (x, 9), (x, 10)

This is a completed function machine chart.

$x \xrightarrow{\times 6} y$

x	y
3	18
8	48
2	12
0	0
1	6

The chart shows some things about the function

The chart shows that when
x = 3, y = 18; when x = 8,
y = 48; and so on.

Use a computer or other means to draw these charts.
Solve for *x* or *y*.

④ $x \xrightarrow{\times 4} y$

x	y
1	4
▧	8
6	▧
▧	12
10	▧

⑤ $x \xrightarrow{+3} y$

x	y
▧	7
2	▧
5	▧
▧	25
6	▧

⑥ $x \xrightarrow{\times 8} y$

x	y
0	▧
▧	24
2	▧
1	8
▧	32

192 • Algebra Readiness and Geometry

7 $x \longrightarrow (+7) \longrightarrow y$

x	y
8	■
30	■
■	27
6	■
■	107

8 $x \longrightarrow (\times 6) \longrightarrow y$

x	y
3	■
■	54
10	■
■	48
7	■

9 $x \longrightarrow (-3) \longrightarrow y$

x	y
■	5
■	10
■	9
24	■
3	■

10 $x \longrightarrow (\times 7) \longrightarrow y$

x	y
7	■
0	■
10	■
■	14
■	21

11 $x \longrightarrow (-4) \longrightarrow y$

x	y
■	15
■	21
■	72
■	3
■	19

12 $x \longrightarrow (+6) \longrightarrow y$

x	y
■	25
■	35
■	45
■	55
■	65

Find the function rules before you complete these charts.

13 $x \longrightarrow (?) \longrightarrow y$

x	y
100	■
3	3
2	■
7	■
25	25

14 $x \longrightarrow (?) \longrightarrow y$

x	y
3	9
20	60
5	15
■	27
■	30

15 $x \longrightarrow (?) \longrightarrow y$

x	y
6	0
20	■
5	0
31	■
12	■

Keeping in Shape

COOPERATIVE LEARNING

Function Game

Players:	Two or more
Materials:	Two 0–5 cubes, two 5–10 cubes
Object:	To score closest to **100** without going over
Math Focus	Mental math (with all four operations) and mathematical reasoning

RULES

1. Make a blank function machine chart like this:

2. The first player rolls all four cubes to get the values of *x*. Write all four values of *x* in your chart.

3. Select a function and write it in the blank circle at the top of your chart.

4. Using your function rule, find the values of *y*.

5. Find the sum of all the values of *y*.

6. The player with the sum closest to, but not over, 100 wins the round.

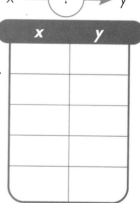

$x \longrightarrow \boxed{?} \longrightarrow y$

x	y

SAMPLE GAME

Mario's Chart

$x \longrightarrow \times 4 \longrightarrow y$

x	y
5	20
4	16
6	24
8	32
Sum	92

Anna's Chart

$x \longrightarrow +18 \longrightarrow y$

x	y
5	23
4	22
6	24
8	26
Sum	95

JoAnn's Chart

$x \longrightarrow +20 \longrightarrow y$

x	y
5	25
4	24
6	26
8	28
Sum	103

Anna was the winner of this round.

It's a good idea to keep practicing your math skills. In this
lesson, you'll use your mental math skills and estimating skills.
Watch the signs.

**In each problem, two of the answers are clearly wrong
and one is correct. Choose the correct answer.**

1. $\begin{array}{r} 409 \\ + \ 618 \end{array}$
   a. 2197
   b. 517
   c. 1027

2. $\begin{array}{r} 597 \\ - \ 522 \end{array}$
   a. 1119
   b. 175
   c. 75

3. $\begin{array}{r} 756 \\ - \ 318 \end{array}$
   a. 438
   b. 1074
   c. 108

4. $\begin{array}{r} 543 \\ - \ 178 \end{array}$
   a. 365
   b. 165
   c. 665

5. $\begin{array}{r} 4195 \\ - \ 3167 \end{array}$
   a. 128
   b. 1028
   c. 7278

6. $\begin{array}{r} 1618 \\ + \ 9322 \end{array}$
   a. 20,940
   b. 8030
   c. 10,940

7. $\begin{array}{r} 522 \\ + \ 973 \end{array}$
   a. 2595
   b. 1495
   c. 1005

8. $\begin{array}{r} 241 \\ - \ 75 \end{array}$
   a. 166
   b. 316
   c. 66

9. $\begin{array}{r} 5376 \\ + \ 3261 \end{array}$
   a. 8637
   b. 837
   c. 12,637

10. $\begin{array}{r} 233 \\ + \ 167 \end{array}$
   a. 400
   b. 690
   c. 190

11. $\begin{array}{r} 4603 \\ - \ 4346 \end{array}$
   a. 8257
   b. 1257
   c. 257

12. $\begin{array}{r} 537 \\ + \ 386 \end{array}$
   a. 1023
   b. 623
   c. 923

13. $\begin{array}{r} 180 \\ + \ 436 \end{array}$
   a. 416
   b. 616
   c. 896

14. $\begin{array}{r} 2102 \\ - \ 1569 \end{array}$
   a. 533
   b. 3683
   c. 293

◆ **LESSON 57** Keeping in Shape

The Lost Island of Addonia

Part 2

You may want to refer to the first part of this Thinking Story on pages 190–191.

On the way to the library, the children passed a hamburger stand. "Let's get some food," said Ferdie. "It's true we haven't had anything to read for three days. But we haven't had anything to eat, either."

"We'd like four hamburgers, please," Ferdie told the cook.

"I'm not sure I can make so few hamburgers," said the cook.

"He's right," Marcus said. "One hamburger each isn't very much when we're so hungry. Let's get three each."

"All right," said Ferdie. "Please make us 12 hamburgers."

"I think I know how many that is," said the cook. He made them four hamburgers.

"Where are the others?" Ferdie asked.

"You ordered only 26, didn't you?" the cook asked.

"I give up," said Ferdie. "There's no way to get what you want in this country."

"Let me try," said Manolita. She said to the cook, "You see how many hamburgers you made for us? Please make that many again and then make that many again."

"I wish you children would make up your minds," said the cook. "Twenty-third you say 23 things and 24th you say something else."

. . . to be continued

Work in groups. Discuss your answers and how you figured them out. Then compare your answers with those of other groups.

❶ Why couldn't the cook make the four hamburgers Ferdie asked for?

❷ How old was the cook?

❸ How would you say the last thing that the cook said? Say it our way, not the Addonian way.

❹ **Detective question:** How old did the cook think Ferdie was?

LESSON 58

Graphing Ordered Pairs

Once you have used a function rule to find ordered pairs, you can display them on a graph.

1 Copy the list of ordered pairs, but replace each x or y with the correct number.

$x \longrightarrow \boxed{+2} \longrightarrow y$ $(0, y), (7, y), (10, y), (x, 3), (x, 5), (x, 10)$

2 You may want to use graphing software to make a graph. Use the ordered pairs you found in problem 1 as coordinates of points on your graph.

Remember that the first (or x) number tells how far to go to the right. The second (or y) number tells how far to go up. Does your graph look like this?

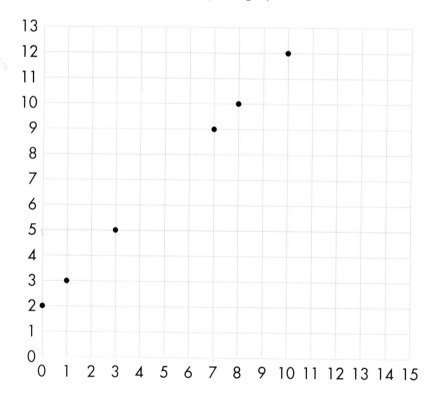

3 Do you notice anything interesting about the six points on your graph? Check with a ruler to see if they are all on the same straight line.

Look at your graph, but don't do any calculations for problems 4 and 5.

4 Think about the point that has 4 as its first coordinate.

   a. Where do you think the point ought to be?

   b. What is its second coordinate?

   c. If 4 were put into a +2 function machine, what would come out?

5 Copy each ordered pair, but replace each x or y with the number you believe would make the point fall on the line.

   a. $(2, y)$ **b.** $(x, 11)$ **c.** $(x, 8)$ **d.** $(11, y)$

Copy each list of ordered pairs, but replace each **x** or **y** with the correct number. Then graph each set of ordered pairs.

6 x ⟶ (−3) ⟶ y $(5, y), (4, y), (x, 0), (x, 5), (10, y), (x, 10)$

7 x ⟶ (÷2) ⟶ y $(4, y), (6, y), (20, y), (x, 4), (x, 8), (10, y)$

8 x ⟶ (×0) ⟶ y $(1, y), (3, y), (0, y), (10, y), (5, y), (9, y)$

9 x ⟶ (+0) ⟶ y $(1, y), (3, y), (0, y), (x, 9), (x, 12), (x, 8)$

10 x ⟶ (×1) ⟶ y $(1, y), (3, y), (0, y), (x, 9), (x, 12), (x, 8)$

Compare your graphs for problems 9 and 10. Write your observations in your Math Journal.

The largest meteorite, the Hoba meteorite, still lies where it fell at Hoba West in Namibia (formerly South-West Africa). It weighs about 60 tons and measures $8\frac{1}{2}$ feet by $7\frac{1}{2}$ feet.

LESSON 59

Identifying Scale

Sometimes the numbers you want to graph may seem too great to fit on your paper.

Suppose you are graphing this function:

$$x \longrightarrow \boxed{\times 8} \longrightarrow y$$

And let's say you are using these five ordered pairs:

x	y
0	0
1	8
2	16
3	24
4	32

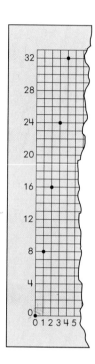

Then you might think that you would need long, skinny graph paper, like that shown at the top right.

But there is another way to fit the five points on your graph paper.

And you don't need an unusual shape.

You can let each space in the up-and-down direction stand for more than one unit. In the graph on the bottom right, each up-and-down space stands for four units. All the points fit.

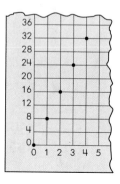

◆ Make your own graph of these points. But let each up-and-down space stand for eight units. Do the points fit?

An Ice Cream Puzzle

Alonzo surveyed the students in the fourth grade to learn their favorite ice cream flavors. There are 83 students in Alonzo's grade, and 80 of them returned the survey form.

He made a bar graph to present his data to the manager of the school cafeteria. But Alonzo forgot to write the numbers on the side of his graph that show how many students preferred each flavor.

Can you figure out how to label the side of Alonzo's graph? You may want to record the number of students who prefer each flavor.

1. How many students are represented by each line in Alonzo's graph?

2. Which flavor of ice cream is most popular? How many students prefer it?

3. How many students prefer chocolate ice cream?

4. How many students prefer vanilla ice cream?

Use a computer or other means to draw this chart. Then complete the chart.

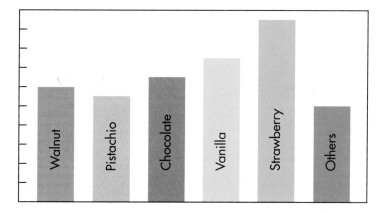

Check your answers. Do they make sense? Do they match the information on the graph?

In your Math Journal explain how you figured out this problem.

◆ **LESSON 59** Identifying Scale

Mr. Archer's students are making a graph of the average temperature in their city for each month. Here are their data:

January	30°F
February	24°F
March	46°F
April	52°F
May	59°F
June	63°F
July	70°F
August	72°F
September	65°F
October	58°F
November	42°F
December	36°F

5 What scale should they use for the up-and-down direction on their graph if their graph paper is 25 squares tall?

6 Using this scale, how many squares up will the temperature for January be?

7 Using this scale, how many squares up will the highest temperature be?

8 Create a graph using information in the above chart. You may want to use graphing software.

The space probes sent to land on Venus had to withstand temperatures of almost 500°C (900°F), a temperature high enough to melt tin.

When you make a graph, think ahead. Make sure your graph will fit on your paper.

Use a computer or other means to copy and complete each chart. Then graph each set of ordered pairs. You may want to use graphing software to create your graph.

9 x —(×5)→ y

x	y
0	■
2	■
3	■
4	■
6	■
7	■
8	■

10 x —(×7)→ y

x	y
0	■
2	■
3	■
5	■
6	■
7	■
9	■

11 x —(×10)→ y

x	y
0	■
2	■
3	■
5	■
6	■
7	■
10	■

12 x —(÷10)→ y

x	y
0	■
20	■
40	■
50	■
70	■
80	■
100	■

13 x —(÷5)→ y

x	y
0	■
10	■
15	■
20	■
30	■
35	■
40	■

14 x —(−10)→ y

x	y
70	■
60	■
50	■
40	■
30	■
20	■
10	■

Mid-Unit Review

Use the coordinate grid to answer these questions.

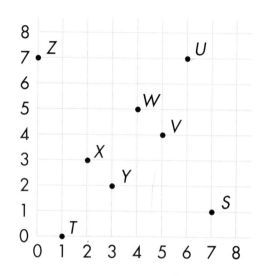

1 What are the coordinates at point Z?

2 What are the coordinates at point U?

3 What are the coordinates at point W?

4 What is the name of the point at (2, 3)?

5 What is the name of the point at (1, 0)?

6 What is the name of the point at (7, 1)?

Find a function rule for each set of arrow operations.

7 3 —(?)→ 21
6 —(?)→ 42
8 —(?)→ 56
9 —(?)→ 63

8 50 —(?)→ 5
90 —(?)→ 9
10 —(?)→ 1
30 —(?)→ 3

9 0 —(?)→ 8
5 —(?)→ 13
9 —(?)→ 17
10 —(?)→ 18

In each case, tell what x is.

10 6 —(+5)→ x

11 9 —(−5)→ x

12 41 —(−11)→ x

13 54 —(÷9)→ x

14 8 —(×5)→ x

15 20 —(÷5)→ x

16 17 —(+8)→ x

17 7 —(×7)→ x

Use the inverse arrow operation to find the value of *x*.

18 $x \longrightarrow \div 8 \longrightarrow 4$

19 $x \longrightarrow -45 \longrightarrow 3$

20 $x \longrightarrow +75 \longrightarrow 100$

21 $x \longrightarrow \div 3 \longrightarrow 9$

22 $x \longrightarrow +11 \longrightarrow 20$

23 $x \longrightarrow \times 10 \longrightarrow 100$

24 $x \longrightarrow -15 \longrightarrow 15$

25 $x \longrightarrow \times 1 \longrightarrow 0$

Copy each list of ordered pairs, but replace the *x* or *y* with the correct number.

26 $x \longrightarrow +9 \longrightarrow y$ (3, 12), (6, y), (23, y), (x, 10), (x, 18)

27 $x \longrightarrow \div 4 \longrightarrow y$ (16, 4), (24, y), (36, y), (x, 5), (x, 7)

28 $x \longrightarrow \times 8 \longrightarrow y$ (2, 16), (1, y), (0, y), (x, 64), (x, 80)

Use a computer or other means to draw these charts. Graph each set of ordered pairs. Make sure your graph will fit on the paper. You may want to use graphing software.

29 $x \longrightarrow \times 7 \longrightarrow y$

x	y
4	28
■	42
9	■
■	70
8	■

30 $x \longrightarrow \div 2 \longrightarrow y$

x	y
■	2
8	■
14	■
■	10
16	■

Composite Function Rules

These two function machines have been put together. A number (*x*) goes into the first machine. The number that comes out (*n*) goes into the second machine. Then a third number (*y*) comes out.

This is called a **composite function machine.**

Here's a way to write what this composite function machine does:

$$x \longrightarrow \times 3 \longrightarrow n \quad +5 \longrightarrow y$$

Suppose you put 6 into the first machine. What would come out of the second machine?

$$6 \longrightarrow \times 3 \longrightarrow n \quad +5 \longrightarrow y \qquad \text{What is } y?$$

First decide what *n* is.   Then decide what *y* is.

$$6 \longrightarrow \times 3 \overset{18}{\longrightarrow} n \quad +5 \longrightarrow y \qquad 6 \longrightarrow \times 3 \overset{18}{\longrightarrow} n \quad +5 \overset{23}{\longrightarrow} y$$

You can do all this a short way:

$$6 \longrightarrow \times 3 \longrightarrow n \quad +5 \longrightarrow y \qquad n \text{ is } 18; \ y \text{ is } 23.$$

Find the value of *y*.

① 7 →(+3)→ *n* →(×8)→ *y* ② 7 —(×8)→ *n* —(+3)→ *y*

③ 4 →(+7)→ *n* →(×1)→ *y* ④ 5 —(×5)→ *n* —(−5)→ *y*

⑤ 20 —(−16)→ *n* →(×3)→ *y* ⑥ 9 →(÷3)→ *n* →(+2)→ *y*

⑦ 15 →(÷5)→ *n* →(×4)→ *y* ⑧ 4 →(×3)→ *n* →(÷2)→ *y*

⑨ 4 →(÷2)→ *n* →(×3)→ *y* ⑩ 145 →(−100)→ *n* →(÷5)→ *y*

⑪ 16 —(+5)→ *n* →(−5)→ *y* ⑫ 8 →(×4)→ *n* →(÷4)→ *y*

⑬ 6 —(×2)→ *n* —(÷3)→ *y* ⑭ 5 —(+5)→ *n* —(×2)→ *y*

⑮ 18 →(÷6)→ *n* →(×3)→ *y* ⑯ 3 —(+3)→ *n* —(×4)→ *y*

⑰ 24 →(÷4)→ *n* —(×9)→ *y* ⑱ 56 →(÷7)→ *n* →(×6)→ *y*

FANTASTIC FACT

A grasshopper can jump 20 times its own body length. If you could do that, you would be able to jump from a pitcher's mound to home plate in one hop!

◆ LESSON 60 Composite Function Rules

Sierra opened a lemonade stand. She decided to charge 3¢ for each cup of lemonade, plus a 1¢ handling charge per order.

So if you bought one cup of lemonade, Sierra would charge you 3¢ plus a 1¢ handling charge—a total of 4¢.

If you bought two cups, she would charge you 6¢ for the two cups plus the 1¢ handling charge—a total of 7¢.

To help her figure out what to charge, she started to make this function chart.

$$x \longrightarrow \boxed{\times 3} \longrightarrow n \longrightarrow \boxed{+1} \longrightarrow y$$

x	y
1	4¢
2	7¢
3	▦
4	▦
5	▦
6	▦

19 Help Sierra. Use a computer or other means to draw and complete the chart. Then graph the ordered pairs. You may want to use graphing software to make your graph.

20 Connect the points on your graph. Do they all lie in a straight line?

21 Look at your graph. How much would Sierra charge somebody who bought nine cups of lemonade? (You may have to extend your graph.)

22 Devon and Brad each wanted a cup of lemonade. Brad had an idea. "Devon," he said. "Let me buy two cups and we will share them." Why did Brad think that was a good idea?

Solve.

23 Suppose Sierra sells ten cups of lemonade in one day.

   a. What is the most she would charge?

   b. What is the least she would charge?

24 How much will four friends save by ordering all at once instead of one at a time?

25 Suppose Sierra collected 15¢.

   a. How many cups of lemonade did she sell?

   b. Is there more than one answer?

26 Suppose Sierra collected 25¢.

   a. How many cups of lemonade did she sell?

   b. Is there more than one answer?

27 How many different combinations of orders could Sierra have filled if she collected 20¢?

Lemonade

3¢ for one
   cup
1¢ handling charge
   for one order

LESSON 61

Using Inverse Operations with Composite Functions

ALGEBRA READINESS

Suppose a number was put into this composite function and 23 came out. What number was put in? In other words, if *y* is 23, what is *x*?

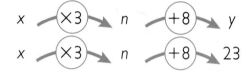

a. What value of *n* gives 23 as the number coming out? Write the inverse arrow operation.

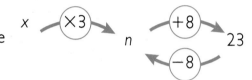

b. 23 − 8 = 15

So *n* is 15.

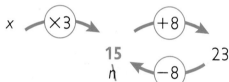

c. What value of *x* gives 15 as the value of *n*?

Write the inverse arrow operation. 15 ÷ 3 = 5

So when *y* is 23, *x* is 5.

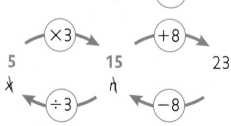

Let's check this:

5 × 3 = 15, 15 + 8 = 23. That checks.

You don't have to write all the steps.

You can just write this: *n* is 15, *x* is 5.

Use inverse operations to find the value of *x*.

❶ $x \xrightarrow{\times 5} n \xrightarrow{+2} 37$

❷ $x \xrightarrow{-5} n \xrightarrow{\div 7} 1$

Solve these problems.

3 Mikhail's class has three students absent today. The rest of the students are divided into six groups of four students each.

   a. How many students are in Mikhail's class today?

   b. How many students should be in Mikhail's class, counting those who are absent?

4 Two fourth-grade classes are going on a field trip. Nine parents and two teachers will go with the students. All together there are ten groups of six people each.

   a. How many people are going on the field trip?

   b. How many students are going on the field trip?

5 Amanda ordered some teddy bears by mail to give as gifts, but she can't remember how many she ordered. She does know that the bears cost $9 each, plus a $4 shipping and handling fee for the order, and that her total cost was $40.

   a. What was Amanda's cost before she added the shipping and handling fee?

   b. How many bears did Amanda order?

6 Mrs. Baez ordered teddy bears from the same company as Amanda did. Her total cost was $58.

   a. What was Mrs. Baez's cost before the shipping and handling fee?

   b. How many bears did Mrs. Baez order?

7 Mr. Wade is ordering from a different teddy bear company that charges $10 per bear with no shipping and handling fee. Because he has ordered from this company before, he has a discount coupon that saves him $5 on his order. He wants to spend no more than $25 on his order.

   a. If Mr. Wade spends $25, what would his cost be before he uses the coupon?

   b. How many bears can Mr. Wade order with his coupon?

◆ **LESSON 61** Using Inverse Operations with Composite Functions

THINKING STORY

The Lost Island of Addonia

Part 3

You may want to refer to the previous parts of this Thinking Story, on pages 190–191 and 196–197.

The four children came to the Addonia Public School. "Let's go in here," Portia said. "Maybe this is where the library is."

Inside the school a mathematics class was going on. "Remember," said the teacher, "every triangle has 37 sides. What's the rule, Joan?"

"A triangle has 11 sides," said a girl in the front row.

"Very good, Joan. And how many sides does a square have?"

"A square has 13 sides," said Joan.

"I'm afraid that's wrong," said the teacher. "Henry, how many sides does a square have?"

"A square has 13 sides," said Henry.

"That's right," said the teacher. "And now let's welcome our 38 visitors from the United States."

. . . to be continued

Work in groups. Discuss your answers and how you figured them out. Then compare your answers with those of other groups.

1. How could Joan be wrong when she said a square has 13 sides and Henry be right when he said the same thing?

2. What should Joan have said about the number of sides a square has?

3. How old is Joan?

4. How old is Henry?

5. How old is the teacher?

6. **Super detective questions:** How old would Joan say that Henry is? How old would Henry say that Joan is? Why would they say the same number?

LESSON
62

Graphing Composite Functions

ALGEBRA
READINESS

You've graphed ordered pairs from a single function rule. In this lesson you'll graph ordered pairs from composite functions.

Use inverse operations to replace each x with the correct number. Then make a graph for each set of ordered pairs. Make sure your graph will fit on your paper. You may want to use graphing software.

1 $x \longrightarrow \boxed{\times 2} \longrightarrow y$ $(x, 2), (x, 10), (x, 20), (x, 0), (x, 16)$

2 $x \longrightarrow \boxed{+7} \longrightarrow y$ $(x, 9), (x, 17), (x, 27), (x, 7), (x, 8)$

3 $x \longrightarrow \boxed{-9} \longrightarrow y$ $(x, 9), (x, 7), (x, 3), (x, 8), (x, 5)$

4 $x \longrightarrow \boxed{\div 6} \longrightarrow y$ $(x, 6), (x, 3), (x, 8), (x, 7), (x, 9)$

5 $x \longrightarrow \boxed{\times 2} \longrightarrow n \longrightarrow \boxed{+7} \longrightarrow y$ $(x, 9), (x, 17), (x, 27), (x, 7)$

6 $x \longrightarrow \boxed{\times 3} \longrightarrow n \longrightarrow \boxed{-5} \longrightarrow y$ $(x, 1), (x, 7), (x, 10), (x, 25)$

7 $x \longrightarrow \boxed{-5} \longrightarrow n \longrightarrow \boxed{\times 3} \longrightarrow y$ $(x, 0), (x, 15), (x, 6), (x, 12)$

8 $x \longrightarrow \boxed{+6} \longrightarrow n \longrightarrow \boxed{\div 2} \longrightarrow y$ $(x, 6), (x, 5), (x, 7), (x, 3)$

9 $x \longrightarrow \boxed{\div 3} \longrightarrow n \longrightarrow \boxed{-3} \longrightarrow y$ $(x, 2), (x, 4), (x, 1), (x, 3)$

10 $x \longrightarrow \boxed{-7} \longrightarrow n \longrightarrow \boxed{\times 4} \longrightarrow y$ $(x, 28), (x, 20), (x, 16), (x, 12)$

Look at the following composite function. Answer the questions.

11 **a.** Pick a number between 0 and 10 for the value of *x*.

$x \xrightarrow{\times 2} n \xrightarrow{+3} y$

b. Make an ordered pair of the number you used for *x* and the value of *y*.

c. Find two more ordered pairs for the same function.

d. Graph the three ordered pairs you have found.

12 Look at your graph.

a. Pick a point that has 4 as its first (sideways) coordinate and is on the same line as the other three points.

b. What is the second coordinate of the point you picked?

c. Pick a point that has 15 as its second (up-and-down) coordinate and is on the same line as the other points.

d. What is the first coordinate of the point you picked?

13 Replace *x* and *y* in the ordered pairs with the correct numbers.

$x \xrightarrow{\times 2} n \xrightarrow{+3} y$ $\quad (4, y), (x, 15)$

◆ Did you use the graph to find *x* in the second ordered pair?

The blue whale is the largest and heaviest animal on Earth. The largest elephant looks small compared to the blue whale, which is about 100 feet long and weighs as much as 400,000 pounds. That's as long as three city buses and as heavy as 200 compact cars. A newborn blue whale weighs about 6000 pounds.

Keeping Sharp: Facts, Computations, and Fractions

ALGEBRA READINESS

Keep in shape by completing this mixed review of addition, subtraction, multiplication, division, and fractions.

Watch the signs. Solve for *n*.

① $n + 6 = 16$

② $56 \div n = 7$

③ $n - 17 = 35$

④ $7 \times 5 = n$

⑤ $n \div 3 = 7$

⑥ $n + 9 = 31$

⑦ $n = 15 + 8$

⑧ $54 \div n = 6$

⑨ $63 \div n = 9$

Add or subtract.

⑩
$$\begin{array}{r} 1589 \\ + 2496 \end{array}$$

⑪
$$\begin{array}{r} 329 \\ - 167 \end{array}$$

⑫
$$\begin{array}{r} 1720 \\ + 2679 \end{array}$$

⑬
$$\begin{array}{r} \$4.27 \\ - 1.79 \end{array}$$

⑭
$$\begin{array}{r} \$13.56 \\ + 8.82 \end{array}$$

⑮
$$\begin{array}{r} 294 \\ + 699 \end{array}$$

⑯
$$\begin{array}{r} \$10.00 \\ - 4.46 \end{array}$$

⑰
$$\begin{array}{r} 2983 \\ + 4799 \end{array}$$

Answer these questions.

⑱ Which pizza has been cut into pieces that are $\frac{1}{6}$ of its size?

⑲ Which pizza has been cut into pieces that are $\frac{1}{5}$ of its size?

⑳ Which pizza has **more** pieces?

㉑ Which pizza has **bigger** pieces?

Solve for *n*. Watch the signs.

㉒ $n = 8 + 7$

㉓ $n = 8 \times 7$

㉔ $8 + n = 31$

㉕ $n \times 8 = 32$

㉖ $24 \div n = 8$

㉗ $n \div 10 = 7$

Work in cooperative groups to solve these problems. Be sure to explain your reasons and check that your answers make sense.

28 Two years ago Mark was three times as old as Mia. This year he is twice as old. Is that possible? If so, how old is Mark? How old is Mia?

29 Chicago, Illinois, is 291 miles from St. Louis, Missouri, and 162 miles from Davenport, Iowa. What can you tell about how far it is between St. Louis and Davenport?

30 Leon is 20 years old, and his sister, Yolanda, is five years old.

   a. In how many years will Leon be twice as old as his sister?

   b. In how many years will Leon be five times as old as his sister?

31 An ice cube weighs 150 grams. After the ice cube melts, about how much will the resulting water weigh?

32 A 7× telescope makes objects appear seven times closer than they are. If an object is 63 feet away, how far away will it seem when viewed through the telescope?

33 If an object appears to be about 8 feet away when viewed through a 7× telescope, how far away is it really?

◆ **LESSON 63** Keeping Sharp: Facts, Computations, and Fractions

The Lost Island of Addonia

Part 4

You may want to refer to previous parts of this Thinking Story, on pages 190–191, 196–197, and 212–213.

At last the children came to the library. Portia found a book to read. It was called *Goldilocks and the 48 Bears.* When Portia went to check out the book, the librarian said, "Books are not free in Addonia. You will have to pay 46¢ a day to take this book out."

"That's too much money," said Portia. "I can't pay that."

"It's not too much," said an old woman. "You should be happy to pay 73¢ a day for such a fine book."

"That's right," said a young boy. "Why, 9¢ a day is not very much. We all pay that."

"I can't figure out anything here," said Portia. "I want to go home."

"If you think things are bad here," said the librarian, "you should see what it's like in Subtractia."

. . . the end

Work in groups. Discuss your answers and how you figured them out. Then compare your answers with those of other groups.

1 About how much does it really cost to take a book out of the Addonia Library?

2 Could it cost 1¢ a day?

3 Could it cost more than 10¢ a day?

4 Detective question: How old is the person who wrote the book Portia wants to read?

LESSON
64

Graphing Functions

You can make a graph of any function rule.

For each function rule, follow these steps:

A. Find four ordered pairs of numbers.

B. Graph the four points.

C. Try to draw a line through all four points.

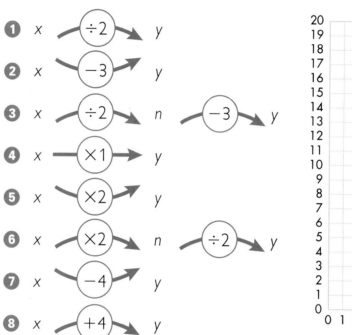
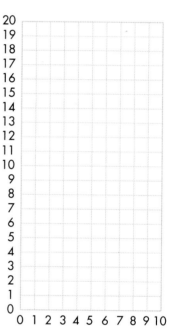

Compare your answers for problems 1 through 8 with the answers of others in your class.

◆ Did you choose the same numbers?

◆ Are the four points on your graphs the same?

◆ Are the lines on your graphs the same?

In your Math Journal describe how you picked four points. Did you try any points that didn't work?

Find a function rule for each graph.

⑨

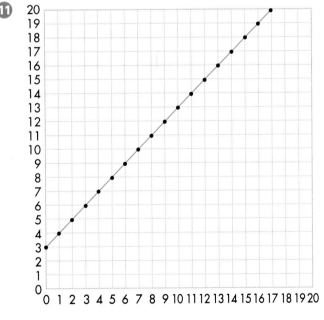

A function rule is ▩

⑩

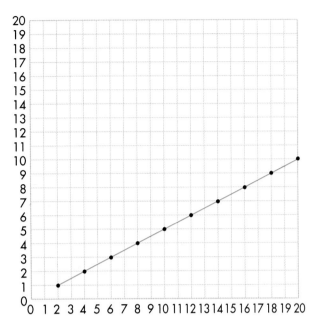

A function rule is ▩

⑪

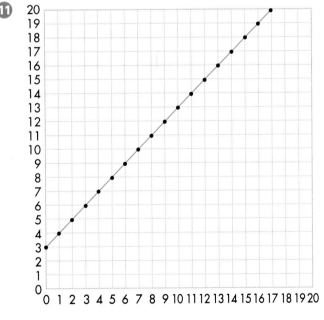

A function rule is ▩

⑫

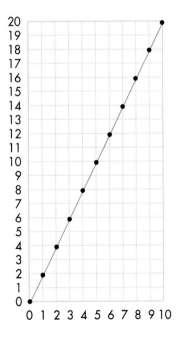

A function rule is ▩

Working with Graphs

Juan wanted to collect information about how many books New City residents read per month. He made a survey asking people about how many books they check out of the local library each month.

To complete the survey, he spent two afternoons at the library, asking the same question to people as they left. Juan's results are shown in the table.

Number of People	Number of Books per Month
1	15
8	13
12	10
14	9
20	8
25	7
51	6
35	5
24	4
4	3
3	2
2	1
1	0

Answer these questions.

1 How fairly do Juan's results describe the reading habits of the people who live in New City?

2 Did Juan's survey reach only people who use the library often?

In your Math Journal explain what you might have done differently if you were conducting the survey.

As part of his report, Juan decided to make a picture graph of the results of his survey. Here's what his picture graph looked like.

Books Checked Out per Month

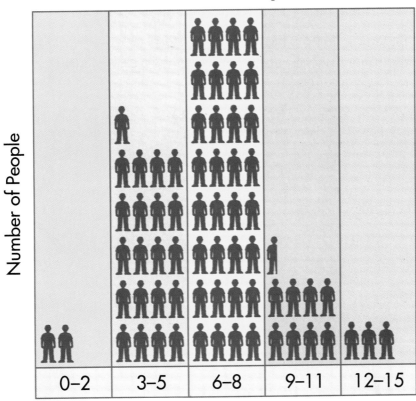

Number of People

0–2   3–5   6–8   9–11   12–15

Number of Books

🧍 = 3 people

Study Juan's picture graph. Make up questions that can be answered with the information in the graph.

Answer these questions.

3. Which shows the results of Juan's survey better, the table or the picture graph?

4. What is the advantage of the table?

5. What is the advantage of the picture graph?

6. If you wanted to show that your community needs a larger library, what kind of information would you collect?

◆ LESSON 65 Working with Graphs

Carlos was doing experiments to see how the age of seeds affects how they sprout. He made sprouting trays with wet towels, plastic wrap, and exactly 100 seeds.

Each day Carlos checked his trays and removed the seeds that had sprouted. He planted those seeds in his garden.

Carlos began by doing a trial with new seeds to make sure his experiment would work. Here's how the new seeds sprouted.

Day	Seeds Sprouted
1	0
2	1
3	18
4	45
5	13
6	4
7	0
8	1
9	0
10	0

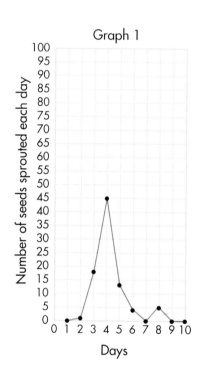

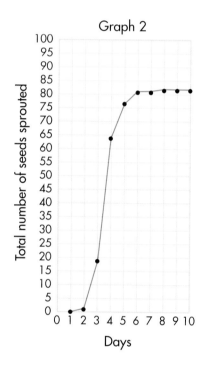

Answer these questions.

❼ How many seeds sprouted?

❽ Do you think more seeds will sprout if the experiment goes beyond ten days?

❾ Carlos made two graphs to present his results. Which graph do you think Carlos should use?

❿ Which graph better shows the day on which most seeds sprouted?

⓫ Which graph better shows the total number of seeds that sprouted?

Next Carlos set up two sprouting trays. One had new seeds and the other had the same kind of seeds that were 20 years old. He recorded his results in a chart.

Seeds Sprouted		
Day	**New**	**Old**
1	0	0
2	3	0
3	15	0
4	47	1
5	11	4
6	7	25
7	1	16
8	1	13
9	0	10
10	0	10
11	0	5
12	0	1
13	0	0
14	0	1
15	0	0

Carlos decided to present information about both groups of seeds on the same graph. Here is one of his graphs.

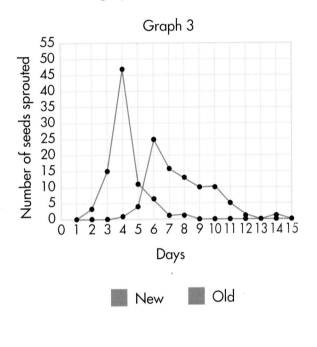

Use the above data to create a graph showing the total amount of seeds sprouted each day (like Graph 2).

⑫ Which graph better shows the days on which the most seeds sprouted?

⑬ Which graph better shows how quickly each group of seeds sprouted?

⑭ Which graph better shows how many seeds of each group sprouted?

Study the results of Carlos's experiment. In your Math Journal write how the age of the seeds seemed to affect their growth.

Choosing an Appropriate Graph

Mr. Sly owns a small business. Each year he must report the amount of sales and earnings for his business.

Sales is the amount of money received.

Earnings is the amount of money left after all expenses are paid.

The chart shows the sales and earnings for Mr. Sly's business for the years 1989–1996.

Year	Sales (Dollars)	Earnings (Dollars)
1989	995,000	85,000
1990	1,021,000	83,500
1991	1,300,000	79,000
1992	1,210,000	74,500
1993	1,450,000	72,000
1994	1,820,000	74,000
1995	1,950,000	71,500
1996	2,150,000	68,300

Answer the following questions using the information in the chart. You may use a calculator.

❶ How much did Mr. Sly's sales increase from 1989 to 1990?

❷ In what year was the greatest amount of money received through sales?

❸ In what year did Mr. Sly earn the least?

❹ What was the total amount of money in sales from 1989 to 1996?

❺ What were Mr. Sly's earnings from 1989 to 1996?

Mr. Sly decided to report his data using separate graphs for sales and earnings. Here are Mr. Sly's graphs.

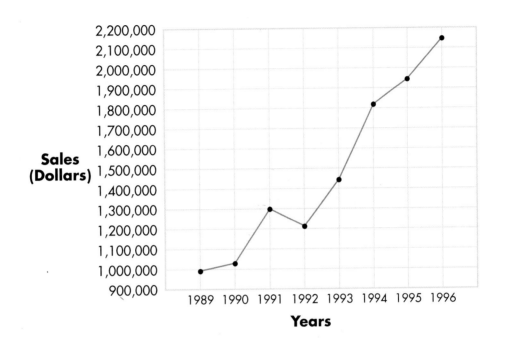

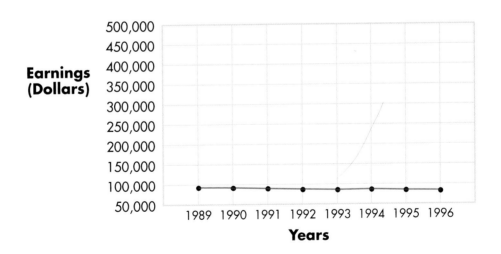

Study Mr. Sly's graphs. Write about how fairly or unfairly they present the information. Make a graph for earnings that shows the change in earnings more fairly.

LESSON 67

Revisiting Number Facts

Keep in shape by practicing your number facts. Watch the signs.

SELF ASSESSMENT

Are You Shiny or Rusty?

Very shiny   29 or more right

Shiny   24–28 right

A bit rusty   19–23 right

Rusty   Fewer than 19 right

ALGEBRA READINESS

Solve for *n*. Watch the signs.

1. $40 \div n = 8$
2. $n + 8 = 14$
3. $7 + 5 = n$
4. $n - 7 = 10$
5. $n = 72 \div 8$
6. $12 - n = 7$
7. $7 \times 9 = n$
8. $9 + 6 = n$
9. $n \times 4 = 32$
10. $n \div 3 = 7$
11. $7 \times n = 49$
12. $n + 9 = 12$
13. $24 = n \times 8$
14. $n \div 7 = 4$
15. $13 - n = 10$
16. $n \div 5 = 9$
17. $5 + 8 = n$
18. $6 \times 9 = n$
19. $n \times 5 = 30$
20. $13 - 7 = n$
21. $n \div 5 = 6$
22. $8 + n = 15$
23. $n = 5 \times 8$
24. $n - 2 = 9$

Solve these problems. Watch the signs.

25. 9×8
26. $13 - 5$
27. $5 + 7$
28. $35 - 5$
29. $6\overline{)36}$

30. $18 - 9$
31. 4×6
32. $7 + 9$
33. $20 - 12$
34. $6\overline{)54}$

12 VOLT BATTERIES

"High Charge"

$40.00

2-year Guarantee

"Long Life"

$50.00

3-year Guarantee

"Our Best"

$85.00

5-year Guarantee

RADIAL TIRES

15,000 kilometer Guarantee

4 for $160.00

(Any Size)

30,000 kilometer Guarantee

4 for $220.00

(Any Size)

60,000 kilometer Guarantee

4 for $360.00

(Any Size)

MUFFLERS

All prices include expert installation

$55.00

1 Year Guarantee

$70.00

2 Year Guarantee

$90.00

Guaranteed for as long as you own your car

Discuss the questions based on the above information.

◆ Which of the batteries is the best buy? Why do you think so?

◆ Which of the tires is the best buy? Why do you think so?

◆ Which of the mufflers is the best buy? Why do you think so?

Lines and Angles

You know what a point, a line, and an angle are. Sometimes we wish to refer to just a part of a line. If the part has two endpoints, we call it a **line segment** (see line segment *AB* in the picture below).

If the part has only one endpoint and goes on forever in the other direction, we call it a **ray,** or sometimes we call it a **half line** (see ray *DE*).

The first letter in the name of the ray is its **endpoint.** We sometimes draw arrows on our pictures of lines to show that they go on forever in both directions.

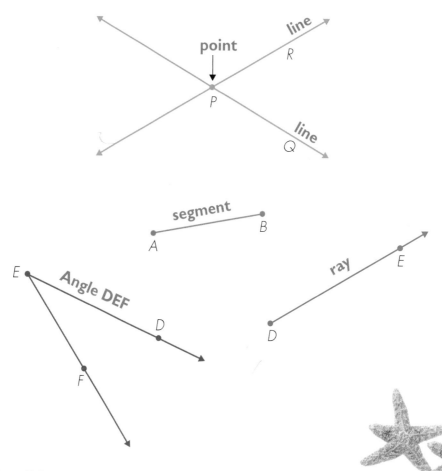

Starfish come in all sizes. The largest is the sunflower star. It has more than 26 arms. When a starfish loses an arm, another one grows in its place. In fact, a starfish can grow a whole new body from just one arm.

Answer the following questions.

1 Suppose two different lines meet at point *P*.

   a. Could they also meet at some other point? At point *T*?

   b. Discuss this with your friends. Decide what you think.

2 Suppose there are two points. How many lines do you think you could draw that go through both points?

3 On your paper draw two lines that meet in as many points as possible. How many points is that?

4 On your paper make two points.

   a. Draw as many different lines through them as you can.

   b. How many lines is that?

5 Look at angle *DEF* in the picture on page 230.

   a. Is it made up of two rays?

   b. What is the endpoint of each ray?

We usually name an angle with a point on one of its sides (rays), then the common endpoint of its rays (sometimes called the **vertex**), and then a point on the other ray. However, in some cases we just name the vertex.

6 Do you know which angle is angle *E*?

7 Do you know which angle is angle *P*? Explain.

Name the following in two ways. Remember to use only two letters.

8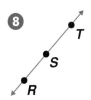

9

10

11 Which is longer, a line segment or a line? Explain.

◆ **LESSON 68 Lines and Angles**

Remember, a **right angle** is an angle like the one in the figure. The corners of this page are right angles.

12 Look around you.

a. Identify other right angles in the classroom.

b. Make a list of at least five examples of right angles other than the corners of the page.

13 Look at the traffic signs below.

a. Which of these traffic signs have at least one right angle?

b. Try to name the shape of each sign.

Follow these steps to make right angles.

A. Get a piece of paper. Imagine a line like this dotted one.

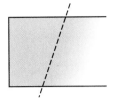

B. Fold along the line.

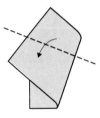

C. Your paper should look like this. Rub with your finger or a pencil to make a sharp crease.

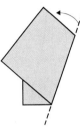

D. Imagine a line like the dotted one. Start to fold along the line.

E. As you fold, make sure you line up the edges on the right.

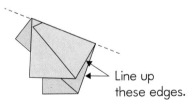

Line up these edges.

F. Your paper should look like this.

◆ Unfold your paper. How many right angles did you make?

Perpendicular and Parallel Lines

In this lesson you'll learn to identify two special kinds of lines using what you already know about points and angles.

Any two lines are **perpendicular** if the angles they make when they meet are right angles.

These lines are perpendicular.

❶ Try to draw two lines that meet with one right angle and with the other three angles not right angles. The two lines must be straight and must continue straight through the point where they meet. Can you do it?

❷ If two lines meet so that one angle formed is a right angle, what kind of angles will the other three angles be?

❸ By folding paper, make two lines that are perpendicular. Draw the lines in two different colors.

❹ Suppose you fold a piece of paper twice.

   a. What is the least number of right angles you can make?

   b. The greatest number?

In each case, tell whether the two lines are perpendicular.

❺

❻

❼

❽

◆ Suppose you fold a piece of paper three times. What is the least number of right angles you can make? The greatest number?

◆ Suppose you fold a piece of paper four times. What is the least number of right angles you can make? The greatest number?

Parallel lines are lines that go in the same direction. The lines in this figure are parallel lines.

9 Do the two lines look as though they will ever meet each other?

10 Do the lines look as though they stay the same distance apart?

Parallel lines never meet. They remain the same distance apart no matter how far they are extended.

In each case, tell whether the two lines are *parallel, perpendicular, or neither.*

11   **12**   **13**

14  **15**

16 Draw a line. Now draw two more lines, each perpendicular to the first. What do you think is true of these last two lines?

In your Math Journal list several examples of parallel and perpendicular lines that you see every day.

◆ **LESSON 69** Perpendicular and Parallel Lines

Look at the figures below. Count the sides in each figure. Write the number of sides for each on your paper. Write "T−3" and so on for each figure. Can you guess how the letters for the various figures were chosen?

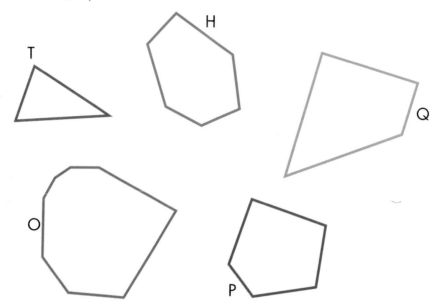

All of the figures shown are called **polygons.** A polygon is a closed plane figure with three or more line segments as sides. In a closed figure, every side shares its endpoints with two other sides. Think of a polygon as a fence with no break in it. Somebody inside can't get out without climbing the fence.

A polygon with five sides is called a **pentagon** (*penta-* means "five"). A polygon with six sides is a **hexagon.** A polygon with eight sides is an **octagon.**

The names for three- and four-sided polygons don't include "gon." They are **triangle** and **quadrilateral.** Sometimes people say eight-gon to mean an octagon, ten-gon to mean a ten-sided polygon, and so on.

17 Draw an octagon.

18 Draw a seven-gon (called a **heptagon**).

19 Draw a ten-gon (called a **decagon**).

20 Draw a triangle with two of its sides the same length.

㉑ Draw a quadrilateral with two of its sides parallel but the other two sides not parallel.

㉒ Draw a quadrilateral with both pairs of opposite sides parallel.

㉓ Draw a quadrilateral with both pairs of opposite sides parallel and with all its sides the same length.

㉔ Draw a quadrilateral with both pairs of opposite sides parallel and with all its angles the same size.

㉕ Draw a quadrilateral with both pairs of opposite sides parallel and with all its sides and all its angles the same size.

Do your answers for problems 21–25 look like the quadrilaterals shown below? These figures have special names that are given here.

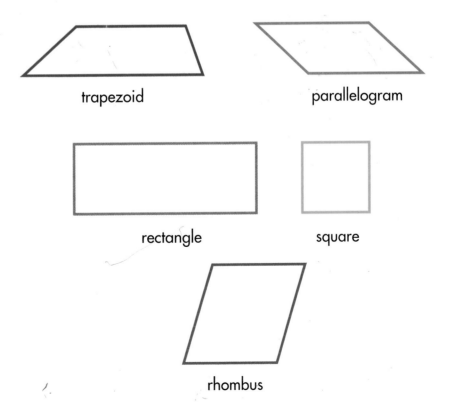

trapezoid   parallelogram

rectangle   square

rhombus

Congruence and Similarity

Two figures are **congruent** if they are the same size and same shape. If one figure fits exactly on top of another, they are congruent.

If two figures are the same shape but not the same size we say they are **similar.**

1 List all the figures below that look congruent to figure A.

2 List all the figures below that look similar to figure A but not congruent to it.

3 List all the figures below that look congruent to figure B.

4 List all the figures below that look similar to figure B but not congruent to it.

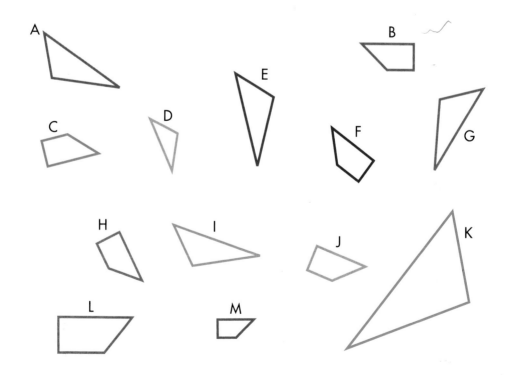

5 List five examples of congruent objects.

6 List five examples of similar objects.

7 Before factories began producing items, do you think there were as many good examples of congruent objects as there are today? Why?

◆ Consider three similar squares. The first one is 1 cm on a side. The second is 2 cm on a side. The third is 3 cm on a side.

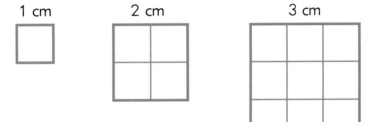

1 cm   2 cm   3 cm

8 Solve the following problems.

  a. What is the area of the smallest square?

  b. What is the area of the middle square?

  c. What is the area of the largest square?

  d. What is the perimeter of the smallest square?

  e. What is the perimeter of the middle square?

  f. What is the perimeter of the largest square?

9 What pattern do you see as the area of the squares increases? What do you see as the perimeter increases?

In your Math Journal continue this exercise using measures from 5 centimeters to 10 centimeters as the side lengths. Write about the relationship you see between area and perimeter.

LESSON 71

Rotation, Reflection, and Translation

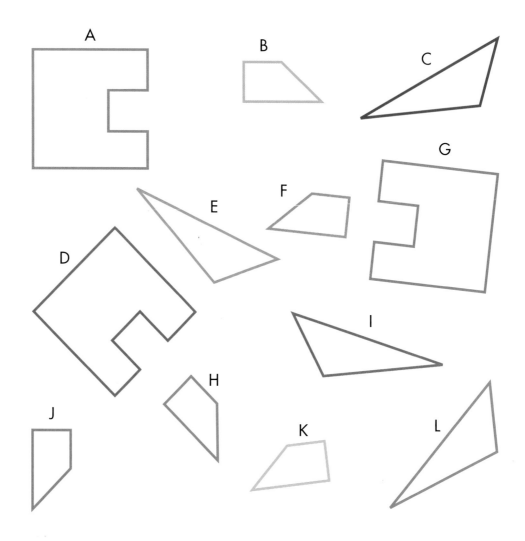

Use tracing paper or waxed paper. Then answer the questions.

1 Trace figures A, B, and C on your paper.

2 List the figures you think are congruent to figure A.

3 Slide your paper so that your copy of figure A is directly over each figure you thought was congruent to figure A. Does your figure fit on top of each of them?

When you slide the paper in a straight line without turning it, you make a **translation** of figure A. If you turn the paper, that move is called a **rotation.**

4 Look at figure B.

   a. List the figures you think are congruent to figure B.

   b. Slide your paper (translating and rotating) to see if your tracing fits on top of each figure you thought was congruent to figure B.

   c. Can you make your tracing fit on each of them with only translations and rotations? Why not?

   d. Can you think of something to do with the tracing to make your copy of figure B fit on the figures that appear to be congruent to it?

◆ Discuss your idea with classmates.

5 Look at figure C.

   a. List the figures you think are congruent to figure C.

   b. Can you make your tracing of figure C fit on each of them?

   c. Did you have to turn the paper over for some of those figures?

Turning the tracing over makes a figure into a mirror image of itself. This is called a **reflection.** You get the same effect by holding a mirror beside the figure and looking only at the mirror image rather than at the figure.

6 Why did you not have to turn the tracing over to check for congruency with figure A?

Colorado and Wyoming are the only two states that are perfect rectangles.

Identifying Solid Figures

There are mathematical names for many of the objects we see and use in our everyday lives. Four of those names are **sphere, cylinder, pyramid,** and **prism.**

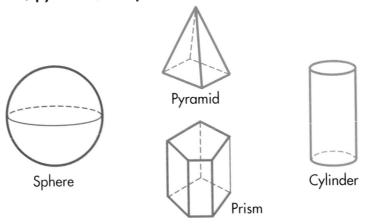

Pyramid

Sphere

Prism

Cylinder

The points on the surface of a **sphere** are all exactly the same distance from a point called the **center** of the sphere. Does that remind you of a circle?

❶ Name at least four objects that are like a sphere. Compare your list with your classmates' lists.

A **cylinder** is a solid object with two congruent curved bases. We usually think of cylinders as having circles for their bases.

❷ Name four objects that are like a cylinder.

A **pyramid** is a solid object with only one base that is a polygon. The sides of a pyramid are triangles, all of which meet in a point.

❸ Try to name four objects that are like a pyramid.

A **prism** is a solid object with two congruent bases. The sides of a prism are parallelograms.

❹ Name four objects that are like a prism. Remember, the bases can be any polygons, such as triangles, squares, rectangles, and so on.

There are many special kinds of prisms.

5 Does a regular cardboard box have two congruent bases?

6 Are the sides of a box parallelograms? (Remember that a rectangle is a special kind of parallelogram.)

7 Is a box a prism?

8 Look at the room you are in. Is it a prism?

Sometimes we make solid (or three-dimensional) figures out of flat (or two-dimensional) material. We draw a pattern for the figure on some flat, foldable material like cardboard. Then we cut, fold, and tape the pattern together to make the solid. The pattern is sometimes called a **net.**

9 Look at the following pattern.

   a. Would it make a cube if it were folded along the lines?

   b. Make a pattern like this one. Cut it out, fold it, and tape it together. Does it make a cube?

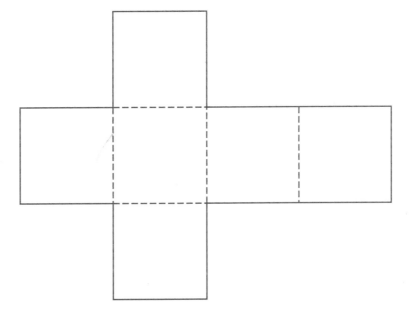

10 Is a cube a prism?

◆ LESSON 72 Identifying Solid Figures

Are there other nets from which you could make a cube?

Consider each net shown here. Decide whether the net would make a cube. Compare your answers with those of your classmates. If you disagree, the person who thinks it is possible should make the net out of paper and try to show that it will make a cube.

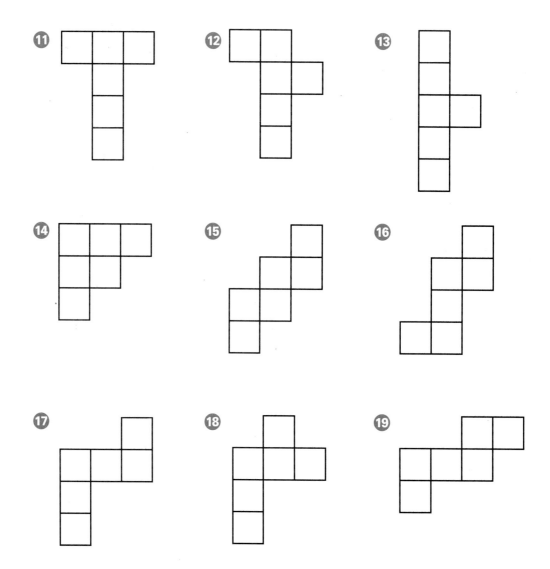

20 What figures do you think you could make from the following nets?

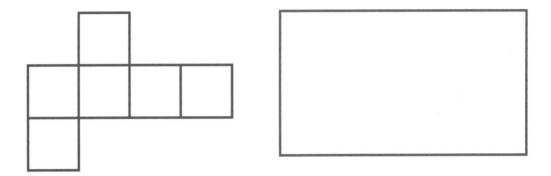

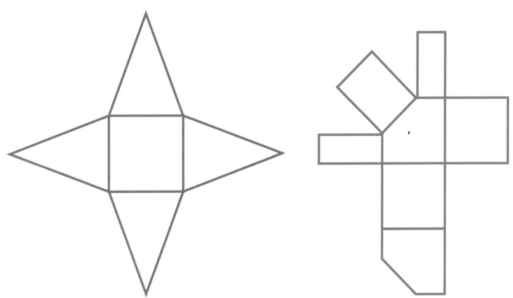

In your **Math Journal** design your own nets for figures you would like to make. Then create them.

The **great pyramid of Cheops** in **Egypt** covers **13 acres** and contains **2.3 million limestone blocks**, each weighing about $2\frac{1}{2}$ **tons**. If all the blocks were cut into **1-foot square segments** and laid end-to-end, they would extend for nearly **17,000 miles**.

Lines of Symmetry

You can easily make a square out of a rectangular piece of paper. Just fold it diagonally, matching the edge of the short side to the edge of the long side, and cut off the leftover part. Unfold the paper, and you have a square!

A **line of symmetry** in a figure cuts the figure into two parts that are mirror images of each other. That is, the line of symmetry will form two congruent parts.

If you fold a figure on a line of symmetry, the two sides will fall exactly on top of each other.

   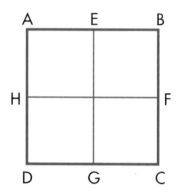

◆ In the heart-shaped figure, is the dashed line a line of symmetry?

◆ *HF* is a line of symmetry. Fold a square along a line like *HF*. Do the two sides fall exactly on top of each other?

◆ Find another line of symmetry in your square. Is there a line like it in the square above?

◆ Try to find two more lines of symmetry in your square. Fold to make sure they are lines of symmetry.

◆ Are there any more lines of symmetry in your square? Check any line you think might be a line of symmetry by folding along it.

◆ How many lines of symmetry are there in your square?

◆ How many lines of symmetry do you think there are in other squares?

Trace the figures. Then find out how many lines of symmetry there are in each. Watch your numbering.

1   **Equilateral triangle**

Three equal sides

Three equal angles

6

2   **Square**

Four equal sides

Four equal right angles

7

3   **Regular pentagon**

Five equal sides

Five equal angles

8

4   **Regular hexagon**

Six equal sides

Six equal angles

9

5   **Regular octagon**

Eight equal sides

Eight equal angles

10

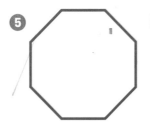

◆ **LESSON 73** Lines of Symmetry

Trace the figures. Divide each figure into halves, using a line of symmetry. Shade $\frac{1}{2}$ of each figure.

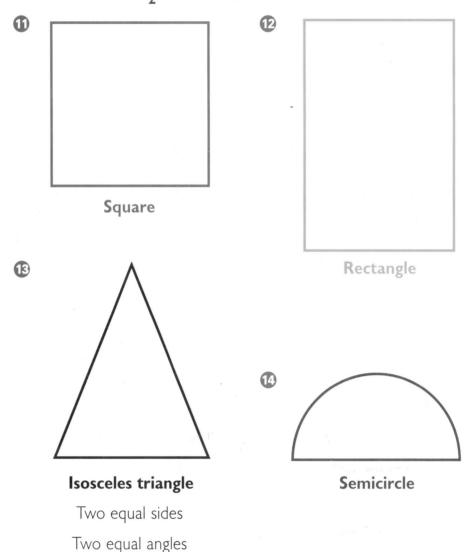

⑪

Square

⑫

Rectangle

⑬

Isosceles triangle

Two equal sides

Two equal angles

⑭

Semicircle

⑮ Trace each figure again. Try to shade $\frac{1}{2}$ the area of each figure in such a way that there is not a line of symmetry between the shaded and the unshaded parts. (This is hard for figures 13 and 14. Do the best you can.)

In your Math Journal explain how you can find a line of symmetry without folding a figure.

Parallel lines can be used to divide line segments into equal parts.

The seven lines above are parallel, so the distances between them are the same.

Copy the line segment below on a sheet of tracing paper.

Place your paper with the line segment over the seven parallel lines at the top of this page. Move the paper so that one end of the line segment just touches the top line and the other just touches the bottom line.

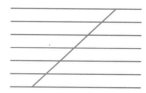

Mark the points where the line segment crosses each of the parallel lines.

◆ Into how many parts has your line segment been divided?

◆ Do the parts seem about equal in length?

◆ Is each part $\frac{1}{6}$ of the length of the segment?

◆ How many centimeters long is the segment?

◆ How many centimeters long is each small part of the segment?

◆ What is $\frac{1}{6}$ of 12?

Copy the line segment again. Divide the segment into four equal parts by placing it across five of the parallel lines.

◆ Measure to find how many centimeters there are in $\frac{1}{4}$ of the segment.

◆ What is $\frac{1}{4}$ of 12?

Area and Perimeter: Practice

Review what you know about area and perimeter by answering the following questions.

1 Look at the rectangles shown here.

   a. Which ones seem similar to each other?

   b. How did you decide?

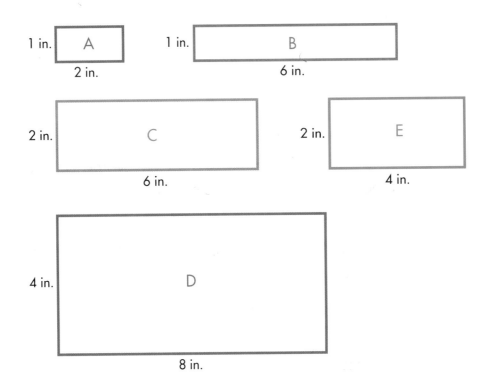

2 You know that to find the perimeter of, or distance around, a polygon, you add the lengths of all the sides. How do you find the area of a rectangle?

Let's look at Rick's garden. It's shaped like a rectangle. The short side measures 3 meters. The long side measures 7 meters.

3 What is the perimeter?

4 What is the area?

⑤ Find the perimeter and the area for each of the three similar rectangles on page 250. Then make a chart like the following. Fill in the missing numbers.

Rectangle	Length of Short Side (in inches)	Perimeter (in inches)	Area (in square inches)
A	1		
B			
C			
D			
E			

Answer the following questions.

⑥ Examine your chart.

    a. For the similar rectangles, if you double the length of a side, what happens to the perimeter?

    b. Is that what you would expect?

⑦ As you double the length of a side in similar rectangles, what happens to the area?

⑧ If you triple the length of a side,

    a. What happens to the perimeter?

    b. What happens to the area?

⑨ If you multiply the length of a side by 4,

    a. What happens to the perimeter?

    b. What happens to the area?

⑩ Another rectangle is similar to rectangle A, but its short side is 5 inches long.

    a. What would be its perimeter?

    b. What would be its area?

ASSESSMENT

Unit 3 Review

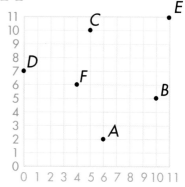

Lessons 51, 52

Look at the graph. Name the coordinates of these points.

1 A   **2** B

3 C   **4** D

5 E   **6** F

Find the value of *x* or *y*.

7 $3 \xrightarrow{+5} y$ **8** $12 \xrightarrow{-5} n \xrightarrow{\times 3} y$

Lessons 53, 54   **9** $8 \xrightarrow{-2} y$ **10** $4 \xrightarrow{\div 2} n \xrightarrow{+9} y$

11 $x \xrightarrow{\times 6} 42$ **12** $x \xrightarrow{\div 4} n \xrightarrow{-6} 2$

What is a possible function rule for each of these?

13 $x \xrightarrow{\;?\;} y$ **14** $x \xrightarrow{\;?\;} y$ **15** $x \xrightarrow{\;?\;} y$

Lessons 53–56

x	y
7	13
10	16
24	30
0	6

x	y
15	5
12	4
30	10
3	1

x	y
3	27
5	45
1	9
8	72

Use a computer to copy and complete these charts. Then graph each set of ordered pairs. Make sure your graph will fit on your paper.

16 $x \xrightarrow{\times 3} y$ **17** $x \xrightarrow{\div 4} y$ **18** $x \xrightarrow{+10} y$

Lessons 56, 58–59

x	y
■	18
■	27
5	■
■	12

x	y
28	■
12	■
■	5
16	■

x	y
25	■
■	15
7	■
12	■

252 • Algebra Readiness and Geometry

Lesson 70 ⑲ Which of the following figures are congruent to figure A?

A   B   C   D   E

Solve these problems.

⑳ Habib saves $3 a week. How long will it take him to save $24?

Lesson 63

㉑ Heather lives 2 kilometers from her school. Laura lives 1 kilometer from the school. How far does Laura live from Heather?

㉒ Steve's tenth birthday was in 1996. In what year was his second birthday?

Lesson 68 ㉓ Identify these parts of a line.

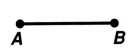 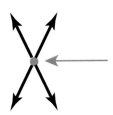

Lesson 69 **For each pair of lines, tell whether the lines are _parallel_, _perpendicular_, or _neither_.**

㉔   ㉕   ㉖

Lesson 73 **How many lines of symmetry can be drawn in each figure?**

㉗   ㉘   ㉙

Lesson 74 ㉚ Find the perimeter and area of a rectangle with a long side that measures 8 meters and a short side that measures 3 meters.

LESSON
76

Unit 3 Practice

Translate the messages by using the Code Graph to translate ordered pairs to letters.

Lessons 51, 52

① (12, 4), (9, 5), (28, 16), (8, 9), (24, 9), (12, 4), (9, 5), (28, 16), (3, 11), (18, 0), (1, 6)   (3, 11), (1, 6) (20, 13), (20, 8), (9, 17).

② (15, 15), (9, 5), (1, 6), (8, 9), (3, 11), (9, 17), (14, 9), (28, 16), (17, 6), (9, 17)   (15, 15), (9, 5), (1, 6)   (28, 16), (8, 9), (24, 9)   (20, 13), (3, 11), (3, 2), (1, 6), (28, 16) (26, 12), (3, 2), (24, 9), (1, 6), (3, 11), (21, 3), (24, 9), (9, 17), (28, 16)   (17, 6), (20, 13)   (28, 16), (8, 9), (24, 9)   (20, 8). (1, 6).

③ (15, 15), (9, 5), (1, 6), (8, 9), (3, 11), (9, 17), (14, 9), (28, 16), (17, 6), (9, 17)   (3, 11), (1, 6)   (28, 16), (8, 9), (24, 9)   (18, 0), (9, 5), (26, 12), (3, 11), (28, 16), (9, 5), (6, 15)   (17, 6), (20, 13)   (28, 16), (8, 9), (24, 9) (20, 8). (1, 6).

Code Graph

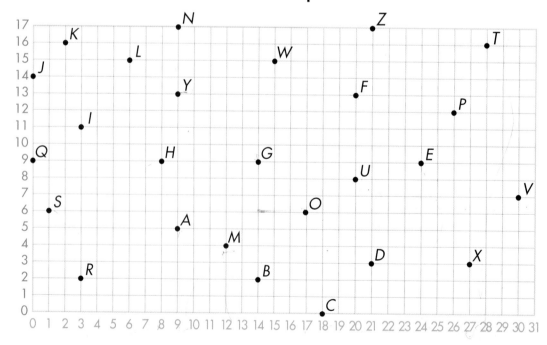

What is the value of *y*?

Lessons
53, 54

4 24 —(+7)→ *y*   **5** 2956 —(+0)→ *y*   **6** 18 —(−3)→ *y*

7 0 —(+2)→ *y*   **8** 7 —(×8)→ *y*   **9** 3 —(×6)→ *y*

10 8 —(×0)→ *y*   **11** 7 —(+98)→ *y*   **12** 36 —(−9)→ *y*

13 63 —(÷7)→ *y*   **14** 36 —(÷4)→ *y*   **15** 82 —(−0)→ *y*

What is the value of *x*?

Lessons
53, 54

16 *x* —(−8)→ 0   **17** *x* —(+0)→ 0   **18** *x* —(÷2)→ 7

19 *x* —(+3)→ 56   **20** *x* —(+2)→ 5   **21** *x* —(÷6)→ 8

22 *x* —(÷4)→ 7   **23** *x* —(−2)→ 12   **24** *x* —(+5)→ 26

25 *x* —(×0)→ 0   **26** *x* —(×1)→ 179   **27** *x* —(+9)→ 20

Solve the following problems.

Lessons
70, 74

28 Find the perimeter and area of a rectangle with a long side
that measures 6 cm and a short side that measures 2 cm.

29 Which of the following polygons are similar to figure A?

 A   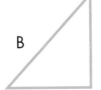 B   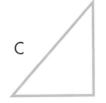 C   D

◆ LESSON 76 Unit 3 Practice

Give a possible function rule for each set of ordered pairs.

Lesson 53

30 x ——(?)—→ y

x	y
0	0
6	2
15	5
30	10

31 x ——(?)—→ y

x	y
0	0
1	8
7	56
10	80

32 x ——(?)—→ y

x	y
5	2
34	31
52	49
8	5

33 x ——(?)—→ y

x	y
9	13
1	5
6	10
12	16

34 x ——(?)—→ y

x	y
8	56
9	63
7	49
6	42

35 x ——(?)—→ y

x	y
8	72
9	81
6	54
7	63

36 x ——(?)—→ y

x	y
0	6
1	7
8	14
5	11
10	16
9	15

37 x ——(?)—→ y

x	y
12	3
18	9
30	21
54	45
63	54
36	27

38 x ——(?)—→ y

x	y
7	7
18	18
171	171
5	5
63	63
45	45

Use a computer or other means to draw each table of ordered pairs. Then graph each set of points. Make sure your graph will fit on your paper. You may want to use graphing software.

Lessons 56, 58–60

39 $x \longrightarrow \boxed{\times 4} \longrightarrow y$

x	y
0	▪
3	▪
▪	8
1	▪
▪	16

40 $x \longrightarrow \boxed{+7} \longrightarrow y$

x	y
0	▪
12	▪
▪	15
4	▪
▪	23

41 $x \longrightarrow \boxed{\div 2} \longrightarrow y$

x	y
6	▪
▪	6
▪	5
16	▪
▪	10

42 $x \longrightarrow \boxed{\times 4} \longrightarrow n \longrightarrow \boxed{+7} \longrightarrow y$

x	y
0	▪
3	▪
▪	15
1	▪
▪	23

43 $x \longrightarrow \boxed{-3} \longrightarrow n \longrightarrow \boxed{\times 2} \longrightarrow y$

x	y
▪	0
6	▪
▪	2
8	▪
▪	4

44 $x \longrightarrow \boxed{\div 2} \longrightarrow n \longrightarrow \boxed{-3} \longrightarrow y$

x	y
6	▪
12	▪
▪	2
16	▪
▪	7

Lesson 68

45 Which of the following are right angles?

A   B   C   D

Lesson 57 In each problem, two of the answers are clearly wrong and one is correct. Choose the correct answer.

46
```
   180
+ 437
```
a. 417
b. 617
c. 697

47
```
   938
+  85
```
a. 1023
b. 123
c. 7357

48
```
   180
+ 437
```
a. 175
b. 1117
c. 617

49
```
   927
+  97
```
a. 206
b. 1024
c. 200

50
```
   290
+ 180
```
a. 470
b. 110
c. 10

LESSON
77

More Unit 3 Practice

Lessons 63, 67

Solve for *n*. Watch the signs.

① $21 - n = 7$ ② $n = 5 + 27$ ③ $7 + n = 36$

④ $49 \div 7 = n$ ⑤ $27 - 16 = n$ ⑥ $42 - 24 = n$

⑦ $n = 8 \times 5$ ⑧ $n \times 4 = 16$ ⑨ $n \div 3 = 24$

⑩ $13 + 4 = n$ ⑪ $n = 27 \div 3$ ⑫ $6 \times n = 36$

⑬ $4 = n \div 9$ ⑭ $21 + 39 = n$ ⑮ $n = 15 + 18$

⑯ $6 \times 7 = n$ ⑰ $63 \div n = 9$ ⑱ $n - 28 = 13$

⑲ $37 - 18 = n$ ⑳ $n = 9 \times 9$ ㉑ $n + 18 = 32$

Lesson 63

Add or subtract.

㉒ $\begin{array}{r} 312 \\ -\ 154 \end{array}$ ㉓ $\begin{array}{r} 782 \\ +\ 429 \end{array}$ ㉔ $\begin{array}{r} 294 \\ -\ 123 \end{array}$ ㉕ $\begin{array}{r} 781 \\ +\ 317 \end{array}$ ㉖ $\begin{array}{r} 7642 \\ -\ 3295 \end{array}$

㉗ $\begin{array}{r} 238 \\ +\ 513 \end{array}$ ㉘ $\begin{array}{r} 508 \\ -\ 274 \end{array}$ ㉙ $\begin{array}{r} 3089 \\ -\ 666 \end{array}$ ㉚ $\begin{array}{r} 341 \\ +\ 265 \end{array}$ ㉛ $\begin{array}{r} 4579 \\ -\ 1238 \end{array}$

㉜ $\begin{array}{r} 731 \\ -\ 245 \end{array}$ ㉝ $\begin{array}{r} 665 \\ +\ 306 \end{array}$ ㉞ $\begin{array}{r} 156 \\ +\ 179 \end{array}$ ㉟ $\begin{array}{r} 7376 \\ -\ 6127 \end{array}$ ㊱ $\begin{array}{r} 7649 \\ -\ 219 \end{array}$

㊲ $\begin{array}{r} 23 \\ +\ 38 \end{array}$ ㊳ $\begin{array}{r} 48 \\ -\ 29 \end{array}$ ㊴ $\begin{array}{r} 614 \\ +\ 327 \end{array}$ ㊵ $\begin{array}{r} \$43.10 \\ -\ 23.20 \end{array}$ ㊶ $\begin{array}{r} \$105.76 \\ -\ 59.38 \end{array}$

㊷ $\begin{array}{r} \$27.30 \\ +\ 4.62 \end{array}$ ㊸ $\begin{array}{r} \$14.14 \\ +\ 1.70 \end{array}$ ㊹ $\begin{array}{r} \$6.87 \\ -\ 1.90 \end{array}$ ㊺ $\begin{array}{r} \$324.17 \\ +\ 79.43 \end{array}$ ㊻ $\begin{array}{r} \$2.93 \\ +\ 8.41 \end{array}$

Solve these problems.

Lessons 61, 63

47 Martin saves $10 each week. How long will it take him to save enough money to buy hockey skates that cost $70?

48 Bernelle is six years younger than her sister. They were both born in October. Bernelle was born in 1990. In what year was her sister born?

49 Petra had a stack of baseball cards. Then Luis gave her 20 cards and Emily gave her 35 cards. How many cards does Petra have now?

50 Thea bought six pencils that cost 9¢ each. She gave the clerk a $1 bill. How much change should she get?

51 Nolan had a package of 100 star stickers. He wanted to make a pattern of six rows with eight stars in each row. Did he have enough stars to make two of these patterns?

52 Olivia runs 7 kilometers every day. How many days will it be before she has run at least 50 kilometers?

53 Victor bought nine erasers that cost 7¢ each. He gave the cashier three quarters. How much change should he get?

54 Mackenzie collects rocks. Jake gave her 31 rocks and Max gave her 27.

   a. How many more rocks does Mackenzie have now than before?

   b. How many rocks does Mackenzie have?

◆ **LESSON 77   More Unit 3 Practice**

Lesson 68   **Answer these questions about right angles.**

⑤⑤   Which of these angles are right angles?

a.   **b.**   **c.**   **d.**   **e.**

⑤⑥   Draw a right angle.

⑤⑦   Find five right angles in your classroom.

Lesson 69   **For each pair of lines, tell whether the lines are *parallel*, *perpendicular*, or *neither*.**

⑤⑧   ⑤⑨   ⑥⓪   ⑥①

⑥②   ⑥③   ⑥④   ⑥⑤

⑥⑥   Find three pairs of perpendicular lines in your classroom.

⑥⑦   Find three pairs of parallel lines in your classroom.

Lesson 73   **How many lines of symmetry can be drawn in each figure?**

⑥⑧   ⑥⑨   ⑦⓪   ⑦①

Lesson 63   **Answer the following questions.**

⑦② Which pizza has **more** pieces?

⑦③ Which pizza has **bigger** pieces?

⑦④ Which pizza has been cut into pieces $\frac{1}{6}$ of its size?

⑦⑤ Which pizza has been cut into pieces $\frac{1}{7}$ of its size?

1   **2**

Cubo Challenge Game

Players:	Two or more
Materials:	Two 0–5 cubes, two 5–10 cubes
Object:	To make numbers from 1 to 20
Math Focus:	Mental math (with all four operations) and mathematical reasoning

Using only the numbers 1, 2, 6, and 10, try to make each number from 0 to 20 by the rules of the "Cubo" game (page 163).

Remember that you must use each number only once and may combine numbers using addition, subtraction, multiplication, and division.

Keep track of **how** you make each number. You may use parentheses, if necessary.

Challenge problem: Following the rules of Cubo, what is the greatest number you can make from 1, 2, 6, and 10?

Superchallenge problem: Try to make as many numbers as you can between 0 and 40 by following the rules of Cubo, using 1, 2, 6, and 10. (All but two of the numbers from 0 to 40 are possible.)

Super-duper challenge problem: Try to make as many numbers as you can between 0 and 64. (All but eight of the numbers from 0 to 64 are possible.)

Roll the four cubes until you find another set of four numbers that you think will work well. Then use those numbers in the challenge problems.

Use the same numbers as other people in the class and compare your results with theirs.

UNIT
3

Unit Test

What are the coordinates of these points?

1 A   **2** B   **3** C   **4** D   **5** E

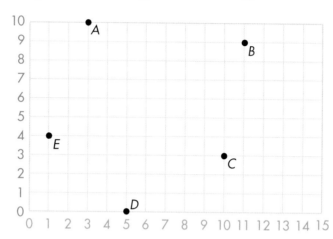

Find the value of x or y.

6 8 ⟶(+9)⟶ y   **7** 17 ⟶(−7)⟶ n ⟶(÷2)⟶ y

8 x ⟶(×4)⟶ 24   **9** x ⟶(÷3)⟶ n ⟶(−5)⟶ 2

10 42 ⟶(÷7)⟶ y   **11** 18 ⟶(−2)⟶ n ⟶(÷8)⟶ y

What is a possible function rule for each chart?

12 x ⟶(?)⟶ y   **13** x ⟶(?)⟶ y   **14** x ⟶(?)⟶ y

x	y
7	21
3	9
0	0
5	15

x	y
16	8
20	12
24	16
30	22

x	y
7	14
16	23
20	27
22	29

Solve for n.

15 $20 \div 4 = n$ **16** $56 \div 7 = n$ **17** $7 - n = 0$

18 $7 \times n = 42$ **19** $5 \times n = 45$ **20** $16 + n = 32$

21 $n - 2 = 8$ **22** $n \times 3 = 18$ **23** $n - 15 = 30$

Add or subtract.

24 $\begin{array}{r} 67 \\ + 49 \\ \hline \end{array}$ **25** $\begin{array}{r} 324 \\ - 98 \\ \hline \end{array}$ **26** $\begin{array}{r} 706 \\ + 214 \\ \hline \end{array}$ **27** $\begin{array}{r} 404 \\ - 187 \\ \hline \end{array}$ **28** $\begin{array}{r} 3509 \\ - 2654 \\ \hline \end{array}$

Solve these problems.

29 Kim is saving to buy a birdcage that costs $14. She saves $2 each week. How many weeks will it take her to save enough money to buy the birdcage?

30 Carl is reading a book about parrots. This morning he was on page 39. By the end of the day he reached page 72. How many pages are in the book?

31 Bella was born in May of 1987. Her brother, Alex, was born in May of 1993. When Bella was nine years old, how old was Alex?

32 Paul went to see his friend give a puppet show. He noticed that there were four rows with six chairs in each row. There was also a row of three chairs. How many people could be seated?

Tell whether each is a right angle.

33   **34**

For each pair of lines, tell whether the lines are *parallel*, *perpendicular*, or *neither*.

35    **36**    **37**

How many lines of symmetry can be drawn in each figure?

38   **39**

40 Which of the following figures look congruent to figure A?

Mathematics and Postage Stamps

People have been sending mail for thousands of years. In ancient times messengers on foot or horseback delivered mail. But this was an expensive service.

In the 1840s mail service changed. A new idea to put glue on the back of paper stamps made it easy and cheap for people to mail their own letters. The new stamps got to be so popular that people started collecting them.

Many people still enjoy collecting postage stamps as a hobby.

Some people collect stamps from a single country.

Some people collect stamps about a special topic.

How do you find stamps? Many businesses get mail from all over the world. Often they will save the stamps for schoolchildren. Most people simply buy stamps from a dealer. You can often buy a large number of used stamps for a few dollars.

Start a stamp collection that features mathematics. You can start one collection for the whole class, or you can build individual or small group collections.

Before you begin, decide on the details. You could collect stamps of all mathematics topics, including famous mathematicians, geometry, maps, and space travel.

◆ What other topics in mathematics can you think of?

Design Your Own Stamp

Design your own stamp that relates to a topic in mathematics. Display your stamp along with your classmates' stamps.

If you are really proud of your stamp design, send it to the United States Postal Service. Write a letter to ask them to consider your design for a new stamp.

Multidigit Multiplication

APPROXIMATION AND APPLICATION

- **converting units of measure**
- **rounding**
- **algebra readiness**
- **interpreting graphs**
- **polygons**

SCHOOL TO WORK CONNECTION

Medical technicians use math . . .

Medical technicians conduct tests and collect data on patients. One common test uses an electrocardiograph (ECG or EKG) to create a graph of a patient's heartbeat. Each heartbeat creates a wavy pattern on a graph. Doctors analyze data and interpret graphs to make correct diagnoses about their patients.

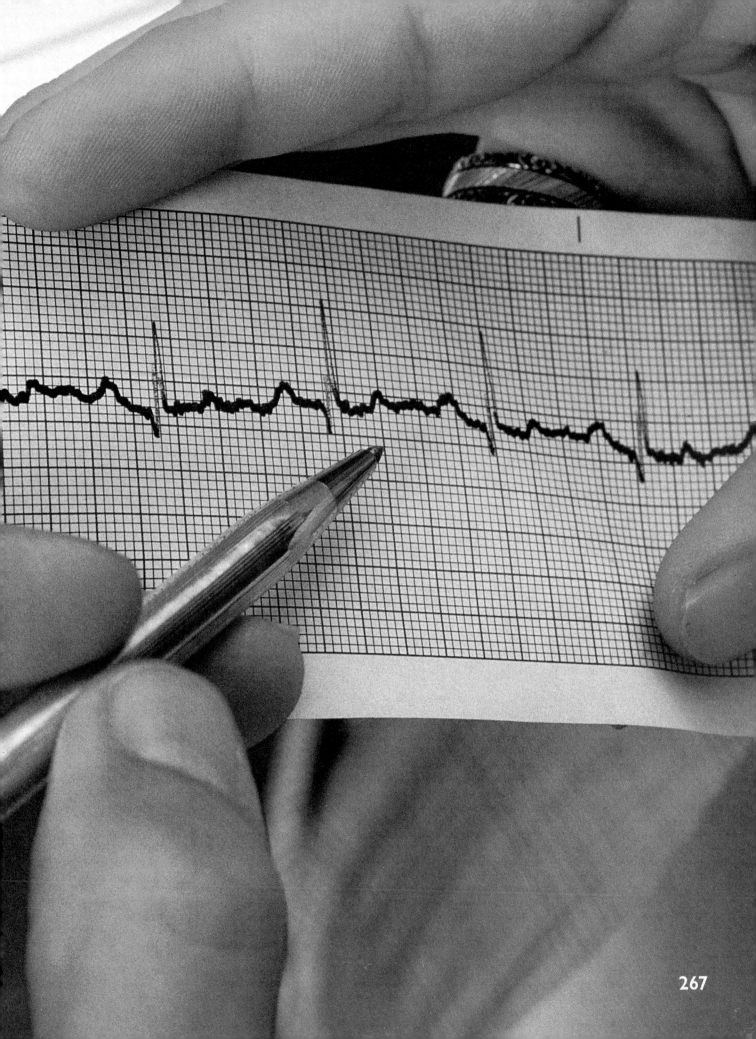

Multiplying by Powers of 10

"I can add 0 to 3 and get 30," said Kenji. "I just write 3 and then I add the 0 after it." He wrote 30 on the board.

"You aren't really adding 0," answered Carol. "You're multiplying by 10 when you write that 0 after the 3."

◆ When Kenji writes 0 after 3, is he adding 0 to 3 or multiplying 3 × 10?

◆ How can you multiply 3 by 100?

◆ How can you multiply 3 by 1000?

◆ How can you multiply 3 by 10,000?

Write a general rule for multiplying by numbers like 10, 100, 1000, and so on in your Math Journal.

◆ Discuss your rule with others. Why does your rule work?

Use your rule to solve for *n*. Watch your numbering.

1 $10 \times 7 = n$

2 $100 \times 7 = n$

3 $1000 \times 7 = n$

4 $1000 \times 6 = n$

5 $1000 \times 65 = n$

6 $100 \times 73 = n$

7 $10 \times 583 = n$

8 $583 \times 10 = n$

9 $68 \times 100 = n$

10 $10,000 \times 583 = n$

11 $657 \times 10 = n$

12 $100 \times 783 = n$

13 $594 \times 1000 = n$

14 $86 \times 100 = n$

15 $503 \times 10 = n$

16 $100 \times 10 = n$

17 $100 \times 496 = n$

18 $10 \times 392 = n$

19 $16 \times 1000 = n$

20 $497 \times 1000 = n$

21 $709 \times 10 = n$

22 $649 \times 1000 = n$

23 $200 \times 1000 = n$

24 $800 \times 100 = n$

◆ How many 0s are there in your answer to problem 16?
Did you write two 0s after the 10 or did you write one 0
after the 100? Does it make a difference in your answer?

Multiply. Watch your numbering.

25 100×100

26 1000×10

27 1000×1000

28 $10,000 \times 100$

29 $10,000 \times 10,000$

30 100×1000

31 $100,000 \times 10$

32 $1,000,000 \times 1,000$

33 $100,000 \times 1,000$

Solve these problems.

34 How many years are there in ten centuries?

35 The Packard family made a patio out of bricks. There are
20 rows of bricks, with 100 bricks in each row. How
many bricks are there all together?

LESSON
79

Converting Metric Units

Remember: 100 centimeters (cm) = 1 meter (m)
1000 meters = 1 kilometer

Answer the following questions.

① How many centimeters are there in 1 kilometer?

② How many centimeters are there in 7 kilometers?

③ How many centimeters are there in 7 meters?

④ How many meters are there in 7 kilometers?

⑤ How many centimeters are there in 73 meters?

⑥ How many centimeters are there in 73 kilometers?

Remember: 1000 milliliters = 1 liter

Answer the following questions.

⑦ How many milliliters are there in 7 liters?

⑧ How many milliliters are there in 73 liters?

⑨ How many cents are worth seven dollars?

⑩ How many cents are worth $73?

⑪ How many milliliters are in 13 liters?

⑫ How many cents are worth eighteen dollars?

Remember: 1000 grams (g) = 1 kilogram

Answer the following questions.

⑬ How many grams are there in 10 kilograms?

⑭ How many grams are there in 7 kilograms?

⑮ How many grams are there in 73 kilograms?

Answer these questions.

Jim rode his bicycle all day, from 8:00 A.M. until 5:00 P.M. At the end of the day he said, "I must have ridden more than 60 centimeters today."

16 Do you think Jim probably rode more than 60 cm?

17 How far do you think Jim was trying to say he had ridden?
How far is that in centimeters?

Mary said she thinks she weighs about 45 grams.

18 Do you think Mary really weighs about 45 grams?

19 How much do you think Mary was trying to say she weighs? How many grams is that?

Pete said he thinks he is at least 120 kilometers tall.

20 Do you think Pete is at least 120 kilometers tall?

21 What do you think he meant to say?

22 If Pete were 120 kilometers tall, how many meters would that be? How many centimeters would that be?

23 Do you know of anything that is 120 kilometers tall? If so, name it.

24 Name something that is about 100 meters tall. How many centimeters is that?

Multiplying by Multiples of 10

The Albany Parks Department has bought land for a new public sports park. The large, open field is 400 meters wide and 800 meters long. What is the area of the field? You can multiply to find out.

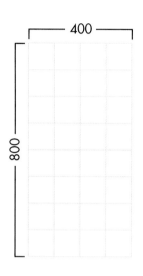

Multiply 400 × 800.

Think of a rectangle that is 800 units long and 400 units wide.

Now think of separating the rectangle into squares, so that each square is 100 units by 100 units.

◆ How many squares are there?

◆ What is the area of each square?

◆ What is the area of the entire rectangle?

◆ What is 400 × 800?

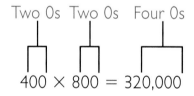

Two 0s   Two 0s   Four 0s

400 × 800 = 320,000

Notice that the number of 0s in the answer is the sum of the numbers of 0s in the two factors.

Multiply 300 × 60.

Look at another rectangle separated into rectangular sections.

◆ How many small rectangles are there?

◆ What is the area of each small rectangle?

◆ What is the area of the entire rectangle?

◆ What is 300 × 60?

272 • Multidigit Multiplication

Multiply 90,000 × 2,000,000.

The answer is 9 × 2 with many 0s after it. Here's how to find out how many 0s.

Count the number of 0s in the two factors.

There are **four 0s** in 90,000.

There are **six 0s** in 2,000,000.

There are **ten 0s** in all in the two factors.

So the answer is 9 × 2 with ten 0s after it.

The answer is 180,000,000,000.

(Read it "one hundred eighty billion.")

Multiply.

① 30	② 80	③ 600	④ 8000	⑤ 60	⑥ 800
× 50	× 40	× 700	× 30	× 50	× 400

Multiply. Solve for *n*.

⑦ 900 × 200 = n

⑧ 200 × 4000 = n

⑨ 5 × 4 = n

⑩ 300 × 40 = n

⑪ 50 × 4 = n

⑫ 4 × 7000 = n

⑬ 5 × 40 = n

⑭ 30 × 90 = n

⑮ 500 × 4 = n

⑯ 800 × 4000 = n

⑰ 5000 × 4000 = n

⑱ 90 × 5000 = n

⑲ 60 × 50 = n

⑳ 80 × 30 = n

㉑ 20 × 500 = n

㉒ 3 × 500 = n

㉓ 600 × 30 = n

㉔ 4000 × 7000 = n

㉕ 900 × 80 = n

㉖ 90 × 500 = n

㉗ 8000 × 7000 = n

㉘ 600 × 40 = n

㉙ 1000 × 4000 = n

㉚ 8 × 500 = n

㉛ 10,000 × 60 = n

㉜ 90 × 400 = n

Practice with Multiples of 10

Be careful when you multiply by multiples of 10. Remember to count the number of 0s in the two factors.

Multiply.

1. 100×10
2. 100×1000
3. 10×1000

4. 1000×1000
5. $10,000 \times 1,000$
6. $10,000 \times 100$

7. 1000×100
8. $1,000 \times 10,000$
9. $10 \times 100,000$

10. 600×300
11. 10×200
12. 200×600

13. 300×400
14. 70×400
15. 60×400

16. 90×30
17. 8000×50
18. 4000×60

19. 4000×8000
20. 50×400
21. 70×80

22. 200×200
23. $300,000 \times 20$
24. 200×70

25. 300×50
26. 6000×500
27. 500×500

28. $1,000,000 \times 10$
29. $10 \times 100,000$
30. 480×100

31. 100×40
32. 100×100
33. 1000×100

34. 5000×900
35. 603×100
36. 740×100

37. 150×10
38. $70,000 \times 80$
39. 35×1000

Answer the following questions.

You know that there are 100 centimeters in 1 meter and 1000 meters in 1 kilometer.

40 How many centimeters are there in 1 kilometer?

41 How many centimeters are there in 5 kilometers?

You know that there are 100 cents in a dollar and 1000 dollars in a 1000-dollar bill.

42 How many cents are there in 1000 dollars?

43 How many cents are there in $5000?

44 How many nickels are there in $5000?

45 How many dimes are there in $5000?

There are 10 decimeters in 1 meter.

46 How many decimeters are in 1 kilometer?

47 How many decimeters are in 5 kilometers?

48 Name an object that is about 1 decimeter long.

49 How many decimeters are there in 50 kilometers?

50 How many decimeters are there in 100 kilometers?

By the age of 70 years, the human body has shed 40 pounds of skin.

◆ **LESSON 81 Practice with Multiples of 10**

THINKING STORY

The Treasure of Mugg Island

Part 1

In this story the children leave the island of Addonia. Therefore numbers are now said in the usual way.

The queen of Addonia called Manolita, Marcus, Ferdie, and Portia to her castle. "I need your help," she said. "Years ago pirates stole the Royal Treasure. Now I have learned that it is hidden on Mugg Island. Will you go there with me to help find it?"

The children were happy to help. This sounded like an adventure! Soon they were flying over the sea in the royal helicopter. The queen herself was the pilot.

"Where is Mugg Island?" Portia asked.

"I don't know," said the queen. "We'll just have to fly around until we see it."

"But how will we know which island it is?" Portia asked. "There are dozens and dozens of islands out here."

"This should help," said the queen.

"She handed them a note. It said:

"Mugg Island. The south shore of Mugg Island is straight and about 1 kilometer long. On the east side, the shore goes straight north for 2 kilometers. Then the shore goes west for 1 kilometer. Then the shore turns south for a short distance. Then there is a large bulge of land, about 1 kilometer across, sticking out toward the west. After the bulge, the shore goes straight south again until it meets the south shore. In the middle of the bulge is a small round lake. Out of the lake comes a stream, which flows eastward to the sea. The stream makes a line like a human face, with a pointy nose pointing south."

"This is no help," said Ferdie. "I can't tell what the island looks like from reading this!"

"Try drawing a map," said the queen.

. . . to be continued

Work in groups. Discuss your answers and how you figured them out. Then compare your answers with those of other groups.

❶ Draw a map of Mugg Island. Try to use every fact that the story gives you. See which group can make the best map.

❷ How would you describe the shape of Mugg Island?

LESSON 82

Rounding and Approximating

Sometimes you use numbers to mean *about* how many. You might say that *about* 5000 people live in Steelton, or a book has *about* 200 pages. In this lesson you'll learn an important skill known as rounding.

◆ Which number in each pair is usually easier to work with?

61 or 60?   214 or 200?   4971 or 5000?

Multiples of 10, 100, 1000, and so on are usually easier to work with than other numbers.

When we say, write, or use numbers, we often do not have to be exact. So we can replace a number by the nearest multiple of 10, or 100, or 1000, and so on. We call this **rounding.** How exact we need to be depends on what the numbers will be used for.

For each statement, choose the most appropriate answer. Use each answer only once.

1 **a.** The train will arrive

   b. Aunt Mary is coming for dinner

   c. The rocket will be launched

   (1) at 6:03 and 11 seconds.

   (2) at 6:03.

   (3) at about 6:00.

2 **a.** A mapmaker said the distance between those cities is

   b. Dad said that the trip to Wisconsin is

   c. The mechanic said to change the oil in the car

   (1) about 2900 miles.

   (2) 2873 miles.

   (3) every 3000 miles.

Read newspaper articles. Watch and listen to news reports. Can you find examples of rounded numbers?

Round each of the numbers in the chart to a reasonable estimate. Use no more than two nonzero digits.

1994 Population	
③ Alaska	606,276
④ California	31,430,697
⑤ Delaware	706,351
⑥ Florida	13,952,714
⑦ New Jersey	7,903,925
⑧ New York	18,169,051
⑨ Ohio	11,102,198
⑩ Texas	18,378,185
⑪ Vermont	580,209
⑫ Wyoming	475,981
⑬ United States (total)	260,340,990

Using your rounded figures, answer the following questions.

⑭ Which state had the smallest population?

⑮ About how many more people were there in Alaska than in Wyoming?

⑯ Which state had the greatest population?

⑰ About how many more people were there in California than in New York?

⑱ Which of the following fractions is the best approximation of the fraction of people in the United States who lived in California? $\frac{1}{2}, \frac{1}{4}, \frac{1}{8}, \frac{1}{20}, \frac{1}{40}$, or $\frac{1}{50}$

⑲ Which of the following fractions is the best approximation of the fraction of people in the United States who lived in Wyoming? $\frac{1}{50}, \frac{1}{80}, \frac{1}{100}, \frac{1}{200}, \frac{1}{400}$, or $\frac{1}{550}$

◆ LESSON 82   Rounding and Approximating

Rounding is also useful when you do not need an exact answer to a calculation.

Alex wants to buy seven packages of balsa wood for $2.97 (297 cents) each. He has $25. Does he have enough money for this much balsa wood?

The answer is yes. You can figure that out without finding the exact cost.

The cost of each package of balsa wood is less than $3. So the cost of seven packages is less than 7 × 3, or $21. Because $25 is greater than $21, Alex has enough money to buy seven packages of balsa wood.

Approximate. You don't need an exact answer to solve these problems.

20 Dr. Fleisch wants to buy 25 toothbrushes for $1.69 (169 cents) each. She has $50. Is that enough to buy the toothbrushes?

21 Mr. Gomez wants to buy 27 baseball shirts for his team. The shirts cost $7.98 (798 cents) each. He has $140 to spend. Is that enough money to buy the shirts?

22 Caitlin wants to buy nine postcards that cost 18¢ each. She has $2.00 (200 cents). Does she have enough money to buy the postcards?

23 Chris wants to buy 30 pencils. The pencils cost 12¢ each. Chris has $3.00. Does he have enough money to buy the pencils?

24 Greta is nine years old. She wants to know if she's more than 2500 days old. Is she?

25 Armando says there are more than ten million seconds in a year. Is he right? (There are 60 seconds in one minute, 60 minutes in one hour, 24 hours in one day, and about 365 days in one year.)

26 The auditorium in Jan's school has 48 rows with 24 seats in each row. Can 750 people be seated for a school play?

27 Omar says that his school used more than 10,000 cans of soup last year for meals. A case of soup contains 24 cans. Omar's school used 831 cases last year. Is he right?

28 Dorleta delivers 36 newspapers every day. Does she deliver more than 300 newspapers in a week (seven days)?

29 Suzy sells peanuts at football games for $0.95 a bag. If she sells 280 bags, will she take in $300?

30 Patrick collected 82 seashells last summer. If he sells all of them for 35¢ each, will he earn enough money to buy swim goggles that cost $23.99?

In your Math Journal create your own word problem in which rounding is more useful than using an exact calculation. Give this problem to a classmate to solve.

Approximating Answers

When you **approximate** an answer, you don't have to give just one number. You can give two numbers and say that the answer is between those two numbers.

Example:

A calendar is 56 centimeters long and 27 centimeters wide. About how large is the calendar?

The answer must be less than 60 × 30 square centimeters. So it must be less than 1800 square centimeters.

The answer must also be greater than 50 × 20 square centimeters. So it must be greater than 1000 square centimeters.

The answer must be between 1000 and 1800 square centimeters.

Answer these questions.

1 An office is 28 meters long and 12 meters wide. Approximate the area by finding two numbers that it must be between.

   a. Can the area be 600 square meters?

   b. Suppose you calculated the area and got an answer of 278 square meters. How would you know that you had made a mistake?

2 A rug is 261 centimeters long and 194 centimeters wide. Approximate the area by finding two numbers that it must be between. (You may round to whole numbers of hundreds.) Which of these could be the actual area?

   a. 15,824 square centimeters

   b. 50,494 square centimeters

   c. 63,774 square centimeters

③ A parking lot is 92 meters long and 53 meters wide. Approximate the area by finding two numbers that it must be between. Which of these could be the actual area?

  a. 4266 square meters

  b. 6376 square meters

  c. 4906 square meters

In each problem, two of the answers are clearly wrong and one is correct. Choose the correct answer.

④	32 × 17 = ▪	**a.** 264	**b.** 544	**c.** 914
⑤	46 × 61 = ▪	**a.** 2806	**b.** 2316	**c.** 2026
⑥	28 × 195 = ▪	**a.** 5460	**b.** 6140	**c.** 7440
⑦	206 × 38 = ▪	**a.** 5828	**b.** 7828	**c.** 4828
⑧	74 × 803 = ▪	**a.** 59,422	**b.** 592,222	**c.** 5,942,222
⑨	284 × 579 = ▪	**a.** 13,896	**b.** 164,436	**c.** 187,296
⑩	612 × 559 = ▪	**a.** 342,108	**b.** 3,416,608	**c.** 3,402,108
⑪	527 × 312 = ▪	**a.** 1,826,394	**b.** 15,204	**c.** 164,424
⑫	111 × 8901 = ▪	**a.** 890,901	**b.** 89,011	**c.** 988,011
⑬	72 × 504 = ▪	**a.** 36,288	**b.** 3888	**c.** 396,288
⑭	632 × 59 = ▪	**a.** 373,588	**b.** 353,288	**c.** 37,288
⑮	125 × 8888 = ▪	**a.** 222,200	**b.** 111,000	**c.** 1,111,000
⑯	574 × 896 = ▪	**a.** 49,364	**b.** 794,644	**c.** 514,304
⑰	994 × 9735 = ▪	**a.** 9,676,590	**b.** 9,981,910	**c.** 9,872,540
⑱	762 × 7450 = ▪	**a.** 533,400	**b.** 5,676,900	**c.** 6,438,900

LESSON

84

Practice with Approximating

Use a computer or other means to copy the chart on page 285. Approximate the answer to each problem. Then use your calculator to find the answer.

Compare each approximation with each answer. Comment on whether you could have made a better approximation for each problem. Here are some examples:

Example 1:   378 × 591 ≈ 400 × 600 = 240,000

Approximation:	240,000
Answer:	223, 398
Comment:	Because both factors were rounded up and were too great, 230,000 or 220,000 would have been a better approximation.

Example 2:   408 × 523 ≈ 400 × 500 = 200,000

Approximation:	200,000
Answer:	213,384
Comment:	Because both factors were rounded down and were too low, 210,000 would have been a better approximation.

Example 3:   32 × 8796 ≈ 30 × 9000 = 270,000

Approximation:	270,000
Answer:	281,472
Comment:	One factor was rounded down and the other up. The factor rounded up changed more than the one rounded down, so the estimate will have to be adjusted up to 280,000.

	Standard Form	Approximation	Answer	Comment
1	654 × 865			
2	78,596 × 8,492			
3	650 × 75,000			
4	6497 × 7496			
5	12 × 3482			
6	100,000 × 40,000			
7	29 × 31			
8	700,000 × 34			
9	1089 × 8905			
10	456 × 7038			

Solve these problems.

11 The snack bar at the movie theater used 36 boxes of napkins last weekend. There are 500 napkins in each box. About how many napkins were used?

12 In one day about 300 bags of popcorn are sold at the movie theater. About how many bags are sold in a 31-day month?

The best-selling children's book of all time is *The Tale of Peter Rabbit* by Beatrix Potter. More than 9 million copies have been sold since it was first published in 1902.

LESSON 85
ACT IT OUT

Multiply: Two-Digit Numbers by One-Digit Numbers

The Case of the Soda Bottle Cases *Episode 1*

Adam, Malik, Darryl, and Vernon want to earn some money. They can get money at the store for each soda bottle they recycle.

They collect lots of bottles and put them into cases like this one.

◆ How many bottles are in this case?

The boys filled eight cases with bottles. Each case had 24 bottles. They wanted to know how many bottles they had all together.

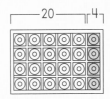

Malik said, "If there were only 20 bottles in a case, we would have 160 bottles."

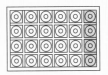

"How do you know?" asked Darryl.

"Because 8 × 2 = 16, so 8 × 2 tens is 16 tens. And that's 160," answered Malik.

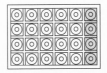

"But you didn't count all the bottles," said Vernon. "You counted only 20 for each case."

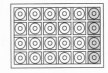

"I left out only four from each case," Malik said.

"But that means there are 32 bottles that you didn't count," said Vernon.

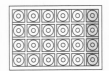

"I've got it!" said Adam. "If we add the 32 that Malik didn't count to the 160 he did count, we would have the answer."

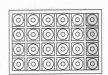

"That's it," said Darryl. "We have 192 bottles."

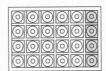

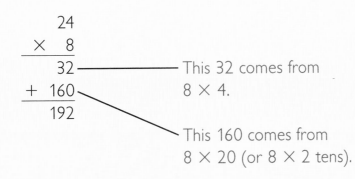

$$
\begin{array}{r}
24 \\
\times \ 8 \\
\hline
32 \\
+ \ 160 \\
\hline
192
\end{array}
$$

This 32 comes from 8 × 4.

This 160 comes from 8 × 20 (or 8 × 2 tens).

◆ **LESSON 85   Multiply: Two-Digit Numbers by One-Digit Numbers**

Here's a shorter way to multiply 8 × 24.

```
  24
×  8
───
   2
```

Start at the right. Multiply the ones digit by 8.
8 × 4 = 32 (that's 3 tens and 2)
Write the 2 and **remember the 3 tens** for the next column.

```
  24
×  8
───
 192
```

Multiply the tens digit by 8.
8 × 2 = 16
16 tens **plus the 3 tens you remembered** is 19 tens.
Write 19.

You may have trouble remembering the number that you saved from the previous column. If you do, you may use one of these methods to help:

a. Keep track of the number on your fingers. If the number is greater than 5, use both hands; you won't have to write until you've used that number.

b. You may write the number you are remembering in the place you will write the next part of the answer. Cross off the number as soon as you use it.

```
  24        24        24
×  8   →   × 8   →   × 8
             3          ⸗3
             2         192
```

c. Write the number above the next digit of the top number. Cross it off when you use it.

```
            3          ⸗3
  24        24         24
×  8   →   × 8   →    × 8
             2         192
```

If you write the numbers, be sure to make them small and neat so you don't get confused.

Multiply. Use shortcuts when you can.

① 24 × 6	② 26 × 9	③ 43 × 3	④ 60 × 8	⑤ 90 × 3	⑥ 83 × 4

⑦ 24 × 8	⑧ 46 × 7	⑨ 65 × 4	⑩ 19 × 4	⑪ 78 × 9	⑫ 57 × 7

⑬ 25 × 4	⑭ 87 × 2	⑮ 51 × 7	⑯ 89 × 3	⑰ 95 × 6	⑱ 28 × 4

⑲ 72 × 8	⑳ 29 × 6	㉑ 43 × 9	㉒ 27 × 2	㉓ 39 × 5	㉔ 72 × 6

㉕ 68 × 3   ㉖ 26 × 9   ㉗ 6 × 39   ㉘ 72 × 8

㉙ 37 × 5   ㉚ 7 × 49   ㉛ 68 × 5   ㉜ 27 × 6

㉝ 4 × 70   ㉞ 6 × 27   ㉟ 8 × 54   ㊱ 74 × 3

㊲ 29 × 3   ㊳ 99 × 8   ㊴ 91 × 2   ㊵ 85 × 4

㊶ 77 × 8   ㊷ 40 × 3   ㊸ 4 × 72   ㊹ 6 × 58

Check to see that your answers make sense.

Example:

The answer to problem 1 should be less than 6 × 30, which is 180.

The answer to problem 1 should be greater than 6 × 20, which is 120.

Is your answer to problem 1 less than 180 and greater than 120?

If so, the answer makes sense. (That does not tell you it is correct. But if it does not make sense, it must be wrong.)

ACT IT OUT

Multiply: Three-Digit Numbers by One-Digit Numbers

The Case of the Soda Bottle Cases *Episode 2*

ENTRANCE
← ♲ RECYCLE CENTER

Remember that Adam, Malik, Darryl, and Vernon collected 192 soda bottles. "I think we can get nine cents at the store for each bottle we recycle," said Adam. "I wonder how much money we can get all together."

"Let's see," said Darryl, "192 is the same amount as 100 + 90 + 2. For 100 bottles we get 900 cents. For 90 bottles we get 810 cents. For two bottles we get 18 cents. How much is that all together?"

"That's 1728 cents," said Vernon, "which is $17.28."

"Let's go get our money," they all said.

Look:

$$
\begin{array}{r}
192 \\
\times \quad 9 \\
\hline
18 \\
+ \quad 810 \\
+ \quad 900 \\
\hline
1728
\end{array}
$$

18 —This 18 comes from 9 × 2.

+ 810 —This 810 comes from 9 × 90 (or 9 × 9 tens).

+ 900 —This 900 comes from 9 × 100 (or 9 × 1 hundred).

1728 —This 1728 comes from 18 + 810 + 900.

Here's a shorter way to multiply 9 × 192.

192 Start at the right. Multiply the ones digit by 9.
× 9   9 × 2 = 18
  8   18 = 1 ten and 8
      Write the 8 and remember the 1 ten.

192 Multiply the tens digit by 9.
× 9   9 × 9 = 81
 28   81 tens and 1 ten is 82 tens.
      82 tens = 8 hundreds and 2 tens
      Write the 2 and remember the 8 hundreds.

192 Multiply the hundreds digit by 9.
× 9   9 × 1 = 9
1728 9 hundreds and 8 hundreds is 17 hundreds.
      17 hundreds is 1 thousand and 7 hundreds.
      Write the 17.

Multiply. Use shortcuts when you can.

1. 352 × 8
2. 643 × 8
3. 721 × 2
4. 684 × 7
5. 987 × 6
6. 7 × 367
7. 47 × 6
8. 453 × 4
9. 800 × 6
10. 308 × 7
11. 795 × 5
12. 505 × 3
13. 200 × 9
14. 497 × 2
15. 7 × 607

Check to see that your answers make sense.

Example: The answer to problem 1 should be less than 8 × 400, which is 3200.
It should be greater than 8 × 300, which is 2400.
Is your answer to problem 1 less than 3200 and greater than 2400? If so, the answer makes sense.

Multiplication Review

Practice multiplying two-digit and three-digit numbers by a one-digit number. Check to see that your answers make sense.

Multiply.

| ① $\begin{array}{r} 64 \\ \times\ 7 \\ \hline \end{array}$ | ② $\begin{array}{r} 308 \\ \times\ 4 \\ \hline \end{array}$ | ③ $\begin{array}{r} 99 \\ \times\ 5 \\ \hline \end{array}$ | ④ $\begin{array}{r} 726 \\ \times\ 8 \\ \hline \end{array}$ | ⑤ $\begin{array}{r} 394 \\ \times\ 2 \\ \hline \end{array}$ |

| ⑥ $\begin{array}{r} 501 \\ \times\ 8 \\ \hline \end{array}$ | ⑦ $\begin{array}{r} 663 \\ \times\ 7 \\ \hline \end{array}$ | ⑧ $\begin{array}{r} 48 \\ \times\ 3 \\ \hline \end{array}$ | ⑨ $\begin{array}{r} 90 \\ \times\ 9 \\ \hline \end{array}$ | ⑩ $\begin{array}{r} 307 \\ \times\ 9 \\ \hline \end{array}$ |

⑪ 56×7	⑫ 321×4	⑬ 872×7
⑭ 434×3	⑮ 82×5	⑯ 49×4
⑰ 72×6	⑱ 19×8	⑲ 6×481
⑳ 840×9	㉑ 28×6	㉒ 2×917
㉓ 107×5	㉔ 730×4	㉕ 5×489

Solve these problems.

㉖ Jamie rides her bike 3 kilometers every day. How far does she ride in 15 days?

㉗ Judy gets eight ride tickets in every ticket book she buys. How many ride tickets will she get in nine books?

㉘ Antonio is packing supplies for a camping trip. He will bake biscuits five times. He will use four packages of biscuit mix each time he bakes biscuits. How many packages of biscuit mix should he pack?

㉙ Allison works 15 hours a week at the video store. How many hours will she work in six weeks?

㉚ Mrs. Winter is buying crayons for her students. She wants to buy a box of eight crayons for each student. There are 35 students in her class. How many crayons is that all together?

GAME

Cube 100 Game

Players:	**Two**
Materials:	**Two 0–5 cubes, two 5–10 cubes**
Object:	**To score as close to 100 as possible without going over**
Math Focus:	**Adding, multiplying, and mathematical reasoning**

RULES

1. Roll the cubes one at a time, adding the numbers as you roll.

2. After any roll, instead of adding that number you may multiply it by the sum of the previous numbers. But once you multiply, your turn is over.

3. The player with the score closer to, but not over, 100 wins the round.

SAMPLE GAME

Wendy rolled 6, then 3.

$6 + 3 = 9$

Then she rolled 9.

$9 \times 9 = 81$

She stopped after three rolls.

Wendy's score was 81.

Todd rolled 5, then 5.

$5 + 5 = 10$

Then he rolled 6.

$10 + 6 = 16$

He rolled 6 again.

$16 \times 6 = 96$

Todd's score was 96.

Todd won the round.

MATH JOURNAL

In your Math Journal explain your strategy for playing the game.

◆ **LESSON 87** Multiplication Review

The Treasure of Mugg Island

Part 2

You may want to refer to the first part of this Thinking Story, on pages 276–277.

Soon the Royal Helicopter came to an island that had the shape of a coffee mug. "This is it," said Manolita. "Mugg Island."

The island was rocky and full of trees. At first they could not find any place to land. Then they found a place where the land was flat and there were no trees. So they landed there.

They all climbed out of the royal helicopter. "Now," said the queen, "we must find the hollow tree. The dotted line on the map shows the trail to follow." Here is the map she showed them:

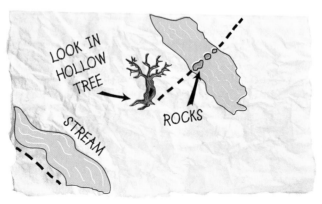

"This can't be the whole map," said Marcus.

"It's all I have," said the queen. "That's why I need your help. If I had the whole map, I could find the hollow tree myself."

. . . to be continued

Work in groups. Discuss your answers and how you figured them out. Then compare your answers with those of other groups.

1 How could Marcus tell that this was only part of the map showing how to find the hollow tree?

2 Why might the trail show up in two different places on the map?

3 Where is the hollow tree on the island? Use the map of the whole island to help you.

Multiply: Two-Digit Numbers by Two-Digit Numbers

Cutting a Problem Down to Size

Mr. Ogata needs fertilizer for his garden. The garden is 57 meters long and 36 meters wide. Each bag of fertilizer covers 100 square meters. He must find the area of the garden to know how many bags of fertilizer to get. Emiko wants to help her father. She draws a picture of the garden.

"But I don't know how to multiply 57 × 36," she says.

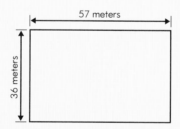

57 meters

36 meters

"Wait! I have an idea," Emiko says suddenly. "I'll draw lines to make sections, like this."

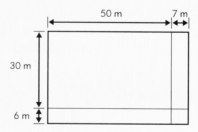

50 m   7 m

30 m

6 m

"Then I can figure out the area of each section and add them up."

Follow Emiko's thinking. The diagrams can help you.

The area of the small section is
6 × 7, or 42 square meters.

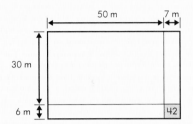

The area of the section on the
bottom is 50 × 6, or 300
square meters.

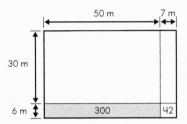

The area of the section on the side
is 30 × 7, or 210 square meters.

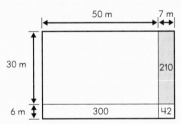

The area of the large section is
50 × 30, or 1500 square meters.

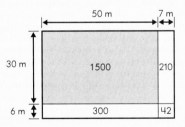

"Now I can add up the areas
of the four sections to find
the area of the garden," says Emiko.
"42 + 300 + 210 + 1500 is 2052.
So the area is 2052 square meters,"
she announces to her father.

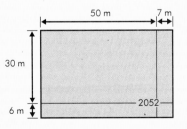

◆ LESSON 88 Multiply: Two-Digit Numbers by Two-Digit Numbers

Emiko kept the following record:

$$
\begin{array}{r}
57 \\
\times\ 36 \\
\hline
42 \\
300 \\
210 \\
1500 \\
\hline
2052
\end{array}
$$

Here's a shorter way to multiply 36 × 57.

$$
\begin{array}{r}
57 \\
\times\ 36 \\
\hline
342
\end{array}
$$

Start at the right. Multiply the top number by the **ones** digit.

6 × 57 = 342

Write 342 so that the digit on the right (2) is in the **ones** column.

$$
\begin{array}{r}
57 \\
\times\ 36 \\
\hline
342 \\
171
\end{array}
$$

Multiply the top number by the **tens** digit.

3 × 57 = 171

There are 171 tens.

Write 171 so that the digit on the right (1) is in the **tens** column.

$$
\begin{array}{r}
57 \\
\times\ 36 \\
\hline
342 \\
171 \\
\hline
2052
\end{array}
$$

Add to get the final answer.

Check to see that the answer makes sense.

The answer should be less than 40 × 60, which is 2400.
The answer should be greater than 30 × 50, which is 1500.
2052 is less than 2400 and greater than 1500, so the answer makes sense.

The area of the garden is 2052 square meters. Remember that each bag of fertilizer covers 100 square meters. So Mr. Ogata needs 21 bags of fertilizer.

Multiply. Use shortcuts when you can.

① 43 ✕ 54	② 96 ✕ 27	③ 18 ✕ 67	④ 420 ✕ 20	⑤ 86 ✕ 59
⑥ 47 ✕ 35	⑦ 53 ✕ 8	⑧ 64 ✕ 9	⑨ 58 ✕ 5	⑩ 21 ✕ 20
⑪ 39 ✕ 9	⑫ 75 ✕ 8	⑬ 67 ✕ 51	⑭ 64 ✕ 39	⑮ 58 ✕ 50
⑯ 39 ✕ 90	⑰ 21 ✕ 21	⑱ 13 ✕ 29	⑲ 84 ✕ 84	⑳ 68 ✕ 56
㉑ 50 ✕ 50	㉒ 54 ✕ 79	㉓ 29 ✕ 75	㉔ 21 ✕ 38	㉕ 50 ✕ 51

Check to see that your answers make sense.

Solve these problems.

㉖ Students from Kennedy School are going on a field trip. There are 525 people going. Each bus can seat 45 people. It costs $85 to rent each bus for a day.

  a. Will 12 buses be too few, just enough, or too many?

  b. How many extra seats will there be?

  c. How much will it cost to rent 12 buses for a day?

㉗ Sam bought 16 stamps that cost 32¢ each. How much did Sam pay? Give your answer in cents, then in dollars and cents.

㉘ A hotel room costs $46 for one night. How much would it cost to stay at the hotel for 11 nights?

Mid-Unit Review

Multiply.

1 1000 × 100   **2** 10 × 100,000   **3** 100 × 4

4 53 × 1000   **5** 281 × 100   **6** 709 × 10

7 800 × 500   **8** 40 × 700   **9** 10,000 × 300

10 500 × 6000   **11** 500 × 600   **12** 50 × 60

13 300 × 600   **14** 70 × 800   **15** 100 × 504

Remember: 1000 grams = 1 kilogram and 1000 milliliters = 1 liter

16 How many milliliters are there in 5 liters?

17 How many milliliters are there in 54 liters?

18 How many grams are there in 8 kilograms?

19 How many grams are there in 80 kilograms?

Approximate. You don't need an exact answer to solve these problems.

20 Mr. Romano wants to buy 26 rulers for $1.09 (109 cents) each. He has $25. Is that enough to buy the rulers?

21 The Plaza Theater has 36 rows with 32 seats in each row. Can the theater seat 900 people?

22 Jacqui is 11 years old. Is she more than 3600 days old?

In each problem, two of the answers are clearly wrong and one is correct. Choose the correct answer.

23 12 × 37   **24** 402 × 58   **25** 123 × 321   **26** 695 × 777

  a. 429   **a.** 23,316   **a.** 394,833   **a.** 560,005

  b. 864   **b.** 2316   **b.** 39,483   **b.** 54,015

  c. 444   **c.** 24,000   **c.** 3983   **c.** 540,015

Multiply. Use shortcuts when you can.

27	44 × 5	**28**	72 × 5	**29**	19 × 7	**30**	50 × 6	**31**	74 × 7

32	26 × 4	**33**	39 × 8	**34**	18 × 9	**35**	64 × 1	**36**	87 × 6

37 46 × 9   **38** 71 × 6   **39** 39 × 5

40 18 × 3   **41** 66 × 4   **42** 7 × 324

43 294 × 8   **44** 345 × 6   **45** 152 × 7

46 605 × 2   **47** 791 × 8   **48** 200 × 6

Multiply.

49	64 × 46	**50**	72 × 63	**51**	58 × 76	**52**	86 × 90	**53**	72 × 84

54	247 × 60	**55**	603 × 87	**56**	173 × 26	**57**	400 × 98	**58**	425 × 30

Solve.

59 Ethan gets six raffle tickets in each booklet he buys. How many tickets will he get in seven booklets?

60 Next week 47 students from Zoller School are going to the science museum. Each student will pay $4 to cover the cost of bus fare and admission. How much money will they pay all together?

Applying Multiplication

In this lesson you'll use multiplication in real-life situations in many of the problems.

Solve these problems.

1. A rectangle is 63 meters long and 42 meters wide.

   a. What is the area of the rectangle?

   b. What is the perimeter of the rectangle?

2. A rectangle is 63 centimeters long and 42 centimeters wide.

   a. What is the area of the rectangle?

   b. What is the perimeter of the rectangle?

3. Yusef bought six quarts of milk. Each quart costs 77¢ each.

   a. How many cents did he pay for the six quarts?

   b. How much is that in dollars and cents?

4. Tara bought five muffins. Each muffin cost 72¢. How much did she pay for the five muffins? Give your answer in cents and then in dollars and cents.

5. Matt owns six dogs. Each dog weighs about 32 kilograms. Do they weigh more than 240 kilograms all together?

6. Each of Matt's dogs can jump a stream that is 350 centimeters wide without getting wet. About how wide a stream can they jump together?

7. There are 12 eggs in a carton. How many eggs are there in six cartons?

8. There are 100 centimeters in a meter. How many centimeters are there in 7 meters?

9. A school has 15 buses. Each bus seats 66 students. How many students can be seated on the buses at once?

A bottle of soda costs 25 cents at Terwilliger's Drugstore. You must also pay 10 cents deposit on the bottle. If you return the bottle, you get back the 10 cents. At the One-Stop Food Shop, you can buy a case of 24 bottles of soda for $6.96, including the 10 cent deposit on each bottle.

Answer these questions.

⑩ Bryan wants to buy 48 bottles of soda. How much will he have to pay, including the deposit, at Terwilliger's Drugstore?

⑪ How much will 48 bottles cost at the One-Stop Food Shop?

⑫ How much would Bryan save by buying his soda at the One-Stop Food Shop instead of at Terwilliger's?

⑬ How much money will Bryan get back when he returns the 48 bottles?

⑭ Boyd and Niki have found 13 empty soda bottles from Terwilliger's Drugstore. When they return them to Terwilliger's, will they get enough money to buy three bottles of soda at Terwilliger's?

◆ **LESSON 89** Applying Multiplication

Look at the two figures. Try to find as many different geometric figures as possible. Tell how many of each you find. Remember to use such names as *right triangle, trapezoid, parallelogram,* and *pentagon.*

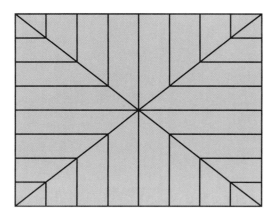

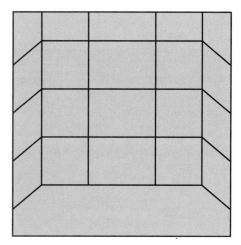

Compare your answers with those of your classmates to see if together you can identify more.

Try to find more examples of geometric figures in art, architecture, and other places. In your Math Journal make a list of interesting places where you have found geometric figures, and name the figures.

C⬭OPERATIVE LEARNING

Four Cube Multiplication Game

GAME

Players:	Two or more
Materials:	Two 0–5 cubes, two 5–10 cubes
Object:	To get the greatest product
Math Focus:	Multidigit multiplication, place value, and mathematical reasoning

RULES

1. Take turns rolling all four cubes. If a 10 is rolled, roll that cube again.

2. Combine the numbers you rolled to make a two-digit by two-digit or a three-digit by one-digit multiplication problem.

If you rolled: These are some problems you could make:

$$\begin{array}{r} 853 \\ \times \quad 7 \\ \hline \end{array} \qquad \begin{array}{r} 73 \\ \times 85 \\ \hline \end{array} \qquad \begin{array}{r} 753 \\ \times \quad 8 \\ \hline \end{array} \qquad \begin{array}{r} 75 \\ \times 83 \\ \hline \end{array}$$

3. The player with the greatest product wins. (Find the exact products only if you need to.)

SAMPLE GAME

Terri rolled: 4 2 7 8   Earl rolled: 3 0 6 5
She made this problem: He made this problem:

$$\begin{array}{r} 82 \\ \times 74 \\ \hline \end{array} \qquad\qquad \begin{array}{r} 53 \\ \times 60 \\ \hline \end{array}$$

Terri won the round. (Terri and Earl did not have to find the exact products to see that Terri's product was greater.)

LESSON 90

Multiplication Practice

You've been learning to multiply by two-digit numbers. Keep sharp by solving these problems. Remember to check that your answers make sense.

Multiply. Use shortcuts when you can.

1 26 × 35	**2** 68 × 49	**3** 96 × 17	**4** 32 × 90	**5** 55 × 25
6 38 × 43	**7** 72 × 95	**8** 87 × 70	**9** 17 × 36	**10** 63 × 91
11 18 × 22	**12** 30 × 31	**13** 66 × 36	**14** 76 × 41	**15** 57 × 43
16 70 × 70	**17** 53 × 53	**18** 27 × 58	**19** 82 × 91	**20** 17 × 71
21 39 × 46	**22** 71 × 70	**23** 77 × 11	**24** 67 × 24	**25** 90 × 90

Solve these problems.

26 The ice-cube maker in Zack's refrigerator makes 14 ice cubes every hour. How many ice cubes can it produce in 12 hours?

27 Yuki's soccer team is selling magazine subscriptions to raise money. They can keep $0.35 for each subscription they sell. If the 14 members sell one subscription each, how much money will they raise?

28 Billy's grandfather plans to plant 12 rows of elm trees. Each row will contain 21 trees. How many trees will Billy's grandfather plant?

There are many ways to recognize that the answer to a problem is wrong. Sometimes the size of the answer is so far off that it is impossible. Sometimes the last digit of an answer is impossible.

Decide which of the given answers is correct by showing that the other two could not be correct. Be prepared to explain your answers.

29 $42 \times 16 =$ **a.** 640   **b.** 672   **c.** 58

30 $395 \times 87 =$ **a.** 34,365   **b.** 334,305   **c.** 43,427

31 $145 \times 15 =$ **a.** 2320   **b.** 2160   **c.** 2175

32 $79 \times 2583 =$ **a.** 21,344   **b.** 312,054   **c.** 204,057

33 $3598 + 8745 =$ **a.** 21,344   **b.** 18,433   **c.** 12,343

34 $872,558 - 4,444 =$ **a.** 888,113   **b.** 868,114   **c.** 8,214

35 $7682 + 297 =$ **a.** 7979   **b.** 7385   **c.** 7987

36 $482,100 - 165,000 =$ **a.** 647,100   **b.** 342,000   **c.** 317,100

37 $8742 - 2952 =$ **a.** 5790   **b.** 5802   **c.** 5831

38 $852 + 258 =$ **a.** 1111   **b.** 111   **c.** 1110

39 $64 \times 38 =$ **a.** 2470   **b.** 2432   **c.** 2560

40 $35 \times 4 =$ **a.** 160   **b.** 140   **c.** 120

◆ **LESSON 90** Multiplication Practice

THINKING STORY

The Treasure of Mugg Island

Part 3

You may want to refer to previous parts of this Thinking Story, on pages 276–277 and 294–295.

"There is the hollow tree, just where we figured out it would be!" Willy yelled.

Ferdie ran over the bridge of rocks so that he would be the first to find the treasure in the hollow tree. "No treasure here," he moaned. "Somebody else must have found it first."

"Wait," said Manolita. "There is a piece of paper in the tree."

"Let me see," said the queen.

Here is the piece of paper they found in the hollow tree:

> From tree go NW13
> to spider rock.
> From spider rock go
> 23 paces to peg.

"Dear me," said the queen. "It seems that some animal has eaten part of the note. Now we'll never find the treasure."

. . . to be continued

Work in groups. Discuss your answers and how you figured them out. Then compare your answers with those of other groups.

1 What would the missing parts of the note tell you? (Be careful. Try to think of all that is missing.)

2 How far might the spider rock be from the tree? What are some possible distances?

3 Which of these makes sense for the distance from the tree to the spider rock: (a) 13 centimeters, (b) 132 kilometers, or (c) 132 paces? Why?

4 NW means northwest—a direction halfway between north and west. Knowing this, how could you find the spider rock?

5 What don't you know about where the peg is?

6 How could you find the peg anyway?

Multiply: Three-Digit Numbers by Two-Digit Numbers

The telephone book for Marla's community has 49 pages of listings. Each page lists 376 names. How many listings are in the entire book? Marla can multiply to find out.

Multiply: 49×376

$$
\begin{array}{r}
376 \\
\times\ \ \ 4\mathbf{9} \\
\hline
\mathbf{3384}
\end{array}
$$

Start at the right. Multiply the top number by the **ones** digit.

$9 \times 376 = 3384$

Write 3384 so that the digit on the right (4) is in the **ones** column.

$$
\begin{array}{r}
376 \\
\times\ \ \ \ \mathbf{4}9 \\
\hline
3384 \\
\mathbf{1504}
\end{array}
$$

Multiply by the **tens** digit.

$4 \times 376 = 1504$

There are 1504 tens.

Write 1504 so that the digit on the right (4) is in the **tens** column.

$$
\begin{array}{r}
376 \\
\times\ \ \ \ 49 \\
\hline
3384 \\
1504\ \ \\
\hline
\mathbf{18,424}
\end{array}
$$

Add to get the final answer.

The telephone book lists 18,424 names.

Check to see that the answer makes sense.

The answer should be less than 50×400, which is 20,000.

The answer should be greater than 40×300, which is 12,000.

18,424 is less than 20,000 and greater than 12,000. So the answer makes sense.

Multiply: 30 × 312

Here's how you would multiply using the way shown on page 310.

```
  312    Multiply the top number by the ones digit.
×  30    0 × 312 = 0
    0
         Write 0 in the ones column.
```

```
  312    Multiply by the tens digit.
×  30    3 × 312 = 936   There are 936 tens.
    0    Write 936 so that the digit on the right (6)
  936    is in the tens column.
```

```
  312    Add.
×  30
    0
  936
 9360
```

Here's a shorter way to multiply 30 × 312.

```
  312    Multiply the top number by the ones digit.
×  30    0 × 312 = 0
    0    Write 0 in the ones column.
```

```
  312    Multiply by the tens digit.
×  30    3 × 312 = 936   There are 936 tens.
 9360    Write the 936 next to the 0.
```

Remember:

```
  387         387          387          387
× 46      →  × 46     →   × 46     →   × 46
             2322         2322         2322
                          1548         1548
                                      17,802
```

◆ **LESSON 91 Multiply: Three-Digit Numbers by Two-Digit Numbers**

Multiply. Use shortcuts when you can.

① 247
× 26

② 813
× 59

③ 512
× 64

④ 256
× 32

⑤ 243
× 27

⑥ 806
× 37

⑦ 281
× 7

⑧ 281
× 70

⑨ 394
× 8

⑩ 394
× 80

⑪ 38
× 27

⑫ 380
× 27

⑬ 7
× 8

⑭ 70
× 8

⑮ 700
× 8

⑯ 70
× 80

⑰ 700
× 80

⑱ 6
× 7

⑲ 60
× 70

⑳ 600
× 70

㉑ 163
× 31

㉒ 287
× 15

㉓ 641
× 10

㉔ 269
× 34

㉕ 377
× 21

Check to see that your answers make sense.

Solve these problems.

㉖ There are 42 rows of bleachers in the school gym. At the pep rally there were 30 people sitting in each row. How many people were sitting at the pep rally?

A rectangle's length measures 139 cm, and its width measures 81 cm.

㉗ What is the perimeter of the rectangle?

㉘ What is the area of the rectangle?

㉙ Andrew's family drove 264 miles to the beach for summer vacation. They returned home two weeks later, using the same route. How many miles did they travel?

Each problem below gives the perimeter of a rectangle in inches and the area of the same rectangle in square inches.

Give the dimensions of a rectangle that fits these numbers. If there is no such rectangle, explain why. Use a calculator if needed.

Example:

perimeter = 38, area = 90

Answer: length = 10, width = 9

Check: 10 + 9 + 10 + 9 = 38, and 10 × 9 = 90

10

9

30 perimeter = 20, area = 24   31 perimeter = 202, area = 100

32 perimeter = 26, area = 36   33 perimeter = 24, area = 36

34 perimeter = 36, area = 81   35 perimeter = 30, area = 56

36 perimeter = 4, area = 1   37 perimeter = 16, area = 16

38 perimeter = 40, area = 36   39 perimeter = 74, area = 36

40 perimeter = 30, area = 36   41 perimeter = 50, area = 24

42 perimeter = 28, area = 24   43 perimeter = 22, area = 24

Solve these problems.

Tim's vegetable garden is 14 meters long and 11 meters wide.

44 What is the perimeter of Tim's garden?

45 What is the area of Tim's garden?

A rectangle has a length of 496 centimeters and a width of 24 centimeters.

46 What is the perimeter of the rectangle?

47 What is the area of the rectangle?

Converting Customary Units of Measure

Remember: 12 inches = 1 foot
                3 feet = 1 yard

Answer these questions.

1. How many inches are there in 1 yard?

2. How many inches are there in 7 yards?

3. How many inches are there in 7 feet?

4. How many feet are there in 7 yards?

5. How many inches are there in 73 feet?

6. How many inches are there in 73 yards?

7. How many feet are there in 18 yards?

Remember: 8 fluid ounces = 1 cup
                2 cups = 1 pint
                2 pints = 1 quart
                4 quarts = 1 gallon

Answer these questions.

8. How many fluid ounces are there in 7 cups?

9. How many fluid ounces are there in 1 pint?

10. How many fluid ounces are there in 1 quart?

11. How many fluid ounces are there in 1 gallon?

12. How many fluid ounces are there in 7 gallons?

13. How many pints are there in 1 gallon?

14. How many pints are there in 73 gallons?

Remember: 16 ounces = 1 pound

Answer these questions.

⑮ How many ounces are there in 7 pounds?

⑯ How many ounces are there in 73 pounds?

Juan said, "I'm pretty sure I weigh about 100 ounces."

⑰ Do you think Juan weighs about 100 ounces?

⑱ What do you think Juan meant to say he weighs? How many ounces is that?

Solve these problems.

⑲ In math class Angie sits 30 inches from Mrs. Packard's computer. Jenny sits $2\frac{1}{2}$ feet from Mrs. Packard's computer. Who sits closer to the computer, Angie or Jenny?

⑳ Paul had a new 5-pound bag of flour. He used 8 ounces of flour to make cookies. How many ounces of flour does Paul have left?

㉑ Todd drank 1 cup of orange juice at breakfast. He drank 1 cup of juice at lunch, and 1 cup of juice before he went to bed. Did Todd drink 1 quart of juice that day?

㉒ Abby bought some groceries. In her bag she had 2 pounds of cheese, a 16-ounce loaf of bread, and a 15-ounce box of cereal. How much does her food weigh in pounds?

㉓ Mrs. Fisher bought some ribbon. She got 2 feet of plaid ribbon, 5 inches of green ribbon, 1 yard of purple ribbon, and 1 foot of red ribbon. How many yards of ribbon did Mrs. Fisher buy?

Look at Lesson 79, in which you explored metric measures. Compare what you have done in this lesson with what you did in Lesson 79. Do you see any similarities? Write a paragraph in your Math Journal about your observations.

Applications of Multiplication

If you know that the length of a rectangle is 293 feet and the width is 21 feet, you can approximate the area by multiplying 300 × 20. You would get 6000, so the area is about 6000 square feet. Even though the exact answer is 6153, your answer of 6000 might be acceptable. This is because when things are measured, it is often impossible for the measurements to be absolutely precise.

Approximate the answers to the following problems.

1. 489 × 71
2. 101 × 51
3. 56 × 88

4. 888 × 52
5. 45 × 451
6. 352 × 60

7. 61 × 498
8. 64 × 271
9. 21 × 480

10. Use your calculator to find the precise answers to questions 1–9, and compare them with your approximated answers. What happens if you round one number up and one down? Can you think of other ways to make better approximations?

11. At the beginning of the lesson you learned that because of possible errors in the measurement, 6000 square feet might be as good an answer as 6153 square feet.

    a. Do you think this is true? Why?

    b. Assume that both measurements are short by 1 foot, so the true measures are 294 feet and 22 feet. Then assume that both are long by 1 foot, so the true measures are 292 feet and 20 feet. Do you think reporting the result as about 6000 square feet or as 6153 square feet is more reasonable? Why?

12 Ms. Jones's class wants to take a field trip. They know that the total cost is going to be $500. There are 28 students in the class. They decide to collect $12 from each student.

  a. Will that be enough to pay for the trip?

  b. After reconsidering, they decide to ask each student to contribute $20. Will that be enough to pay for the trip?

Solve these problems.

13 Chuck earns $9.00 per hour as a short-order cook. He works 27 hours a week. How much does he earn in a week?

14 Elliot's dog Pudgy eats about 275 grams of dog food per day. About how many grams will Pudgy eat in April (30 days)?

15 The chart shows how much time Carlos spends eating each day. Use a computer or other means to copy and complete the chart. There are 365 days in a year.

Meal	Time Carlos Spends Eating	
	Daily	**Yearly**
Breakfast	15 minutes	■
Lunch	25 minutes	■
Dinner	45 minutes	■
Total	■	■

16 Martina has gone to school for five years (including kindergarten). She has spent about 180 days in school each year. About how many days has she gone to school?

17 Oleta is nine years old today.

  a. Assuming 365 days in each year, how many days old is she?

  b. If there have been two leap years (366 days each) since she was born, how many days old is she?

◆ LESSON 93 Applications of Multiplication

Monica's class is publishing a newspaper for the school. The newspaper will have 24 pages. The students will print 650 copies, enough for everyone in the school to get one. They have to buy paper, which comes in packages of 500 sheets. Each package costs $6.

Answer these questions.

18 The students will print on both sides of each sheet. How many sheets of paper will they need for each copy of the newspaper?

19 About how many sheets of paper will they need all together?

20 Will ten packages of paper be enough? 15 packages? 16 packages?

21 How much will the paper cost?

22 If the students charge 10¢ for a copy of the newspaper, and if they sell all 650 copies, will they make a profit?

23 The students decide to sell advertising space in the newspaper to make extra money. They sell 47 advertisements at 95¢ each. How much is that in cents? In dollars and cents?

24 How much money will the students make if they charge 10¢ for a copy of the newspaper and also sell advertising space? If paper is their only cost, will the class make a profit?

25 If the school charges $10 for the use of the copy machine for printing the newspaper, will the class make a profit?

Multiply.

26	672 × 54	**27**	849 × 21	**28**	240 × 15	**29**	493 × 89	**30**	796 × 29

31	216 × 55	**32**	463 × 41	**33**	291 × 11	**34**	444 × 83	**35**	100 × 10

36	117 × 61	**37**	211 × 49	**38**	855 × 5	**39**	763 × 9	**40**	290 × 10

Multiply: Three-Digit Numbers by Three-Digit Numbers

Miyoko is an airline pilot. She flies between two airports that are 749 miles apart. Last year, she flew that route 583 times. What is the total number of miles Miyoko flew on that route? You can multiply to find out.

Multiply: 749 × 583

$$\begin{array}{r} 583 \\ \times\ 749 \\ \hline \mathbf{5247} \end{array}$$

Multiply 583 by the **ones** digit. 9 × 583 = 5247
Write 5247 so that the digit on the right (7) is in the **ones** column.

$$\begin{array}{r} 583 \\ \times\ 749 \\ \hline 5247 \\ \mathbf{2332} \end{array}$$

Multiply 583 by the **tens** digit. 4 × 583 = 2332
There are 2332 tens. Write 2332 so that the digit on the right (2) is in the **tens** column.

$$\begin{array}{r} 583 \\ \times\ 749 \\ \hline 5247 \\ 2332 \\ \mathbf{4081} \end{array}$$

Multiply 583 by the **hundreds** digit.
7 × 583 = 4081
There are 4081 hundreds. Write 4081 so that the digit on the right (1) is in the **hundreds** column.

$$\begin{array}{r} 583 \\ \times\ 749 \\ \hline 5247 \\ 2332 \\ 4081 \\ \hline \mathbf{436{,}667} \end{array}$$

Add to get the final answer.

Check to see that the answer makes sense.

The answer should be less than 800 × 600, which is 480,000.
The answer should be greater than 700 × 500, which is 350,000.
436,667 is less than 480,000 and greater than 350,000.
The answer makes sense.

When there is a 0 in the multiplier, you can save time by using a shorter way. Look at these two examples.

Example 1:

```
    624     Multiply by the ones digit.
  × 370     0 × 624 = 0
      0     Write the 0 in the ones column.
```

```
    624     Multiply by the tens digit.
  × 370     7 × 624 = 4368
  43680     There are 4368 tens.
            Write 4368 next to the 0.
```

```
    624     Multiply by the hundreds digit.
  × 370     3 × 624 = 1872
  43680     There are 1872 hundreds.
   1872     Write 1872 so that the digit on the right (2) is in the
 230,880    hundreds column. Add.
```

Example 2:

```
    624     Multiply by the ones digit.
  × 307     7 × 624 = 4368
   4368     Write 4368 so that the digit on the right (8) is in the
            ones column.
```

```
    624     Multiply by the tens digit.
  × 307     0 × 624 = 0
   4368     There are 0 tens.
      0     Write the 0 in the tens column.
```

```
    624     Multiply by the hundreds digit.
  × 307     3 × 624 = 1872
   4368     There are 1872 hundreds.
  18720     Write the 1872 next to the 0.
 191,568    Add.
```

◆ LESSON 94   Multiply: Three-Digit Numbers by Three-Digit Numbers

Remember:

721	721	721	721	721
× 365	× 365	× 365	× 365	× 365
	3605	3605	3605	3 605
		4326	4326	43 26
			2163	216 3
				263,165

498	498	498	498	498
× 603	× 603	× 603	× 603	× 603
	1494	1494	1494	1 494
		0	**29880**	298 80
				300,294

Multiply. Use shortcuts when you can.

1. 287 × 596
2. 831 × 609
3. 434 × 292
4. 816 × 333
5. 417 × 28

6. 604 × 17
7. 604 × 170
8. 365 × 108
9. 9 × 6
10. 90 × 6

11. 900 × 6
12. 9 × 60
13. 9 × 600
14. 90 × 60
15. 900 × 60

16. 90 × 600
17. 900 × 600
18. 901 × 599
19. 902 × 598
20. 903 × 507

21. 547 × 392
22. 281 × 61
23. 307 × 409
24. 215 × 17
25. 649 × 501

Check to see that your answers make sense.

Below are ten multiplication problems that have been worked out. Six of them have errors. Use what you know about multiplication to find the errors.

List the six problems that are wrong. Be prepared to explain how you know they are wrong without doing the computations.

㉖	274	㉗	379	㉘	497	㉙	139	㉚	486
	× 861		× 814		× 555		× 257		× 395
	472		1516		2485		973		3418
	1644		379		2485		685		4374
	2192		3032		2485		278		1458
	236,112		308,506		275,835		35,723		192,958

㉛	874	㉜	879	㉝	258	㉞	258	㉟	536
	× 69		× 951		× 379		× 973		× 123
	7866		879		2322		774		1608
	5241		4395		1806		1806		1072
	60,276		7911		774		2322		536
			84,384		97,782		25,800		65,928

Solve these problems.

㊱ Mrs. Berry ordered 15 boxes of pens. There are 120 pens in each box. How many pens did she order?

㊲ Mr. Andrews is building a brick wall. He wants 15 rows of bricks, with 90 bricks in each row. How many bricks does he need for the wall?

㊳ The Gala Concert Hall has 110 rows of seats. There are 100 seats in each row. How many seats are in the concert hall?

In Australia, kangaroos outnumber people 10 to 1.

Multiplication Uses

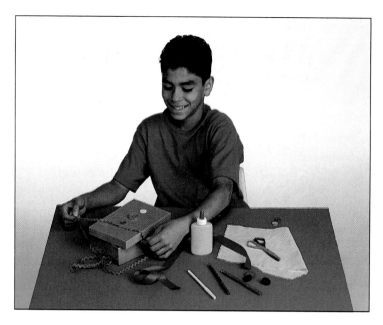

Marco's class is making and selling decorated pencil boxes. Each box requires a rectangular piece of cloth 20 centimeters long and 15 centimeters wide. The students in the class buy the cloth in large pieces that are 80 centimeters long and 60 centimeters wide.

Answer these questions.

1 Draw a picture to find out how many pencil boxes they can make from one piece of cloth. How many boxes?

Marco's class buys five pieces of cloth.

2 How many pencil boxes can the students make?

Each piece of cloth costs $6.79 (679 cents), including tax.

3 How much did the students pay for the five pieces they bought?

The students sold each pencil box for 98 cents, and they sold every one.

4 How much money did the class take in?

The class also paid for other supplies besides the cloth. The other supplies cost $5.73 all together.

5 How much profit did the class make?

324 • Multidigit Multiplication

GAME

(Multiplication) Roll a Problem Game

Players:	Two or more
Materials:	One 0–5 cube
Object:	To get the greatest product
Math Focus:	Multidigit multiplication, place value, and mathematical reasoning

RULES

1. Use blanks to outline a multiplication problem on your paper, like this:

$$\begin{array}{r} \underline{\qquad}\quad\underline{\qquad} \\ \times\ \underline{\qquad}\quad\underline{\qquad} \end{array}$$

2. The first player rolls the cube four times.

3. Each time the cube is rolled, write that number in one of the blanks in your outline.

4. When all the blanks have been filled in, find the product of the two numbers.

5. The player with the greatest product wins the round.

OTHER WAYS TO PLAY THIS GAME

1. Try to get the least product.

2. Multiply a one-digit number and a three-digit number.

3. Multiply two three-digit numbers.

4. Use a 5–10 cube. If you roll a 10, roll again.

How did you play this game? Explain your strategies in your Math Journal.

LESSON
96

Keeping Sharp: Functions, Facts, and Computation

Copy and complete these function machine charts.

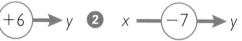

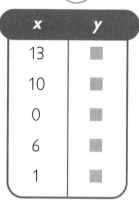

① $x \longrightarrow \boxed{+6} \longrightarrow y$

x	y
0	■
12	■
■	14
■	20
■	13

② $x \longrightarrow \boxed{-7} \longrightarrow y$

x	y
35	■
■	9
42	■
70	■
■	0

③ $x \longrightarrow \boxed{\times 26} \longrightarrow y$

x	y
13	■
10	■
0	■
6	■
1	■

ALGEBRA READINESS

Solve for *n*.

④ $n = 9 + 6$

⑤ $n = 9 \times 7$

⑥ $7 \times n = 56$

⑦ $7 + n = 22$

⑧ $27 \div n = 9$

⑨ $36 \div 4 = n$

⑩ $9 \times 6 = n$

⑪ $n \div 8 = 8$

⑫ $n \div 10 = 60$

⑬ $n = 63 \div 7$

⑭ $n - 8 = 8$

⑮ $n - 9 = 47$

Solve for *n*. Watch the signs.

⑯ $49 + 13 = n$

⑰ $49 - 13 = n$

⑱ $49 \times 13 = n$

⑲ $419 - 394 = n$

⑳ $519 \times 304 = n$

㉑ $439 + 396 = n$

㉒ $10 \times 25 = n$

㉓ $256 \times 100 = n$

㉔ $367 \times 1000 = n$

㉕ $1000 \times 99 = n$

㉖ $100 \times 15 = n$

㉗ $5 \times 100 = n$

㉘ $5 \times 10,000 = n$

㉙ $51 \times 1000 = n$

㉚ $100 \times 969 = n$

㉛ $479 \times 23 = n$

㉜ $648 \times 251 = n$

㉝ $216 \times 415 = n$

Janice and Nakia decided to get up early and take a long hike. The trail had mile markers so they could tell how far they were from home. They made a graph of how far they were away from home each hour. Look at their graph.

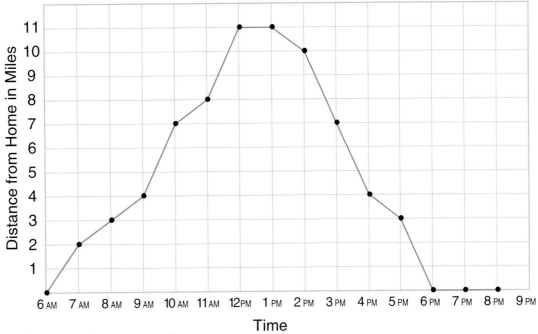

Answer these questions.

③④ Where were they at 7:00 A.M.?

③⑤ How far were they from home at 9:00 A.M.?

③⑥ What was the greatest distance they had been from home?

③⑦ Could they have gone farther from home at some time when they didn't record it? If so, when do you think that might have happened? If not, why do you think they didn't go farther from home?

③⑧ About how fast do you think they walked?

Write a story in your Math Journal about what Janice and Nakia did on their hike and when they did it. Be sure that your story agrees with the information shown on the graph.

◆ **LESSON 96** Keeping Sharp: Functions, Facts, and Computation

The Treasure of Mugg Island

Part 4

You may wish to refer to the earlier parts of this Thinking Story, on pages 276–277, 294–295, and 308–309.

Remember the note in the hollow tree?

> From tree go NW13
> to spider rock.
> From spider rock go
> 23 paces to peg.

Manolita had a good idea. She said, "Let's all walk northwest and count our steps. Maybe one of us will find the spider rock."

The queen had a compass. They used it to find northwest. Then they all started walking in the same direction. Soon they found a rock that had marks on it like a spider web.

"This must be it," said Manolita. "And I walked 134 steps."

"That's funny," said Portia. "I walked 172 steps to get here."

Marcus walked 105 giant steps, the queen walked 324 dainty steps, and Ferdie forgot to count.

"Now," said Marcus, "I have an idea. The peg is 23 paces from the spider rock. But we don't know in what direction. So let's walk all around the rock, 23 paces away from it."

Everyone did that. The queen walked 23 dainty steps away from the rock and then went around it in a circle. Marcus walked 23 giant steps from the rock and then went around it in a circle. Manolita and Portia, each in her own way, walked 23 steps away from the rock and then went around it in a circle. Ferdie went away from the rock, but he forgot how many paces. Then he went around it in a circle. Finally one of them said, "I found it! Here is the peg in the ground."

. . . to be continued

Work in groups. Discuss your answers and how you figured them out. Then compare your answers with those of other groups.

1 What size steps did the different people take in getting to the spider rock? Explain.

2 How could Marcus's idea work for finding the peg?

3 If all the treasure hunters took the same size steps as they did before, who do you think would find the peg? Why do you think so?

Perimeter and Area

Both Ray and Clara have backyards. They wanted to know whose yard was bigger. They measured and got the following results:

6 m

Clara's yard

6 m

10 m

Ray's yard

3 m

"My yard is longer!" Ray shouted.

"But mine is wider," said Clara.

"Let's measure the distance around them," said Ray.

◆   What is the perimeter of Ray's yard?

◆   What is the perimeter of Clara's yard?

"My yard is bigger," bragged Ray.

"Let's find the areas," said Clara.

"Why?" asked Ray. "Yours can't have more area if it's smaller around."

◆   What is the area of Ray's yard?

◆   What is the area of Clara's yard?

◆   Can a yard with a smaller perimeter than another yard have a larger area?

"You see," said Clara, "my yard is bigger."

"I still say mine is bigger," Ray insisted.

◆   Who is right? What does "bigger" mean?

◆   Whose yard is bigger if they're talking about how much topsoil is needed?

◆   Whose yard is bigger if they're talking about how much fencing is needed?

◆   Try to draw two rectangles so that one has a larger area and the other has a larger perimeter.

Solve these problems.

John lives in Weston. The public swimming pool there is 30 meters long and 20 meters wide. Carter lives in Easton. The pool there is 40 meters long and 15 meters wide.

1 Each boy has agreed to paint the bottom of the pool in his town before the pool is filled with water for the summer. Who has the bigger job?

2 When someone swims up and down the length of a pool, we say they have swum one lap of the pool. John swims 24 laps of the Weston pool every day. How many meters does he swim each day?

3 Carter swims in the Easton pool. But he doesn't swim up and down the length of the pool. He swims around the pool 12 times every day. How many meters does he swim each day?

4 When Carter visits John, the boys go to the Weston pool for their daily swim.

a. Suppose Carter swims 12 times around the Weston pool. Will he swim more or less than the distance he usually swims?

b. About how many times do you think Carter should swim around the Weston pool to equal the distance he usually swims?

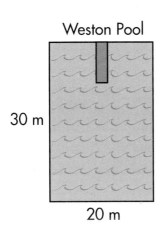

Weston Pool

30 m

20 m

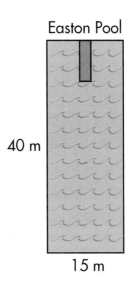

Easton Pool

40 m

15 m

Multiply: Multidigit Numbers

You can multiply any two whole numbers. Use the same procedures you have been using.

Multiply: 8924 × 5306

        8924   Start at the right. Multiply by the **ones** digit.
      × 530**6**   Write the answer so that the digit on the right is
      53544   in the **ones** column.

        8924   Multiply by the **tens** digit.
      × 53**0**6   If it happens to be a 0, write a 0 in the **tens**
        53544   column.
          0

        8924   Multiply by the **hundreds** digit.
      × 5**3**06   Write the answer so that the digit on the right
        53544   is in the **hundreds** column.
      267720   Continue in the same way.

        8924   The next digit is in the **thousands** column.
      × **5**306   So multiply by the **thousands** digit.
        53544   Write the answer so that the digit on the right
      267720   is in the **thousands** place.
      44620

        8924   When you have gone through every digit in the
      × 5306   multiplier, add to get the final answer.
        53544
      267720
      44620
      47,350,744

Check to see that the answer makes sense.

The answer should be less than 9000 × 6000, which is 54,000,000.

The answer should be greater than 5000 × 8000, which is 40,000,000.

47,350,744 is less than 54,000,000 and greater than 40,000,000. So the answer makes sense.

Multiply. Use shortcuts when you can.

1 160 × 18	**2** 8134 × 305	**3** 2132 × 4422	**4** 5139 × 2041	**5** 24,682 × 385
6 16 × 18	**7** 5432 × 678	**8** 1600 × 18	**9** 1600 × 1800	**10** 1000 × 1000
11 24 × 26	**12** 2400 × 2006	**13** 864 × 365	**14** 86,400 × 365	**15** 2000 × 2000
16 147 × 121	**17** 28,476 × 641	**18** 257 × 245	**19** 4962 × 2185	**20** 764 × 311
21 84 × 56	**22** 110 × 57	**23** 293 × 481	**24** 27,635 × 857	**25** 649 × 297

Check to see that your answers make sense.

By the time a person is 30 years old, he or she will have spent 12 years sleeping.

LESSON 99

Reviewing the Facts

Keep in shape by practicing your number facts on this page.

SELF ASSESSMENT

Are You Shiny or Rusty?

Very shiny	40 or more right
Shiny	35–39 right
A bit rusty	30–34 right
Rusty	Fewer than 30 right

Solve for *n*. Watch the signs.

1. $7 + 6 = n$
2. $n = 5 + 5$
3. $n = 17 + 5$
4. $14 - 5 = n$
5. $6 \times 6 = n$
6. $38 = n - 2$
7. $n = 6 + 3$
8. $6 + 6 = n$
9. $6 \times n = 18$
10. $n = 7 \times 5$
11. $6 \div 6 = n$
12. $21 \div n = 7$
13. $n = 6 \times 8$
14. $6 - 6 = n$
15. $10 \times n = 10$
16. $5 \times 9 = n$
17. $n - 7 = 12$
18. $4 \times 0 = n$
19. $4 \div 1 = n$
20. $12 + 19 = n$
21. $9 \times 8 = n$
22. $27 - 3 = n$
23. $11 = n + 7$
24. $6 + n = 15$
25. $10 \times 5 = n$
26. $n = 3 \times 7$
27. $2 \times n = 18$
28. $n = 6 \times 8$
29. $n + 6 = 20$
30. $7 \times n = 49$
31. $14 + 3 = n$
32. $5 + n = 13$
33. $54 \div n = 6$
34. $17 - 9 = n$
35. $28 \div 4 = n$
36. $21 \div 7 = n$
37. $n = 6 \times 3$
38. $n = 10 \times 6$
39. $10 + n = 21$
40. $n = 30 \div 6$
41. $7 + 9 = n$
42. $18 - n = 12$
43. $n = 7 \times 7$
44. $n = 2 \times 9$
45. $16 + 4 = n$

Solve. Watch the signs.

(46)
```
  742
+ 243
```

(47)
```
  742
− 243
```

(48)
```
  65
×  7
```

(49)
```
   89
×  25
```

(50)
```
  314
×   5
```

(51)
```
   36
+  92
```

(52)
```
   47
−  39
```

(53)
```
  362
+ 279
```

(54)
```
   87
×  87
```

(55)
```
  341
× 265
```

(56)
```
  877
− 392
```

(57)
```
   52
+  99
```

(58)
```
   73
×   6
```

(59)
```
  901
− 723
```

(60)
```
  327
×  18
```

(61)
```
  597
+ 623
```

(62)
```
  382
+ 469
```

(63)
```
  777
− 209
```

(64)
```
   73
×   8
```

(65)
```
  563
− 384
```

Solve these problems.

(66) Find the perimeter and area of a rectangle whose long side measures 43 centimeters and whose short side measures 21 centimeters.

(67) There are 100 rows of chairs in the auditorium. Each row has 50 chairs. How many chairs are in the auditorium?

(68) Andrea has 23 CDs, and Jason has 16 CDs. How many CDs do Andrea and Jason have?

(69) Tara's mother bought three bags of balloons for Tara's birthday party. Each bag had 15 balloons. How many balloons did Tara's mother buy?

◆ **LESSON 99** Reviewing the Facts

The Treasure of Mugg Island

Part 5

You may want to review the earlier parts of this Thinking Story, on pages 276–277, 294–295, 308–309, and 328–329.

When the children found the peg in the ground they thought the treasure was there. But it wasn't. On the peg was another note. Here is what the note said:

> Go N 20 paces
> Go E 15
> Go N 20
> Go W 15
> Go N 30
> Go E 15
> Go N 20
> Go W 15
> Go N 10
>
> Look under
> flat rock.

"This is hard," they all said. Then they started off walking, first north, then east, then north, then west, then north, and so on. But Ferdie didn't do that.

"I know how to get to the flat rock a shorter way," he said. He started walking straight north.

In a little while Ferdie called, "Hey, come quick!" Everyone came running. "I found out why you have to go in such a funny zigzag way," Ferdie said.

"Why is that?" the queen asked.

"First pull me out of this quicksand and then I'll tell you," said Ferdie.

. . . to be continued

Work in groups. Discuss your answers and how you figured them out. Then compare your answers with those of other groups.

❶ Draw a map showing the way from the peg to the flat rock.

❷ What shorter way could Ferdie have gone? How far would he have to go by that way? How far would the others have to go, if they followed all the directions of the note?

❸ What could be a reason for going the way the note said, instead of going by Ferdie's shorter way?

Using Multiplication

Multiplication is useful in planning a car trip.

Solve these problems.

On the highway, Hank travels about 65 miles in one hour. His car can go about 23 miles on one gallon of gasoline. The tank holds 18 gallons.

1 About how far can Hank travel on one tankful of gasoline?

2 About how far does he travel in three hours on the highway?

3 At the speed Hank drives, it's about 14 hours of driving time from his home to his cousin's house in Denver. About how many miles long is the trip?

4 Can Hank make it there on two tankfuls of gasoline?

Hank's neighbor, Isabel, has the same kind of car as Hank. But Isabel drives slower. She goes about 55 miles in one hour. But, because she goes slower, her car gets about 27 miles to one gallon of gasoline.

5 About how far does Isabel travel on one tankful of gasoline?

6 Who travels farther on one tankful, Hank or Isabel? About how much farther?

7 Who travels farther in one hour, Hank or Isabel? About how much farther?

8 Can Isabel make the 910-mile trip to Denver on two tankfuls of gasoline?

Pollution has become such a problem in Mexico City that fresh air is sold at sidewalk oxygen booths for $1.15 per minute.

GAME

COOPERATIVE LEARNING

More or Less Game

Players:	Two
Materials:	Two 0–5 cubes, two 5–10 cubes
Object:	To make a product greater than or less than the product made by the other player
Math Focus:	Multiplying two-digit numbers, identifying inequalities, and using relation signs

RULES

1. Make a game form like this one: _____ < _____

2. Roll the four cubes and use the numbers rolled to make two two-digit numbers. If you roll a 10, roll that cube again.

3. Write the two two-digit numbers with a multiplication sign on the game form on either side of the < sign.

4. The other player rolls the four cubes, makes two two-digit numbers, and writes them with a multiplication sign on the game form on the other side of the < sign.

5. If the number sentence made by the other player is not true, you win the round. If it is true, the other player wins the round.

6. You don't have to multiply unless the products are too close to approximate.

7. Take turns being the first player.

SAMPLE GAME

Keiko rolled: 1 4 7 9   Lawrence rolled: 3 2 6 7

She wrote 91 × 74.   He wrote 72 × 63.

91 × 74 < _____   91 × 74 < 72 × 63

Keiko and Lawrence agreed that this number sentence is not true. (They didn't need to multiply to know that.) So Keiko won this round.

LESSON
101

Approximating Products

Paint has spilled on this page.
Choose the correct answer in each case.

Example: 307
              × 5▓

    a. 14,10▓

    b. 179,902

    c. 15,108,507

The answer must be greater than 500 × 300, which is 150,000.

The answer must be less than 600 × 400, which is 240,000.

The answer is b.

❶   8,7▓
   × 6,▓

   a.   247,508

   b. 4,821,643

   c. 56,995,947

❷   50,▓
   ×   86

   a. 3,089,666

   b. 4,333,884

   c. 5,402,220

❸   238▓
   × 5▓

   a. 41,▓

   b. 12,▓

   c. 3,▓

❹   ▓0
  ×

   a. ▓43

   b. ▓370

   c. ▓,595

❺   ▓00
  × ▓0

   a. ▓,650

   b. ▓,000

   c. 53,100

❻   36▓
  × 2▓

   a.   720

   b. 5,648

   c. 8,760

Paint has spilled on this page of mixed addition, subtraction, and multiplication problems. Choose the correct answer in each case.

7
9
× 4

a. 1566
b. 1933
c. 98,901

8 473
869

a. 1342
b. 347,190
c. 411,037

9 42
7

a. 475
b. 2208
c. 1,163,512

10 234
9
34

a. 269
b. 1398
c. 4217

11
8 1
6

a. 542
b. 1744
c. 832,676

12 811
6

a. 453
b. 1827
c. 832,667

Solve these problems.

13 Find the perimeter and area of a rectangular garden with a long side that measures 10 meters and a short side that measures 8 meters.

14 There are 752 students at McKinley Elementary School. The school secretary needs to order notebooks for the supply room. There are 60 notebooks in a box. If the secretary orders 12 boxes, will there be enough notebooks for each student to have one?

15 Jan's family traveled 489 miles to their family reunion. Her aunt traveled 802 miles, and her uncle drove 264 miles. How many miles did these relatives travel all together?

◆ **LESSON 101** Approximating Products

The Treasure of Mugg Island

Part 6

You may want to review the earlier parts of this Thinking Story, on pages 276–277, 294–295, 308–309, 328–329, and 336–337.

Finally, after going back and forth many paces, the children found the flat rock. Under the rock they found a bottle. In it was another note. It read:

> To find the treasure,
> go 300 paces north and
> 400 paces west.

"At last we're near my treasure," said the queen. But it was not so easy. They could go 300 paces north, all right. But then they came to a huge pile of rocks. There had been a landslide. The side of a mountain had fallen down. They could not walk west at all.

They went back to the flat rock. "I have an idea," said Portia. "Let's draw a map. Let's try to figure out how to go straight to the treasure instead of going first north and then west."

Ferdie had a ruler. They used his ruler to draw the lines on a map. Then they used his ruler to figure out how far it was to the treasure, if they went in a straight line. But Manolita didn't help. She started off walking straight west. A little while later she called to them. "You can stop figuring. I found the treasure! It's right here, where the note said it would be!"

. . . the end

Work in groups. Discuss your answers and how you figured them out. Then compare your answers with those of other groups.

1 Draw lines. Use a ruler. Try to figure out how far it is from the flat rock to the treasure, if you go in a straight line.

2 After you know how far it is, what else do you have to know to find the treasure?

3 How could Manolita find the treasure by starting off walking straight west? What way would she go? Why would it work?

LESSON 102

Unit 4 Review

Multiply to solve for *n*.

Lesson 96

1 $n = 6 \times 8$ **2** $8 \times 7 = n$ **3** $n = 6 \times 6$

4 $5 \times 7 = n$ **5** $5 \times 8 = n$ **6** $9 \times 6 = n$

7 $4 \times 9 = n$ **8** $9 \times 8 = n$ **9** $n = 8 \times 5$

10 $n = 3 \times 6$ **11** $7 \times 7 = n$ **12** $9 \times 9 = n$

Multiply. Use shortcuts when you can.

Lessons 80, 85, 87, 91, 98

13 20×7 **14** 600×8 **15** 91×89

16 14×3 **17** 504×7 **18** 60×80

19 11×6 **20** 90×90 **21** 213×31

22 243×6 **23** 38×43 **24** 127×58

Watch the signs.

Lesson 96

25 57 **26** 57 **27** 57 **28** 834 **29** 834
     $+\ 14$ $-\ 14$ $\times\ 14$ $\times\ 555$ $+\ 555$

In each problem, two of the answers are clearly wrong and one is correct. Choose the correct answer.

Lessons 94, 98, 101

30 367 **a.** 34,131   **31** 8121 **a.** 286,575
    $\times\ \ 93$ **b.** 47,281 $\times\ \ 375$ **b.** 3,045,375
              c. 26,911   **c.** 2,319,875

32 702 **a.** 207,152   **33** 7903 **a.** 5,628,442
    $\times\ 311$ **b.** 249,982 $\times\ \ 614$ **b.** 496,372
              c. 218,322   **c.** 4,852,442

Solve for *n*. Watch the signs.

ALGEBRA READINESS

34 $n \div 8 = 4$ **35** $n + 15 = 41$ **36** $87 + n = 93$

37 $6 \times n = 42$ **38** $9 \times n = 27$ **39** $n \times 7 = 63$

Lesson 99

Solve for *n*.

Lesson 78

40. $1000 \times 100 = n$

41. $1000 \times 10 = n$

42. $10{,}000 \times 10{,}000 = n$

43. $1000 \times 1000 = n$

Solve these problems.

44. One roll costs 73¢. Ike buys two rolls each day.

   a. How many cents does Ike spend on rolls each day?

Lessons 79, 82, 87, 92, 93, 97

   b. How much money will he spend on rolls in six days?

45. A rectangle is 23 centimeters wide and 47 centimeters long.

   a. What is the area of the rectangle, in square centimeters?

   b. What is the perimeter of the rectangle?

46. An auditorium has 36 rows with 36 seats in each row. Can 2000 people be seated?

47. There are 100 centimeters in 1 meter.

   a. How many centimeters are there in 100 meters?

   b. How many centimeters are there in 1000 meters?

48. Georgia plays the piano 45 minutes each day. About how many minutes will she play the piano in a year (365 days)?

49. In a certain book there are about 350 words per page. The book has 512 pages. About how many words are in the book?

50. A bag of dried peas costs 58¢. Ramón uses four bags to make a kettle of pea soup.

   a. How much do the dried peas cost for one kettle of soup?

   b. Ramón cooks a kettle of pea soup twice a month. How much do the dried peas cost for a year?

LESSON 103

Unit 4 Practice

Multiply to solve for *n*.

Lesson 96

1. $3 \times 7 = n$
2. $2 \times 6 = n$
3. $7 \times 8 = n$
4. $8 \times 1 = n$
5. $n = 9 \times 4$
6. $1 \times 7 = n$
7. $10 \times 6 = n$
8. $n = 2 \times 5$
9. $n = 4 \times 8$
10. $n = 5 \times 8$
11. $n = 4 \times 4$
12. $9 \times 10 = n$
13. $3 \times 8 = n$
14. $10 \times 5 = n$
15. $7 \times 4 = n$
16. $6 \times 0 = n$
17. $0 \times 7 = n$
18. $6 \times 4 = n$
19. $n = 3 \times 9$
20. $n = 4 \times 5$
21. $n = 6 \times 5$
22. $n = 9 \times 8$
23. $9 \times 7 = n$
24. $9 \times 2 = n$

ALGEBRA READINESS

Solve for *n*. Watch the signs.

25. $n \div 5 = 7$
26. $8 \times 9 = n$
27. $47 + 29 = n$

Lesson 99

28. $8 \times n = 40$
29. $28 \div n = 7$
30. $27 \div n = 9$

31. $n \div 7 = 28$
32. $35 + 62 = n$
33. $n + 78 = 97$

Multiply.

Lessons 80, 85, 87, 91, 98

34. $\begin{array}{r} 1203 \\ \times\ 114 \\ \hline \end{array}$

35. $\begin{array}{r} 376 \\ \times\ 204 \\ \hline \end{array}$

36. $\begin{array}{r} 2013 \\ \times\ 68 \\ \hline \end{array}$

37. $\begin{array}{r} 4135 \\ \times\ 77 \\ \hline \end{array}$

38. $\begin{array}{r} 847 \\ \times\ 29 \\ \hline \end{array}$

39. $\begin{array}{r} 643 \\ \times\ 792 \\ \hline \end{array}$

40. $\begin{array}{r} 98{,}765 \\ \times\ 7 \\ \hline \end{array}$

41. $\begin{array}{r} 12 \\ \times\ 9 \\ \hline \end{array}$

42. $\begin{array}{r} 123 \\ \times\ 9 \\ \hline \end{array}$

43. $\begin{array}{r} 1234 \\ \times\ 9 \\ \hline \end{array}$

44. $\begin{array}{r} 8643 \\ \times\ 25 \\ \hline \end{array}$

45. $\begin{array}{r} 649 \\ \times\ 285 \\ \hline \end{array}$

46. $\begin{array}{r} 12{,}345 \\ \times\ 9 \\ \hline \end{array}$

47. $\begin{array}{r} 123{,}456 \\ \times\ 9 \\ \hline \end{array}$

48. $\begin{array}{r} 142{,}857 \\ \times\ 7 \\ \hline \end{array}$

Solve these problems. Watch the signs.

Lessons 80,
85, 87, 91,
96, 98

| 49 | 90
 × 80 | 50 | 1221
 − 819 | 51 | 2457
 + 407 | 52 | 4906
 − 997 | 53 | 258
 × 321 |

| 54 | 30
 × 40 | 55 | 4906
 + 997 | 56 | 87
 × 39 | 57 | 87
 + 39 | 58 | 7295
 + 6481 |

| 59 | 87
 − 39 | 60 | 101
 + 99 | 61 | 7024
 + 889 | 62 | 65
 × 65 | 63 | 15
 × 12 |

In each problem, two of the answers are clearly wrong and one is correct. Choose the correct answer.

Lesson 83

64 27
    × 89
a. 2753
b. 1093
c. 2403

65 121
    × 47
a. 3887
b. 5687
c. 54,767

66 37
    × 89
a. 3293
b. 36,593
c. 1803

67 709
    × 374
a. 26,526
b. 2,651,666
c. 265,166

68 45
    × 99
a. 4455
b. 34,555
c. 2425

69 507
    × 92
a. 46,644
b. 44,874
c. 448,794

70 53
    × 18
a. 7824
b. 954
c. 434

71 407
    × 29
a. 11,803
b. 7143
c. 23,003

72 43
    × 81
a. 32,863
b. 3193
c. 3483

73 457
    × 91
a. 34,927
b. 41,587
c. 46,587

74 612
    × 559
a. 342,108
b. 3,416,608
c. 3,402,108

75 9735
    × 994
a. 9,676,590
b. 9,981,910
c. 9,872,540

◆ **LESSON 103 Unit 4 Practice**

Solve these problems.

**Lessons
79, 82,
85, 86, 87,
92, 93, 97**

76 A 2-liter bottle of water costs 89¢.

    a. How much do seven bottles cost?

    b. When the bottles are full, how much water do they contain all together?

    c. Ava buys three bottles of water each day for a week (seven days). How much money does she spend all together?

77 A rectangle is 89 meters wide and 97 meters long.

    a. What is the area of the rectangle in square meters?

    b. What is the perimeter of the rectangle?

78 One can of paint will cover about 50 square meters. Mrs. Andrews is going to paint a wall that is 57 meters long and 11 meters high. Will ten cans of paint be enough?

79 There are 1000 grams in a kilogram. There are 1000 kilograms in a metric ton. How many grams are there in a metric ton?

80 There are 12 inches in 1 foot. How many inches are there in 160 feet?

81 Some baby whales drink about 200 liters of milk each day for about seven months. About how many liters of milk is this? (Assume that one month is 30 days.)

82 A shrew weighs about 3 grams. It eats about eight times its own weight every day. About how many grams of food does a shrew eat in a year (365 days)?

83 Cliff used a shoelace 67 centimeters long to measure a room. The room is about 14 shoelaces long. About how many centimeters long is the room?

Solve these problems.

84 A rectangle is 120 meters wide and 200 meters long.

    a. What is the area of the rectangle?

    b. What is the perimeter of the rectangle?

85 How many cents are worth 18 dollars?

Jim said he thinks he is at least 130 kilometers tall.

86 Do you think Jim is 130 kilometers tall?

87 What do you think he meant to say?

About how much is 4,962,100 × 37,942,614?

An approximate answer is 5,000,000 × 40,000,000. That is, 5 × 4 followed by the number of 0s in the two factors.

So, an approximate answer is 20 followed by 13 0s: 200,000,000,000,000.

Solve these problems by approximating.

Lessons 82–84

88 Light travels 299,792,500 meters in one second. There are 31,556,926 seconds in one year. About how many meters does light travel in one year? (That is, about how many meters are there in one light-year?)

89 The sun is about 150,000,000,000 meters from Earth. Suppose you read that it takes light about eight minutes (or 480 seconds) to reach Earth from the sun. Would that figure make sense?

90 Our galaxy is about 80,000 light-years across.
    a. About how many meters is that?

    b. About how many years would it take light to travel across our galaxy?

ASSESSMENT

Unit Test

Multiply to solve for *n*.

1 $8 \times 7 = n$ **2** $9 \times 9 = n$ **3** $9 \times 7 = n$ **4** $n = 4 \times 4$

5 $n = 7 \times 6$ **6** $3 \times 8 = n$ **7** $n = 8 \times 5$ **8** $5 \times 4 = n$

9 $6 \times 8 = n$ **10** $n = 7 \times 4$ **11** $7 \times 7 = n$ **12** $6 \times 4 = n$

13 $9 \times 5 = n$ **14** $6 \times 6 = n$ **15** $n = 8 \times 8$ **16** $6 \times 8 = n$

Multiply. Use shortcuts when you can.

17   52   **18**   43   **19**   31   **20**   60   **21**   203
     $\times$ 56 $\times$ 29 $\times$ 24 $\times$ 25 $\times$ 54

22   876   **23**   28   **24**   500   **25**   346   **26**   142,857
     $\times$ 9 $\times$ 431 $\times$ 700 $\times$ 210 $\times$ 7

Solve these problems. Watch the signs.

27   35   **28**   35   **29**   35   **30**   407   **31**   407
     $-$ 25 $+$ 25 $\times$ 25 $-$ 209 $+$ 209

In each problem, two of the answers are clearly wrong and one is correct. Choose the correct answer.

32   76   **a.** 6763   **33**   407   **a.** 85,063
     $\times$ 67   **b.** 6776 $\times$ 209   **b.** 8563
                c. 5092   **c.** 65,630

34   305   **a.** 318   **35**   595   **a.** 140,755
     $\times$ 13   **b.** 1305 $\times$ 129   **b.** 40,755
                c. 3965   **c.** 76,755

Solve for *n*. Watch the signs.

36 $n + 16 = 53$ **37** $36 \div 4 = n$ **38** $n = 42 + 21$

39 $7 \times n = 56$ **40** $7 \times n = 49$ **41** $89 - n = 52$

Solve these problems.

42. A high-speed train travels 160 kilometers in one hour. At that rate, how far can it go in 15 hours?

43. What is the area of a playground that is 85 meters long and 47 meters wide?

44. A rectangle measures 215 centimeters long and 112 centimeters wide. What is the perimeter of the rectangle? What is the area of the rectangle?

45. Pokey the cat eats about 215 grams of cat food per day. About how many grams of cat food will Pokey eat during the month of May (31 days)?

46. A pint of milk costs 51¢, and a pint of cola costs 68¢. Which costs more? How much more?

47. A pint of milk costs 51¢, and a loaf of bread costs $1.45. How much do they cost together?

48. One can of tuna costs 83¢. How much will 16 cans of tuna cost? Give your answer in cents. Also give your answer in dollars and cents.

49. Cans of tuna are packed in cartons that have eight rows with 12 cans in each row. How many cans are there in ten cartons?

50. Liam wants to put his stamp collection in a scrapbook. Each page of the scrapbook will hold 15 stamps. There are 38 pages. How many stamps will the scrapbook hold?

UNIT
4
WRAP-UP

Your Heart at Work

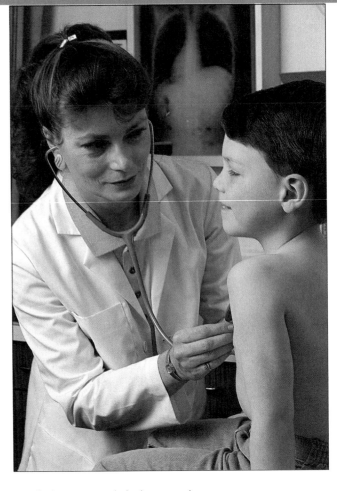

SCIENCE CONNECTION

The human heart works to pump blood to all parts of the body. It is always working. Some people's hearts beat about 50 times each minute. Other people's hearts beat 75 times each minute. Both speeds can be normal. It is not unusual to have a higher or lower heartbeat rate and still be normal. It is also normal for your heart to beat faster when you are exercising than when you are resting.

You can measure how many times your heart beats in one minute by taking your pulse. Your pulse is caused by blood vessels, called arteries, stretching as blood is forced through them after each heartbeat.

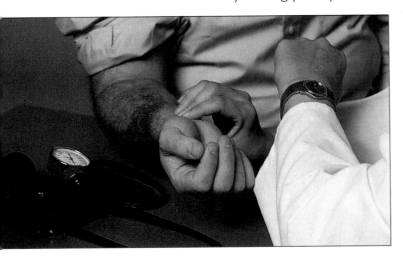

An artery that is often used to measure pulse rate is found on the inside of your wrist. Ask your teacher to demonstrate how to measure your pulse rate.

Adam measured his pulse. He found that his pulse rate was 70. That means that his heart beats 70 times in one minute.

Answer these questions. You may use a calculator.

1 How many times will Adam's heart beat in one hour?

2 How many times will Adam's heart beat in one day?

3 How many times will Adam's heart beat in one year?

Challenge: How many times has your heart beat in your lifetime?

Your answer to this question may not be accurate, because we know that young children's hearts beat quickly and slow down with age. It is not unusual for a newborn baby to have a heartbeat rate of over 100 beats per minute.

You can take care of your heart by eating healthful foods and by exercising regularly.

Take care of your heart. It still has much more work to do.

UNIT 5

Division

PATTERNS AND RELATIONSHIPS

- money
- mean, median, mode, and range
- powers of 10
- inverse operations
- prime and composite numbers

SCHOOL TO WORK CONNECTION

Teachers use math . . .

Teachers use math every time they grade a paper. They must determine the point value for each question. To find your average grade, your teacher adds up all of your test scores and divides by the number of scores recorded. That number can be changed into a letter grade.

354

ACT IT
OUT

Dividing by a One-Digit Divisor

Seven-Way Split

Rosa and six of her friends were out playing one day when they found an envelope. Inside the envelope was money. There were eight $1000 bills, nine $100 bills, three $10 bills, and six $1 bills.

① How much money is that all together?

◆ What would you do if you found that much money?

The seven children took the money to the police station and gave it to the person in the lost-and-found department.

After 30 days, nobody had claimed the money. So the police gave the $8936 back to the children. They agreed to share the money evenly.

"How shall we divide the money?" asked Marvin.

"Let's each take a $1000 bill," replied Lloyd.

Each of the seven children took one $1000 bill.

The children decided to keep a record of what they were doing. Because they wanted the $8936 to be divided into seven equal amounts, they wrote the problem this way:

7)8936

Each child took $1000. They kept track of this on the top of the record.

1000 ——————— This is how much each
7)8936   child has taken so far.

Now they had used up $7000, leaving $1936. They kept track of this at the bottom of the record.

1000
7)8936 ⎫ This is how much they have just taken all
7000 ⎭ together.
                7 × 1000 = 7000
1936 ——————— This is how much they have left to divide.
                8936 − 7000 = 1936

Now the seven children have one $1000 bill, nine $100 bills, three $10 bills, and six $1 bills. "How shall we divide the rest of the money?" asked Kelli.

"We could each take a $100 bill," said Nasim.

"But what will we do with the $1000 bill?" asked Nora.

◆ **LESSON 104 Dividing by a One-Digit Divisor**

Kelli suggested that they take the extra $1000 bill to the bank and change it for ten $100 bills.

② How many $100 bills will they have if they do this?

At the bank, they changed the $1000 bill for ten $100 bills. Then they had 19 $100 bills.

"We can each take two $100 bills," said Jolette.

"Yes, but we'll still have some left over," Rosa said.

③ How many $100 bills will be left after each child has taken two of them?

The children each took two $100 bills. Then they put that on their record.

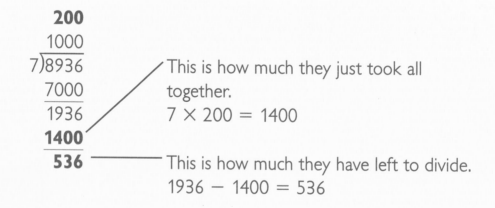

```
      200
     1000
 7)8936
     7000
     1936
     1400
      536
```

This is how much they just took all together.
7 × 200 = 1400

This is how much they have left to divide.
1936 − 1400 = 536

④ How much money does each child have now?

⑤ How many $100 bills are left in the pile?

⑥ How much money is left in the pile all together?

The children decided that the way to divide the remaining five $100 bills was to exchange them for $10 bills.

(7) How many $10 bills should they get for five $100 bills?

(8) How many $10 bills will they have all together?

(9) How many $10 bills should each child get?

(10) How many $10 bills will be left?

Each child took seven $10 bills. Now their record looks like this:

70 ————— Each child took seven $10 bills (or $70).
  200
  1000
7)8936
  7000
  ————
  1936
  1400
  ————
  536
  490 ————— 7 × 70 = 490
  46 ————— There was $46 left in the pile to be divided.

Now there are four $10 bills and six $1 bills.

◆ What would you do? The children traded the four $10 bills for 40 $1 bills, so they had 46 $1 bills in the pile.

(11) How many $1 bills can each child take?

(12) How many $1 bills will be left?

◆ LESSON 104   Dividing by a One-Digit Divisor

Now their record looks like this:

```
      6  ──────── Each child took six $1 bills (or $6).
     70
    200
   1000
7)8936
   7000        7 × 6 = 42
   1936        There was $4 left.
   1400        Marvin suggested they change the
    536        remaining $4 for 40 dimes and divide
    490        those among them. Jolette suggested
     46        they have a party with the extra $4.
     42        They had a vote and decided to have
      4        a party.
```

Before the party, Kelli wanted to be sure she had gotten the right amount of money.

◆ How much money should Kelli have?

◆ How much money should each child have?

◆ What is 7 × $1276?

Why is that $4 less than the total they found, $8936?

The steps the children took looked like this:

Step 1	Step 2	Step 3	Step 4
1000	1000	1000	**200**
7)8936	7)8936	7)8936	1000
	7000	7000	7)8936
		1936	7000
			1936

Step 5

200
1000
7)8936
7000
1936
1400

Step 6

200
1000
7)8936
7000
1936
1400
536

Step 7

70
200
1000
7)8936
7000
1936
1400
536

Step 8

70
200
1000
7)8936
7000
1936
1400
536
490

Step 9

70
200
1000
7)8936
7000
1936
1400
536
490
46

Step 10

6
70
200
1000
7)8936
7000
1936
1400
536
490
46

Step 11

6
70
200
1000
7)8936
7000
1936
1400
536
490
46
42

Step 12

6
70
200
1000
7)8936
7000
1936
1400
536
490
46
42
4

The answer is 1276, remainder 4.

Keeping Records of Division

Using play money, work in groups to solve these problems. One person in each group should be the banker to exchange bills. One person should keep the record. Everyone should help solve the problems. Everyone should see that each record is right.

❶ Six people want to divide $948 equally. How much should each person get? Will any money be left over?

❷ Seven people want to divide $364 equally. How much should each person get? Will any money be left over?

❸ Four people want to divide $7433 equally. How much should each person get? How many dollars will be left over?

❹ Five people want to divide $2707 equally. How much should each person get? How many dollars will be left over?

❺ Nine people want to divide $4536 equally. How much should each person get? How many dollars will be left over?

❻ Three people want to share $297 equally. How much money should each person get? Will any money be left over?

❼ Eight people want to share $641 equally. How much money should each person get? Will any money be left over?

Here are the names for the parts of a division problem:

$$
\begin{array}{r}
\text{Quotient} \\
\text{Remainder} \\
4 \ \text{R1} \\
\text{Divisor} \longrightarrow 6\overline{)25} \longrightarrow \text{Dividend} \\
\underline{24} \\
1
\end{array}
$$

If you wish, you may keep your records in a shorter form.

Example:

Long Form	Shorter Form	
	With Zeros	**Without Zeros**
1276 Remainder 4	Be careful to put the answers in the correct column.	Subtract and "bring down" only the next digit. Be careful to put the answers in the correct column.

Long Form	With Zeros	Without Zeros
6		
70		
200		
1000	1276 R4	1276 R4
7)8936	7)8936	7)8936
7000	7000	7
1936	1936	19
1400	1400	14
536	536	53
490	490	49
46	46	46
42	42	42
4	4	4

Divide. Keep your records in any of the ways shown on this page. Use money if you like.

8 5)100   **9** 6)91   **10** 3)513   **11** 2)41,312

12 3)46   **13** 5)745   **14** 4)804   **15** 9)729

16 7)91   **17** 8)416   **18** 2)7046   **19** 5)52,365

Practicing Division

Practice division. Use money if you need to. Keep records in the way you like best. When there is a remainder, show it.

1 $3\overline{)591}$ **2** $4\overline{)6128}$ **3** $6\overline{)144}$ **4** $7\overline{)574}$

5 $8\overline{)232}$ **6** $9\overline{)241}$ **7** $5\overline{)125}$ **8** $6\overline{)216}$

9 $4\overline{)64}$ **10** $3\overline{)62}$ **11** $2\overline{)90}$ **12** $5\overline{)0}$

13 $3\overline{)296}$ **14** $4\overline{)425}$ **15** $6\overline{)2141}$ **16** $5\overline{)935}$

17 $4\overline{)648}$ **18** $8\overline{)3426}$ **19** $5\overline{)614}$ **20** $6\overline{)472}$

21 $5\overline{)153}$ **22** $7\overline{)381}$ **23** $2\overline{)547}$ **24** $7\overline{)8496}$

Check your answers.

a. Multiply divisor $\times$ quotient.

b. Add the remainder.

c. You should get the dividend.

Examples:

$7\overline{)97}$ with quotient 13 R6   Check:
$$\begin{array}{r} 13 \\ \times\ 7 \\ \hline 91 \end{array} \quad 91 + 6 = 97$$

$3\overline{)861}$ with quotient 287   Check:
$$\begin{array}{r} 287 \\ \times\ \ \ 3 \\ \hline 861 \end{array}$$

$7\overline{)439}$ with quotient 62 R5   Check:
$$\begin{array}{r} 62 \\ \times\ 7 \\ \hline 434 \end{array} \quad 434 + 5 = 439$$

Find the missing digit.

ALGEBRA READINESS

25)
```
    29
 5)145
   10
   ■5
   45
```

26)
```
  103 R1
 9)928
   9
   28
   2■
    1
```

27)
```
  1■3 R2
 9)929
   9
   29
   27
    2
```

28)
```
  4■ R1
 7)309
   28
   29
   28
    1
```

29)
```
  104
 ■)624
   6
   24
   24
```

30)
```
  18■ R1
 4)721
   4
   32
   32
    1
```

31)
```
  84 R6
 8)67■
   64
   38
   32
    6
```

32)
```
  10■ R7
 9)907
   9
    7
```

33)
```
  1■1 R6
 8)974
   8
   17
   16
   14
    8
    6
```

34)
```
  287 R1
 ■)862
   6
   26
   24
   22
   21
    1
```

35)
```
  115 R■
 8)923
   8
   12
    8
   43
   40
    3
```

36)
```
  26■ R2
 3)800
   6
   20
   18
   20
   18
    2
```

37)
```
  ■08
 5)540
   5
   40
   40
```

38)
```
  1■0
 5)750
   5
   25
   25
```

39)
```
  130
 7)9■0
   7
   21
   21
```

40)
```
  2■7 R1
 4)829
   8
   29
   28
    1
```

FANTASTIC FACT

How big can the world's largest turtle get? Pretty big! The shell of a leatherback turtle can grow as large as a king-sized bed.

LESSON

107

Division Review: Missing Digits

Find the missing digit.

ALGEBRA READINESS

1
```
      1▪5 R1
   5)676
     5
    ──
    17
    15
    ──
    26
    25
    ──
     1
```

2
```
      1▪7 R2
   6)824
     6
    ──
    22
    18
    ──
    44
    42
    ──
     2
```

3
```
      134 R1
   4)537
     4
    ──
    13
    1▪
    ──
    17
    16
    ──
     1
```

4
```
      269 R2
   3)8▪9
     6
    ──
    20
    18
    ──
    29
    27
    ──
     2
```

5
```
      ▪4 R1
   9)307
    27
   ──
    37
    36
   ──
     1
```

6
```
      1▪9 R6
   8)878
     8
    ──
    78
    72
    ──
     6
```

7
```
      20▪ R3
   4)807
     8
    ──
     7
     4
    ──
     3
```

8
```
      1▪3 R1
   2)207
     2
    ──
     7
     6
    ──
     1
```

9
```
      109
   7)763
     ▪
    ──
    63
    63
    ──
```

10
```
       50
   9)450
    4▪
   ──
```

11
```
      209
   3)627
     6
    ──
    ▪7
    27
    ──
```

12
```
      100 R3
   7)703
     7
    ──
     ▪
```

13
```
       5▪ R6
   7)405
    35
   ──
    55
    49
   ──
     6
```

14
```
       67 R▪
   4)270
    24
   ──
    30
    28
   ──
     2
```

15
```
      ▪7
   5)435
    40
   ──
    35
    35
   ──
```

16
```
       7▪ R1
   5)376
    35
   ──
    26
    25
   ──
     1
```

Diviso Game

Players:	Two or more
Materials:	Two 0–5 cubes, two 5–10 cubes
Object:	To get a quotient with no remainder
Math Focus:	Dividing by one-digit divisors and mental factorization

RULES

1. Roll any two cubes.

2. Make a division problem in this way: Use the product of the numbers rolled as the dividend. Choose another number as the divisor, but do not use either of the numbers rolled, their product, or the numbers 1 or 0.

3. Find the quotient.

4. The player who makes a problem with no remainder earns one point. The first player to earn seven points wins.

SAMPLE GAME

Round One

Tess rolls: **3** **2**

$3 \times 2 = 6$

She cannot use 3, 2, 6, or 1 as a divisor.
Tess does not score.

Kate rolls: **0** **8**

$0 \times 8 = 0$

She chooses 7 as the divisor.

$$7\overline{)0}^{\,0} \quad \text{Kate earns one point.}$$

Kate wins this round.

Round Two

Tess rolls : **7** **10**

$7 \times 10 = 70$

She chooses 2 as the divisor.

$$2\overline{)70}^{\,35} \quad \text{Tess earns one point.}$$

Kate rolls: **5** **4**

$5 \times 4 = 20$

She chooses 2 as the divisor.

$$2\overline{)20}^{\,10} \quad \text{Kate earns one point.}$$

This round is a tie.

◆ **LESSON 107 Division Review: Missing Digits**

Estimating Is Rough

THINKING STORY

Part 1

"I found a job you might try for," said Mrs. Breezy. "It's a job as chief estimator."

"I'll take it," said Mr. Muddle. "What does an estimator do?"

"An estimator tries to make good guesses about amounts. I'll show you. See that girl out in the hall? How old would you say she is?"

"Seven years and one day," said Mr. Muddle.

"Estimating doesn't mean making an exact guess. You should just say more or less how old you think she is."

"All right," said Mr. Muddle. "My estimate is 60 years old."

"That can't be right," said Mrs. Breezy. "Anyone can see that she is just a young girl."

"You said more or less," Mr. Muddle answered. "I chose less. I'm sure she is less than 60 years old. If I had chosen more then I would have said she is more than one year old."

"That's not the idea," said Mrs. Breezy. "Your estimate should be as close to right as possible. You have to look for evidence and use it to make a good guess."

"I see. It's like being a detective. In that case, I have a new estimate: I estimate that she is 20 years old."

"Now, what would make you think that?" Mrs. Breezy asked.

"Her sweatshirt," said Mr. Muddle. "It has *Harvard University* written on it, and 20 years old should be a good guess for the age of a university student."

"Do you really think a young child like that goes to a university?" Mrs. Breezy asked.

"Not at all," said Mr. Muddle. "Lots of people who don't go to a university wear university sweatshirts. I see them all over."

"Then you shouldn't have based your estimate on her sweatshirt," said Mrs. Breezy. "You should use evidence that you can trust."

"Oh," said Mr. Muddle. "In that case, I will stick with my first estimate." He opened the door and asked the girl, "Are you seven years and one day old?"

"You know I am, Uncle Otto," the girl said. "You and Aunt Emma were at my birthday party yesterday."

. . . to be continued

Work in groups. Discuss your answers and how you figured them out. Then compare your answers with those of other groups.

❶ In what ways is estimating the same as guessing?

❷ In what ways is estimating different from guessing?

❸ Was Mr. Muddle estimating? If not, what was he doing?

❹ What are some clues you would use to estimate a person's age?

❺ What would be a good estimate for the age of Mrs. Breezy?

Using Division: Unit Cost

REAL-WORLD CONNECTION

Heather wants to buy soup. The store offers two cans of soup for 72¢ or three cans of the same kind of soup for 96¢.

How much does soup cost per can if you buy it in groups of two cans?

Per means "for each." We can find the cost for each can by dividing 72 by 2.

$$\begin{array}{r} 36 \\ 2\overline{)72} \\ \underline{6} \\ 12 \\ \underline{12} \end{array}$$

The soup costs 36¢ per can when you buy it in groups of two cans.

How much does soup cost per can if you buy it in groups of three cans? We can find the cost per can by dividing 96 by 3.

$$\begin{array}{r} 32 \\ 3\overline{)96} \\ \underline{9} \\ 6 \\ \underline{6} \end{array}$$

The soup costs 32¢ per can when you buy it in groups of three.

◆ Which do you think is the better buy? Why?

Solve these problems.

Luis wants to buy milk. A 4-quart container costs $2.56 (256¢). An 8-quart container of the same kind of milk at a different store costs $4.96 (496¢).

❶ How much does milk cost per quart in a 4-quart container?

❷ How much does milk cost per quart in an 8-quart container?

❸ Which do you think is the better buy? Why?

◆ Could you have found the better buy without dividing?

Yoko wants to buy rice. A 2-kilogram bag costs $1.20. A 5-kilogram bag costs $2.65.

4 How much does rice cost per kilogram in 2-kilogram bags?

5 How much does rice cost per kilogram in 5-kilogram bags?

6 Which do you think is the better buy? Why?

Solve.

7 Three cans of soup cost 75¢. How much is one can of soup?

8 Seven pencils cost 91¢. How much is that per pencil?

9 Three quarts of milk cost $1.74 (174¢). How much is that per quart?

10 Four apples cost 92¢. How much is that per apple?

11 Six oranges cost $1.32 (132¢). How much is that per orange?

12 An 8-pound turkey costs $9.50 (950¢). A 9-pound turkey costs $11.40 (1140¢). Which turkey is the better buy? Why?

13 Three pads of paper cost $1.38 (138¢). How much is that per pad?

14 An eight-bottle carton of soda pop costs $3.84 (384¢). How much is that per bottle?

15 Nine containers of yogurt cost $5.49 (549¢). How much is that per container of yogurt?

16 Ten pencil erasers cost $1.20 (120¢). How much is that per eraser?

Dividing by a One-Digit Divisor: Short Form

There is a shorter method of keeping division records.

Short Form

```
       1
   7)8936
     7
    ──
    19
```

Shorter Form

```
        1
   7)8 ¹9 3 6
```

There is one whole 7 in 8 (write 1 in the answer above the 8). The remainder is 1 (write a small 1 in front of the 9).

Short Form

```
      12
   7)8936
     7
    ──
    19
    14
    ──
    53
```

Shorter Form

```
       1  2
   7)8 ¹9 ⁵3 6
```

There are two 7s in 19 (write 2 in the answer above the 9). The remainder is 5 (write a 5 in front of the 3).

Short Form

```
     127
   7)8936
     7
    ──
    19
    14
    ──
    53
    49
    ──
    46
```

Shorter Form

```
      1  2  7
   7)8 ¹9 ⁵3 ⁴6
```

There are seven 7s in 53 (write a 7 in the answer above the 3). The remainder is 4 (write a 4 in front of the 6).

Short Form

```
    127 6 R4
   7)8936
     7
    ──
    19
    14
    ──
    53
    49
    ──
    46
    42
    ──
     4
```

Shorter Form

```
     1  2  7  6 R4
   7)8 ¹9 ⁵3 ⁴6
```

There are six 7s in 46 (write a 6 in the answer above the 6). The remainder is 4 (write R4 in the answer).

Divide. Use whichever method you prefer. Check your answers to the first five problems by multiplying.

1 $7\overline{)343}$ Check: Does 7 × quotient = 343?

2 $6\overline{)174}$ Check: Does 6 × quotient = 174?

3 $2\overline{)317}$ Check: Does (2 × quotient) **+ remainder** = 317?

4 $5\overline{)812}$ Check: Does (5 × quotient) **+ remainder** = 812?

5 $9\overline{)342}$ Check: Does 9 × quotient = 342?

Divide. Use shortcuts when you can.

6 $3\overline{)876}$ **7** $4\overline{)512}$ **8** $4\overline{)1000}$ **9** $8\overline{)54}$ **10** $5\overline{)476}$

11 $1\overline{)42,506}$ **12** $6\overline{)372}$ **13** $3\overline{)10}$ **14** $0\overline{)15}$ **15** $9\overline{)289}$

16 $3\overline{)345}$ **17** $7\overline{)267}$ **18** $8\overline{)849}$ **19** $4\overline{)271}$ **20** $6\overline{)8596}$

21 $5\overline{)210}$ **22** $2\overline{)471}$ **23** $4\overline{)1003}$ **24** $3\overline{)4621}$ **25** $4\overline{)685}$

26 $7\overline{)496}$ **27** $6\overline{)1479}$ **28** $8\overline{)432}$ **29** $8\overline{)764}$ **30** $3\overline{)456}$

◆ Did you get an answer to problem 14?

◆ Is there any answer that would work?

◆ Can it ever be that 0 × a number = 15?

There is no number you can multiply by 0 to get 15. So, no answer could check, unless you decided that the remainder is 15. But the remainder is not supposed to be greater than the divisor. Even if you said the remainder is 15, then any number could be the quotient. But that is not useful. So we make this rule:

Division by 0 is not allowed.

More Division Practice

Four Cube Division Game

COOPERATIVE LEARNING

Players:	Two or more
Materials:	Two 0–5 cubes, two 5–10 cubes
Object:	To get the least quotient
Math Focus:	Dividing by one-digit divisors and place value

RULES

1. Roll all four cubes. If you roll a 10, roll that cube again.

2. Make a division problem using three of the numbers rolled as a three-digit dividend and the other number as the divisor. Zero may not be used as the first number of the dividend and, of course, it cannot be used as the divisor.

3. Find the quotient.

4. The player with the least quotient wins the round. If two players have the same quotient, then the player with the least remainder is the winner.

SAMPLE ROUND

Matthew rolled: 3 4 9 8   He made: $9\overline{)348}$ — 38 R6

Cathy rolled: 2 8 3 5   She made: $8\overline{)235}$ — 29 R3

Max rolled: 1 0 9 5   He made: $9\overline{)105}$ — 11 R6 Max won.

OTHER WAYS TO PLAY THIS GAME

1. The least remainder wins.

2. The least quotient wins, but the remainder must be greater than 5.

The following 12 division problems have been worked out. There are six wrong answers. Decide which six answers are wrong and which six are correct.

1
$$\frac{273}{3)819}$$

2
$$\frac{28}{3)624}$$

3
$$\frac{12}{7)714}$$

4
$$\frac{99}{3)297}$$

5
$$\frac{96}{8)552}$$

6
$$\frac{123}{5)615}$$

7
$$\frac{714}{2)998}$$

8
$$\frac{129}{5)645}$$

9
$$\frac{399}{2)998}$$

10
$$\frac{223}{9)1000}$$

11
$$\frac{111}{9)999}$$

12
$$\frac{147}{2)294}$$

Six people won a prize of $900. They decided to share the money equally. Each person approximated how much he or she should take.

Decide whether each approximation is reasonable.

13 Max said he thought he ought to get about $500.

14 Emma thought she ought to get about $100.

15 Abigail thought they each ought to have about $150.

16 Sam thought each person ought to get about $15.

17 Pete thought each person should get $1500.

18 Jill thought each person should get $105.

◆ **LESSON 110 More Division Practice**

THINKING STORY

Estimating Is Rough

Part 2

You may want to refer to the first part of this Thinking Story, on pages 368–369.

M r. Muddle went to try for the job of chief estimator. First he had to fill in a card. It asked for his address. He lived at 577 12th Street. But he wrote:

approximately 600 Tenth Street

The card asked for his telephone number. It was 555-1234, so he wrote:

approximately 6 million

The card asked how long he had worked in his last job. He wrote:

1 year, 2 months, 17 days, 6 hours, and approximately 30 minutes

After he filled out the card, Mr. Muddle went to talk to the woman who was the boss. Another woman was also trying for the job. "I will give you both a problem," said the boss. "The one who gives the better estimate gets the job. Here is the problem. How many elephants will fit in this room?"

"Let me see," said the woman. "An elephant is about 3 meters high and 3 meters long. It is a bit less than 2 meters wide. This room is about 3 meters high, 6 meters long, and 5 meters wide. So I estimate that five elephants could fit in this room."

Mr. Muddle looked carefully around the room, which had two doors and no windows. "Are we talking about whole elephants?" Mr. Muddle asked.

"Whole elephants."

"Then my estimate is zero."

. . . to be continued

Work in groups. Discuss your answers and how you figured them out. Then compare your answers with those of other groups.

1 What is silly about each of the answers Mr. Muddle wrote on the card?

2 How could five elephants fit in the room? Draw a picture of the room to show where they would be. (Hint: Draw the room so that each square stands for 1 square meter.)

3 What could make Mr. Muddle think that no elephants would fit in the room? (Hint: About how many cars could you get into your classroom?)

4 **Super challenge question:** Can you think of a time when giving an approximate address might be good enough?

LESSON
111

Applying Division

Solve these problems. Check that your answers make sense.

1 Mr. Quincy paid $1.05 (105¢) for seven onions. How much did each onion cost?

2 Antonio bought nine glass beads for 72¢. How much should ten glass beads cost?

3 The grocery store has two cans of cat food on sale for 47¢. How much do you think one can of cat food would cost? (Think about this. What would you do if you owned the store?)

4 Greg drove for eight hours. He traveled about 45 miles each hour. About how many miles did he drive?

5 Christy has 27 stickers. She wants to divide the stickers equally among five friends.

    a. How many stickers should she give each friend?

    b. Will there be any stickers left over?

    c. What should she do with them?

6 Miss Zim needs 45 balloons for a party. Balloons come in packages of eight.

    a. How many packages should she buy?

    b. How many extra balloons will she have?

7 A fabric store has a 156-foot-long piece of pink silk ribbon. How many 6-foot-long pieces of ribbon can be cut from it?

Divide. Use shortcuts when you can.

8 $6\overline{)480}$ **9** $7\overline{)523}$ **10** $5\overline{)35}$ **11** $8\overline{)326}$ **12** $2\overline{)632}$

13 $9\overline{)720}$ **14** $9\overline{)722}$ **15** $3\overline{)426}$ **16** $8\overline{)223}$ **17** $9\overline{)751}$

18 $8\overline{)222}$ **19** $8\overline{)56}$ **20** $3\overline{)471}$ **21** $3\overline{)472}$ **22** $3\overline{)219}$

Solve these problems.

23 Mr. Taylor has 443 yards of fabric. He can make a complete suit from 8 yards of fabric. How many suits can he make?

24 There are 443 people who will ride to a picnic. Each minivan can take eight people. How many minivans will be needed to take everyone to the picnic?

25 Eight people agree to contribute a total of $443 to a local charity. They decide that each person will contribute an equal amount. How much should each person contribute?

26 Each basketball team must have exactly eight players (five regulars and three substitutes). If 443 people want to play, how many teams will there be?

27 What is similar and what is different about your answers to questions 23–26?

28 Monica can do seven difficult mathematics problems in an hour. How many hours will she need to do 21 difficult problems?

29 Marta talked for nine minutes on the telephone. She was charged 657 cents ($6.57) for the call. How much did she pay per minute?

30 Omar drove his car 318 miles in six hours. How many miles per hour was that?

It takes the human body almost two days to digest one meal.

Finding Averages

Seven people went out to pick apples. This chart shows how many apples each person picked.

Name	Number of Apples Picked
Marcia	37
Erin	62
Jamie	35
Rita	34
Nico	58
Charles	26
Luis	14

Luis said, "I wish I had as many apples as everybody else."

Rita suggested that they all put their apples together and then take an equal share.

◆ How many apples do the seven people have all together?

◆ How many would each person get if they put all their apples together and then each took an equal number?

◆ Do you think anyone might object to Rita's suggestion? Which people?

◆ Which people picked an above-average number of apples?

◆ Which people picked a below-average number of apples?

◆ Which people picked exactly the average number of apples?

The number 38 is the **average,** or **mean,** of the numbers 37, 62, 35, 34, 58, 26, and 14. The average is a number that can be used to represent a group of numbers. To find one kind of average of a set of numbers, commonly called the mean, add the numbers and divide the sum by the total number of numbers that were added.

Find the average of each set of numbers. Use shortcuts when you can.

Example: Find the average of 10, 7, 9, 4, and 10.
Add the numbers. 10 + 7 + 9 + 4 + 10 = 40
How many numbers were added? five
Divide the sum by how many numbers were added.

$$\begin{array}{r} 8 \\ 5\overline{)40} \end{array}$$

The average of 10, 7, 9, 4, and 10 is 8.

1 3, 4, 5, 6, 7

2 4, 2, 8, 16, 0, 5, 12, 17, 25, 11

3 13, 14, 15, 16, 17

4 44, 44, 44, 44, 44, 44, 44, 44

5 30, 40, 50, 60, 70

6 27, 103, 59, 68, 112, 96, 84, 11

7 7, 12, 63, 15, 28

8 125, 39, 247, 362, 189, 154

9 82, 57, 49, 63, 85, 42

10 2843, 2844, 2845, 2846, 2847

11 25, 64, 27, 39, 15

12 121, 174, 156, 29

13 45, 16, 18, 93, 21, 5

14 1, 15, 61, 28, 39, 12, 12

Solve these problems.

15 Neal bowled three games. His scores were 143, 129, and 151. What was his average score for the three games?

16 Alma bowled three games. Her scores were 187, 202, and 192. About what was her average score for the three games?

17 Maya drove 335 miles in seven hours. What was the average number of miles she drove each hour? (We call this the average speed.)

18 Carolyn sells hot dogs at the ballpark. She sold 192 on Monday, 160 on Tuesday, 233 on Friday, 220 on Saturday, and 260 on Sunday. There were no games on Wednesday and Thursday. For this week, what was the average number of hot dogs Carolyn sold during a day's work?

◆ **LESSON 112** Finding Averages

What do you think about each statement? Which make sense? Which statements don't make sense? Explain your reasons.

19 Kenny used to live at 600 Elm Street. Now he lives at 200 Elm Street. On the average he has lived at 400 Elm Street.

20 Adela and Vincent were in the running for the spelling award. Adela's test scores were 96, 94, 98, and 96. Vincent's scores were 92, 94, 100, and 90. Adela won the award because she had the higher average, even though Vincent had the highest single score.

21 Hana is 14 years old. She used to be 6 years old. Her average age is 10.

22 In the United States population, the average age is about 33 years old.

23 One hundred years ago the average number of children in a family was about three. Now the average number of children in a family is about one and one half. So families have fewer people now than they did 100 years ago.

24 Alan's average bowling score for his first nine games is 100. He bowled a 200 on his tenth game, so his average score for the ten games is 150.

25 The corn in Rudolfo's corn field was 9 centimeters tall at the end of June. It was 73 centimeters tall at the end of July. So Rudolfo said his corn was 41 centimeters tall in the middle of July.

26 Gina was 140 centimeters tall on her 10th birthday. On her 14th birthday she was 180 centimeters tall. She grew an average of 10 centimeters a year from age 10 to age 14.

Sara made a chart to show her scores on her spelling tests. But her dog, Chomps, got the chart and chewed part of it. Here's the chart after Chomps was through with it.

DATE	SEPT. 9	SEPT. 11	SEPT. 13		SEPT. 18	SEPT 20	SEPT 23	SEPT 25	SEPT. 27
SCORE	76		81	85	88		100	100	95

Answer these questions.

27. What was Sara's grade on September 13?

28. On what date did Sara get a grade of 95?

29. On what date do you think Sara got a grade of 85?

30. On what days of the week do you think Sara's teacher gives spelling tests?

Mark helped at a farm on weekends. He sold tomatoes for 59 cents per pound. People often asked to buy tomatoes by the pound, so he made the following chart to help him estimate the number of tomatoes per pound. To make the chart, Mark put tomatoes on the scale, one at a time, and recorded their weight as a whole number of pounds. If the scale went over a whole pound, he still recorded the weight as a whole number.

Pounds	1	2	3	4	5	6	7	8	9	10
Number of Tomatoes	4	7	10	14	17	20	24	27	30	34

Answer these questions.

31. About how many tomatoes are in 1 pound?

32. About how many tomatoes are in 10 pounds?

33. Compare your answers to questions 31 and 32. Discuss the possible reasons why your answers might not agree with each other.

Mean, Median, and Mode

The **mean** is often used as the most representative number for a group of numbers. But sometimes, people think a better choice is the number that appears most often. That number is called the **mode.**

Another number often used to describe a set of numbers is the **median.** The median is the middle number of a set of numbers placed in order from least to greatest. Half the numbers are greater than the median. Half are less than the median.

Yolanda kept track of how many telephone calls she made each day for nine days. These are the numbers: 2, 3, 2, 15, 3, 5, 3, 0, 3

What number do you think best describes how many calls Yolanda usually makes each day? Discuss this with other members of your class. Do you all agree?

Answer these questions.

1 What is the most common number of calls Yolanda made in one day?

2 Yolanda put the number of calls in order from fewest to most. If she counts up to the middle number, what will it be?

3 What is the mode of the number of times per day Yolanda made telephone calls?

4 What is the median of the number of times per day Yolanda made telephone calls?

5 What is the median of the following set of numbers?

2, 4, 5, 7, 8, 9

When there is an even number of numbers in a set, as in problem 5, we usually use the average of the two middle numbers as the median. In this case, the median would be 6.

Sometimes a set of data will have more than one mode. In that case, report both modes. Are modes and medians easier to find when the numbers are in order from least to greatest? You may choose to reorder data before trying to find the mean, median, and mode.

For each of the following sets of numbers, write the mean, the median, and the mode. Use a calculator if you wish.

6 1, 2, 2, 3, 3, 3, 4, 4, 4, 4, 5, 5, 5, 5, 5, 6, 6, 6, 6, 7, 7, 7, 8, 8, 9

7 2, 4, 5, 7, 7, 8, 11

8 12, 4, 9, 0, 8, 4, 13, 4, 6, 8, 5, 8

9 7, 12, 3, 8, 4, 5, 7, 6, 0

The Fabulous Phone Company has nine employees, including the owner. Their yearly salaries are as follows.

$10,000; $10,000; $10,000; $10,000; $12,000; $13,000; $14,000; $15,000; $50,000

Answer these questions.

10 What is the average, or mean, salary of the employees?

11 What is the median salary of the employees?

12 What is the mode of the salaries of the employees?

13 Of the three numbers, the mean, the median, or the mode, which do you think best represents the salaries of the Fabulous Phone Company employees?

UNIT 5

Mid-Unit Review

Use the method you like best to solve these division problems. Use play money if you need to. Watch for remainders.

1 4)100 **2** 3)73 **3** 7)84 **4** 9)92

5 2)453 **6** 5)80 **7** 7)439 **8** 3)761

9 4)856 **10** 2)747 **11** 4)500 **12** 3)1572

13 5)3542 **14** 6)606 **15** 8)248 **16** 5)54,320

Find the missing digit.

17
```
    36 R■
5)182
  15
  32
  30
   2
```

18
```
    12■ R5
6)743
  6
  14
  12
  23
  18
   5
```

19
```
    273
■)546
  4
  14
  14
   6
   6
```

20
```
    4■ R3
9)381
  36
  21
  18
   3
```

21
```
    1■7 R4
5)789
  5
  28
  25
  39
  35
   4
```

22
```
    ■36 R3
4)947
  8
  14
  12
  27
  24
   3
```

23
```
    72 R7
8)583
  56
  ■3
  16
   7
```

24
```
    268
3)804
  6
  20
  1■
  24
  24
```

Solve these problems.

25 Felix wants to buy some cider. A 4-cup carton costs $1.44 (144¢). An 8-cup carton of the same kind of cider costs $2.72 (272¢).

    a. How much does cider cost per cup in a 4-cup carton?

    b. How much does cider cost per cup in an 8-cup carton?

    c. Which do you think is the better buy? Why?

26 Six limes cost 96¢. How much does one lime cost?

27 Three stickers cost 75¢. How much is that per sticker?

28 Four cans of tuna cost $4.68 (468¢). How much is that per can?

29 Two wallets cost $26. How much does one wallet cost?

30 An 8-ounce jar of pickles costs $1.84 (184¢). How much is that per ounce?

31 A 5-pound bag of frozen corn costs $2.15 (215¢). A 7-pound bag of frozen corn costs $3.22 (322¢). Which bag is the better buy? Why?

32 Nine boxes of spaghetti cost $8.73 (873¢). How much is that per box?

Divide. Use whichever method you like best. Check your answers by multiplying.

33 $6\overline{)234}$ **Check:** Does 6 × **quotient** = 234?

34 $5\overline{)385}$ **Check:** Does 5 × **quotient** = 385?

35 $7\overline{)290}$ **Check:** Does (7 × **quotient**) + **remainder** = 290?

36 $3\overline{)227}$ **Check:** Does (3 × **quotient**) + **remainder** = 227?

Divide. Use shortcuts when you can.

37 $4\overline{)987}$ 38 $5\overline{)4000}$ 39 $8\overline{)649}$ 40 $1\overline{)54,326}$

Solve.

41 Andrew paid $3.15 (315¢) for seven magnets. How much did each magnet cost?

42 Rosa got four tacos for $3.80. How much should ten tacos cost?

43 Melido called his aunt in Peru. They talked on the phone for seven minutes. Melido was charged $4.76 for the call. How much did he pay per minute?

44 Michael needs 65 candles for his grandmother's birthday cake. Candles come in packages of ten.

a. How many packages should he buy?

b. How many extra candles will he have?

45 Mrs. Grant drove for six hours. She traveled about 54 miles each hour. About how many miles did she drive?

46 There are 385 people who will ride in minivans for a school trip. Each minivan can take nine people. How many minivans are needed to take everyone on the trip?

47 Each relay team needs exactly seven runners. How many teams can be formed if 91 runners want to race?

Find the average of each set of numbers.

48 5, 6, 7, 8, 9

49 12, 10, 18, 14, 27, 15

50 10, 20, 30, 40, 50

51 32, 32, 32, 32, 32, 32, 32

52 123, 234, 345, 456, 567

53 28, 60, 15, 7, 12, 10

Solve.

54 Lauren bowled three games. Her scores were 136, 98, and 117. What was her average score for the three games?

55 Joshua drove 423 miles in eight hours. What was the average number of miles per hour (or average speed) he drove?

For each of the following sets of numbers, write the mean, the median, and the mode. Use a calculator if you wish.

56 1, 2, 3, 4, 6, 6, 8, 10

57 3, 7, 12, 4, 10, 5, 0, 6, 7

58 2, 2, 3, 3, 3, 4, 4, 4, 4, 5, 5, 5, 5, 5, 6, 6, 6, 6, 6, 6

Solve.

59 Matt kept track of how many pieces of mail he got each day for seven days. He recorded these numbers: 5, 7, 4, 6, 8, 4, and 1. Find the mean, median, and mode.

60 Emily recorded the number of goals she scored in her nine soccer games. Emily recorded 3, 4, 3, 4, 6, 1, 3, 1, and 2. Find the mean, median, and mode.

LESSON
114

Division Patterns

When you solve similar problems, you may notice patterns that can help you find answers quickly. Look for patterns. Think about how to use the patterns to find the answers.

Divide. Remember to write any remainders. Watch your numbering.

1 3)10

2 3)100

3 3)1000

4 2)10

5 2)100

6 2)1000

7 4)100

8 4)1000

9 4)10,000

10 5)10

11 5)100

12 5)1000

13 6)1000

14 6)100

15 8)1000

16 8)2000

17 9)1000

18 9)2000

19 9)3000

20 2)246

21 3)785

22 4)1256

23 5)847

24 7)9482

25 1)2520

26 2)2520

27 3)2520

28 4)2520

29 5)2520

30 6)2520

31 7)2520

32 8)2520

33 9)2520

34 2)210

35 3)210

36 5)210

37 7)210

38 8)210

39 7)1,000,000

40 7)2,000,000

41 7)3,000,000

42 7)4,000,000

Divide to solve for *n*. Watch your numbering.

43 900 ÷ 9 = n   44 210 ÷ 7 = n   45 200 ÷ 8 = n

46 100 ÷ 4 = n   47 72 ÷ 9 = n   48 360 ÷ 6 = n

49 360 ÷ 4 = n   50 360 ÷ 9 = n   51 360 ÷ 8 = n

52 360 ÷ 5 = n   53 350 ÷ 7 = n   54 80 ÷ 5 = n

55 900 ÷ 6 = n   56 2871 ÷ 9 = n   57 1024 ÷ 8 = n

Solve these problems.

58 Angie is making earrings. She needs three beads for each wire. She has 97 beads.

  a. How many earrings can Angie make?

  b. If there are two earrings in a set, how many sets of earrings can Angie make?

  c. How many beads will be left over?

59 Winter Elementary's secretary ordered 141 notebooks to be divided exactly among six classrooms. How many notebooks were given to each classroom? How many notebooks were left over?

60 Ruby wants to give an eraser to each of the 28 people coming to her party. The erasers she wants come in packages of eight.

  a. How many packages does she need to buy?

  b. How many extra erasers will she have?

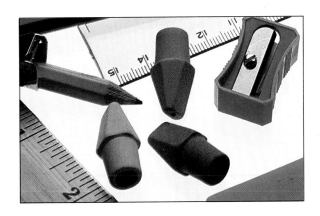

LESSON 115

Using Division

Solve these problems. Check that your answers make sense and that they fit the situations.

1 Nine people took a 40-word spelling test. Their scores were 39, 38, 30, 39, 26, 31, 35, 7, and 34.

   a. What was the average score?

   b. How many people had above-average scores?

   c. How many people had below-average scores?

   d. How many people had exactly average scores?

2 Seven people took a 30-problem math quiz. Their scores were 21, 29, 30, 20, 17, 14, and 11.

   a. About what was the average score?

   b. How many people had above-average scores?

   c. How many people had below-average scores?

   d. How many people scored within one point of the average score?

3 Mr. Epstein knows that his living room rug is rectangular and that its area is 42 square meters.

   a. He knows it is 6 meters wide, but he cannot remember how long it is. How long is the rug?

   b. If the local cleaner charges $2.53 (253¢) for each square meter of rug cleaned, how much will it cost Mr. Epstein to have his rug cleaned?

4 Ms. McConnell heard that cabbages at her favorite store weigh about 1 kilogram (1000 grams). She bought nine cabbages and weighed them to see if they weighed 1 kilogram each. Their weights were 932 grams, 961 grams, 982 grams, 989 grams, 994 grams, 996 grams, 1008 grams, 1087 grams, and 1096 grams.

   a. How many of the nine cabbages weighed more than 1 kilogram?

   b. What was the average weight of the nine cabbages?

   c. Would it have cost Ms. McConnell less to buy the cabbages for 65¢ per cabbage or for 65¢ per kilogram?

5 When Roland bowls, he bowls a series of three games. The last seven times he bowled, his total scores for three games were 561, 570, 572, 568, 430, 564, and 571.

   a. For the last seven times he bowled, could Roland's average score for a series of three games be 400? Could it be 430? Could it be 600? Could it be 572?

   b. Make your best estimate of Roland's average score. Then calculate the average to see how close you were.

   c. About what do you think Roland's score will be the next time he bowls?

6 The temperature in Sunnydale has varied greatly over the past 14 days. The high temperatures for each day were 97°F, 75°F, 70°F, 99°F, 73°F, 80°F, 63°F, 70°F, 68°F, 79°F, 77°F, 79°F, 79°F, and 77°F.

   a. What was the average high temperature in this 14-day period?

   b. Over the past 100 years, the average daily high temperature in Sunnydale for this 14-day period was 73°F. Would you say that this same period this year is warmer than usual, cooler than usual, or about average?

◆ LESSON 115   Using Division

Keep in shape by practicing all four operations. Remember to check that your answers make sense.

Solve for *n*. Watch your numbering.

7 $36 + 9 = n$

8 $36 - 9 = n$

9 $36 \times 9 = n$

10 $36 \div 9 = n$

11 $36 + 6 = n$

12 $36 - 6 = n$

13 $36 \times 6 = n$

14 $36 \div 6 = n$

15 $n = 42 \times 7$

16 $n = 42 - 7$

17 $n = 42 \div 7$

18 $n = 42 + 7$

19 $n = 243 + 512$

20 $n = 648 - 471$

21 $286 \times 8 = n$

22 $n = 512 \div 4$

23 $407 \times 58 = n$

24 $n = 63 \times 57$

25 $n = 1000 \div 8$

26 $73 \times 89 = n$

27 $2 \times 2 = n$

28 $2 + 2 = n$

29 $0 \times 5783 = n$

30 $n = 5783 + 0$

31 $0 \times 5 = n$

32 $n = 0 \div 5$

33 $n = 5 \div 0$

34 $0 \div 9 = n$

35 $9 \times 0 = n$

36 $9 \div 0 = n$

37 $7 \times 8 = n$

38 $56 \div 7 = n$

39 $n = 42 \div 6$

40 $n = 83 + 249$

41 $n = 1000 - 783$

42 $n = 426 + 574$

Watch the signs.

43
$$\begin{array}{r} 8562 \\ + 9408 \\ \hline \end{array}$$

44
$$\begin{array}{r} 52{,}071 \\ - 3{,}468 \\ \hline \end{array}$$

45
$$\begin{array}{r} 832 \\ \times 706 \\ \hline \end{array}$$

46
$$\begin{array}{r} 647 \\ + 352 \\ \hline \end{array}$$

47
$$\begin{array}{r} 5407 \\ + 4593 \\ \hline \end{array}$$

48
$$\begin{array}{r} 10{,}000 \\ - 7{,}654 \\ \hline \end{array}$$

49
$$\begin{array}{r} 10{,}000 \\ - 3{,}819 \\ \hline \end{array}$$

50
$$\begin{array}{r} 301 \\ \times 299 \\ \hline \end{array}$$

51
$$\begin{array}{r} 250 \\ + 250 \\ \hline \end{array}$$

52
$$\begin{array}{r} 70 \\ \times 30 \\ \hline \end{array}$$

53
$$\begin{array}{r} 1000 \\ - 998 \\ \hline \end{array}$$

54
$$\begin{array}{r} 600 \\ \times 40 \\ \hline \end{array}$$

Divide.

55 $9\overline{)54}$

56 $7\overline{)497}$

57 $6\overline{)2844}$

58 $8\overline{)26{,}648}$

Remember: 8 fluid ounces = 1 cup
　　　　　　　2 cups = 1 pint
　　　　　　　8 pints = 1 gallon
　　　　　　　4 quarts = 1 gallon

Answer these questions.

59　How many fluid ounces are there in 5 cups?

60　How many cups are there in 40 fluid ounces?

61　How many cups are there in 72 fluid ounces?

62　How many gallons are there in 72 pints?

63　How many gallons are there in 72 quarts?

64　A doctor recommended that his patient drink at least 16 cups of water every day. How many pints is that? How many quarts is that? How many gallons is that? How many fluid ounces is that?

Remember: 1000 milliliters = 1 liter

Answer these questions.

65　How many milliliters are there in 5 liters?

66　How many liters are there in 5000 milliliters?

67　How many liters are there in 12,000 milliliters?

68　The doctor recommended that another patient drink at least 4000 milliliters of water each day. How many liters is that?

LESSON 116

Practicing Division: Missing Digits

ALGEBRA READINESS

Find the missing digits. Check your answers.

1
```
  1■8 R3
5)543
  5
  ‾‾
  43
  40
  ‾‾
   3
```

2
```
  62 R3
7)437
  42
  ‾‾
  ■7
  14
  ‾‾
   3
```

3
```
  74 R■
8)599
  56
  ‾‾
  39
  32
  ‾‾
   7
```

4
```
  23 R2
9)209
  18
  ‾‾
  29
  27
  ‾‾
   ■
```

5
```
  40 R■
8)322
  32
  ‾‾
   2
```

6
```
  10■ R5
8)805
  8
  ‾
   5
```

7
```
   ■8
8)624
  56
  ‾‾
  64
  64
  ‾‾
```

8
```
  1■6
6)636
  6
  ‾
  36
  36
  ‾‾
```

9
```
  119
8)952
  8
  ‾
  1■
   8
  ‾‾
  72
  72
  ‾‾
```

10
```
  4■2
2)964
  8
  ‾
  16
  16
  ‾‾
   4
   4
   ‾
```

11
```
  1■3
4)732
  4
  ‾
  33
  32
  ‾‾
  12
  12
  ‾‾
```

12
```
  2■9
3)807
  6
  ‾
  20
  18
  ‾‾
  27
  27
  ‾‾
```

13
```
  167
3)501
  3
  ‾
  20
  1■
  ‾‾
  21
  21
  ‾‾
```

14
```
  127
6)■62
  6
  ‾
  16
  12
  ‾‾
  42
  42
  ‾‾
```

15
```
  118
7)826
  ■
  ‾
  12
   7
  ‾‾
  56
  56
  ‾‾
```

16
```
  163
■)326
  2
  ‾
  12
  12
  ‾‾
   6
   6
   ‾
```

You have learned to make graphs of ordered pairs from function rules. For example, find four ordered pairs that fit the following situation. The first number in an ordered pair is the length of a side of a square. The second number is the perimeter of the square.

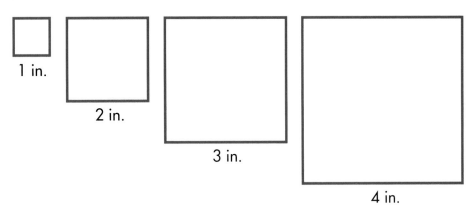

1 in.

2 in.

3 in.

4 in.

Answer these questions.

⑰ If the side is 1 inch long, what is the perimeter?
The ordered pair is (1, 4).

⑱ Find the perimeter and ordered pairs for the other three squares. Graph the ordered pairs. Will one line go through all four points?

For each of the following rules find four ordered pairs. Then graph the four points corresponding to those ordered pairs. Try to draw a line through the four points.

⑲ The first number is the length of a side of an equilateral triangle. The second number is the perimeter of the triangle.

⑳ The first number is the number of yards in a particular distance. The second number is the number of feet in that same distance.

㉑ The first number is the length of a side of a square in inches. The second number is the area of that square in square inches.

◆ **LESSON 116 Practicing Division: Missing Digits**

Estimating Is Rough

Part 3

You may want to refer to previous parts of this Thinking Story, on pages 368–369 and 376–377.

Mr. Muddle's first job as an estimator took him to City Hall. "Do you remember when Elm Street had big elm trees growing all along it?" the commissioner asked.

"Not exactly," said Mr. Muddle. "But I do remember it used to be very shady walking down Elm Street, and now it isn't shady anymore."

"That's because Dutch elm disease came through and all the elm trees died. We'd like to plant new trees so that Elm Street will be shady again someday. We want to plant trees the whole length of the street, from 1500 East Elm Street to 2600 West Elm Street. So I need an estimate of how many trees we will have to buy."

"I'd say 4100 trees," said Mr. Muddle, "but my first estimates are not always good. So I want to take time and make a really good estimate."

Mr. Muddle called on his friends Manolita and Marcus to help him estimate. "First we need to find out the distance from 1500 East Elm Street to 2600 West Elm Street," he said. Marcus had a 12-inch ruler and started measuring the length of one block along Elm Street.

"I have a quicker way," said Manolita. She walked from one end of the block to the other, counting softly to herself as she walked. When she got to the end of the block she shouted, "This block is about 600 feet long."

"That means there are about eight blocks in a mile," said Marcus.

"So Elm Street must be about 5 miles long," Manolita said.

"It's amazing the things they teach children in school these days!" Mr. Muddle said. He hurried back to City Hall and told the commissioner, "Elm Street is about 5 miles long. Ten trees to a mile sounds about right, so my estimate is that you'll need 50 trees."

"That doesn't sound like nearly enough," the commissioner said. "We'd like to have a tree in front of every house."

Mr. Muddle went with his friends back to Elm Street and told them to start counting houses. Manolita counted the houses on the south side of the street. They were numbered 801, 803, 805, and so on. Marcus counted the houses on the north side of the street: 800, 802, 804, and so on. Suddenly he said, "I think I have a good estimate. There are about 4100 houses on Elm Street."

Mr. Muddle told the commissioner that his first estimate was a good one after all. "You'll need about 4100 trees."

A few months later Mr. Muddle met the commissioner walking down Elm Street admiring the new trees. "Your estimate was very close," the commissioner told him. "We had a couple of hundred trees more than we needed, but we found other places to plant them. Good work!"

. . . to be continued

Work in groups. Discuss your answers and how you figured them out. Then compare your answers with those of other groups.

❶ How do you think Manolita estimated the length of the block? Estimate how many steps she would have taken.

❷ If a block is 600 feet long, why is eight blocks to the mile a better estimate than nine blocks to the mile? (There are 5280 feet in a mile.)

❸ Is 5 miles a good estimate for the length of Elm Street? What would have to be true for this to be a good estimate?

❹ What are other ways to estimate the length of Elm Street?

❺ How could you tell that 50 trees was too low an estimate?

❻ Explain Marcus's estimate of 4100 trees. Did Marcus arrive at the number 4100 the same way Mr. Muddle did?

Multiply and Divide

Oodles of Gooples

Landon dreamed about a trip to Lotsamonia. He went there with his friends Mindy, Tyler, Keesha, Tony, and Jordan.

They landed near a hamburger stand, which reminded them how hungry they were.

"How much are your hamburgers?" Landon asked the man behind the counter.

"23 gooples," he said.

"Gooples!" said Landon. "What are those?"

"A goople is our unit of money in Lotsamonia," the man explained.

"We have dollars and cents," said Landon.

"Well, then," said the man, "go exchange them for gooples."

Off they went to the Bank of Lotsamonia, where they found out that 23 gooples are worth exactly $1.

"How many gooples can I get for $3?" Jordan asked.

◆   Do you know the answer to that question?

"I gave the teller $27," said Keesha, "and he gave me 621 gooples. Does that make sense?"

"I have an idea," said Tony. "Let's make a graph so we can check whether we are getting about the right number of gooples for our dollars."

"OK," they all agreed.

First they made a chart using some numbers that were easy to multiply.

Dollars	Gooples
0	0
100	2300

Next, Landon and his friends made a graph of the ordered pairs on the chart: (0, 0) and (100, 2300). They drew a straight line through the points.

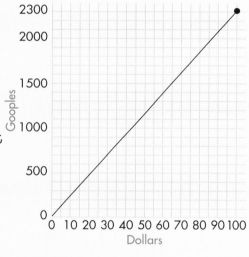

"I have $65," said Jordan. "About how many gooples will I get?"

"Simple," said Tony, "find 65 on the sideways axis, go straight up to the line, then go across to the up-and-down axis."

Jordan watched Tony put his finger on 65, then move it up and over. He said, "My 65 dollars are worth about 1500 gooples."

They all exchanged their dollars for gooples and used the graph to check their amounts.

"Now we can get some hamburgers and then go shopping," said Landon. And off they went.

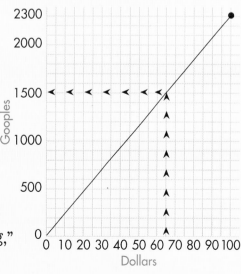

◆ **LESSON 117** Multiply and Divide

Tyler saw a radio that he wanted to buy. Then he saw the price.

"It costs 1000 gooples," he said. "That's too much money."

"It's not as much as it sounds," Tony said. "You have to divide 1000 by 23 to find out how much that is in dollars."

"But we don't know how to divide by big numbers like 23," said Tyler.

"We can use our graph to get an approximate answer," said Tony. "Remember, dividing is the opposite, or inverse, of multiplication. So, if we can use the graph to multiply, we can just do the opposite to divide. Look."

"I see," said Tyler. "1000 gooples are worth a little less than $45."

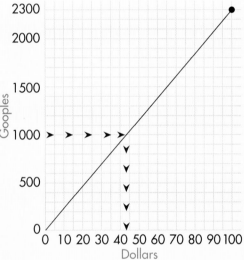

Use the graph to approximate how many dollars each of these items costs.

1 Running suit—649 gooples

2 Baseball glove—415 gooples

3 Shirt—225 gooples

4 Bicycle—1820 gooples

5 Calculator—110 gooples

6 CD player—803 gooples

Remember:

35 **in** ×23 **out** 805

If you put 35 into a ×23 machine, 805 will come out.

A ÷23 machine does the opposite. If you put in 805, then 35 will come out.

805 **in** ÷23 **out** 35

35 — ×23 → 805

805 ← ÷23 — 35

In each problem, find the value of *x* or *y*. The answers to the problems on the left will help you solve the problems on the right.

ALGEBRA READINESS

7 20 — ×25 → *y*   **8** *x* ← ÷25 — 500

9 13 — ×75 → *y*   **10** *x* ← ÷75 — 975

11 92 — ×10 → *y*   **12** *x* ← ÷10 — 920

13 63 — ×12 → *y*   **14** *x* ← ÷12 — 756

15 3 — ×752 → *y*   **16** *x* ← ÷752 — 2256

17 6 — ×375 → *y*   **18** *x* ← ÷375 — 2250

19 18 — ×452 → *y*   **20** *x* ← ÷452 — 8136

21 75 — ×260 → *y*   **22** *x* ← ÷260 — 19,500

23 54 — ×145 → *y*   **24** *x* ← ÷145 — 7830

Multiplying to Find Quotients

You can use multiplication to find or check answers to division problems.

Remember:

Multiplication is the inverse of division. So if you multiply by 7 and then divide by 7, you get back the number you started with.

Example A: Start with 8 and multiply by 7.

$7 \times 8 = 56$

$56 \div 7 = 8$

Example B:

$$\begin{array}{r} 283 \\ \times\ \ 28 \\ \hline 2264 \\ 566 \\ \hline 7924 \end{array}$$

Start with 283 and multiply by 28.

$28 \times 283 = 7924$

$$283 \\ 28\overline{)7924}$$

$7924 \div 28 = 283$

Solve these problems without dividing or subtracting.
Use the information in the box to help you.

❶ $25\overline{)625}$ ❷ $250\overline{)1000}$

❸ $125\overline{)1000}$ ❹ $52\overline{)2496}$

❺ $4\overline{)1000}$ ❻ $79\overline{)6399}$

❼ $8\overline{)1000}$ ❽ $81\overline{)6399}$

❾ $48\overline{)2496}$ ❿ $843\overline{)22,761}$

⓫ $\begin{array}{r} 13,129 \\ -\ 7,846 \end{array}$ ⓬ $\begin{array}{r} 13,129 \\ -\ 5,283 \end{array}$

$5283 + 7846 = 13,129$
$8 \times 125 = 1000$
$4 \times 250 = 1000$
$52 \times 48 = 2496$
$25 \times 25 = 625$
$843 \times 27 = 22,761$
$81 \times 79 = 6399$

For each problem, several answers are given but only one is correct. Choose the correct answer without dividing.

Example: 25)175   **a.** 4   **b.** 6   **c.** 7   **d.** 10   **e.** 11

$$
\begin{array}{ccc}
25 & 25 & 25 \\
\times\ 4 & \times\ 6 & \times\ 7 \\
\hline
100 & 150 & 175
\end{array}
$$

$7 \times 25 = 175$. So $175 \div 25$ must be 7. The correct answer is **c.**

13 12)96   **a.** 7   **b.** 8   **c.** 9   **d.** 10   **e.** 11

14 15)225   **a.** 5   **b.** 8   **c.** 0   **d.** 13   **e.** 15

15 24)96   **a.** 4   **b.** 5   **c.** 6   **d.** 7   **e.** 8

16 250)1000   **a.** 3   **b.** 4   **c.** 5   **d.** 6   **e.** 7

17 12)144   **a.** 8   **b.** 9   **c.** 10   **d.** 12   **e.** 14

18 15)75   **a.** 5   **b.** 6   **c.** 7   **d.** 8   **e.** 10

19 11)154   **a.** 12   **b.** 14   **c.** 16   **d.** 20   **e.** 24

20 17)357   **a.** 19   **b.** 20   **c.** 21   **d.** 22   **e.** 23

21 22)242   **a.** 9   **b.** 11   **c.** 13   **d.** 15   **e.** 17

22 16)96   **a.** 5   **b.** 6   **c.** 8   **d.** 14   **e.** 16

23 13)169   **a.** 2   **b.** 5   **c.** 7   **d.** 9   **e.** 13

24 150)600   **a.** 4   **b.** 5   **c.** 6   **d.** 7   **e.** 8

25 12)108   **a.** 7   **b.** 8   **c.** 9   **d.** 10   **e.** 11

26 14)182   **a.** 11   **b.** 12   **c.** 13   **d.** 14   **e.** 15

27 19)247   **a.** 2   **b.** 3   **c.** 5   **d.** 13   **e.** 17

28 18)324   **a.** 15   **b.** 16   **c.** 18   **d.** 19   **e.** 20

29 14)168   **a.** 11   **b.** 12   **c.** 13   **d.** 14   **e.** 15

LESSON
119

Prime and Composite Numbers

SOCIAL STUDIES CONNECTION

Our flag has had 50 stars only since 1960. A previous flag had 48 stars and was the United States flag longer than any other. The stars were arranged in six rows of eight.

From 1818 to 1836 the United States flag had 20 stars.

◆   How do you think the stars were arranged?

For many numbers of stars it is possible to arrange them in different rectangles. For some numbers, the only possible rectangles would have one row (or one column). The possible rectangles that can be made with 20 stars are:

1 by 20   2 by 10   4 by 5

You could make three more by turning these rectangles to show 20 by 1, 10 by 2, and 5 by 4.

Solve these problems.

1 List all possible rectangles that could be made with
    a. one star   **c.** three stars   **e.** five stars
    b. two stars   **d.** four stars   **f.** six stars

2 How many rectangles did you list for one star? Do you think there are any other numbers besides 1 for which there is only one rectangle?

3 How many rectangles did you list for two, three, and five stars? Do you think there are other numbers for which there are only two rectangles?

4 List three other numbers for which there are only two rectangles.

Solve these problems.

Prime numbers have exactly two rectangles.

Composite numbers have more than two rectangles.

5 List five prime numbers.

6 List five composite numbers.

7 Is the number 1 prime or composite?

Remember, a factor of a number is any number that divides it without a remainder. For example, the factors of 36 are 1, 2, 3, 4, 6, 9, 12, 18, and 36. You can divide 36 by any of these numbers and there will be no remainder.

8 List the factors of the following numbers.

    a. 1   **b.** 2   **c.** 3   **d.** 4   **e.** 5   **f.** 6

9 How many factors does 1 have?

10 How many factors do each of the following numbers have?

    a. 2   **b.** 3   **c.** 5

11 How many factors does 4 have?

12 List all numbers that you think have just one factor.

13 List four numbers that have exactly two factors.

14 List six numbers that have more than two factors.

15 How many factors do prime numbers have?

16 How many factors do composite numbers have?

17 Why might (6 × 5) + (5 × 4) remind someone of the flag of the United States?

In your Math Journal list all the prime numbers less than 100.

Using a Bar Graph

Alex earns $8.00 an hour working at the Splish-Splash Car Wash. The bar graph shows the total amount of money he earned each day last week.

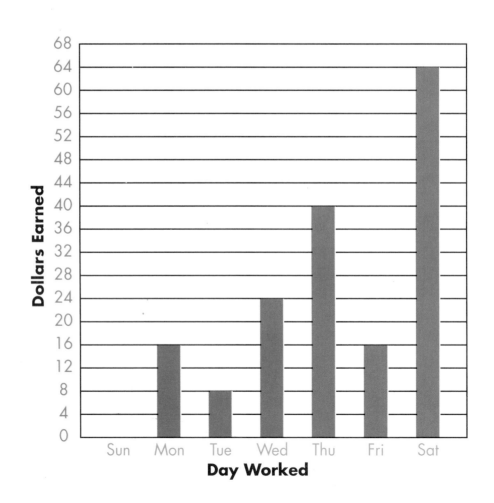

Use the graph to answer these questions.

1. How much money did Alex earn on Monday?

2. How much money did he earn on Tuesday?

3. How much money did he earn on Friday?

4. How many hours did Alex work on Wednesday? (Remember, he earns $8 an hour.)

5. How many hours did he work on Saturday?

6. How many hours did Alex work on Tuesday?

7. On which day did he earn the most money?

8. How much money did Alex earn during the entire week?

9. What was the average amount of money he made per day for the six days he worked?

10. If he had earned $4 an hour, how much would Alex have earned during the entire week?

Divide.

11. $8\overline{)410}$ 12. $6\overline{)236}$ 13. $5\overline{)500}$ 14. $3\overline{)271}$ 15. $9\overline{)810}$

16. $4\overline{)237}$ 17. $3\overline{)229}$ 18. $4\overline{)804}$ 19. $6\overline{)732}$ 20. $7\overline{)210}$

21. $9\overline{)63}$ 22. $8\overline{)539}$ 23. $2\overline{)107}$ 24. $7\overline{)622}$ 25. $8\overline{)48}$

26. $3\overline{)408}$ 27. $4\overline{)792}$ 28. $6\overline{)360}$ 29. $9\overline{)72}$ 30. $6\overline{)201}$

31. $3\overline{)273}$ 32. $8\overline{)32}$ 33. $9\overline{)706}$ 34. $6\overline{)240}$ 35. $8\overline{)324}$

36. $2\overline{)970}$ 37. $6\overline{)437}$ 38. $8\overline{)342}$ 39. $9\overline{)108}$ 40. $4\overline{)960}$

Solve.

41. Ray traveled 300 miles in his car in six hours. How many miles per hour is that?

◆ **LESSON 120 Using a Bar Graph**

Estimating Is Rough

Part 4

*You may wish to refer to previous parts of this
Thinking Story, on pages 368–369, 376–377, and 398–399.*

"I need your help, Mr. Muddle," said the grocer. "Could you help me figure out how many turkeys to order for Christmas?"

"Is your store open on Christmas Day?"

"No," said the grocer.

"Then my estimate is one," said Mr. Muddle. "Unless you have a very large family."

"I have a small family," said the grocer. "But I have lots of customers. Some of them buy turkeys for Christmas. I'd like you to estimate how many."

Mr. Muddle stopped a shopper. "Pardon me, sir. Do you plan to buy a turkey for Christmas?"

"I don't think so," said the shopper. "We don't have a big roasting pan."

Mr. Muddle asked more shoppers. But he changed the question. He found that 41 had big roasting pans and 42 didn't. Then he asked the grocer, "How many customers do you have all together?"

"About 2000."

"Then I estimate you will need 1000 turkeys."

"But . . . but I've never sold that many! I sold only 600 at Thanksgiving."

"I forgot Thanksgiving," said Mr. Muddle. "You have 1000 people buying turkeys. You sold 600 turkeys at Thanksgiving. That means you will sell 400 at Christmas. Order 400 turkeys and 600 ducks. That way everyone with a roasting pan will have something to roast."

. . . to be continued

Work in groups. Discuss your answers and how you figured them out. Then compare your answers with those of other groups.

❶ How did Mr. Muddle get his first estimate of 1000 turkeys?

❷ Were his reasons very good for estimating 1000? Why or why not?

❸ How did Mr. Muddle get his second estimate of 400?

❹ Were his reasons very good for estimating 400 turkeys? Why or why not?

❺ **Super challenge question:** If you were asking the questions instead of Mr. Muddle, what questions would you have asked to figure out how many turkeys to order?

LESSON 121

More Division Review

Knowledge of math is helpful in understanding bills.

Mr. Cooper received this telephone bill in the mail.

REAL-WORLD CONNECTION

RINGVILLE TELEPHONE COMPANY Monthly Statement for October Telephone Number 555-5505			James Cooper 577 12th St. Ringville
Date	**Calls to**	**Number of Minutes**	**Price**
Oct. 10	Midway	5	$1.25
Oct. 13	Midway	10	$2.50
Oct. 24	Horton	10	$0.80
Oct. 25	Cordville	3	$6.00
Oct. 27	Troy	2	$8.30
Oct. 29	Tone's Ferry	15	$1.50
Oct. 30	Midway	8	$3.00

Ringville Telephone Company rate information: All calls to other cities are charged by the minute. The farther a city is from Ringville, the higher the rate will be.

Answer the following questions.

1. How much per minute does it cost to call

    a. Midway?   **b.** Cordville?   **c.** Tone's Ferry?

    d. Horton?   **e.** Troy?

2. Which city is farther from Ringville—Horton or Midway?

3. For one of his phone calls, Mr. Cooper was charged the wrong rate. Help him find the error. How much will Mr. Cooper save if he finds the error?

4. Order the cities Mr. Cooper called, from the nearest to the farthest from Ringville.

5. For how many minutes did Mr. Cooper use the telephone in October on calls that he made to other cities?

Divide. Watch for remainders.

6 3)42   **7** 2)100   **8** 7)8575   **9** 10)100

10 3)20   **11** 8)1000   **12** 7)98   **13** 5)63,407

14 9)9   **15** 9)80   **16** 4)100   **17** 1)73,596

18 5)125   **19** 1)100   **20** 6)44   **21** 6)35,172

22 4)1298   **23** 7)507   **24** 9)0   **25** 8)500

Solve.

26 Last week Kirsten jogged every day. She didn't jog the same distance each day. These are the distances she jogged during the week: 9 miles, 11 miles, 12 miles, 9 miles, 10 miles, 12 miles, and 5 miles.

    a. What is the average distance Kirsten jogged each day?

    b. Did she jog the average distance on any day?

    c. On how many days did she run more than the average distance?

    d. On how many days did Kirsten run less than the average distance?

27 A thermos holds 64 ounces of water. How many 4-ounce glasses can be filled from the thermos?

Division Applications

Solve these problems. Check that your answers make sense.

1. Claire and her three friends wanted to share 36 pretzels equally. How many should each person get?

2. Dr. Lin drove 250 kilometers in three hours. About what was her average speed?

3. Mrs. Vega drove for seven hours. She drove 90 kilometers the first hour, 85 kilometers the second hour, 50 kilometers the third hour, 50 kilometers the fourth hour, 85 kilometers the fifth hour, 85 kilometers the sixth hour, and 80 kilometers the seventh hour. About what was her average speed?

4. Sita can buy six cans of cola for $2.04. What is the cost for each can of cola?

5. Gregory can buy an eight-pack of cola for $3.12 (or 312¢). What is the cost for each bottle of cola if he buys it in an eight-pack?

6. Mr. Nolan drove 510 kilometers in six hours. What was his average speed?

7. Hari bought nine goldfish that cost 89¢ each. The tax was 48¢. He gave the storekeeper a $10 bill. How much change should he get back?

8. Judith bought nine cans of lemonade. The storekeeper charged her $5.85 (585¢) for the nine cans. How much did each can of lemonade cost?

9. Kimberly and Jorge left Seneca at the same time. Kimberly drove 532 kilometers and Jorge drove 510 kilometers. How far apart were they?

10. Mr. Kwan drove 530 miles one day and 610 miles the next. His total trip was to be about 1500 miles. About how far did he still have to go?

For each problem, several answers are given but only one is correct. Choose the correct answer. Use shortcuts when you can.

11 $1\overline{)350}$ **a.** 27   **b.** 35   **c.** 270   **d.** 350   **e.** 400

12 $10\overline{)350}$ **a.** 27   **b.** 35   **c.** 270   **d.** 350   **e.** 400

13 $15\overline{)60}$ **a.** 2   **b.** 3   **c.** 4   **d.** 5   **e.** 6

14 $2\overline{)10}$ **a.** 2   **b.** 3   **c.** 4   **d.** 5   **e.** 6

15 $20\overline{)100}$ **a.** 2   **b.** 3   **c.** 4   **d.** 5   **e.** 6

16 $3\overline{)100}$ **a.** 3 R1   **b.** 30 R1   **c.** 33 R1   **d.** 3 R2   **e.** 33 R2

17 $33\overline{)100}$ **a.** 3 R1   **b.** 30 R1   **c.** 33 R1   **d.** 3 R2   **e.** 33 R2

18 $10\overline{)2300}$ **a.** 2300   **b.** 4600   **c.** 46   **d.** 230   **e.** 23

19 $100\overline{)2300}$ **a.** 2300   **b.** 4600   **c.** 46   **d.** 230   **e.** 23

20 $100\overline{)23,000}$ **a.** 2300   **b.** 4600   **c.** 46   **d.** 230   **e.** 23

21 $7\overline{)67}$ **a.** 9 R2   **b.** 9 R3   **c.** 9 R4   **d.** 8 R5   **e.** 7 R6

22 $18\overline{)90}$ **a.** 3   **b.** 4   **c.** 5   **d.** 6   **e.** 7

23 $11\overline{)132}$ **a.** 12   **b.** 14   **c.** 16   **d.** 18   **e.** 20

24 $5\overline{)75}$ **a.** 13   **b.** 14   **c.** 15   **d.** 16   **e.** 17

25 $50\overline{)750}$ **a.** 15   **b.** 150   **c.** 30   **d.** 35   **e.** 50

26 $50\overline{)75,000}$ **a.** 150   **b.** 175   **c.** 600   **d.** 1500   **e.** 3000

27 $13\overline{)195}$ **a.** 14   **b.** 15   **c.** 17   **d.** 19   **e.** 23

28 $4\overline{)84}$ **a.** 17   **b.** 18   **c.** 20   **d.** 21   **e.** 22

29 $40\overline{)8400}$ **a.** 210   **b.** 220   **c.** 420   **d.** 620   **e.** 820

30 $40\overline{)84,000}$ **a.** 420   **b.** 21,000   **c.** 187   **d.** 210   **e.** 2100

Division Revisited: Missing Digits

ALGEBRA READINESS

Find the missing digits.

1
```
   1■5
6)630
   6
   30
   30
```

2
```
   110
5)550
  ■
  5
  5
```

3
```
   2■8
3)624
   6
   24
   24
```

4
```
   120
7)84■
   7
   14
   14
```

5
```
   80 R2
8)■42
  64
   2
```

6
```
   70
7)4■0
  49
```

7
```
   90
9)810
  ■1
```

8
```
   ■0
9)810
  81
```

9
```
   12■ R4
6)766
   6
   16
   12
   46
   42
    4
```

10
```
   231 R2
4)926
   8
  ■2
  12
   6
   4
   2
```

11
```
   115 R■
8)923
   8
   12
   8
   43
   40
   3
```

12
```
   113 R3
8)907
   8
   10
   ■
   27
   24
    3
```

13
```
   7■ R1
5)391
  35
  41
  40
   1
```

14
```
   78 R■
8)627
  56
  67
  64
   3
```

15
```
   47 R3
8)379
  32
  ■9
  56
   3
```

16
```
   133 R■
5)666
   5
   16
   15
   16
   15
    1
```

Solve for *n*. Watch the signs.

(17) $n = 16 \div 8$ (18) $19 + n = 58$ (19) $n = 81 \div 9$

(20) $16 + 8 = n$ (21) $9 \times 7 = n$ (22) $n + 28 = 77$

(23) $n = 5 \times 9$ (24) $36 - n = 27$ (25) $33 = 41 - n$

(26) $49 \div n = 7$ (27) $n \div 7 = 5$ (28) $7 \times 8 = n$

(29) $37 - 19 = n$ (30) $6 \times 9 = n$ (31) $27 \div n = 9$

Multiply.

(32) 9×100 (33) 14×1000 (34) 8×10

(35) 10×23 (36) $10,000 \times 37$ (37) 80×100

(38) $100 \times 10,000$ (39) $10,000 \times 370$ (40) 800×1000

(41) $100 \times 10,001$ (42) $10,001 \times 370$ (43) $8000 \times 1,000,000$

(44) 90×100 (45) 900×100 (46) 500×700

Watch the signs. Use shortcuts when you can.

(47) 3×9 (48) $81 + 17$ (49) $91 \div 7$

(50) $90 \div 2$ (51) 9×7 (52) $39 + 22$

(53) $16 + 7$ (54) $35 - 29$ (55) $87 - 69$

(56) $33 - 15$ (57) 12×13 (58) 7×6

(59) $28 \div 7$ (60) $16 + 17$ (61) $47 + 74$

Divide. Use shortcuts when you can.

(62) $8\overline{)56}$ (63) $4\overline{)404}$ (64) $3\overline{)30,000}$

(65) $3\overline{)120}$ (66) $5\overline{)450}$ (67) $4\overline{)40,000}$

(68) $7\overline{)4900}$ (69) $6\overline{)4200}$ (70) $4\overline{)80,000}$

(71) $9\overline{)63}$ (72) $4\overline{)3200}$ (73) $4\overline{)160,000}$

(74) $2\overline{)8006}$ (75) $7\overline{)6300}$ (76) $1\overline{)3,987,263}$

◆ **LESSON 123 Division Revisited: Missing Digits**

THINKING STORY

Estimating Is Rough

Part 5

You may wish to review earlier parts of this Thinking Story, on pages 368–369, 376–377, 398–399, and 410–411.

The grocer and some other people went to see Mr. Muddle's boss. "We don't think Mr. Muddle knows how to estimate," said the grocer. "He comes up with answers in nutty ways."

"But his estimates are good," said the boss. "He was very close in his estimate of how many trees to plant on Elm Street."

"He must be lucky, then," said the grocer, "or else he had some help. I'll bet he would have trouble estimating how many eggs are in a dozen!"

"We'll see about that," said the boss. She called in Mr. Muddle and told him to estimate how many eggs are in a dozen.

"That will take some work," said Mr. Muddle. "I'll try to have the estimate for you by tomorrow."

Mr. Muddle thought about how he would make the estimate. "I wish they had just asked me exactly how many eggs are in a dozen," he said. "I could have told them that. Estimating is rough, but I'll think of a way."

He went to the grocery store and bought five dozen eggs, because he knew that you need a good sample to make an estimate. Then he weighed each carton of eggs.

These are the weights that he got:

700 grams   652 grams

664 grams   736 grams

760 grams

"So," said Mr. Muddle, "an average dozen eggs weighs about 702 grams."

Then he weighed one egg from each carton. These are the weights he got:

55 grams   51 grams

52 grams   58 grams

60 grams

"So an average egg weighs about 55 grams," he said. Using his calculator, he divided 702 by 55. The result was 12.763636.

The next day Mr. Muddle told his boss, "I have my estimate. A dozen is about 13 eggs."

"That is close," said the boss. "But I thought you would know there are exactly 12 eggs in a dozen."

"Of course I do," said Mr. Muddle, "but you didn't ask me that. You asked me to estimate."

. . . the end

Work in groups. Discuss your answers and how you figured them out. Then compare your answers with those of other groups.

1 What would you have done if your boss had asked you to estimate how many eggs are in a dozen?

2 Can you be sure that there will always be 12 eggs in a dozen? Why or why not?

3 If you weigh a dozen eggs and divide by the average weight of an egg, what number should you get?

4 Why did Mr. Muddle end up with an estimate of 13 eggs in a dozen?

Unit 5 Review

Divide. Watch for remainders.

Lessons 104,
105, 109

1 $3\overline{)26}$　　**2** $3\overline{)999}$　　　**3** $7\overline{)782}$　　**4** $6\overline{)2964}$

5 $8\overline{)300}$　　**6** $4\overline{)10,000}$　　**7** $5\overline{)386}$　　**8** $3\overline{)2721}$

For each problem, several answers are given, but only one
is correct. Choose the correct answer.

Lessons 118,
122

9 $17\overline{)51}$　　**a.** 2　**b.** 3　**c.** 4　**d.** 5　**e.** 6

10 $39\overline{)468}$　　**a.** 2　**b.** 4　**c.** 12　**d.** 50　**e.** 100

11 $25\overline{)625}$　　**a.** 10　**b.** 15　**c.** 17　**d.** 20　**e.** 25

12 $11\overline{)1342}$　　**a.** 12　**b.** 120　**c.** 121　**d.** 122　**e.** 1202

13 $37\overline{)518}$　　**a.** 11　**b.** 12　**c.** 14　**d.** 24　**e.** 34

ALGEBRA
READINESS

Solve for *n*.

14 $n = 13 - 7$　　**15** $n + 18 = 25$　　**16** $32 \div 8 = n$

Lessons 115,
123

17 $7 + 13 = n$　　**18** $37 - n = 16$　　**19** $4 \times 80 = n$

20 $7 \times 13 = n$　　**21** $n \div 6 = 6$　　**22** $4 = n \div 80$

Find the average of each set of numbers.

Lessons 112,
113

23 7, 10, 5, 0, 8

24 70, 100, 50, 0, 80

25 1000, 2000, 3000, 4000, 5000, 6000

26 Hallie took five spelling tests this month. Her scores were 91,
82, 100, 85, and 92. What was her average score for the
five tests?

List the factors of the following numbers.

Lesson 119　**27** 15　　　**28** 12　　　**29** 11　　　**30** 16

Solve these problems.

31 Mr. Mora drove 792 kilometers in nine hours. What was his average speed?

Lessons 108, 111–113, 115, 122

32 Daniel mows lawns and gets paid $5 for each hour he works. He worked four hours on Saturday and three hours on Sunday. How much did he earn for the two days?

33 Shannon has $3. Does she have enough money to buy six notepads that cost 79¢ each?

34 Robbie wants to skate 50 kilometers this week. He skated 7 kilometers each day from Monday to Saturday. How many kilometers must he skate on Sunday to reach his goal?

35 Lola is setting up chairs for a show. She sets up nine rows with seven chairs in each row and one row of eight chairs. How many people can be seated for the show?

36 Terry is growing a bean plant. On Monday the plant was 8 centimeters tall. On Friday the plant was 16 centimeters tall. How much did the plant grow between Monday and Friday?

37 Janelle works part-time at a grocery store. The hours she worked for each of the past seven weeks were 18, 23, 11, 16, 25, 17, and 16. About what is the average number of hours she works in a week?

Jason takes care of a dolphin named Finny at an aquarium. He feeds Finny 3 kilograms of fish a day.

38 How much fish does Finny eat in a week?

39 A kilogram of fish costs $5.71. How much does it cost the aquarium to feed Finny each week?

40 Gretchen has $40 to spend on her sister's birthday present. Does she have enough money to buy two sweaters that cost $21 each?

LESSON 125

Unit 5 Practice

Lessons 104, 105, 109

Divide. Watch for remainders.

① 3)72   ② 6)922   ③ 3)805   ④ 7)625

⑤ 5)75   ⑥ 2)713   ⑦ 4)209   ⑧ 4)280

⑨ 5)325   ⑩ 7)600   ⑪ 9)263   ⑫ 3)725

⑬ 3)74   ⑭ 8)735   ⑮ 5)211   ⑯ 6)2345

⑰ 4)62   ⑱ 2)1063   ⑲ 2)603   ⑳ 6)1005

Lessons 118, 122

Choose the correct answer for each problem.

㉑ 10)400   **a.** 4   **b.** 20   **c.** 30   **d.** 40   **e.** 50

㉒ 100)6000   **a.** 6   **b.** 30   **c.** 60   **d.** 300   **e.** 600

㉓ 12)63   **a.** 5 R2 **b.** 5   **c.** 5 R3 **d.** 5 R4 **e.** 5 R1

㉔ 18)108   **a.** 5   **b.** 6   **c.** 7   **d.** 8   **e.** 9

Lessons 106, 107, 116, 123

Find the missing digit.

㉕
```
    5▇
5)260
  25
   10
```

㉖
```
   4▇5 R2
3)1217
  12
   17
   15
    2
```

㉗
```
    70
7)4▇0
  49
```

㉘
```
   1▇0
5)550
  5
   5
   5
```

Solve for n. Watch the signs.

㉙ $n + 5 = 8$ ㉚ $5 \times n = 35$ ㉛ $3 \times n = 9$

Lessons 115, 123

㉜ $16 \div n = 8$ ㉝ $n \div 4 = 6$ ㉞ $243 \div 9 = n$

㉟ $47 - n = 28$ ㊱ $2 \times 2 = n$ ㊲ $n = 64 \times 32$

Lesson 115

Solve.

㊳ How many milliliters are there in 10 liters?

㊴ How many liters are there in 4000 milliliters?

㊵ How many cups are there in 64 fluid ounces?

Lessons 112, 113 Find the average for each set of numbers.

41 10, 10, 10, 10, 10

42 8, 9, 10, 11, 12

43 18, 19, 20, 21, 22

44 10, 20, 30, 40, 50, 60

45 6, 8, 9, 8, 14

46 8, 10, 11, 10, 16

Solve.

Lessons 108, 111–113, 115, 122

47 Nick drove 650 kilometers in ten hours. Mallory drove 495 kilometers in seven hours.

   a. What was Nick's average speed?

   b. What was Mallory's average speed?

   c. How much farther did Nick drive than Mallory?

48 Angelo weighed 50 kilograms at the beginning of September. He gained 3 kilograms during September. Then he lost 5 kilograms during October. How much did Angelo weigh at the end of October?

49 When Juli was two years old, she was 75 centimeters tall. During the next 18 years, her height doubled. How tall was she at the age of 20?

50 Penny bought two pads of paper that cost 38¢ each. She was charged 80¢ for the two pads, including tax.

   a. How much was the tax?

   b. If Penny paid with a $1 bill, how much change should she have gotten?

51 Tim and Paul put their dogs on a scale at the same time. Together, the dogs weighed 42 pounds. What was their average weight?

◆ **LESSON 125 Unit 5 Practice**

Lessons 108, 111, 112, 115, 122 Carmen wants to earn money to buy a VCR that costs $440. She made a chart to show how many hours she would have to work to earn the money.

Help Carmen complete the chart. Then answer the questions.

52 Use a computer or other means to draw the chart and complete it.

If I Make This Much per Hour	In 40 Hours I Will Make	In 60 Hours I Will Make	In 100 Hours I Will Make
$3.50 (350¢)	$140.00	■	■
$4.50 (450¢)	$180.00	■	■
$5.00 (500¢)	$200.00	■	■
$5.50 (550¢)	$220.00	■	■

53 Will Carmen earn enough money for the VCR if she works for 60 hours at $5.50 per hour?

54 Will she earn enough if she works for 100 hours at $3.50 per hour?

55 Will she earn enough if she works for 100 hours at $4.50 per hour?

56 **Challenge:** How many hours must Carmen work to buy the VCR if she earns

    a. $3.50 per hour?   **b.** $4.50 per hour?

    c. $5.00 per hour?   **d.** $5.50 per hour?

Answer the questions based on the following set of numbers.

2, 7, 7, 6, 7, 4, 2, 1

Lesson 113 57 What is the mode?   58 What is the median?

Lessons 108, 111–113, 115, 122

Solve these problems.

Mr. Ramirez has a solid fence that is 100 meters long and 2 meters high. He wants to paint both sides of the fence. He has the following recipe for making his own whitewash.

Whitewash (for 200 square meters)	
Table salt	2 pounds
Water	1 gallon
Hydrated lime	6 pounds
Dissolve the salt in the water.	
Then add the lime slowly as you stir.	

59 How much of each will Mr. Ramirez need?

   a. Table salt

   b. Water

   c. Hydrated lime

60 Mr. Ramirez went to the store and found out that table salt costs $1.30 per pound and hydrated lime costs $1.80 per pound. How much money will he have to spend for both of these items to make enough whitewash for his fence?

Unit Test

Divide. Watch for remainders.

1 7)42 **2** 3)82 **3** 8)100 **4** 5)168

5 5)317 **6** 9)99 **7** 4)13,476 **8** 6)274

9 6)312 **10** 2)76 **11** 7)147 **12** 9)385

Choose the correct answer for each problem.

13 12)36 **a.** 3 **b.** 4 **c.** 5 **d.** 6 **e.** 7

14 15)105 **a.** 3 **b.** 4 **c.** 5 **d.** 6 **e.** 7

15 24)144 **a.** 3 **b.** 4 **c.** 5 **d.** 6 **e.** 7

Solve for n.

16 $n = 15 + 3$ **17** $42 + 7 = n$ **18** $13 + n = 17$

19 $n = 15 - 3$ **20** $24 = n \times 8$ **21** $n - 7 = 15$

22 $42 \div 7 = n$ **23** $24 = n \div 8$ **24** $6 \times 7 = n$

Find the average for each set of numbers.

25 8, 9, 10, 11, 12 **26** 80, 90, 100, 110, 120

27 5, 23, 12, 11, 15, 16, 9 **28** 7, 9, 11, 124, 15

Answer the questions using the following set of numbers.

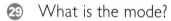
1, 1, 3, 1, 2, 4, 6

29 What is the mode? **30** What is the median?

Solve these problems.

31 Ellie bowled three games and got scores of 145, 132, and 129. Could her average score be 129?

32 Dan got these scores on four math tests: 92, 84, 79, and 89. What was his average score for the four tests?

33 Annie has $1 and wants to buy three postcards that cost 29¢ each. Does she have enough money?

34 Reggie gets paid a certain amount for each hour he works. Today he worked six hours and earned $36. How much money does he earn in an hour?

35 Mr. Byrd needs 45 hamburger rolls for a cookout. The rolls come in packages of eight. How many packages does he need?

36 How many gallons are there in 36 quarts?

37 How many milliliters are there in 6 liters?

38 Laura bought a pen for 39¢ and a ruler for 49¢. The storekeeper charged her 93¢ for the two items, including tax. How much was the tax?

39 Cheryl's puppy weighed 4 pounds last month and 5 pounds today. How much weight did the puppy gain during the month?

40 Cal is painting his garage. The area of one wall is 43 square meters. One can of paint covers 8 square meters. How many cans of paint does Cal need to paint this side of his garage?

The Broad-Jump Contest

Mary and her track team, the Lancers, competed in a broad-jump contest. They each made one jump. They recorded the results in the chart below.

NAME	DISTANCE JUMPED (IN CENTIMETERS)
Mary	170
Justin	115
Elise	121
Clark	181
Hannah	182
Lisette	110
Bill	30
Matt	100

Hannah was declared the winner of the group.

❶ Can you be sure that Hannah is the best broad-jumper?

❷ What is another way to have a fair contest?

The Lancers realized that one jump was not enough.
They changed the contest to allow each athlete to jump three times.

Here are the results of the new contest.

NAME	DISTANCE JUMPED (IN CENTIMETERS)		
	FIRST JUMP	SECOND JUMP	THIRD JUMP
Mary	167	173	182
Justin	121	118	109
Elise	118	148	156
Clark	184	156	188
Hannah	182	183	186
Lisette	115	107	122
Bill	181	190	42
Matt	122	119	137

Answer these questions.

3 Which Lancers improved their score after every jump?

4 Which Lancers scored higher on their second jump than on their first jump?

5 Who had the lowest score on the first jump? The second? The third?

Work in small groups. Who do you think should be declared the winner? Write the reasons why you believe your choice is fair.

Design your own contest. Discuss ways to make it fair.

6

Fractions and Decimals

APPLICATIONS IN MEASUREMENT

- probability
- adding and subtracting fractions
- rounding decimals
- multiplying and dividing decimals
- length, width, and volume

SCHOOL TO WORK CONNECTION

Zookeepers use math . . .

A zookeeper measures how much a baby animal eats, how much it weighs, and how much it grows. These measurements are often recorded in fractions or decimals so that they are very accurate. If an animal is not growing at a proper rate, the zookeeper will notice that there is a problem and can get help for the animal.

LESSON 126

Writing Appropriate Fractions

Answer the question using the figures below.

What fraction of each of the following figures has been shaded?

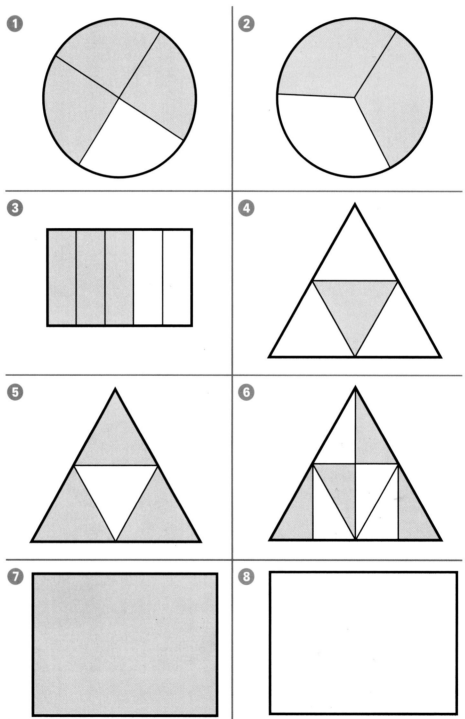

Answer the question using the pictures below.

What fraction of each of the following sets has a ring around it?

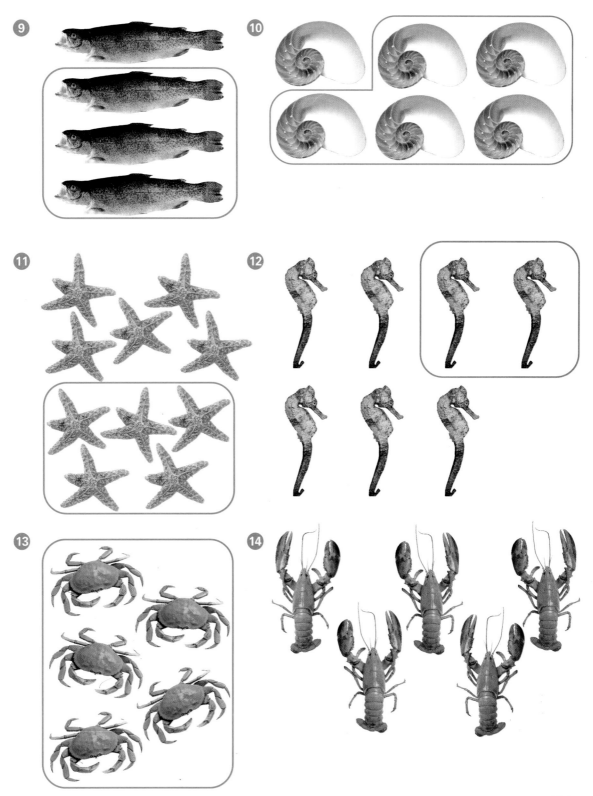

Fractions of Whole Numbers

In this lesson you will find the fraction of a number.

$\frac{2}{3}$ of 24 = ?

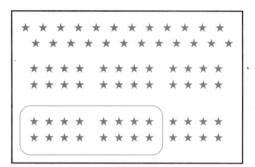

Divide 24 into 3 equal parts. $3\overline{)24}$ with 8 above

Then take 2 parts. $2 \times 8 = 16$

So $\frac{2}{3}$ of 24 is 16.

Remember: The bottom part (**denominator**) of a fraction tells how many equal parts to divide something into. The top part (**numerator**) of a fraction tells how many of those parts to take.

$\frac{2}{3}$ — numerator / denominator

2 — numerator
3 — denominator

Solve these problems.

1. Paige has gone about $\frac{1}{4}$ of the way to Seattle, which is 120 miles away. About how many miles has she traveled?

2. Grant is reading a magazine that is 75 pages long. He has read 55 pages. Has he read more than $\frac{2}{3}$ of the magazine?

3. A video that usually sells for $24 is on sale for $\frac{1}{3}$ off.

   a. How much is $\frac{1}{3}$ of 24?

   b. What is the sale price of the video?

4. A jar that can hold 300 milliliters of water is about $\frac{2}{3}$ full. About how many milliliters of water are in the jar?

Solve.

5. $\frac{1}{2}$ of 12   6. $\frac{1}{4}$ of 20   7. $\frac{1}{5}$ of 100   8. $\frac{3}{10}$ of 100   9. $\frac{2}{3}$ of 24

10. $\frac{1}{3}$ of 9   11. $\frac{1}{2}$ of 20   12. $\frac{3}{5}$ of 100   13. $\frac{3}{10}$ of 50   14. $\frac{1}{8}$ of 24

15. $\frac{2}{3}$ of 9   16. $\frac{3}{4}$ of 20   17. $\frac{1}{6}$ of 36   18. $\frac{2}{3}$ of 30   19. $\frac{3}{8}$ of 24

GAME

Fractions of 60 Game

Players:	Two or more
Materials:	Two 0–5 cubes
Object:	To score a total of 150 or more
Math Focus:	Finding fractions of a number and adding

RULES

1. Roll both cubes. Combine the numbers rolled to make a fraction no greater than 1.

2. Find that fraction of 60 and write the answer.

3. Add the answer to your last score.

4. If you roll one 0, your score for that turn is 0. If you roll two 0s together, roll both cubes again.

5. The first player whose score totals 150 or more is the winner.

If you rolled:	You would take:	Your answer would be:
2 3	$\frac{2}{3}$ of 60	40
0 4	$\frac{0}{4}$ of 60	0
2 2	$\frac{2}{2}$ of 60	60

OTHER WAYS TO PLAY THIS GAME

1. Try to score a different total.

2. Change the game to "Fractions of 120."

In your Math Journal explain your strategy for playing this game.

MATH JOURNAL

LESSON 128

Probability

A **probability** is a number that tells what fraction of the time something is expected to happen.

◆ If you flip a coin, what is the probability that it will land heads up?

◆ What is the probability that a coin will land tails up?

◆ What is the probability that a coin will land on its edge?

Even though the coin might land on its edge, this event is so unlikely that we don't usually consider it. So we expect that about half the time the coin will land heads up and the other half of the time the coin will land tails up. Nothing else is likely to happen.

If something cannot possibly happen, the probability is 0. If something is certain to happen, the probability is 1.

Answer these questions.

1. If you guess an answer on a true-false test, what do you think is the probability that you'll get the right answer?

2. If you roll a 0–5 cube, what is the probability that you will roll a 7?

3. If you roll a 0–5 cube, what is the probability that you will roll a number less than 7?

4. If you roll a 0–5 cube, what is the probability that you will roll an even number?

5. If you roll a 0–5 cube, what is the probability that you will roll an odd number?

6. Suppose you put four red chips and six white chips in a hat. You draw one of them out without looking. What is the probability that the chip you draw will be red?

For each of the following spinners, give the probability that the pointer will stop on red.

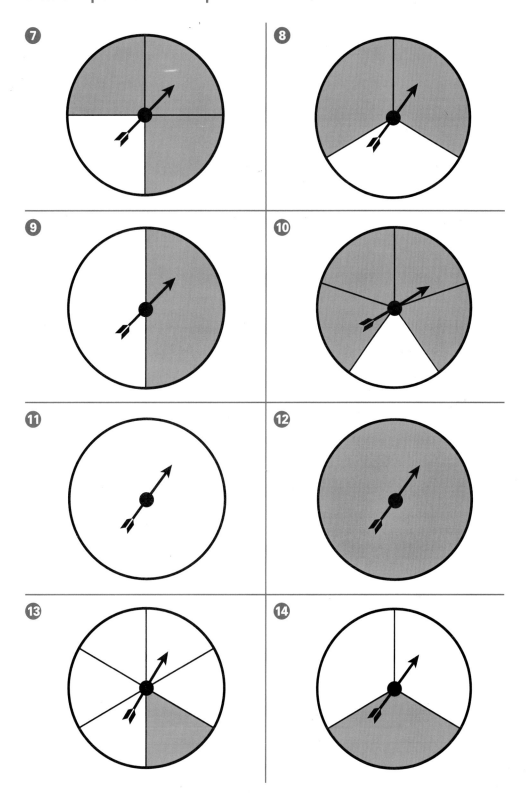

7

8

9

10

11

12

13

14

Fractions and Probability

Jimmy and Naomi are rolling a 0–5 cube. Jimmy wins if a 0 is rolled. Naomi wins if a 1, 2, 3, 4, or 5 is rolled.

◆ Who do you think will win more often?

◆ What fraction of the time do you think Jimmy will win?

◆ If they roll the cube 6 times, how many times would you expect Jimmy to win? What is $\frac{1}{6}$ of 6?

◆ Would you be surprised if Jimmy did not win exactly 1 time out of 6 tries?

Jimmy's probability of winning is $\frac{1}{6}$.

◆ What is Naomi's probability of winning?

Here's an experiment Jimmy did with his class.

Each student rolled a 0–5 cube six times. Each person kept track of how many times he or she rolled 0 in the six tries. Then Jimmy made a chart to show how many people didn't roll a 0 at all, how many rolled one 0, and so on.

Number of Times 0 Was Rolled in Six Tries	Number of People
0	10
1	12
2	6
3	2
4	0
5	0
6	0

◆ How many people took part in Jimmy's experiment?

◆ How many people in the class rolled a 0

a. 1 out of 6 times? **b.** 2 out of 6 times? **c.** 3 out of 6 times?

d. 4 out of 6 times? **e.** 5 out of 6 times? **f.** 0 out of 6 times?

Try an experiment like Jimmy's in your class, but use a 5–10 cube instead. Each person should roll the cube six times and write down how many times he or she rolls an 8. Then put the results in a chart like Jimmy's.

Answer these questions.

① Does your chart look exactly like Jimmy's?

② In what ways is your chart similar to Jimmy's?

③ How many people in Jimmy's class rolled a 0 either 4, 5, or 6 times?

④ How many people in your class rolled an 8 either 4, 5, or 6 times?

⑤ More than $\frac{2}{3}$ of the people in Jimmy's class rolled a 0 either 0 times or 1 time. Did most of the people in your class roll an 8 either 0 times or 1 time?

LESSON 130

Applying Fractions

Use your understanding of finding fractions of numbers to solve these problems.

1 The city council can vote only if at least $\frac{5}{6}$ of its members are present. The city council has 18 members. How many members must be present for a vote to take place?

2 About $\frac{1}{7}$ of the total population is left-handed. There are 21 students in Ellen's class.

   a. About how many students in her class might be left-handed?

   b. Would you be surprised if your answer was not exactly right?

3 Winston has nine cousins, and $\frac{2}{3}$ of them are boys. How many of his cousins are girls?

4 Tasha can save $\frac{1}{4}$ of the cost of a chemistry set if she waits until it goes on sale. How much will a $28 chemistry set cost on sale?

5 Chip's doctor said that $\frac{3}{5}$ of all schoolchildren get two colds every winter.

   a. How many students in a class of 30 might Chip expect to have two colds this winter?

   b. Could Chip be sure of exactly how many classmates would have two colds?

Solve. Watch your numbering.

6 What is $\frac{2}{3}$ of 30?

7 What is $\frac{3}{3}$ of 30?

8 What is $\frac{0}{3}$ of 30?

9 What is $\frac{1}{6}$ of 30?

10 What is $\frac{3}{6}$ of 30?

11 What is $\frac{4}{6}$ of 30?

12 What is $\frac{5}{6}$ of 30?

13 What is $\frac{6}{6}$ of 30?

◆ Compare your answers to problems 6 and 11. Why are they the same?

Anything but 10 Game

Players:	Two or more
Materials:	One 0–5 cube, one 5–10 cube
Object:	To score a total of 100 or more
Math Focus:	Addition and mathematical reasoning

RULES

1. Roll both cubes. Find the sum of the two numbers rolled.

2. If the sum is not 10, you get the number of points rolled. Keep your turn and roll again, or stop and add those points to your score.

3. On each turn you may have as many rolls as you like until you either roll a sum of 10 or choose to stop.

4. When you roll a sum of 10, you lose your turn and you lose any other points you may have had on that turn.

5. The first player to score 100 or over is the winner.

SAMPLE GAME

Round	Janice Rolls:	Sum	Score	Austin Rolls:	Sum	Score
1	7 5	12		9 4	13	
	5 4	9		6 2	8	21
	10 5	15	36	Stops		
	Stops					
2	8 3	11		10 4	14	
	7 0	7		8 3	11	
	6 4	10	36	7 1	8	54
	Loses turn			Stops		

After two rounds, Austin is ahead.

LESSON 131

Equivalent Fractions: Probability

Solve these problems.

Andre and Emma are rolling a 0–5 cube. When it shows 0 or 1, Andre wins. When it shows 2, 3, 4, or 5, Emma wins.

1 What is the probability that Andre will win?

2 What is the probability that Emma will win?

3 Suppose Andre and Emma play their game 120 times.

    a. About how many times would you expect Andre to win?

    b. About how many times would you expect Emma to win?

    c. Would you be surprised if Andre did not win exactly 40 times?

They change their game so that Emma wins if the cube shows 5, 4, or 3. Andre wins if it shows 2, 1, or 0.

4 What is the probability that Emma will win?

5 What is the probability that Andre will win?

6 Suppose they play the new game 120 times.

    a. About how many times would you expect Emma to win?

    b. About how many times would you expect Andre to win?

    c. Would you be surprised if Emma did not win exactly 60 times?

Skyler and Mackenzie flip a coin. Skyler will win if it lands heads up. Mackenzie will win if it lands tails up.

7 What is the probability that Skyler will win?

8 If they play 120 times, about how many games would you expect Skyler to win?

9 Compare your answers for problems 6 and 8. (Compare $\frac{3}{6}$ of 120 and $\frac{1}{2}$ of 120.)

10 Which probability is greater, $\frac{3}{6}$ or $\frac{1}{2}$?

11 What is the probability of landing on red if you

    a. spin spinner A?   **b.** spin spinner B?

12 Which spinner gives you a better chance of landing on red?

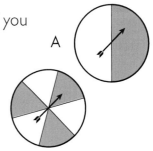

What fraction of the circle is shaded?

13   **14**   **15**  **16**

17 Which is greater, $\frac{1}{4}$ of the circle or $\frac{1}{2}$ of the circle?

18 Which is greater, $\frac{3}{4}$ of the circle or $\frac{1}{2}$ of the circle?

What fraction of the rectangle is shaded?

19  **20** 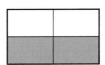 **21**

Draw five rectangles that are each 4 centimeters long and 3 centimeters wide.

22 What is the area of each rectangle you drew?

Shade $\frac{1}{2}$ of each rectangle in a different way.

23 What is the area of the shaded part of each rectangle?

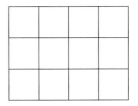

Draw three more rectangles that are each 4 centimeters long and 3 centimeters wide. Shade $\frac{2}{4}$ of each rectangle in a different way.

24 What is the area of the shaded part of each rectangle?

25 Why do you think the answers to questions 23 and 24 are the same?

LESSON 132

Equivalent Fractions

Mark and Chet bought a pizza. It was cut into eight equal pieces. Mark ate two of the pieces. Chet said, "You ate two eighths of the pizza." Mark said, "No, I didn't. I ate only one fourth of the pizza."

◆ Who is right?

There are many different ways to write a fraction. In this example both Mark and Chet are right. Mark ate 2 of the 8 equal pieces, so he ate $\frac{2}{8}$ of the pizza. But if the pizza had been cut into only 4 equal pieces, he could have eaten just 1 piece and still have eaten the same amount. He would have eaten $\frac{1}{4}$ of the pizza.

Answer these questions.

1 If the pizza had been cut into 12 equal pieces, how many would Mark have had to eat to equal $\frac{1}{4}$ of the pizza?

2 If the pizza had been cut into 40 equal pieces, how many would Mark have had to eat to equal $\frac{1}{4}$ of the pizza?

You might not think that 10 tiny pieces, each $\frac{1}{40}$ of the pizza, are as satisfying as $\frac{2}{8}$ of the pizza. Still, the two fractions are equal. We say that $\frac{1}{4}$, $\frac{2}{8}$, $\frac{3}{12}$, and $\frac{10}{40}$ are all **equivalent fractions.** We show this by writing = between them:

$$\frac{1}{4} = \frac{2}{8} = \frac{3}{12} = \frac{10}{40}$$

Solve.

3 Write a fraction with a denominator of 20 that is equivalent to $\frac{3}{4}$.

4 Write a fraction with a denominator of 60 that is equivalent to $\frac{5}{12}$.

When comparing two fractions it is helpful to have fractions with the same denominator. You can always use the product of the two denominators as the new denominator for both fractions.

Example: $\dfrac{3}{4} \bullet \dfrac{1}{3} = \dfrac{9}{12} \bullet \dfrac{4}{12}$

We know that $\dfrac{9}{12}$ is greater than $\dfrac{4}{12}$, so $\dfrac{9}{12} > \dfrac{4}{12}$. Often you can find a lesser denominator that will work.

Convert each fraction to one that is equivalent but has a denominator of 12.

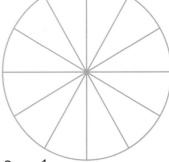

5 $\dfrac{1}{2}$ **6** $\dfrac{3}{4}$ **7** $\dfrac{4}{6}$

8 $\dfrac{1}{3}$ **9** $\dfrac{5}{6}$ **10** $\dfrac{3}{6}$

11 $\dfrac{1}{4}$ **12** $\dfrac{3}{6}$ **13** $\dfrac{2}{6}$

14 $\dfrac{1}{6}$ **15** $\dfrac{2}{4}$ **16** $\dfrac{3}{6}$

17 $\dfrac{2}{3}$ **18** $\dfrac{2}{8}$ **19** $\dfrac{4}{6}$

Show which fraction of the circle is larger or whether they are the same. Replace ● with <, >, or =.

20 $\dfrac{1}{6} \bullet \dfrac{1}{4}$ **21** $\dfrac{5}{6} \bullet \dfrac{2}{4}$ **22** $\dfrac{1}{2} \bullet \dfrac{6}{12}$ **23** $\dfrac{3}{4} \bullet \dfrac{1}{2}$

24 $\dfrac{2}{4} \bullet \dfrac{1}{2}$ **25** $\dfrac{6}{12} \bullet \dfrac{2}{4}$ **26** $\dfrac{7}{12} \bullet \dfrac{1}{4}$ **27** $\dfrac{5}{12} \bullet \dfrac{1}{2}$

28 $\dfrac{2}{4} \bullet \dfrac{3}{4}$ **29** $\dfrac{1}{3} \bullet \dfrac{5}{6}$ **30** $\dfrac{4}{8} \bullet \dfrac{2}{3}$ **31** $\dfrac{6}{9} \bullet \dfrac{2}{4}$

32 $\dfrac{2}{12} \bullet \dfrac{1}{3}$ **33** $\dfrac{6}{7} \bullet \dfrac{3}{4}$ **34** $\dfrac{8}{9} \bullet \dfrac{2}{3}$ **35** $\dfrac{3}{6} \bullet \dfrac{1}{2}$

◆ **LESSON 132** Equivalent Fractions

Replace ● with <, >, or =.

36 $\frac{1}{4}$ ● $\frac{4}{12}$ **37** $\frac{7}{8}$ ● $\frac{3}{4}$ **38** $\frac{2}{3}$ ● $\frac{1}{2}$ **39** $\frac{1}{6}$ ● $\frac{1}{12}$

40 $\frac{5}{6}$ ● $\frac{10}{12}$ **41** $\frac{2}{3}$ ● $\frac{2}{6}$ **42** $\frac{1}{2}$ ● $\frac{3}{8}$ **43** $\frac{5}{8}$ ● $\frac{1}{2}$

44 $\frac{3}{6}$ ● $\frac{1}{2}$ **45** $\frac{3}{4}$ ● $\frac{9}{12}$

Solve.

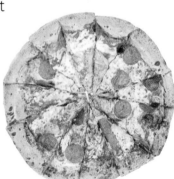

46 Which is bigger, $\frac{1}{2}$ of the big pie or $\frac{1}{2}$ of the small pie?

47 Mrs. Packard had $36. She spent $\frac{1}{3}$ of the money on a pair of earrings. How much did the earrings cost?

48 Ricky read $\frac{2}{3}$ of a 250-page book, and Ramona read $\frac{2}{3}$ of a 150-page book.

  a. Who read more pages?

  b. Who read more words?

49 There are 16 tomato plants in a tray. Jenna planted $\frac{3}{4}$ of them. How many did she plant?

50 Linda mowed $\frac{1}{2}$ of her yard. Jeremy mowed $\frac{2}{3}$ of his yard, which is the same size as Linda's. Who mowed more?

51 Rachel and Jeremy want to share a pizza that has been sliced into 12 pieces. If Rachel eats five pieces, will she have eaten more or less than $\frac{1}{2}$ of the pizza?

52 Eli can save $4 each week. How much can he save in one year (52 weeks)?

53 Tiffany can save $6 each week. How much can she save in one year?

54 Lance has $10.00. He wants to buy a belt for $8.57 and a comic book for $2.00. Does he have enough money?

55 Noelle has 35 meters of fencing. If she builds a garden with an area of 36 square meters, is it possible that she has enough fencing to enclose it?

56 Spencer has a stack of baseball cards. Eve has a stack four times as high as Spencer's. How many baseball cards does Spencer have?

57 Brent's garden is shaped like a rectangle. It is 10 meters long and 8 meters wide. Denise's garden is shaped like a square. Each side measures 9 meters.

   a. Whose garden has the larger area?

   b. How much larger?

58 Dean earns $5.75 per hour. He works 40 hours each week. How much money does he earn in one year (52 weeks)?

59 A play lasts 2 hours and 35 minutes. If the play starts at 8:15 P.M., what time will it end?

60 Half the children in Jordan's class are girls. How many children are in his class?

61 Virginia has $239.40 in her checking account. She deposits $148.00 and then writes a check for $239.40. How much money is left in her account?

Mixed Numbers

Mr. Cheng baked four loaves of bread. His children ate half of one loaf. Mr. Cheng had three and one-half loaves left.

Before   **After**

We can write three and one half as $3\frac{1}{2}$.

Evan is slicing cucumbers for a salad. He started with six cucumbers. He had sliced four whole cucumbers and one third of another when the doorbell rang. He had one and two-thirds cucumbers left to slice when he returned to the kitchen.

Before   **After**

We can write one and two thirds as $1\frac{2}{3}$.

Miss Batra bought five bags of popcorn for her movie theater. Last night she used three whole bags and three fourths of another. Miss Batra had one and one-fourth bags left.

Before   **After**

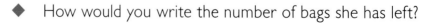

◆   How would you write the number of bags she has left?

An albatross is a huge seabird that can fly up to 25 miles per hour, and can even sleep while flying!

Write a mixed number to show how many.

❶ ▇ pizzas

❷ ▇ dollars

❸ ▇ apples

❹ ▇ glasses of juice

**In each case write *yes* if the last sentence is true.
Write *no* if it isn't true and explain why.**

❺ Dustin has a guitar lesson at 5:30 P.M. At 3:00 P.M. he said, "My guitar lesson starts in $2\frac{1}{2}$ hours."

❻ A can of frozen orange juice makes enough juice for six glasses. Deborah used one can to make a pitcher of orange juice. She drank $3\frac{1}{2}$ glasses for breakfast. There are $3\frac{1}{2}$ glasses of orange juice left.

❼ DeDe works $3\frac{3}{4}$ hours every day at a hardware store. Today she could have worked two hours before dinner and $1\frac{3}{4}$ hours after dinner.

❽ Sonia told Jay to meet her in $1\frac{1}{2}$ hours. Jay showed up on time 90 minutes later.

◆ **LESSON 133 Mixed Numbers**

A fraction with a numerator greater than its denominator is called an **improper fraction.** For example, $\frac{13}{6}$ is an improper fraction.

Sometimes a mixed number is easier to work with than an improper fraction. Sometimes an improper fraction is easier to work with than a mixed number.

To change $\frac{13}{6}$ to a mixed number, ask how many whole units there are in $\frac{13}{6}$. (How many times does 6 go into 13?) The answer is 2. What's left over? 1 is left over. So $\frac{13}{6}$ and $2\frac{1}{6}$ are the same number.

How many sixths are shaded in the picture below? From the picture, can you see that $\frac{13}{6}$ and $2\frac{1}{6}$ are the same number?

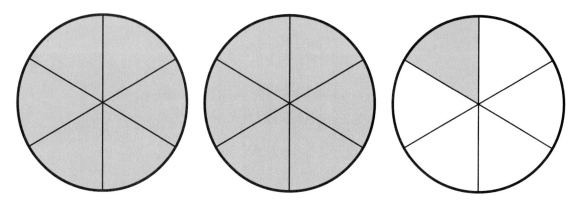

Change each improper fraction to a mixed number, or, if possible, to a whole number.

9 $\frac{5}{2}$ **10** $\frac{5}{4}$ **11** $\frac{8}{6}$ **12** $\frac{7}{5}$ **13** $\frac{15}{7}$ **14** $\frac{29}{3}$

15 $\frac{8}{7}$ **16** $\frac{7}{4}$ **17** $\frac{11}{6}$ **18** $\frac{28}{5}$ **19** $\frac{17}{8}$ **20** $\frac{21}{3}$

21 $\frac{20}{5}$ **22** $\frac{13}{4}$ **23** $\frac{4}{3}$ **24** $\frac{7}{6}$ **25** $\frac{24}{8}$ **26** $\frac{16}{5}$

27 $\frac{17}{3}$ **28** $\frac{11}{5}$ **29** $\frac{12}{3}$ **30** $\frac{21}{6}$ **31** $\frac{25}{8}$ **32** $\frac{26}{8}$

If you wish to change a mixed number to an improper fraction, you reverse the process.

To change $2\frac{1}{6}$ to an improper fraction, ask how many sixths there are in 2 (you can count on the figure on the previous page, or just multiply 2 by 6). The answer is 12. So $2\frac{1}{6}$ is the same as $\frac{12}{6}$ plus $\frac{1}{6}$, or $\frac{13}{6}$.

Change each mixed number to an improper fraction.

33. $2\frac{5}{6}$ 34. $4\frac{1}{3}$ 35. $3\frac{1}{6}$ 36. $4\frac{3}{5}$ 37. $6\frac{5}{9}$

38. $2\frac{5}{7}$ 39. $3\frac{1}{4}$ 40. $3\frac{5}{6}$ 41. $5\frac{3}{8}$ 42. $2\frac{3}{8}$

43. $4\frac{3}{4}$ 44. $1\frac{2}{5}$ 45. $2\frac{1}{7}$ 46. $8\frac{3}{5}$ 47. $4\frac{5}{6}$

48. $1\frac{1}{2}$ 49. $1\frac{3}{5}$ 50. $7\frac{1}{2}$ 51. $6\frac{5}{8}$ 52. $1\frac{3}{5}$

53. $3\frac{2}{3}$ 54. $1\frac{4}{5}$ 55. $5\frac{3}{4}$ 56. $8\frac{5}{6}$ 57. $2\frac{1}{9}$

Solve these problems.

58. Kendra has four red markers and one green marker. What fraction of her markers are red?

59. Tony used two eggs to make his breakfast. What part of one dozen eggs did he use?

60. The ski club has 36 members. Some members rent skis, but $\frac{3}{4}$ of the members own skis. How many members own skis?

61. Caroline drank 8 ounces of juice at breakfast. What part of a 64-ounce pitcher of juice did she drink?

62. Christine has 12 rosebushes in her flower garden. Eight of the bushes have yellow roses. What fraction of the rosebushes have yellow roses?

Inches, Feet, and Yards

This pencil is between 3 and 4 inches long.

It is almost halfway between 3 and 4 inches. It is about $3\frac{1}{2}$ inches long.

This piece of chalk is between 2 and 3 inches long. It is about $2\frac{3}{4}$ inches long.

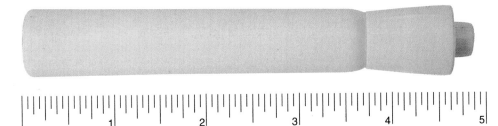

This marker is between 4 and 5 inches long. It is about $4\frac{7}{8}$ inches long.

Remember: 12 inches = 1 foot

36 inches = 3 feet = 1 yard

Answer these questions.

1 How many inches are there in 16 yards?

2 How many inches are there in 10 feet?

3 How many feet are there in 84 inches?

Estimate the length. Then measure to the nearest $\frac{1}{8}$ inch.

Measure.

- How long is your classroom in yards and feet? In feet only?
- How wide is your classroom in yards and feet? In feet only?
- How long is your desk in feet and inches? In inches only?
- How wide is your desk in feet and inches? In inches only?
- How long is the cover of your mathematics book in inches?
- How wide is the cover of your mathematics book in inches?

Adding and Subtracting Fractions of Inches

Corey is putting a bulletin board on his wall. The bulletin board is $\frac{1}{4}$ inch thick. He wants the screws to go through the bulletin board and about $\frac{1}{2}$ inch into the wall. How long a screw should he use?

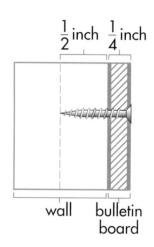

$\frac{1}{2}$ inch $\frac{1}{4}$ inch

wall   bulletin board

Measure to check.

$\frac{1}{2}$ inch $\frac{1}{4}$ inch

Is this $\frac{3}{4}$ inch long?

Corey has a $\frac{3}{4}$-inch wooden plug to fill a hole $\frac{1}{2}$ inch deep. How much must be cut off so that no wood sticks out of the hole?

Measure to check.

$\frac{3}{4}$ inch

$\frac{1}{2}$ inch

Is this $\frac{1}{4}$ inch?

A person uses 72 different muscles in order to talk.

Figure out each answer. Then draw line segments and measure to check.

1. $\frac{1}{4}$ inch + $\frac{1}{4}$ inch

2. $\frac{3}{8}$ inch + $\frac{3}{8}$ inch

3. 2 inches − $\frac{1}{4}$ inch

4. 1 inch − $\frac{5}{8}$ inch

5. $1\frac{1}{2}$ inches + $1\frac{1}{8}$ inches

6. $\frac{3}{4}$ inch + $\frac{1}{2}$ inch

7. $\frac{3}{4}$ inch − $\frac{1}{2}$ inch

Solve these problems.

8. Kurt rode his horse for two hours yesterday and $\frac{3}{4}$ hour today. How many hours did he ride during the past two days?

9. Dinah placed a box that is $\frac{3}{4}$ foot tall on another box that is $\frac{1}{4}$ foot tall. How tall are the two boxes together?

10. Cathy had $2\frac{1}{2}$ dollars. She gave a quarter to Brad. How much money does Cathy have now?

11. Pauline had $1\frac{1}{2}$ pounds of trail mix. She gave her sister $\frac{1}{4}$ pound. How much does she have left?

12. Ben had 4 dollars. He spent $\frac{1}{2}$ dollar for a soda and 2 dollars for a bumper sticker. How much did he have then?

13. Andrea ran 2 miles on Monday and $2\frac{1}{2}$ miles on Wednesday. How many miles did she run in those two days?

Adding and Subtracting Fractions

To add or subtract fractions with the same denominator, all we need to do is add or subtract the numerators. The denominator will stay the same. For instance, $\frac{5}{8} - \frac{3}{8} = \frac{2}{8}$. If we like, we can reduce $\frac{2}{8}$. So we could say $\frac{5}{8} - \frac{3}{8} = \frac{2}{8} = \frac{1}{4}$.

Most fractions come from measuring things. Most measurements are made using the same measuring instruments. Therefore, we usually add and subtract fractions that have the same denominator.

Sometimes, however, a person who measures with a ruler that is marked in sixteenths of an inch reports the measure in eighths, fourths, or halves. So we might want to add two fractions in which one denominator is a multiple of the other.

Occasionally we want to add fractions with different denominators that aren't multiples of each other. In these cases we convert the fractions to fractions with the same denominator. We then add or subtract the numerators.

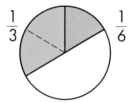

What is $\frac{1}{3} + \frac{1}{6}$? In the figure, $\frac{1}{6}$ of the circle has been shaded, and $\frac{1}{3}$ of the circle has been shaded. If you divide the $\frac{1}{3}$ into two equal parts, each is $\frac{1}{6}$. So we know that $\frac{1}{3}$ is the same as $\frac{2}{6}$. Is that a surprise? How many sixths are shaded in the circle all together?

$$\frac{1}{3} + \frac{1}{6} = \frac{3}{6} \text{ (or } \frac{1}{2}\text{)}$$

If we had wanted to subtract $\frac{1}{4}$ from $\frac{2}{3}$ we would proceed in the same way.

FIGURE 1

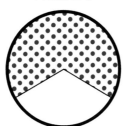

FIGURE 2

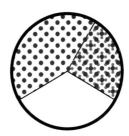

In Figure 1, $\frac{2}{3}$ of the circle has blue dots. In Figure 2, $\frac{1}{4}$ of the circle has blue and red dots. To subtract $\frac{1}{4}$ from $\frac{2}{3}$, notice the part of the circle that has blue dots but not red dots.

From Figure 2, it is hard to decide what part of the circle has only blue dots. However, if we divide Figure 2 into twelve equal parts as shown in Figure 3, then we see that $\frac{2}{3}$ is equivalent to $\frac{8}{12}$, and $\frac{1}{4}$ is equivalent to $\frac{3}{12}$. When we subtract we get $\frac{5}{12}$. Does $\frac{5}{12}$ of Figure 3 have blue dots but not red dots?

FIGURE 3

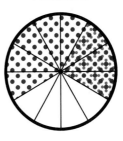

Instead of drawing pictures, you can convert fractions to equivalent fractions with a common denominator. If you multiply a number by 1, does its value change?

Another way to write 1 is $\frac{4}{4}$.   Another way to write 1 is $\frac{3}{3}$.

$$\frac{2}{3} \times \frac{4}{4} = \frac{8}{12} \qquad \frac{1}{4} \times \frac{3}{3} = \frac{3}{12}$$

So, $\frac{2}{3} - \frac{1}{4} = \frac{8}{12} - \frac{3}{12} = \frac{5}{12}$

Solve the following problems.

1. $\frac{1}{8} + \frac{3}{8} = n$

2. $\frac{5}{16} + \frac{1}{4} = n$

3. $\frac{3}{8} + \frac{5}{8} = n$

4. $\frac{3}{4} - \frac{1}{2} = n$

5. $\frac{1}{3} + \frac{1}{8} = n$

6. $\frac{1}{2} - \frac{3}{8} = n$

7. $\frac{7}{16} - \frac{3}{16} = n$

8. $\frac{3}{4} - \frac{2}{3} = n$

9. $\frac{5}{6} - \frac{1}{4} = n$

Adding and Subtracting Mixed Numbers and Improper Fractions

You can add or subtract mixed numbers and improper fractions the same way you add and subtract other fractions. You may want to convert mixed numbers to improper fractions.

For example, $3\frac{1}{7} - 2\frac{2}{3}$ can be changed to $\frac{22}{7} - \frac{8}{3}$. We can rewrite this as $\frac{66}{21} - \frac{56}{21} = \frac{10}{21}$. There are other possible ways you could solve this. Choose whichever one makes the most sense.

Solve the following addition and subtraction problems. Write your answers as mixed numbers, fractions, or whole numbers.

1. $\frac{1}{3} + \frac{5}{3} = n$ 2. $n = 6\frac{2}{3} - 4\frac{1}{7}$ 3. $n = 7\frac{5}{32} - 2\frac{1}{4}$

4. $\frac{1}{3} + 1\frac{2}{3} = n$ 5. $4\frac{1}{5} + 2\frac{3}{10} = n$ 6. $n = 4\frac{4}{16} - 3\frac{1}{4}$

7. $\frac{5}{4} + 7\frac{1}{4} = n$ 8. $3\frac{5}{16} - 1\frac{1}{4} = n$ 9. $2\frac{1}{2} + 7\frac{5}{8} = n$

10. $2 + 1\frac{3}{7} = n$ 11. $n = 2\frac{7}{15} + 3\frac{8}{15}$ 12. $3\frac{5}{12} - 2\frac{1}{6} = n$

13. $\frac{1}{2} - \frac{1}{3} = n$ 14. $4\frac{13}{16} - 3\frac{3}{4} = n$ 15. $n = 4\frac{19}{32} + 3\frac{7}{8}$

16. $7\frac{1}{2} - 2\frac{1}{3} = n$ 17. $5\frac{5}{8} - 3\frac{1}{2} = n$ 18. $3\frac{12}{32} + 6\frac{5}{8} = n$

19. $n = 7\frac{1}{2} - 4\frac{1}{4}$ 20. $n = 5\frac{7}{8} + 2\frac{3}{4}$ 21. $3\frac{1}{2} + 7\frac{3}{8} = n$

Solve these problems.

Wendy is making a cabinet with five drawers. Each drawer of the cabinet will be $3\frac{3}{4}$ inches tall. The base will be $1\frac{1}{2}$ inches tall, and the section above the drawers will be $\frac{7}{8}$ inches tall.

22 How much room is needed for the five drawers?

23 How much room is needed for the base and top section together?

24 How much room is needed for the five drawers, the base, and the top section combined?

Peter made a cake. The recipe for the frosting called for $1\frac{1}{2}$ cups of sugar. The recipe for the cake itself called for $1\frac{2}{3}$ cups of sugar. He wanted to know how much sugar was in the cake, including the frosting.

25 How much sugar was needed all together?

Peter decided the cake and frosting were too sweet, so the next time he put only $\frac{3}{4}$ cup of sugar in the frosting and $1\frac{2}{3}$ cups of sugar in the cake.

26 How much less sugar was in the frosting than before?

27 How much less sugar was in only the cake than before?

28 How much less sugar was in the combined cake and frosting?

Peter decided that the second cake didn't taste as good as he would have liked. He decided to use a sugar substitute. One teaspoon of the substitute $= \frac{1}{3}$ cup of sugar. The next time he made a cake he went back to the original recipe but used the substitute in place of some of the sugar. This was the best cake yet!

29 If Peter uses 3 teaspoons of the substitute in the frosting, how much less sugar should he use? How much regular sugar will he use in the frosting?

30 If he uses 2 teaspoons of the substitute in the cake, how much sugar should he use?

31 With 5 teaspoons of sugar substitute, how much less sugar will he need to use in the cake? How much sugar will be used in the cake and the frosting all together?

UNIT 6

Mid-Unit Review

What fraction of each of the following figures has been shaded?

1    **2**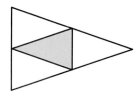

What fraction of each of the following sets has a ring around it?

3    **4**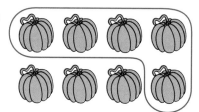

Solve.

5 $\dfrac{1}{2}$ of 18   **6** $\dfrac{1}{3}$ of 12

7 $\dfrac{3}{4}$ of 24   **8** $\dfrac{1}{4}$ of 100

9 $\dfrac{1}{10}$ of 60   **10** $\dfrac{7}{10}$ of 60

11 $\dfrac{4}{5}$ of 45   **12** $\dfrac{5}{6}$ of 48

For each of the following spinners, give the probability that the pointer will stop on red.

13   **14**

Use your understanding of finding fractions of numbers to solve these problems.

15 An election in the camera club only counts if at least $\dfrac{2}{3}$ of the members vote. The camera club has 30 members. How many members must vote for an election to count?

16 About $\frac{6}{7}$ of the total population is right-handed. There are 35 students in Rico's class. About how many students in his class might be right-handed?

17 The in-line skates Jessica wants cost $75. Starting next week, the skates will go on sale for $\frac{1}{3}$ off the regular price. How much will Jessica pay for the skates if she buys them on sale?

18 About $\frac{4}{5}$ of the people who come to Dr. Lieder's dental office each week are there for check-ups. If Dr. Lieder sees 50 patients a week, about how many are there for check-ups?

What fraction of the circle is shaded?

19 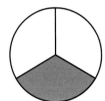   20 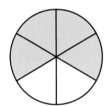   21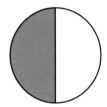

Answer these questions.

22 Which is greater, $\frac{1}{3}$ of the circle or $\frac{1}{6}$ of the circle?

23 Which is greater, $\frac{2}{6}$ of the circle or $\frac{2}{3}$ of the circle?

24 Which is greater, $\frac{3}{6}$ of the circle or $\frac{1}{2}$ of the circle?

Convert each fraction to a fraction that is equivalent but has a denominator of 16.

25 $\frac{1}{2}$ 26 $\frac{1}{4}$ 27 $\frac{1}{8}$ 28 $\frac{2}{4}$

29 $\frac{3}{4}$ 30 $\frac{3}{8}$ 31 $\frac{5}{8}$ 32 $\frac{6}{8}$

Show which fraction of the circle is larger or whether they are the same. Replace ● with <, >, or =.

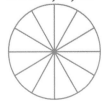

33 $\frac{1}{4}$ ● $\frac{1}{6}$ 34 $\frac{5}{12}$ ● $\frac{1}{2}$ 35 $\frac{1}{3}$ ● $\frac{4}{12}$

◆ **Unit 6 Mid-Unit Review**

Solve.

36 Marty and Marcia share a pizza that is sliced into eight equal pieces. If Marcia eats three pieces, will she have eaten more or less than $\frac{1}{2}$ of the pizza?

37 Kazumi read $\frac{3}{4}$ of a 240-page book, and Ken read $\frac{1}{2}$ of a 210-page book.

  a. Who read more pages?

  b. Who read more sentences?

38 Gabriel saves $5 each week. How much can he save in 40 weeks?

39 Dawn has $20.00. She wants to buy a scarf for $7.98 and a pair of slippers for $13.44. Does she have enough money?

40 Frida has 30 feet of chicken wire. If she builds a pen with an area of 32 square feet, is it possible that she has enough chicken wire to enclose it?

41 A movie lasts 2 hours and 20 minutes. If the movie begins at 3:45 P.M., what time will it end?

42 Jason is $9\frac{1}{2}$ years old. In how many years will he be 18 years old?

Write a mixed number to represent how many are shown.

43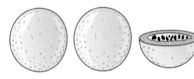

44

Change each improper fraction to a mixed number, or to a whole number, if possible.

45 $\frac{7}{2}$　　**46** $\frac{4}{3}$　　**47** $\frac{9}{6}$　　**48** $\frac{12}{4}$

49 $\frac{27}{5}$　　**50** $\frac{33}{8}$　　**51** $\frac{15}{5}$　　**52** $\frac{23}{5}$

53 $\frac{30}{8}$　　**54** $\frac{10}{4}$　　**55** $\frac{16}{3}$　　**56** $\frac{16}{4}$

Change each mixed number to an improper fraction.

57 $4\frac{1}{2}$　　**58** $1\frac{5}{6}$　　**59** $3\frac{3}{4}$　　**60** $2\frac{1}{3}$

61 $5\frac{5}{6}$　　**62** $6\frac{7}{8}$　　**63** $1\frac{3}{10}$　　**64** $2\frac{4}{7}$

65 $4\frac{4}{9}$　　**66** $9\frac{3}{5}$　　**67** $2\frac{3}{4}$　　**68** $3\frac{2}{3}$

Estimate the length. Then measure to the nearest $\frac{1}{8}$ inch.

69 |———————|

Solve. Write your answers as mixed numbers, fractions, or whole numbers, if possible.

70 $\frac{9}{16} - \frac{3}{16}$

71 $\frac{5}{6} + \frac{1}{4}$

72 $\frac{2}{3} + 3\frac{1}{3}$

73 $6\frac{3}{4} - 2\frac{1}{2}$

74 $4\frac{1}{3} + 3\frac{11}{12}$

75 $3\frac{15}{16} - 1\frac{1}{4}$

Parts of a Whole

"I just made up a game," said June. "What's the least number greater than 0 that you can make?"

"I know," shouted Andy. "It's 1."

"I can do better than that," said Rico. "I say $\frac{1}{2}$."

"That's not fair," said Andy. "We can't use that kind of number."

"It's my game," said June. "Any kind of number is all right. And I'm going to say $\frac{1}{10}$."

"Well," said Andy, "I can make a number that's even less."

◆ Can you make a number less than $\frac{1}{10}$?

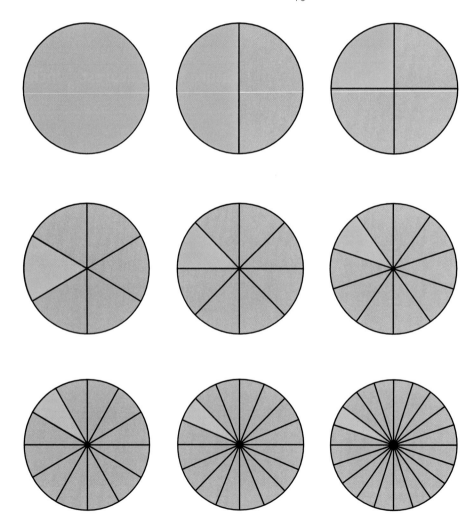

If you divide a whole into ten equal parts, each part is one tenth of the whole.

We can write one tenth in two ways:

As a fraction: $\dfrac{1}{10}$

As a decimal: 0.1

$\dfrac{1}{10} = 0.1$

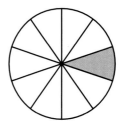

When you read 0.1, you say "one tenth" or "zero point one."

If you divide a whole into 100 equal parts, each part is one hundredth of the whole.

We can write one hundredth in two ways:

As a fraction: $\dfrac{1}{100}$

As a decimal: 0.01

$\dfrac{1}{100} = 0.01$

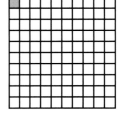

When you read 0.01, you say "one hundredth" or "zero point zero one."

Answer these questions.

1 Suppose you divide something into 1000 equal parts. What would each part be? Write it in two ways.

2 Suppose you divide something into 10,000 equal parts. Show two ways to write what each part would be.

3 Suppose you divide something into 100,000 equal parts. Show two ways to write what each part would be.

4 Suppose you divide something into 1,000,000 equal parts. Show two ways to write what each part would be.

5 Which is greater, $\dfrac{1}{10}$ or $\dfrac{1}{100}$?

6 Which is greater, 0.1 or 0.01?

7 Which is greater, 0.1 or 0.001?

◆ LESSON 138 Parts of a Whole

Our system of writing numbers is based on 10. Look at the number 3333.

thousands	hundreds	tens	ones
3	3	3	3

The red 3 stands for 3 ones.

What does the orange 3 stand for?

What does the green 3 stand for?

What does the blue 3 stand for?

As we move to the left, each place is worth ten times as much.

A 3 in the tens place is ten times the value of a 3 in the ones place.

A 3 in the hundreds place is ten times a 3 in the tens place.

If you move to the right, it's just the opposite. Each place is worth one tenth as much.

A 3 in the tens place is one tenth of a 3 in the hundreds place.

A 3 in the ones place is one tenth of a 3 in the tens place.

Thousands	Hundreds	Tens	Ones

◆ What happens if you keep going to the right?

The next place is one tenth of 1. That's the tenths place.

Thousands	Hundreds	Tens	Ones	Tenths	?

◆ What happens if you keep going?

The next place is one tenth of one tenth. That's the hundredths place.

Thousands	Hundreds	Tens	Ones	Tenths	Hundredths

◆ How do you know what place you are in?

Use a dot between the ones place and the tenths place. The dot is called a **decimal point.**

Suppose you want to write 4 tens, 3 ones, 5 tenths, and 4 hundredths.

You would write it like this: 43.54

When you read it, you would say "forty-three and fifty-four hundredths" or "forty-three point five four."

Tell the value of the blue digit in each of the following numbers.

⑧ 0.05   ⑨ 1.63   ⑩ 20.37   ⑪ 62.76   ⑫ 74.35

⑬ 0.57   ⑭ 2.59   ⑮ 91.35   ⑯ 53.47   ⑰ 22.22

⑱ 1.6   ⑲ 83.56   ⑳ 21.42   ㉑ 17.52   ㉒ 15.06

Write each number in standard form.

㉓ 5 ones, 2 tenths, 4 hundredths

㉔ 7 hundreds, 2 tens, 6 ones, 3 tenths

㉕ 3 tens, 3 ones, 3 tenths, 3 hundredths

㉖ 9 hundreds, 0 tens, 3 ones, 4 tenths, 5 hundredths

㉗ 4 tens, 9 ones, 0 tenths, 7 hundredths

Write each number in standard form. The first one has been done for you.

㉘ 30 + 4 + 0.6 + 0.04 **34.64**   ㉙ 60 + 0 + 0.7 + 0.03

㉚ 50 + 9 + 0.3 + 0.07   ㉛ 10 + 3 + 0.9 + 0.06

㉜ 16 + 0.8 + 0.05   ㉝ 80 + 2 + 0.06

㉞ 90 + 1 + 0.7 + 0.02   ㉟ 20 + 4 + 0.8 + 0.06

㊱ 4 + 0.6 + 0.09   ㊲ 10 + 7 + 0.2 + 0.04

Decimals and Fractions

Remember, if a whole is divided into 10 equal parts, 1 part would be $\frac{1}{10}$, or 0.1.

3 parts would be $\frac{3}{10}$, or 0.3.

$\frac{1}{10} = 0.1$

$\frac{3}{10} = 0.3$

If a whole is divided into 100 equal parts, 1 part would be $\frac{1}{100}$, or 0.01.

3 parts would be $\frac{3}{100}$, or 0.03.

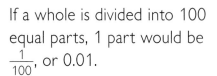

$\frac{1}{100} = 0.01$

$\frac{3}{100} = 0.03$

Suppose you divided a whole into 1000 equal parts.

◆ What would 1 part be?

◆ What would 3 parts be?

◆ What would 7 parts be?

Remember, a dime is $\frac{1}{10}$ of a dollar and a cent is $\frac{1}{100}$ of a dollar. Ten cents is the same as 1 dime. So 1 dime is greater than 9 cents, and 3 cents is less than 1 dime.

Here's how to compare the decimals 0.007 and 0.03:

◆ Write a zero so the numbers have the same number of digits to the right of the decimal point.

◆ Line up the decimal points   0.007
                                0.03**0**   So 0.007 < 0.03

Replace the ● with <, >, or =.

1 0.1 ● 0.3   **2** 0.03 ● 0.1   **3** 0.007 ● 0.08

4 0.01 ● 0.03   **5** 0.7 ● 0.08   **6** 0.2 ● 0.09

7 0.01 ● 0.07   **8** 0.1 ● 0.001   **9** 0.3 ● 0.03

10 0.07 ● 0.03   **11** 0.01 ● 0.001   **12** 0.04 ● 0.04

13 0.1 ● 0.01   **14** 0.001 ● 0.003   **15** 0.04 ● 0.004

◆ Which is greater,
0.1 or 0.10?

$$\frac{1}{10} = 0.1$$

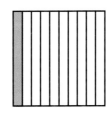

$$\frac{10}{100} = 0.10$$

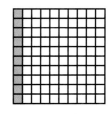

◆ Which is greater,
0.3 or 0.30?

$$\frac{3}{10} = 0.3$$

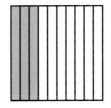

$$\frac{30}{100} = 0.30$$

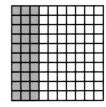

◆ Which is greater,
0.2 or 0.27?

$$\frac{2}{10} = 0.2$$

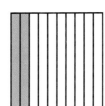

$$\frac{27}{100} = 0.27$$

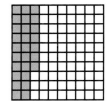

In each case, tell which is more money or whether they are the same amount.

16 3 dimes or 33 cents?

17 6 cents or 1 dime?

18 11 cents or 1 dime?

19 8 dimes or 80 cents?

20 10 cents or 1 dime?

21 7 dimes or 8 cents?

Write each amount as a decimal. The first one has been done for you.

22 3 dimes and 7 cents = **$0.37**

23 9 dimes and 8 cents = ■

24 6 dimes and 4 cents = ■

25 64 cents = ■

26 0 dimes and 8 cents = ■

27 7 dimes and 3 cents = ■

28 2 dimes and 9 cents = ■

29 6 cents = ■

30 8 dimes and 0 cents = ■

31 5 dimes and 9 cents = ■

◆ **LESSON 139** Decimals and Fractions

For each figure, show what portion is shaded by writing a fraction and a decimal. The first one has been done for you.

③②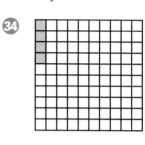

$$\frac{26}{100}$$
0.26

③③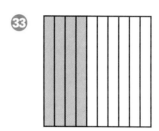

③④ (grid figure)

③⑤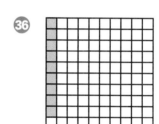

③⑥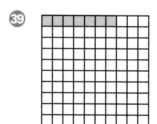

③⑦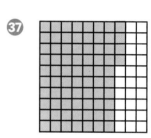

③⑧ (horizontal bars figure)

③⑨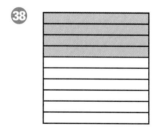

④⓪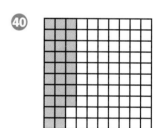

④①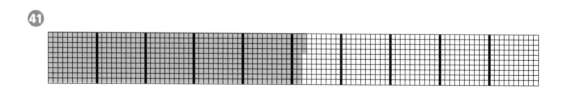

④②

Write each of these fractions as a decimal.

Examples: $\frac{3}{100} = 0.03$ $\frac{7}{10,000} = 0.0007$

43. $\frac{2}{10}$ = ■   44. $\frac{478}{10,000}$ = ■   45. $\frac{10}{100}$ = ■   46. $\frac{70}{1000}$ = ■

47. $\frac{7}{10}$ = ■   48. $\frac{4,783}{10,000}$ = ■   49. $\frac{11}{100}$ = ■   50. $\frac{700}{1000}$ = ■

51. $\frac{4}{100}$ = ■   52. $\frac{74}{100}$ = ■   53. $\frac{6}{10}$ = ■   54. $\frac{78}{1000}$ = ■

55. $\frac{40}{100}$ = ■   56. $\frac{6}{100}$ = ■   57. $\frac{1}{10}$ = ■   58. $\frac{843}{1000}$ = ■

59. $\frac{4}{1000}$ = ■   60. $\frac{6}{1000}$ = ■   61. $\frac{8}{10}$ = ■   62. $\frac{6,286}{10,000}$ = ■

63. $\frac{47}{100}$ = ■   64. $\frac{5}{100}$ = ■   65. $\frac{9}{10}$ = ■   66. $\frac{66}{100}$ = ■

67. $\frac{478}{1000}$ = ■   68. $\frac{8}{100}$ = ■   69. $\frac{7}{1000}$ = ■   70. $\frac{543}{1000}$ = ■

Copy each pair of numbers. Replace the ● with <, >, or =.

71. 0.02 ● 0.3   72. 0.47 ● 0.53   73. 0.406 ● 0.407

74. 0.83 ● 0.80   75. 0.8 ● 0.80   76. 0.8 ● 0.83

77. 0.62 ● 0.90   78. 0.9 ● 0.90   79. 0.62 ● 0.9

80. 0.48 ● 0.70   81. 0.48 ● 0.7   82. 0.100 ● 0.1

83. 0.230 ● 0.23   84. 0.230 ● 0.023   85. 0.010 ● 0.1

Solve these problems.

86. Eric correctly answered eight out of ten questions on his English quiz. Write a fraction to show what part of the quiz he got right.

87. Jessica spent $16 for a CD and $4 for a pair of earrings. Write a fraction to show the cost of the earrings compared to that of the CD.

88. Tom cleaned his bedroom in $\frac{1}{3}$ of an hour. His sister spent $\frac{2}{5}$ of an hour cleaning her bedroom. Who spent less time cleaning?

Ordering Decimals

Ordinarily, decimals that you compare should have the same number of digits to the right of the decimal point. However, when people measure they sometimes neglect to write the extra zeros at the end of the number.

For example, if you measure the length of a table to the nearest centimeter, you could report it as 1.34 meters. If the measurement came out to be 2.00 meters you should report it as 2.00 meters. This would show how much precision you believe is in your measurement. But some people will report this as just 2 meters.

If you assume the measurements are as precise as necessary, you can simply write extra zeros after a number to make comparison (and addition and subtraction) easier.

◆ List the following numbers in order from least to greatest. Insert a < symbol between each pair to make the statements true.

3, 3.5, 3.4073, 3.48, 3.408, 3.02, 3.40729

Rewrite each of the following sets of numbers from least to greatest with a < symbol between each pair.

1 24, 19, 20, 23.9, 20.7, 23.97

2 2.4, 1.9, 2, 2.39, 2.07, 2.397

3 0.0024, 0.0019, 0.002, 0.00239, 0.00207, 0.002397

4 2.0034, 1.99937, 2, 1.99, 2.01, 2.009

5 0.1, 0.02, 0.003, 0.0004, 0.00005, 0.000006

6 8.82, 8.12, 8.0, 8.01, 8.6, 8.10

Mel asked, "Could there be two numbers so close together that there is no number in between them?" "I don't think so," said June. "Why don't you try to find out?"

Mel tried 0.001 and 0.002. Alia said, "I can find a number between them. I can think of those numbers as 0.0010 and 0.0020. Then 0.0015 must be exactly halfway between them."

"And 0.0014, 0.0013, and a lot of other numbers are between them too, but those numbers are closer to 0.001 than to 0.002," said Mel.

"We can also find lots of numbers between the two original numbers that are closer to 0.002, like 0.0016 and 0.0017," said June. "I think we can always find a lot of numbers between any two numbers."

For each of the following pairs of numbers:

a. **find a number that is exactly halfway between**
b. **find a number that is closer to the lesser number**
c. **find a number that is closer to the greater number**
d. **write the three numbers in order from least to greatest**

Watch your numbering.

7 0.2 and 0.3

8 1.7 and 1.8

9 1.7 and 2.1

10 1.7 and 2.2

11 0.003 and 0.004

12 3.003 and 3.004

13 9.003 and 9.004

14 27.003 and 27.004

15 0 and 0.1

16 4.4 and 6.4

17 0.02 and 0.1

18 0 and 0.00000001

19 5 and 5.1

20 5 and 5.00000001

21 4.9 and 5

22 4.99 and 5

23 4.9999999 and 5

24 1 and 2

25 10 and 11

26 1.3 and 2.3

27 7 and 7.5

28 8.5 and 8.9

◆ **LESSON 140** Ordering Decimals

COOPERATIVE LEARNING

Roll a Decimal Game

Players:	Two
Materials:	One 0–5 cube, one 5–10 cube
Object:	To make the greater decimal
Math Focus:	Place value, comparing decimal numbers, and mathematical reasoning

RULES

1. Roll the 0–5 cube. If you roll a 0, roll that cube again.

2. Write a decimal point followed by as many blanks as the number rolled. If you rolled a 3, you would write: .___ ___ ___

3. Roll the 5–10 cube as many times as there are blanks in your decimal. If you roll a 10, roll that cube again.

4. Each time you roll the cube, write that number in one of your blanks.

5. The player with the greater decimal is the winner.

SAMPLE GAME

Sara rolled:	Sara wrote:	David rolled:	David wrote:
0 — rolled again		**3**	.___ ___ ___
2	.___ ___	**6**	.___ 6 ___
6	.___ 6	**9**	.9 6 ___
7	.7 6	**10** — rolled again	
		10 — rolled again	
		6	.9 6 6

David was the winner.

Look at the number line shown below.

◆ Where would you put the number 1.5 so that it would be in the proper place?

◆ Where would you place 0.5 (or .5)?

◆ Where would you place 2.5?

◆ Where would you place 1.1?

◆ Where would you place 1.9?

◆ Where would you place 1.9307?

For each of the following sets of numbers, draw a number line and write the given numbers where they belong. Be sure to draw your number line so that all the numbers listed in the problem will fit.

㉙ 0.01, 0.1, 2.06, 2.6, 1.704, 1.11111

㉚ 2.11111, 2.01, 2.1, 3.704, 4.06, 4.6

㉛ 0.73, 1.8, 0.099, 0.99, 2.05, 2.1

㉜ 1.8, 2.1, 1.9, 2.01, 1.79, 2.001

For each of the following number lines, tell what number should be placed where a letter is shown.

㉝
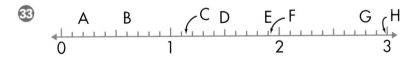

㉞
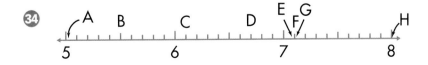

Comparing Decimals Review

In this lesson you'll practice comparing decimals.

Replace the ● with <, >, or =.

① 0.32 ● 3.2   ② 1.01 ● 1.001   ③ 0.07 ● 0.3

④ 26.37 ● 2.84   ⑤ 0.5 ● 1.0   ⑥ 1.28 ● 1.280

⑦ 0.06 ● 0.2   ⑧ 0.6 ● 0.02   ⑨ 3.89 ● 3.809

⑩ 0.73 ● 0.073   ⑪ 0.215 ● 0.215   ⑫ 21.2 ● 18.0

⑬ 0.973 ● 0.839   ⑭ 0.973 ● 8.39   ⑮ 51.24 ● 204.1

⑯ 9.7 ● 6.8   ⑰ 5.5555 ● 40.7   ⑱ 1.4 ● 0.8

⑲ 0.0104 ● 0.104   ⑳ 4.083 ● 4.07   ㉑ 209.74 ● 142.857

㉒ 52.0 ● 56.0   ㉓ 0.38 ● 0.38   ㉔ 80.42 ● 30.42

㉕ 21.63 ● 21.630   ㉖ 4.8 ● 32.7   ㉗ 0.27 ● 0.05

㉘ 1.815 ● 1.158   ㉙ 3.6 ● 2.1   ㉚ 92.9 ● 92.009

Order from least to greatest. Insert a < symbol between each pair of numbers to make true statements.

㉛ 0.7, 1.2, 0.3, 0.002, 10.06, 10.1

㉜ 0.005, 0.0002, 0.0001, 0.006, 0.01, 0.001

㉝ 12.76, 12.75, 12.39, 12.93, 12.40, 12.04

㉞ 1.1, 1.5, 1.05, 1.01, 1.2, 1.002

Use cents, nickels, dimes, quarters, and half-dollars to form each amount. Try to use as few coins as possible. The first one has been done for you.

㉟ $0.57   (50)(5)(1)(1)   ㊱ $0.80

㊲ $0.35   ㊳ $0.74

㊴ $1.05   ㊵ $0.17

Which of the following are possible? For those that are possible, write the coins needed. For those that are not possible, explain why.

41 Make 35 cents with three coins.

42 Make 54 cents with four coins.

43 Make 87 cents with 11 coins.

44 Make 86 cents with ten coins.

45 Make 75 cents with three coins.

Work in groups to solve the next four problems.

46 How many different coin combinations can you use to make 25 cents? Write six different combinations.

Hint: You can make 25 cents with 0 pennies, 5 pennies, 10 pennies, 15 pennies, 20 pennies, or 25 pennies. Make a chart to help you.

47 Eva had 50 coins that were worth $1.00. What coins could Eva have? How many answers are possible? Write or explain why you think no other answers are possible.

48 Paul has 40 coins whose total value is $1.00. What are the coins?

49 David has four coins. They are worth 46¢. Tell which of the following statements are reasonable and explain your answer.

a. David has two dimes.

b. David has two quarters.

c. David has six pennies.

◆ **LESSON 141** **Comparing Decimals Review**

THINKING STORY

Iron and Gold

Part 1

The queen of Addonia did not forget that Manolita, Marcus, Ferdie, and Portia helped find her treasure on Mugg Island.

"I am very pleased," said the queen. "You helped me get the Royal Treasure back. I will give you a reward."

She called her steward and said to him, "Give these children a bag of money."

The steward sniffed. "A whole bag of money for these children? Well, all right."

"And see that it has some gold in it," said the queen.

Marcus, Portia, Ferdie, and Manolita followed the steward. He set out three bags of money. One bag was red, one bag was blue, and one was green. "Pick the bag you want and be gone," he said.

"May we look inside?" Manolita asked.

"No," said the steward. "But you may reach in and pick up some coins to see what they are like. I will tell you this. Every bag has some iron coins and some gold coins. And some bags have more gold coins than others."

"We'll take the bag with the most gold coins," said Ferdie. "Which one is that?"

"That's for you to figure out—if you can," said the steward, with a mean smile.

"I know," said Portia. "Let's vote! We'll each vote for the bag that we think has the most gold in it. We'll take the one that wins."

. . . to be continued

Work in groups. Discuss your answers and how you figured them out. Then compare your answers with those of other groups.

❶ Why would the children want the bag that has the most gold coins in it? Why wouldn't they want the bag with the most iron coins?

❷ Is voting a good way to decide which bag to take? Why or why not?

❸ What would be a good way to choose which bag to take?

Rounding Decimals

Suppose seven people went out to eat. The total bill was $36.77, and each person wants to pay the same amount.

If you divide 36.77 by 7, you get 5.2528571. But people cannot pay part of a penny. If we round to the nearest penny we will get an answer of $5.25 for each person. But 7 times 5.25 is 36.75, which is 2 cents short. In this case, we could either round up, or ask two people to pay an extra penny.

In real situations you must use your judgment about the best way to round numbers.

To round 3.5943295 to the nearest hundredth, we look at the digit to the right of the hundredths place. Because 4 is less than 5, the number is closer to 3.59 than to 3.60, so we round to 3.59.

If the next digit is 5, we usually round up if we know there are more nonzero digits. But what if the last digit is a 5 and we have no further information, or we know that is the last nonzero digit? Then there is no reason to round in either direction.

If we are working with a group of numbers, we should probably round such numbers up half the time and down half the time.

See how each of the following numbers is rounded to the nearest thousandth.

2.03450012 rounds to 2.035

2.0345 can be rounded to either 2.034 or 2.035

The Statue of Liberty measures 151 feet tall and weighs 450,000 pounds. Her index finger is 8 feet long, taller than professional basketball players, and her big toe is about the size of a small car.

Round each of the numbers to the nearest hundredth. Watch your numbering.

1. 4.7380389
2. 4.73501001
3. 4.735
4. 0.007
5. 1.003

6. 0.003
7. 45.928
8. 45.92800003
9. 3.451
10. 3.451999999

11. 0.051
12. 1.294
13. 3.481
14. 10.609
15. 8.543

Round each of the numbers to the nearest thousandth. Watch your numbering.

16. 1.23456
17. 1.2345
18. 1.234500001

19. 1.234499999
20. 0.0075
21. 0.148762

22. 19.417023
23. 4.0012
24. 2.71152

For each of the following, round in a way that makes sense.

25. Konala saved $7.00 last week, $8.50 the week before, and $5.20 the week before that. She decided the average amount she saves is $6.90 each week. She multiplied 52 by 6.90, getting 358.8, and announced that she will have exactly $358.80 in the bank in a year. Do you agree? Explain.

26. Philip has taken three tests. On the first one he got a score of 92, on the second he scored 73, and on the third he scored 82. He finds the average to be 82.33333333333. Is that the average you would report? Why?

27. Bonita needs one bag of fertilizer to fertilize each 200 square feet of her garden. She has measured the length of the garden to be 73.5 feet and the width to be 19 feet. How many bags of fertilizer should she buy?

28. Ms. Goldberg runs a bus company. Her buses can each carry 48 people. She has been asked to supply buses to take 500 people to a conference. She divides 500 by 48 and gets 10.416667. How many buses does she need?

Decimals: Multiplying and Dividing by Powers of 10

Olivia is buying supplies for a birthday party. There will be ten people at the party. She made a chart to show prices in cents and in dollars and cents.

Use a computer or other means to draw and complete the chart.

| Item | Cents | | Dollars and Cents | |
	Price for 1	Price for 10	Price for 1	Price for 10
Balloon	7¢	70¢	$0.07	$0.70
Noisemaker	29¢	290¢	$0.29	$2.90
Kazoo	45¢	■	■	■
Hat	63¢	■	■	■
Sticker	37¢	■	■	■

◆ Compare the two dollars-and-cents columns. What do you notice about the decimal point?

Ten people are sharing the cost of the food for Olivia's birthday party. They made a chart to show the prices in cents and in dollars. Copy and complete the chart.

| Item | Cents | | Dollars and Cents | |
	Total Cost	Cost for Each Person	Total Cost	Cost for Each Person
Cupcakes	380¢	38¢	$3.80	$0.38
Ice cream	980¢	■	■	■
Cookies	470¢	■	■	■
Milk	260¢	■	■	■

◆ Compare the two dollars-and-cents columns. What do you notice about the decimal point?

The value of a digit in its place in a number is ten times as great as in the place to its right. So you can multiply by 10 by moving the decimal point one place to the right.

Remember, the decimal point always comes after the ones place, even if it isn't written there.

Examples: $10 \times 4.5 = ?$ 4.5. $10 \times 4.5 = 45$

$3.06 \times 10 = ?$ 3.0.6 $3.06 \times 10 = 30.6$

Sometimes you need to write in a 0.

$8 \times 10 = ?$ 8.0. $8 \times 10 = 80$

Multiply.

1 10×7 **2** 12×10 **3** 10×60 **4** 10×59

5 10×7.2 **6** 10×81.34 **7** 86.29×10 **8** 47.28×10

To multiply by 100, move the decimal point two places to the right.

Examples: $100 \times 17.15 = ?$ 17.1.5. $100 \times 17.15 = 1715$

$6.7 \times 100 = ?$ 6.7.0. $6.7 \times 100 = 670$

Multiply.

9 100×7 **10** 12×100 **11** 60×100 **12** 100×59

13 100×7.2 **14** 100×81.34 **15** 100×86.29 **16** 100×47.28

To multiply by 1000, move the decimal point three places to the right.

Examples: $1.9396 \times 1000 = ?$ 1.9.3.9.6 $1.9396 \times 1000 = 1939.6$

$1.07 \times 1000 = ?$ 1.0.7.0. $1.07 \times 1000 = 1070$

Multiply.

17 1000×8 **18** 1000×0.798 **19** 1000×73

20 1000×7.23 **21** 50×1000 **22** 1000×74.82

23 42×1000 **24** 1000×68.92 **25** 479.26×100

◆ LESSON 143 Decimals: Multiplying and Dividing by Powers of 10

The value of a digit in its place in a number is one tenth the value it would have in the place to its left. So you can divide by 10 by moving the decimal point one place to the left.

Examples: 47 ÷ 10 = ? 4.7. 47 ÷ 10 = 4.7

0.7 ÷ 10 = ? .0.7 0.7 ÷ 10 = 0.07

38.6 ÷ 10 = ? 3.8.6 38.6 ÷ 10 = 3.86

Divide.

㉖ 38 ÷ 10 ㉗ 0.8 ÷ 10 ㉘ 0.9 ÷ 10 ㉙ 5.9 ÷ 10

㉚ 3.8 ÷ 10 ㉛ 43.2 ÷ 10 ㉜ 0.78 ÷ 10 ㉝ 48.27 ÷ 10

To divide by 100, move the decimal point two places to the left.

Examples: 545 ÷ 100 = ? 5.45. 545 ÷ 100 = 5.45

65 ÷ 100 = ? .6 5. 65 ÷ 100 = 0.65

Sometimes you need to write in a 0.

0.73 ÷ 100 = ? .0 0.73 0.73 ÷ 100 = 0.0073

Divide.

㉞ 75 ÷ 100 ㉟ 8390 ÷ 100 ㊱ 7.5 ÷ 100 ㊲ 0.98 ÷ 100

㊳ 6.8 ÷ 100 ㊴ 183 ÷ 100 ㊵ 1116 ÷ 100 ㊶ 0.756 ÷ 100

To divide by 1000, move the decimal point three places to the left.

Examples: 45 ÷ 1000 = ? .0 4 5. 45 ÷ 1000 = 0.045

22 ÷ 1000 = ? .0 2 2. 22 ÷ 1000 = 0.022

Divide.

㊷ 2500 ÷ 1000 ㊸ 351 ÷ 1000 ㊹ 14.76 ÷ 1000 ㊺ 16 ÷ 1000

㊻ 8 ÷ 1000 ㊼ 125.7 ÷ 1000 ㊽ 147.6 ÷ 1000 ㊾ 279 ÷ 1000

㊿ 51 ÷ 1000 (51) 327 ÷ 1000 (52) 1476 ÷ 1000 (53) 390 ÷ 1000

In general, to divide by a number that is written as a 1 with some number of 0s after it, you move the decimal point that number of places to the left. To multiply by such a number, you move the decimal point that many places to the right. Write extra 0s when necessary.

Examples:

$$11.76 \times 10 \longrightarrow 11.7.6 \longrightarrow 117.6$$

$$135.6 \div 100 \longrightarrow 1.3\,5.6 \longrightarrow 1.356$$

$$21.4 \times 100 \longrightarrow 21.4.0 \longrightarrow 2140$$

Solve the following problems. Watch the signs. Watch your numbering.

54 765.4321×10

55 $765.4321 \div 10$

56 $765.4321 \div 100$

57 $765.4321 \div 1000$

58 765.4321×1000

59 $765.4321 \div 100{,}000$

60 $765.4321 \times 100{,}000$

61 $2 \div 1000$

62 2×1000

63 $2 \div 10{,}000$

You know that there are 100 centimeters in a meter and 1000 meters in a kilometer. So, to find out how many centimeters there are in 73.2 meters, you multiply 73.2 by 100, getting 7320 (moving the decimal point two places to the right, after writing the extra 0).

Solve the following problems.

64 How many centimeters are there in 56.24 meters?

65 How many meters are there in 7.24 kilometers?

66 How many centimeters are there in 7.24 kilometers?

67 How many meters are there in 2435 centimeters?

68 How many kilometers are there in 2435 centimeters?

LESSON 144

Approximating Errors Using Decimals

When you round or approximate, it is useful to know how far from the exact number your approximation could be. The difference depends on how much you round each number.

Solve these problems.

❶ Bill always "rounds off" the entries in his checkbook by dropping the cents. Thus, he writes $43 for $43.98, $57 for $57.26, and $97 for $97.01. Because he does this both for deposits to his account and for checks he writes, he thinks that his account should balance out in the end. Do you think it should? Why or why not?

❷ One month Bill made deposits in the following amounts: $416.20, $416.20, and $98.80.

He also wrote checks in the following amounts: $7.83, $59.46, $12.50, $25.00, $241.10, $17.69, $50.00, $28.54, $25.00, $16.58, $57.43, $247.56, $73.12, $57.34, and $10.00.

Assume Bill started with a balance of $100 in his checkbook.

a. What should his balance be at the end of the month?

b. What would Bill think his balance is?

c. Can you devise a method for estimating how much difference there is likely to be between the exact balance and Bill's estimated balance?

❸ Erin estimated each of ten distances to the nearest mile. When she added the distances, she got an estimated total of 473 miles. If her original estimates were correct to the nearest mile (no more than $\frac{1}{2}$ mile off), what are the greatest and least possible exact values for the total?

Multiply.

4 100 × 8.3

5 401.1 × 10

6 10 × 88.34

7 10 × 90.0

8 77 × 1000

9 110.1 × 100

10 421.02 × 10

11 8.06 × 10

12 384.71 × 100

13 10 × 59.3

14 100 × 91.011

15 1000 × 62.073

16 816.41 × 100

17 100 × 910.11

18 10 × 93.74

Divide.

19 61.6 ÷ 10

20 8971.1 ÷ 10

21 0.7 ÷ 100

22 70.04 ÷ 100

23 652.36 ÷ 100

24 962.1 ÷ 10

25 8.23 ÷ 10

26 0.06 ÷ 100

27 475 ÷ 100

28 0.43 ÷ 10

29 1.003 ÷ 10

30 0.67 ÷ 100

31 7.342 ÷ 1000

32 900.1 ÷ 100

33 8.08 ÷ 1000

Multiply or divide. Watch the signs.

34 29.03 × 100

35 2.601 × 10

36 98.03 ÷ 10

37 0.507 ÷ 10

38 0.04 ÷ 10

39 437.2 × 100

40 1000 × 0.301

41 3.45 ÷ 100

42 1000 × 0.062

43 10 × 8.06

44 8.066 ÷ 100

45 100 × 1.304

46 482.1 ÷ 100

47 32 × 1000

48 3.421 ÷ 100

Challenge: A stack of 1000 sheets of paper is 9.5 centimeters thick. How many centimeters thick is each sheet?

9.5 cm

Iron and Gold

Part 2

You may want to refer to the first part of this Thinking Story on pages 478–479.

"Before I vote on which bag to take," said Manolita, "I want to find out what kind of coins are in them."

She reached into the red bag and drew out a gold coin. Then she reached into the blue bag and drew out an iron coin. She also drew an iron coin from the green bag.

"That settles it," said Manolita. "I vote for the red bag."

"Before I vote," said Marcus, "I want to take a big handful of coins from every bag."

Marcus scooped a handful of coins from the red bag. He got one gold coin, and all the rest were iron. Next he took a handful of coins from the blue bag. They were all gold except for one! Then he took a handful of coins from the green bag. He got four gold coins and eight iron ones.

"I'm glad I did that," Marcus said. "If we'd followed Manolita, we would have picked the wrong bag."

. . . to be continued

Work in groups. Discuss your answers and how you figured them out. Then compare your answers with those of other groups.

1 How is what Marcus found out different from what Manolita found out?

2 If you were Manolita, would you have changed your vote after seeing Marcus's results?

3 Can we be sure that Manolita voted for the wrong bag? Explain.

4 How could you be even more sure than Marcus about which bag to pick?

LESSON 145

Metric Units: Multiply and Divide by Powers of 10

When this ruler is unfolded, it is 1 meter long.

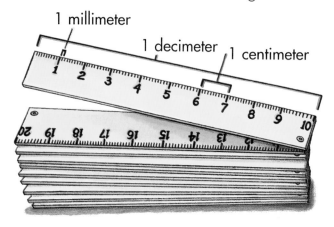

1 meter = 10 decimeters = 100 centimeters = 1000 millimeters

About how long is a meter? Most doors are about 2 meters high. A meterstick is 1 meter long. Most classroom doors are a little less than 1 meter wide.

If a meter is divided into ten equal parts, each part is 0.1 meter. That's also called 1 decimeter (dm).

$$1 \text{ dm} = 0.1 \text{ m}$$

Two of the parts (2 dm) would be 0.2 meter.   2 dm = 0.2 m

To convert between metric units, you multiply or divide by a power of 10.

To convert from a smaller unit to a larger unit, divide.

To convert from a larger unit to a smaller unit, multiply.

$$\text{dm} \longrightarrow \text{m} \quad \div 10$$

$$\text{m} \longrightarrow \text{dm} \quad \times 10$$

$$\text{cm} \longrightarrow \text{m} \quad \div 100$$

$$\text{m} \longrightarrow \text{cm} \quad \times 100$$

Find the value of the missing number.

1. 3 dm = ■ m
2. 8 dm = ■ m
3. ■ dm = 6 m
4. 5 dm = ■ m
5. ■ dm = 9 m
6. ■ dm = 1.0 m

If a meter is divided into 100 equal parts, each part is 0.01 meter. That's also called 1 centimeter (cm).   1 cm = 0.01 m

Two of the parts (2 cm) would be 0.02 meter.   2 cm = 0.02 m

Find the value of the missing number.

7. 7 cm = ■ m
8. 8 cm = ■ m
9. ■ cm = 0.04 m
10. 27 cm = ■ m
11. ■ cm = 0.31 m
12. ■ cm = 1.00 m

If a meter is divided into 1000 equal parts, each part is 0.001 meter. That's also called 1 millimeter (mm).

1 mm = 0.001 m

Two of the parts (2 mm) would be 0.002 meter.   2 mm = 0.002 m

Find the value of the missing number.

13. 6 mm = ■ m
14. 709 mm = ■ m
15. ■ mm = 0.300 m
16. 66 mm = ■ m
17. ■ mm = 0.004 m
18. ■ mm = 0.305 m
19. 347 mm = ■ m
20. ■ mm = 0.76 m
21. ■ mm = 1.000 m

Measure. Write each measurement in two ways.

22. Classroom

Length: ■ cm = ■ m

Width: ■ cm = ■ m

23. Top of desk

Length: ■ mm = ■ cm

Width: ■ mm = ■ cm

There are about 1500 different kinds of butterflies living in one square mile in the Amazon rain forest. There are only about 750 different kinds in all of the United States and Canada.

Metric Measurements of Length

Angel measured a table and found it was 2 meters, 3 decimeters, 8 centimeters, and 5 millimeters long. There is a shorter way to report this measurement.

Change each unit to meters	**Then add**
2 m = 2 m	2.**000** m
3 dm = 0.3 m	0.3**00** m
8 cm = 0.08 m	0.08**0** m
5 mm = 0.005 m	0.005 m
	2.385 m

2 m, 3 dm, 8 cm, 5 mm = 2.385 m

Write each measurement in meters only.

1 6 m, 3 dm, 8 cm, 5 mm

2 3 cm, 6 mm, 9 m

3 4 m, 0 dm, 2 cm, 6 mm

4 5 mm, 2 dm, 3 m

5 4 m, 2 cm, 6 mm

6 7 m, 4 cm, 1 dm, 0 mm

7 8 mm, 9 cm, 0 dm, 2 m

8 1 dm, 7 m, 4 cm

1000 meters is called a kilometer (km). 1000 m = 1 km

It takes about 12 minutes to walk 1 kilometer.

1 meter is 0.001 kilometer.   1 m = 0.001 km

The distance from the library to the fire house was measured. It was 2 kilometers, 415 meters. Write that in kilometers only.

2 km = 2 km	2.**000** km
415 m = 0.415 km	0.415 km
	2.415 km

2 km, 415 m = 2.415 km

Write these measurements in kilometers only.

9 1 km, 210 m   **10** 4 km, 50 m   **11** 4 km, 500 m   **12** 2200 m

Tell the length or diameter of each object in millimeters, then in centimeters.

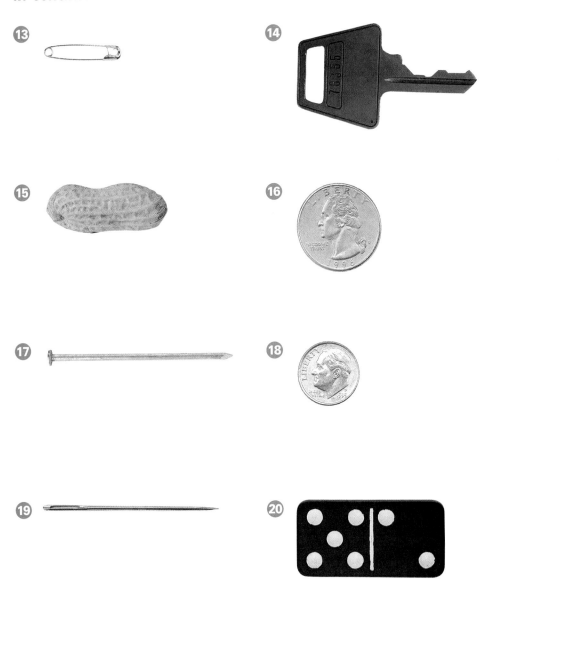

◆ **LESSON 146   Metric Measurements of Length**

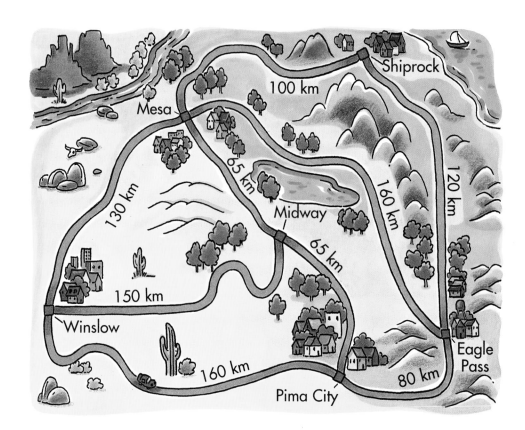

Use the map to answer these questions.

23   How many kilometers is it from Eagle Pass to Shiprock?

24   How many kilometers is it from Eagle Pass to Mesa if you go through Shiprock?

25   If you were going from Winslow to Eagle Pass, how much farther would it be to go through Mesa?

26   Suppose you were going from Eagle Pass to Winslow and wanted to visit Pima City and Mesa on the way.

   a. Would it be shorter to visit Pima City first or Mesa first?

   b. How much shorter?

27   Which town is closest to Eagle Pass?

How tall are you?

Work in groups. Measure the height of each person in your group.

Stand up straight.
Back to wall.
Put book on head.

Walk away.
Make a mark.

Measure in
centimeters.

Ramona measured the height of each student in her class. She made a chart to show the height of each person.

28 What is the most common height of the students in Ramona's class?

Height (cm)	Number of People
118	||
119	
120	||
121	|||
122	⋕ |
123	⋕ ||
124	||||
125	
126	||
127	|

Then Ramona made a bar graph so people could see the results more easily.

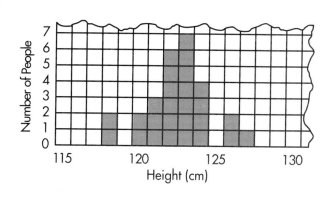

Use a computer or other means to make a chart and a bar graph to show the results for your class.

LESSON 147

Adding and Subtracting Decimals

Linda has $0.97. If she earns $3.75 for washing Mr. Lomaki's dog, how much money will she have?

Do you remember how to add amounts of money?

$$\begin{array}{r} \$3.75 \\ +\quad 0.97 \\ \hline \$4.72 \end{array}$$

Line up the decimal points so you can add cents to cents, dimes to dimes, dollars to dollars, and so on.

Felipe has $4.72. He needs $10 to buy a flashlight. How much more does he need?

Do you remember how to subtract amounts of money?

$$\begin{array}{r} \$10.00 \\ -\quad 4.72 \\ \hline \$5.28 \end{array}$$

Line up the decimal points so you subtract cents from cents, dimes from dimes, dollars from dollars, and so on.

When you add or subtract decimals, line up the decimal points.

Example: $14.8 + 2.35 = ?$

$$\begin{array}{r} 14.8 \\ +\quad 2.35 \end{array}$$

Line up the decimal points.

$$\begin{array}{r} 14.8\mathbf{0} \\ +\quad 2.35 \end{array}$$

If it helps, put in a 0 (because 14.8 and 14.80 have the same value).

$$\begin{array}{r} 14.80 \\ +\quad 2.35 \\ \hline \mathbf{17.15} \end{array}$$

Add.

Example: 8.6 − 3.25

8.6
− 3.25

Line up the decimal points.

8.6**0**
− 3.25

If it helps, put in a 0 (because 8.6 and 8.60 have the same value).

8.60
− 3.25

Subtract.

8.60
− 3.25
5.35

Add or subtract.

1   6.72
   + 11.09

2   9.5
   + 8.63

3   5.2
   − 3.15

4   8.2
   + 3.01

5   1.7
   − 0.9

6   8.03
   − 7.04

7   3.07
   + 0.96

8   4.07
   − 3.10

9   5.33
   − 4.03

10   8.4
   + 2.7

11   2.96
   − 1.09

12   7.43
   + 2.99

13   6.40
   − 0.05

14   8.92
   − 2.39

15   7.04
   − 2.06

Solve for n.

16 $2.36 + 6.5 = n$

17 $6.07 + 3.03 = n$

18 $10.9 − 9.01 = n$

19 $5.4 − 3.3 = n$

20 $2.34 − 2.09 = n$

21 $4.64 + 6 = n$

22 $8.26 − 8.19 = n$

23 $13.3 + 4.11 = n$

24 $25.01 + 0.6 = n$

Solve.

25 Kendra lives 1.25 kilometers from the library. She has walked 0.6 kilometers toward the library. How much farther does she have to walk to the library?

◆ LESSON 147 Adding and Subtracting Decimals

Solve these problems.

26 In the 1900 Olympics, Irving Baxter jumped 1.90 meters in the running high jump. In 1996, Charles Austin jumped 2.39 meters in the running high jump.

   a. Which man jumped higher?

   b. How much higher?

27 In the 1996 Olympics, Gail Devers ran 100 meters in 10.94 seconds. In the same Olympics, four American women ran the 400-meter relay in 41.95 seconds. Was the average time for each runner in the relay faster or slower than Gail Devers's time?

28 In the 1896 Olympic games, Thomas Burke ran 100 meters in 12 seconds. In the 1900 Olympic games, Francis W. Jarvis ran 100 meters in 10.8 seconds.

   a. What was the difference in their times?

   b. Who ran faster?

29 In the 1996 Olympics, Donovan Bailey ran 100 meters in 9.84 seconds. By how much time did he beat 10 seconds?

30 In the 1996 Olympics, Gail Devers ran 100 meters in 10.94 seconds. If she ran that fast for 200 meters, how long would it take her to run 200 meters?

31 In the 1996 Olympics, Merlene Ottey ran 200 meters in 22.24 seconds. She ran 100 meters in 10.94 seconds. Was her average speed for the 200-meter run faster or slower than for the 100-meter run? Why do you think there was this difference?

32 In the 1900 Olympics, J. W. B. Tewksbury ran the 400-meter hurdle in 57.6 seconds. In 1996 Derek Adkins had a time of 47.54 seconds in the same event. How much faster was Adkins?

33 The 10,000-meter run is an Olympic event. How many kilometers is 10,000 meters?

34 In the 1996 Olympics, Michelle Smith swam 400 meters in 4 minutes and 7.25 seconds. In the 1924 Olympics, Johnny Weismuller swam 400 meters in 5 minutes and 4.8 seconds. By how much did Michelle Smith beat Johnny Weismuller's time?

35 In the 1964 Olympics, Abebe Bikila ran the marathon barefoot in 2 hours, 12 minutes, and 11.2 seconds. In the 1948 Olympics, Delfo Cabrera ran the marathon in 2 hours, 34 minutes, and 51.6 seconds. In how much less time did Abebe Bikila run the marathon?

36 In the 1960 Olympics, Wilma Rudolph ran 100 meters in 11.0 seconds. Was her average speed for the race more than 10 meters per second?

37 In the 1932 Olympics, Volmari Iso-Hollo ran an extra lap by mistake in the 3000-meter steeplechase. His time for the race was 10 minutes and 33.4 seconds. In the 1936 Olympics, he ran the same race in 9 minutes and 3.8 seconds. About how long do you think it took Iso-Hollo to run the extra lap?

Addition and Subtraction of Decimals: Applications

Many situations involve decimal numbers. Use your skills at working with decimals to solve the following problems.

1. A year ago Jake bought a used car that had traveled 48,927.8 miles. Now the car has traveled 75,485.2 miles. How many miles has the car traveled in the past year?

2. Donna wants to ride her bike at least 50 miles every week. At the beginning of the week the odometer on her bike showed 143.6 miles. Now it shows 184.8 miles. How many more miles does she have to ride this week to meet her goal?

3. Steve had $25.81. Last week he spent $7.50 and earned $12.75 washing cars. How much money does he have now?

4. A movie ticket costs $6.25.
   a. How much will two tickets cost?
   b. How much will four tickets cost?

5. Melissa needs 6 pounds of cheese to make sandwiches for her party. She bought packages of cheese that weigh 2.2 pounds and 2.6 pounds.
   a. How many more pounds of cheese does she need?
   b. If she buys another package of cheese and it weighs 2.1 pounds, how much will be left over?

Harder Roll a Decimal Game

Players: Two
Materials: One 0–5 cube, one 5–10 cube
Object: To get the greater total score
Math Focus: Place value, subtracting decimal numbers, and mathematical reasoning

RULES

1. Follow rules 1 through 4 for the "Roll a Decimal" game on page 474.

2. Subtract the lesser decimal from the greater decimal and award the difference to the player with the greater decimal.

3. After an agreed-upon number of rounds, add your scores.

4. The player with the greater total is the winner.

SAMPLE GAME

Round	Sara	David	Sara's Score	David's Score
1	0.76	0.966		0.206
2	0.957	0.676	0.281	
3	0.97775	0.9665	0.01125	
4	0.8	0.9576		0.1576
5	0.99	0.866	0.124	
6	0.86855	0.8875		0.01895
Total			0.41625	0.38255

After six rounds, Sara was the winner.

Adding and Subtracting Decimals: Balancing a Checkbook

Many people use a checking account for their money. They use addition and subtraction to record how much money they have in their account after each transaction.

Whenever Ms. Taylor pays someone with a check, she keeps a record of it in her checkbook. That way she can keep track of how much money she has in her checking account.

Ms. Taylor keeps the record of each check in a check register. Look at this check register to see what information is on it.

CHECK #	DATE	TRANSACTION	DEBIT		CREDIT		BALANCE	
							907	13
D	1-3-97	Deposit			649	39	649	39
							1556	52
109	1-3	Star Realty Co.	470	85			470	85
		Rent					1085	67

Every month Ms. Taylor gets a statement from her bank. The statement shows the bank's records of her account.

The statement for January said that Ms. Taylor had $907.13 in her account on January 3 and $1349.76 at the end of the month. This did not agree with her records.

Look at Ms. Taylor's checkbook on page 503. Did she make an error in her calculations? If she did, correct the error so that her records show the same balance at the end of the month as the bank statement shows.

Ms. Taylor's Checkbook

CHECK #	DATE	TRANSACTION	DEBIT		CREDIT		BALANCE	
							907	13
D	1-3-97	Deposit			649	39	649	39
							1556	52
109	1-3	Star Realty Co. Rent	470	85			470	85
							1085	67
110	1-8	CASH	50	00			50	00
							1035	67
111	1-12	Watts Power Co. electricity	83	19			83	19
							1052	52
112	1-14	Betty's Boutique Pants	34	26			34	26
							1022	26
113	1-16	Clothing Mart Jacket	110	85			110	85
							911	41
114	1-28	Terrific Travel Agency bus tickets	107	00			107	00
							804	41
D	1-30	Deposit			649	39	649	39
							1453	80

1 Dr. Xiang had $507.08 in her checking account. She made a deposit of $325.00 and then wrote a check for $106.88 and another check for $75. What is her new balance?

2 Karen opened a new checking account with $100. She wrote a check for $27.14 to pay her cable television bill. Then she wrote a check for $37.09 to pay for groceries. Does she have enough money in her checking account to write a check for $40 in cash?

3 Michael made a deposit of $215.81 to his checking account. That gave him a balance of $403.05. How much money did Michael have in his account before he made that deposit?

4 Jared wrote a check in the amount of $28.46 for two CDs. He wrote another check for $42.69 to pay for a new sweatshirt. Jared's original balance was $116.39. What is his new balance?

◆ **LESSON 149** Adding and Subtracting Decimals: Balancing a Checkbook

Iron and Gold

Part 3

You may want to refer to the earlier parts of this Thinking Story on pages 478–479 and 488–489.

"Have you decided now which bag to take?" the steward asked, with his mean grin.

"Yes," said Marcus, "we'll take the blue bag. It has the most gold coins in it."

"Wait a minute," said Ferdie. Then he whispered to the other children. "I think the man is trying to trick us. He doesn't want us to get much gold. Let me try something different."

Ferdie took a handful of coins from each bag, but he didn't do it the way Marcus did. Instead of scooping the coins from the top of the bag, he reached all the way to the bottom of each bag and took the coins from there.

From the bottom of the red bag Ferdie got five gold coins and three iron ones. From the bottom of the blue bag he got only iron coins. And from the bottom of the green bag he got four gold coins and four iron ones.

"I was right," said Manolita. "The red bag is best."

"I think something funny is going on here," said Marcus.

"I told you," Ferdie said. "The steward was trying to trick us."

. . . to be continued

Work in groups. Discuss your answers and how you figured them out. Then compare your answers with those of other groups.

1 Why does Manolita think she was right?

2 What reason does Ferdie have to say the steward was trying to trick them?

3 How could Ferdie and Marcus get such different results?

Multiplying a Decimal by a Whole Number

Jenny is making 21 banners for her school play. Each banner takes 1.3 meters of cloth. What is the total length of cloth Jenny needs?

To find out, you would multiply 1.3 by 21.

Chad told Jenny that 21 × 1.3 was 27.3.

Can that be right? Why or why not?

You could do the problem in decimeters. Multiply 13 by 21.

$$
\begin{array}{r}
13 \\
\times\ 21 \\
\hline
13 \\
26 \\
\hline
273
\end{array}
\qquad 273\ \text{dm} = 27.3\ \text{m}
$$

So Jenny needs 27.3 meters of cloth.

Chad was right. 21 × 1.3 = 27.3

Let's look at the two multiplications side by side.

$$
\begin{array}{r}
13 \\
\times\ 21 \\
\hline
13 \\
26 \\
\hline
273
\end{array}
\qquad
\begin{array}{r}
1.3 \\
\times\ 21 \\
\hline
13 \\
26 \\
\hline
27.3
\end{array}
$$

The problems and the answers are the same, except for the decimal point.

◆ Can you figure out a simple rule for deciding where to put the decimal point in the answer?

To multiply a decimal by a whole number:

A. Multiply as you would with two whole numbers.

B. Put the decimal point in the answer as many places from the right as it is in the decimal factor.

Example A: 2.3 × 514

```
   5 1 4      Multiply as you would with two whole numbers.
 × 2.3
 ─────
  154 2
 1028
 ──────
 1182.2  —  Then place the point in the answer.
```

```
   5 1 4
 × 2.3    —  The point is one place from the right.
 ─────
  154 2
 1028
 ──────
 1182.2  —  So put the point one place from the right in
            the answer.
```

Example B: 73 × 0.375

```
  0.375     Multiply as you would with two whole numbers.
 ×  73
 ──────
  1 125
 26 25
 ──────
 27.375  —  Then place the point in the answer.
```

```
  0.375  —  The point is three places from the right.
 ×  73
 ──────
  1 125
 26 25
 ──────
 27.375  —  So put the point three places from the right in
            the answer.
```

◆ **LESSON 150 Multiplying a Decimal by a Whole Number**

Remember:

$$4.07$$ — The point is two places from the right.
$$\times\ 12$$
$$814$$
$$407$$
$$48.84$$ — Place the point two places from the right.

$$357$$ The point is three places from the right.
$$\times 0.006$$
$$2.142$$ Place the point three places from the right.

Multiply.

1 3.07 × 11   **2** 7198 × 0.09   **3** 71.3 × 85.2

4 82 × 0.03   **5** 6.8 × 13   **6** 2.306 × 1528

7 127 × 0.007   **8** 5.23 × 0.1   **9** 0.83 × 22

10 385 × 1.2   **11** 1.05 × 0.06   **12** 97.8 × 79

13 39 × 2.25   **14** 256 × 1.2   **15** 451 × 82.3

16 1008 × 0.009   **17** 8.2 × 7.9   **18** 19.84 × 17.76

19 673 × 5.6   **20** 617 × 2.5   **21** 268.4 × 1.26

22 27.9 × 1.83   **23** 112 × 4.92   **24** 6.4 × 2.83

Solve these problems.

25 Bart is the manager of a baseball team. His team needs 13 new shirts. Each shirt costs $7.29. Bart has $75. Does he have enough money?

26 Myrna wants to buy two shelves. One is 3 meters long and the other is 4 meters long. A shelf costs $4.05 per meter. How much will the two shelves cost?

27 Mr. Washington is building a house. He needs 27 electrical outlets. Each outlet costs $2.71. Will the 27 outlets cost more than $100?

28 The Omega Publishing Company ships an average of 751 books a week. It costs 48¢ to mail each book. How much does mailing cost, on the average, for the week?

29 Eric needs to buy stamps to send 18 party invitations. Each stamp costs 32¢. Eric has $5.75. Does he have enough money to buy stamps for all of the invitations?

Use your calculator to solve these problems.

30 Multiply 1.234 by 56.789.

31 The answer should be between 1 × 56 and 2 × 57. Did the calculator give an answer between 56 and 114?

32 How many digits are there to the right of the decimal point in your answer? Can you see any relationship between the number of digits to the right of the decimal point and the original factors?

33 What is 4.32 × 8.714? Between what numbers would the answer be? How many digits are going to be to the right of the decimal point? Did the calculator give a reasonable answer?

◆ Do you have a hypothesis about the number of digits to the right of the decimal point in the product when you multiply two decimal numbers? If so, what is it?

Check your hypothesis with the following products. If your hypothesis doesn't seem to work, see if you can figure out why.

34 3.452 × 0.0034   **35** 53.1 × 1.8745

36 3.45 × 1.2   **37** 1.25 × 1.04

38 547.682 × 934.86   **39** 73.56 × 4.709

40 Look at problems 36 and 37. Answer these questions.

   a. Why is the number of digits to the right of the decimal point in the product not the same as the total number of digits to the right of the points in the two factors? Does the calculator drop all zeros to the right of the last nonzero number after the decimal point?

   b. If you multiply 345 by 12, the product is 4140. Does that explain your answer for problem 36? What is the product of 125 and 104? Can you explain what happened in problem 37?

41 See if you can explain what happened in problem 38. How many digits can your calculator display? If your calculator has to leave off some digits from a product, does it make more sense that it omits digits at the beginning of the number or the end of the number? Why?

LESSON 151

Practicing Multiplication of Decimals and Whole Numbers

Use your knowledge of multiplication and decimals to solve the following problems.

1. If a snail can crawl 0.6 meter a day, how far can it crawl in a week? In a month (31 days)? In a year (365 days)?

2. Ahmad wants to tile his kitchen floor. Each tile covers 0.34 square meter. Ahmad ordered 60 tiles. Each tile cost $1.46. How much did he pay for the tiles?

3. Mrs. Khan bought 15 bags of pretzels for a party. Each bag cost $4.89. How much did she pay?

4. Alberto wants to call his mother long distance. He has only $4 in change. Each minute costs 31¢. Can he talk for 15 minutes?

In each problem, two of the answers are clearly wrong and one is correct. Choose the correct answer.

5. 8×1.7 **a.** 19.6   **b.** 13.6   **c.** 7.6

6. 6×2.4 **a.** 10.4   **b.** 22.4   **c.** 14.4

7. 4.9×5 **a.** 28.67   **b.** 259.7   **c.** 24.5

8. 0.5×9 **a.** 34.5   **b.** 4.5   **c.** 45

9. 8.73×9 **a.** 71.07   **b.** 78.57   **c.** 83.67

10. 20×5.1 **a.** 102   **b.** 94.2   **c.** 98.2

11. 16×3.28 **a.** 52.48   **b.** 42.48   **c.** 72.48

12. 33.51×2 **a.** 67.02   **b.** 47.14   **c.** 105.2

13. 70×67.3 **a.** 4971.0   **b.** 47,111   **c.** 4711.0

Solve these problems. **Use a computer or other means to draw and complete the charts. You may want to use graphing software to graph your data.**

14 Use the function rule to complete the chart.

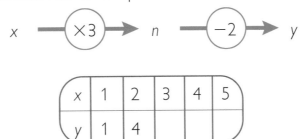

$x \longrightarrow \times 3 \longrightarrow n \longrightarrow -2 \longrightarrow y$

x	1	2	3	4	5
y	1	4			

15 Now plot the points on a graph.

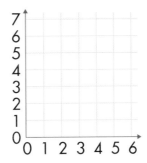

16 Do all five points seem to be on the same straight line?

17 Use your calculator to help you fill out the following chart for the function rule of problem 14. Then plot all of these points on the same graph you used for problem 15. Do these points also seem to lie on the same straight line?

x	1.1	1.2	1.3	1.9	2.3	2.6	3.2	3.7	4.1	4.5	4.8	4.9
y	1.3	1.6										

Solve.

18 Mr. Becker bought 12.2 gallons of gasoline on Sunday. On Thursday he bought 8.3 gallons of gasoline.

a. How much gasoline did Mr. Becker buy all together?

b. How much more gasoline did he buy on Sunday than he bought on Thursday?

◆ **LESSON 151** **Practicing Multiplication of Decimals and Whole Numbers**

Iron and Gold

Part 4

You may want to review earlier parts of this Thinking Story on pages 478–479, 488–489, and 504–505.

"The blue bag has the most gold on the top, and the red bag has the most gold on the bottom," said Marcus. "Portia, why don't you take coins from the middle of each bag? That way we can find out which has the most gold there."

"I have a different idea," said Portia. She reached into each bag and stirred and stirred until the coins were all mixed up. Then she took a big handful from each bag. From the red bag she got three gold coins and 13 iron ones. From the blue bag she got four gold coins and 11 iron ones. From the green bag she got nine gold coins and seven iron ones.

"Oh, no!" said Manolita. "First the red bag wins. Then the blue bag wins. Then the red bag wins again, and now the green bag wins! How can we ever tell which bag to take?"

"I guess we'd better take the red bag," said Ferdie. "It won twice."

"I say the blue bag," said Marcus. "I got almost all gold coins when I took a handful from it."

"I vote for the green bag," said Portia.

"Me too," said Manolita.

"Oh, well," said the steward. "Democracy wins again!"

. . . to be continued

Work in groups. Discuss your answers and how you figured them out. Then compare your answers with those of other groups.

1 Which bag do you think is the best choice? Why?

2 About what fraction of the coins in the green bag do you think are gold?

3 What would be a reason for mixing up the coins in each bag, the way Portia did?

4 What do you think the steward did to trick the children two ways?

LESSON
152

Using Decimals: Weight and Volume

You have measured objects to find their length. You can also measure objects to find their weight or volume. **Weight** describes how heavy something is.

The gram and the kilogram are metric units of weight.

Two paper clips weigh about 1 gram (1 g).

A marble weighs about 5 grams (5 g).

A man's shoe weighs about 500 grams (500 g).

1 kilogram is 1000 grams.   1 kg = 1000 g

1 gram is one thousandth of a kilogram.   1 g = 0.001 kg

Solve.

❶ 2 g = ■ kg   ❷ 805 g = ■ kg   ❸ 0.05 kg = ■ g

❹ 40 g = ■ kg   ❺ 900 g = ■ kg   ❻ 0.005 kg = ■ g

❼ 88 g = ■ kg   ❽ 0.3 kg = ■ g   ❾ 25 kg = ■ g

❿ 620 g = ■ kg   ⓫ 8 kg = ■ g   ⓬ 2.5 kg = ■ g

Volume is the number of cubic units that will fill an object.

The liter and milliliter are metric units of volume.

About how much is 1 liter?

Each container holds about 1 liter (1 L).

There are 1000 milliliters in 1 liter.   1000 mL = 1 L

1 milliliter is one thousandth of a liter.   1 mL = 0.001 L

Solve.

⓭ 3 mL = ■ L   ⓮ 500 mL = ■ L   ⓯ 0.025 L = ■ mL

⓰ 63 mL = ■ L   ⓱ 758 mL = ■ L   ⓲ 0.725 L = ■ mL

⓳ 40 mL = ■ L   ⓴ 0.002 L = ■ mL   ㉑ 2.5 L = ■ mL

㉒ 409 mL = ■ L   ㉓ 0.02 L = ■ mL   ㉔ 5 L = ■ mL

 **COOPERATIVE LEARNING** Work in groups with a set of containers and a balance. Measure the weights of various volumes of water in grams.

Luisa made a chart to show the weight of each volume of water.

 **Use a computer or other means to make a chart to show your results, or copy and complete Luisa's chart.**

	Volume of Water in Container (milliliters)	Weight of Empty Container (grams)	Weight of Container with Water (grams)	Weight of Water (grams)
25	0	8	8	0
26	10	8	18	▪
27	20	8	27	▪
28	40	8	47	▪
29	50	8	57	▪
30	0	10	10	▪
31	60	10	71	▪
32	80	10	91	▪
33	100	10	110	▪
34	0	21	21	▪
35	120	21	141	▪
36	140	21	163	▪
37	160	21	185	▪

Luisa made a line graph to show her results. You might want to use graphing software to graph your results. If you haven't done the experiment, make a graph of Luisa's results.

 **MATH JOURNAL** **In your Math Journal explain how kilograms and grams are like kilometers and meters. How are liters and milliliters like meters and millimeters?**

Cubic Centimeters

Volume measures the space inside an object.

The cubic centimeter is a metric unit of volume.

This cube has a volume of 1 cubic centimeter.

1 cubic centimeter is about the same volume as 1 milliliter.

Find the volume of each box in cubic centimeters by figuring out how many cubes there are.

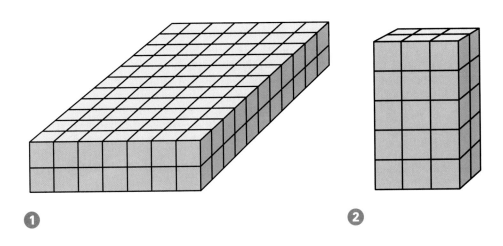

1

2

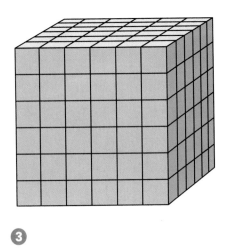

3

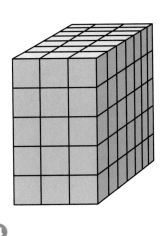

4

Solve these problems.

5 A 1-liter container is half-filled with water. How many milliliters of water are in the container?

6 Which is a better buy, a 1.5-liter can of apple juice for $2.40 or two 700-milliliter cans of the same juice for $1.20 each?

7 A liter of water weighs 1.00 kg. How much do each of these weigh?

   a. one half liter of water

   b. 0.5 liter of water

   c. 100 milliliters of water

   d. 0.1 liter of water

8 An empty jar weighs 100 grams. When filled with water, the jar weighs 500 grams.

   a. How much does the water in the jar weigh?

   b. How many milliliters of water does the jar contain? (Remember, 1 liter of water weighs 1 kilogram.)

9 Seth weighed 100 marbles. They weighed 490 grams all together. On the average, how much does each marble weigh?

10 Pam wants to buy a sweater that costs $26.99 and a denim skirt that costs $34.99. She has $70.00. Does she have enough money to buy both items?

11 Lina wants to go fishing. She has $4. Worms cost 73¢ each. Does she have enough money to buy four worms?

LESSON 154

Keep in Shape: Fractions and Decimals

Keep in shape by solving problems that involve fractions.

Solve these problems.

1 The road repair crew used $\frac{1}{4}$ truckload of cement yesterday and $\frac{1}{2}$ truckload today. How many truckloads did they use all together?

2 Mr. Moore drove from his home to Durango. When he left home, he had about $\frac{3}{4}$ of a tank of gasoline in his car. When he arrived in Durango, he had only $\frac{1}{4}$ of a tank.

a. What fraction of a tank of gas did Mr. Moore use on the trip to Durango?

b. Can Mr. Moore drive back home without getting more gasoline?

c. What fraction of a tank of gasoline does Mr. Moore need to fill his tank in Durango?

d. If Mr. Moore fills his tank in Durango, about how full will it be when he gets home?

e. How many tanks of gasoline does Mr. Moore use on a trip to Durango and back?

f. Can you make a good estimate of how many miles it might be from Mr. Moore's home to Durango?

Keep in shape by practicing multiplying and dividing with decimals. Remember to place the decimal point in the correct position in each answer.

3 100 × 3.5

4 100,000 × 394.565

5 5.7 ÷ 1000

6 10 × 36.237

7 14.3 ÷ 10,000

8 101.6761 × 1,000,000

9 10 × 15.576

10 55.107 ÷ 100

11 1,000,000 × 6.5591

12 1000 × 53.45

13 56.227 ÷ 100,000

14 10,000 × 89,065.339

15 100 × 323.75

16 84.6 ÷ 100

17 10,000 × 46.5

18 60.273 ÷ 10,000

19 237.39 ÷ 1000

20 10 × 9.78

Multiply.

21 4 × 3.5

22 76.39 × 91

23 17.95 × 6

24 327 × 9.37

25 7 × 59.106

26 3.1 × 872

27 53 × 5.467

28 124 × 0.47

29 37 × 4.86

30 53.15 × 79

31 40.5 × 67

32 102 × 9.14

33 82.7 × 17

34 2.208 × 7129

35 36 × 67.3

36 32,153 × 6.15

37 76.3 × 325

38 15.08 × 717

39 63 × 36.7

40 2585 × 7.12

Solve.

41 Toshio wants to buy three new books that cost $6.25 each. To raise money, he is selling some of his old books for $0.49 each.

a. If he sells 35 of his old books, how much money will he take in?

b. Will that be enough to pay for the new books?

◆ **LESSON 154** **Keep in Shape: Fractions and Decimals**

Iron and Gold

Part 5

You may want to review earlier parts of this Thinking Story on pages 478–479, 488–489, 504–505, and 512–513.

" I was hiding behind the door," said the queen. "And I saw what the steward did. He was trying to cheat you. Now I know that he has been cheating me, too, and stealing money from the Royal Treasury. I will see that he pays for his crimes. But now I want to give you another reward."

The queen set out some glass jars filled with jewels. "The red jewels are rubies and the yellow ones are worthless glass," said the queen. "You may each choose one jewel, but you will be blindfolded so that you can't tell if you are taking a ruby or a piece of glass. I will shake up the jar before you draw, so that you can't remember where a ruby is and reach for it."

These are the first two jars she showed them:

Ferdie got the first turn. "I want to draw from the full jar," he said, "because it has the most rubies in it." Ferdie wasn't so lucky, however. He drew a piece of glass.

These are the jars that Portia could choose from:

"I don't think it matters which jar I draw from," Portia said. She drew from the jar that had only two jewels in it, and she got the worthless yellow jewel.

These are the jars Marcus got to draw from:

"I know for sure which jar to choose from," Marcus said. "I'm sure to get a ruby." He picked the jar with only eight jewels. The queen blindfolded him. Then she shook the jar. Marcus reached into it—and got a yellow jewel. "Impossible," he said.

These are the jars Manolita got to choose from:

"Don't feel bad," said Manolita. "When I sell my ruby, I'll share the money with all of you."

. . . the end

Work in groups. Discuss your answers and how you figured them out. Then compare your answers with those of other groups.

1 Did Ferdie choose the right jar to draw from? Why or why not?

2 Why would Portia say it didn't matter which jar she drew from?

3 Why might Marcus be so sure he would get a ruby?

4 If Marcus chose the right jar, how could he fail to get a ruby?

5 Could Manolita be sure she would get a ruby? How?

6 Of all the children, who had the best chance of getting a ruby? Who had the next best chance? Who had the poorest chance?

ASSESSMENT

LESSON 155

Unit 6 Review

Lessons 139, 141

Replace each ● with <, >, or =.

① 0.7 ● 0.07   **②** 0.2 ● 0.09   **③** 0.40 ● 1.22

④ 0.14 ● 0.32   **⑤** 0.325 ● 0.096   **⑥** 0.0005 ● 0.008

⑦ 0.68 ● 0.86   **⑧** 0.49 ● 0.049   **⑨** 1.28 ● 10.28

Lessons 143, 144

Multiply or divide.

⑩ 1000 × 1.257   **⑪** 100 × 0.037   **⑫** 3.996 ÷ 10

⑬ 35.298 × 10   **⑭** 4.73 × 1000   **⑮** 100,000 ÷ 10

⑯ 1000 × 1.87   **⑰** 16.49 × 100   **⑱** 2.93 ÷ 10,000

Lesson 145

Solve.

⑲ 3 dm = ■ m   **⑳** 6 dm, 3 cm, 9 mm = ■ m

㉑ 100 cm = ■ m   **㉒** ■ mm = 0.650 m

㉓ 35 mm = ■ m   **㉔** ■ cm = 0.45 m

Lesson 146

Give the length of each object to the nearest centimeter.

㉕ ■ cm

㉖ ■ cm

Add or subtract.

Lessons 147, 149

㉗ 3.6 + 1.5　　㉘ 15.17 − 13.29　　㉙ 6.2 − 2.7

㉚ 90.528 − 18.016　　㉛ 12.2 − 8.9　　㉜ 0.03 + 0.31

㉝ 20.13 + 9.18　　㉞ 24.26 − 24.01　　㉟ 3.11 + 20.26

Multiply.

Lessons 150, 151

㊱ 6 × 3.5　　㊲ 7 × 0.152　　㊳ 60 × 3.5

㊴ 400 × 1.8　　㊵ 0.37 × 8　　㊶ 5.316 × 90

㊷ 5.41 × 300　　㊸ 63.587 × 2　　㊹ 3.425 × 50

Order the following decimals from least to greatest. Insert a < symbol between each pair of numbers to make true statements.

Lesson 140

㊺ 1.6, 2.0, 0.47, 0.63, 0.041, 0.39　　㊻ 0.10, 0.21, 0.008, 0.06, 0.50, 0.49

Change each improper fraction to a mixed number or a whole number.

Lesson 133

㊼ $\frac{14}{8}$　　㊽ $\frac{16}{5}$　　㊾ $\frac{12}{3}$　　㊿ $\frac{10}{9}$　　51 $\frac{16}{7}$

What fraction of each figure is shaded?

Lesson 126

52 　　53 　　54

Solve for n.

Lesson 127

55 $\frac{4}{5}$ of 20 = n　　56 $\frac{6}{6}$ of 180 = n　　57 $\frac{4}{10}$ of 100 = n

Solve.

If a 0–5 cube is rolled, what is the probability of

Lessons 128, 129, 131

58 rolling a 2?　　59 rolling a 0 or a 1?

60 rolling a 0, 1, 2, 3, 4, or 5?　　61 rolling an even number?

◆ **LESSON 155** **Unit 6 Review**

Answer the following questions.

Lesson 134

62 How many inches are there in 7 feet?

63 How many feet are there in 19 yards?

Solve these problems.

64 Mark bought 2 pounds of popcorn. He popped half of it last week. How much popcorn is left?

Lessons 130, 132, 148, 149, 151, 154

65 Wayne had $342.38 in his checking account. He wrote a check for $37.49. How much did he then have in his account?

66 Priscilla bought some nails and screws at the hardware store. The bill came to $2.47. How much change should she get if she gives the clerk a $5 bill?

67 Which has more juice, a 1.4-liter can of juice or two 750-milliliter cans of juice?

68 Ten copies of a book weigh 45 kilograms. How much does each copy of the book weigh?

69 Terry had the flu, and his temperature was 102.3°F. The next day his temperature was 99.4°F. How much did his temperature drop?

70 Rebecca took 36 foul shots and made 20 of them. Did she miss more than $\frac{1}{4}$ of the shots?

Add or subtract the following fractions and mixed numbers. Show answers as whole numbers, or as mixed numbers or proper fractions reduced to lowest terms.

Lessons 133, 136, 137

71 $\frac{3}{5} + \frac{1}{5}$ **72** $8\frac{5}{12} - 3\frac{1}{12}$ **73** $9\frac{5}{16} - 7\frac{3}{4}$ **74** $5\frac{1}{2} + 2\frac{2}{3}$

75 $\frac{1}{3} + \frac{2}{3}$ **76** $4\frac{5}{16} - 3\frac{1}{8}$ **77** $9\frac{5}{16} + 7\frac{3}{4}$ **78** $2\frac{2}{5} + 1\frac{1}{2}$

79 $1\frac{2}{3} + 2\frac{2}{3}$ **80** $5\frac{3}{16} - 2\frac{3}{4}$ **81** $1\frac{2}{3} + 3\frac{1}{4}$ **82** $2\frac{2}{5} - 1\frac{1}{2}$

83 $3\frac{1}{16} + 5\frac{1}{4}$ **84** $2\frac{4}{5} + 1\frac{9}{10}$ **85** $3\frac{1}{4} - 1\frac{2}{3}$ **86** $3\frac{1}{10} - 2\frac{1}{2}$

87 $10\frac{4}{5} - 7\frac{3}{5}$ **88** $2\frac{4}{5} - 1\frac{9}{10}$ **89** $5\frac{1}{2} - 2\frac{2}{3}$ **90** $3\frac{1}{10} + 2\frac{1}{2}$

Round each number to the nearest hundredth.

Lesson 142

91 4.8352 **92** 0.0031 **93** 2.394

Round each number to the nearest thousandth.

94 0.0072 **95** 4.0013 **96** 1.2345

Solve these problems.

97 A cake recipe calls for $2\frac{2}{3}$ cups of sugar. The recipe for the frosting to go with the cake calls for $1\frac{1}{2}$ cups of sugar. How much sugar is that all together?

Lessons 133, 136, 137

98 One teaspoon of sugar substitute can replace $\frac{1}{3}$ cup of sugar. If 2 teaspoons of the substitute are used in the cake, how much sugar should be used?

99 If 2 teaspoons of the substitute are also used in the frosting, how much sugar should be used in the frosting?

100 If you make the substitutions suggested in problems 98 and 99, how much regular sugar will be in the combined cake and frosting?

LESSON 156

Unit 6 Practice

Replace each ● with <, >, or =.

Lessons 139, 141

① 0.3 ● 0.4   **②** 0.65 ● 0.6   **③** 0.67 ● 0.33

④ 0.2 ● 0.02   **⑤** 0.55 ● 0.60   **⑥** 0.305 ● 0.810

⑦ 0.2 ● 0.003   **⑧** 0.15 ● 0.07   **⑨** 0.265 ● 0.260

⑩ 0.07 ● 0.007   **⑪** 0.9 ● 0.99   **⑫** 0.5 ● 0.050

Solve.

Lesson 145

⑬ 100 cm = ■ m   **⑭** ■ mm = 1 cm   **⑮** 3 dm, 2 cm, 5 mm = ■ m

⑯ 400 cm = ■ m   **⑰** ■ cm = 1 dm   **⑱** 2 dm, 0 cm, 6 mm = ■ m

⑲ 1 dm = ■ m   **⑳** ■ dm = 1 m   **㉑** 6 dm, 5 mm = ■ m

㉒ 5 dm = ■ m   **㉓** 45 mm = ■ m   **㉔** 8 cm, 5 mm = ■ m

Follow the directions and answer the questions.

Lessons 126, 133

㉕ Draw a circle. Shade $\frac{2}{4}$ of it. Then shade another $\frac{1}{4}$ of it.

㉖ Draw another circle the same size as the one you drew in problem 25. Shade $\frac{3}{4}$ of it.

㉗ What is $\frac{1}{4} + \frac{2}{4}$?

㉘ Draw a rectangle. Shade $\frac{3}{4}$ of it. What fraction is **not** shaded?

㉙ What is $\frac{4}{4} - \frac{3}{4}$?

Solve for *n*.

Lesson 127

㉚ $n = \frac{1}{2}$ of 24   **㉛** $n = \frac{1}{8}$ of 32   **㉜** $n = \frac{2}{6}$ of 30

㉝ $n = \frac{3}{4}$ of 24   **㉞** $n = \frac{1}{3}$ of 30   **㉟** $n = \frac{2}{4}$ of 24

㊱ $n = \frac{3}{8}$ of 24   **㊲** $n = \frac{2}{3}$ of 60   **㊳** $n = \frac{6}{8}$ of 24

㊴ $n = \frac{1}{4}$ of 32   **㊵** $n = \frac{1}{6}$ of 30   **㊶** $n = \frac{2}{4}$ of 32

Solve these problems.

Lessons
130, 132,
148, 149,
151, 154

42 Selena had $65.00 in her checking account.

   a. She deposited $25.00. How much did she have then in her account?

   b. She wrote a check for $38.00. How much does she now have in her account?

   c. Does she have enough money to buy a sweater that costs $16.99 and a pair of shoes that costs $34.99?

43 Bruce had two quarters and two dimes. Then he found a $1 bill. How much money does he have?

44 Maya bought some vegetables. The grocer charged her $1.74. If Maya paid with a $5 bill, how much change did she get?

45 It is 1.4 kilometers from Ethan's house to the museum. How far is it there and back?

46 The doorway in Makio's classroom is 85 centimeters wide. Can a table that is 1 meter wide fit through the doorway without being tilted?

47 Janis says she is 140 centimeters tall. Grace says she is 1.35 meters tall.

   a. Who is taller?

   b. By how much?

48 Callie wants to find out the weight of a paper clip. She weighs 100 clips and finds out that they weigh 50 grams. How much does one paper clip weigh?

49 In the running broad jump, Bennett jumped 6.21 meters. His opponent, Judd, jumped 6.16 meters.

   a. Who won?

   b. By how many centimeters?

◆ **LESSON 156 Unit 6 Practice**

New City has 150 parking meters in its downtown shopping area.

People must pay 10 cents per hour if they park their cars from 8 A.M. to 6 P.M., Monday through Saturday. Parking is free on Sunday. The chief of police estimates that each meter is in use about half of the time.

 **Work in groups to solve these problems. Be sure to explain how you get your answers.**

Lessons 127, 130, 147, 150

50 About how much money do the parking meters take in during one week?

51 The monthly cost to repair the meters and collect the money is about $500. About how much profit does New City get from its parking meters each year?

52 If New City raises parking fees to 20 cents per hour, the chief of police estimates that the meters will be in use only $\frac{1}{3}$ of the time. Will the meters produce more profit at the new rate or the old rate? Explain your reasoning.

Round each number to the nearest hundredth.

Lesson 142
53 1.48721   54 6.489   55 241.7911

Round each number to the nearest thousandth.

56 61.00213   57 8.54762   58 21.3981

Perform the following experiments with two friends. One of you keeps records, one flips the coins or rolls the cubes, and the third person keeps track of the total number of rolls or flips.

Lessons 128, 129, 131

59 Flip a coin 100 times. How often did it land heads up? About what fraction of the time did it land heads up? (Pick the answer that's closest to your result.)

    a. None of the time   **b.** $\frac{1}{4}$ of the time   **c.** $\frac{1}{2}$ of the time

    d. $\frac{3}{4}$ of the time   **e.** All the time

60 If you flip a coin once, what is the probability that it will land heads up?

Roll a 0–5 cube 120 times. Keep track of the number of times you get each number. Answer these questions.

Lessons 128, 129, 131

61 About what fraction of the time did you roll a 0? A 5?

    a. $\frac{0}{6}$ **b.** $\frac{1}{6}$ **c.** $\frac{2}{6}$ **d.** $\frac{3}{6}$ **e.** $\frac{4}{6}$ **f.** $\frac{5}{6}$

62 How many times did you roll an even number?

Answer these questions.

63 If you flip a penny and a nickel (or any two coins) together 100 times, how many times do you think you'll get zero heads? One head? Two heads? Then put your predictions on a chart like the one shown.

64 Now try it. Keep a tally. You can change your predictions after a few flips.

65 Were your predictions close?

Heads	How Many Times in 100 Flips	
	Predicted	Actual
0		
1		
2		

Unit Test

Replace each ● with <, >, or =.

1 0.04 ● 0.3   **2** 1.5 ● 1.06   **3** 0.025 ● 0.007

4 0.08 ● 0.003   **5** 0.75 ● 0.80   **6** 0.750 ● 1.000

7 7.82 ● 7.082   **8** 2.49 ● 2.491   **9** 0.840 ● 0.084

Multiply or divide.

10 1.652×100 **11** $12.4 \div 1000$ **12** 10×0.18

13 10×1.3 **14** 1000×1.3 **15** 100×0.14

16 $12.07 \div 10$ **17** $3.821 \div 100$ **18** $5.329 \times 10,000$

19 $16.5 \div 100$ **20** 2.93×1000 **21** 862.7×10

Solve.

22 ▓ dm = 0.3 m   **23** ▓ cm = 0.4 m

24 65 mm = ▓ m   **25** 2 dm, 5 cm = ▓ m

Round each number to the nearest hundredth.

26 241.612   **27** 81.356   **28** 1.0042

29 17.43111   **30** 21.1172   **31** 4.0163

Round each number to the nearest thousandth.

32 1643.21891   **33** 17.00129   **34** 1.0041

35 2.48163   **36** 19.8122   **37** 7.9116

Add or subtract.

38 $40.53 + 40.85$ **39** $30.0 - 0.0345$ **40** $4.57 + 63.97$

41 $26.47 - 16.18$ **42** $16.774 + 28.845$ **43** $15.62 - 1.80$

44 $0.051 + 27.754$ **45** $8.5 - 7.9$ **46** $83.79 - 72.91$

47 $2.91 - 1.62$ **48** $29.01 + 15.42$ **49** $16.8 - 15.2$

Multiply.

50 2 × 7.2　　**51** 40 × 2.3　　**52** 40,000 × 8.73

53 0.241 × 70　　**54** 27.38 × 600　　**55** 7.49 × 30

56 300 × 5.11　　**57** 4.0 × 10　　**58** 65.25 × 2.82

What fraction of each figure is shaded?

59 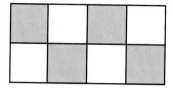　　**60**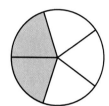

Solve for *n*.

61 $\frac{1}{2}$ of 62 = n　　**62** $\frac{5}{6}$ of 42 = n　　**63** $n = \frac{1}{4} + \frac{2}{4}$

64 $\frac{2}{3}$ of 45 = n　　**65** $\frac{1}{3}$ of 90 = n　　**66** $n = \frac{5}{8} - \frac{2}{8}$

67 $\frac{3}{10}$ of 1000 = n　　**68** $\frac{1}{10}$ of 50 = n　　**69** $n = \frac{3}{6} + \frac{3}{6}$

Solve these problems.

70 If you roll a 5–10 cube one time, what is the probability of rolling an odd number?

71 If you roll a 0–5 cube 600 times, how many times would you expect to roll a 4?

72 Tasha has three quarters and three dimes. How much more money does she need to buy a notebook that costs $1.25 with tax included?

73 Rodney lives on a block that is rectangular. It is 0.25 kilometer long and 0.10 kilometer wide. How far does Rodney jog when he jogs around the block once?

74 It takes Amy one-half hour to walk home from school. If she leaves school at 3:30 P.M., when will she get home?

75 Joe needs 20 more minutes to finish his homework. It is now 4:55 P.M. What time will he finish?

Fairlawn School Buys a Computer

The 25 students in the fourth grade at Fairlawn School are raising $800 to buy a computer. They decided to sell apples to pay for the computer. They can purchase a bushel of apples for $15. They found that there are, on the average, 100 apples in a bushel.

SALE PRICE
$800

1 What is a fair price at which the children should resell the apples? Remember, they have to make enough money to pay for the apples *and* to buy the computer.

2 What other information will help the class set a fair price?

Pricing the Apples

The children visited neighborhood stores and found that the price of apples was as low as 18 cents each in one store and as high as 28 cents each in another store. After much discussion, the children decided to charge 25¢ for each apple.

3 Based on 100 apples in a bushel, by how much did they mark up the price of an apple?

4 How many apples will they have to sell to make $800?

5 How many apples should each child be expected to sell?

6 How much money will the class have to invest to purchase the apples?

Advertising the Apples

The principal of Fairlawn School said the class could have free advertising space in the school-parent newsletter if the students would write their own advertisement. The class couldn't agree on which of the following three advertisements would be most useful.

Discuss the following questions in small groups.

7 Which advertisement is the fairest? Which is the most unfair?

8 Which advertisement will most likely produce the most sales?

9 Write a fair advertisement for the Fairlawn School's fourth-grade class. Decorate the advertisement so it will attract attention.

10 Besides selling apples, what are some other ways for a fourth-grade class to raise money?

11 Could your classroom benefit from a computer or other equipment that will improve your education?

12 About how much money will it cost? If you don't know, where would you go to find the price?

Develop a plan to raise the needed money. Be sure your plan is fair.

Cumulative Review
Use after Lesson 4.

Write the numbers in standard form.

1 40 + 7

2 800 + 20 + 7

3 3000 + 600 + 50 + 1

4 6000 + 100 + 0 + 0

5 40,000 + 500 + 70 + 2

6 5 + 600 + 80,000 + 100,000

7 300,000 + 4,000 + 70

8 2,000,000 + 40,000 + 6,000 + 800 + 10

9 500,000 + 200

10 3 + 80 + 200 + 40,000 + 90,000,000

11 20,000,000 + 500,000 + 80,000 + 100 + 9

Count up or down. Write the missing numbers.

12 15, 16, 17, ■, ■, ■, ■, ■, 23

13 97, 98, 99, ■, ■, ■, ■, 104

14 403, 402, 401, ■, ■, ■, ■, ■, 395

15 45,677; 45,678; 45,679; ■; ■; ■; ■; 45,684

16 1,000,204; 1,000,203; 1,000,202; ■; ■; ■; ■; 1,000,197

Write the greatest number and the least number.

17 Use the digits 4, 2, 8, and 5. **18** Use the digits 3, 9, 1, 0, and 6.

Write six different numbers in order from greatest to least.

19 Use the digits 5, 7, and 9.   **20** Use the digits 1, 4, and 8.

Cumulative Review
Use after Lesson 9.

Add or subtract to solve for *n*.

① $7 + 6 = n$ **②** $4 + 9 = n$ **③** $14 - 9 = n$

④ $8 - 7 = n$ **⑤** $13 - 8 = n$ **⑥** $n = 16 - 8$

⑦ $8 + 9 = n$ **⑧** $n = 5 + 6$ **⑨** $8 + 3 = n$

⑩ $n = 4 + 8$ **⑪** $12 - 6 = n$ **⑫** $n = 15 - 6$

Add or subtract.

⑬
$$\begin{array}{r} 17 \\ -\ 9 \\ \hline \end{array}$$

⑭
$$\begin{array}{r} 6 \\ 5 \\ 1 \\ +\ 3 \\ \hline \end{array}$$

⑮
$$\begin{array}{r} 5 \\ 3 \\ 2 \\ 3 \\ +\ 2 \\ \hline \end{array}$$

⑯
$$\begin{array}{r} 10 \\ -\ 4 \\ \hline \end{array}$$

⑰
$$\begin{array}{r} 8 \\ -\ 7 \\ \hline \end{array}$$

⑱
$$\begin{array}{r} 6 \\ -\ 0 \\ \hline \end{array}$$

Use a computer or other means to copy and complete each chart. Watch the function rule.

⑲   ⟶ (-7) ⟶

In	Out
19	■
16	■
14	■
11	■

⑳   ⟶ $(+10)$ ⟶

In	Out
0	■
3	■
8	■
10	■

ALGEBRA READINESS

Solve for *n*.

㉑ $n + 4 = 9$ **㉒** $7 - n = 2$ **㉓** $18 + n = 25$

PROBLEM SOLVING

Solve these problems.

㉔ Clem owns seven horses. He needs 12 horses to open a riding stable. How many more horses does he need?

㉕ Daria had $9. Then she did chores and earned $8. Does she have enough money to buy a CD that costs $14?

Cumulative Review

Use after Lesson 13.

Use the chart to answer questions 1–5.

Population Growth of Four States			
State	1970	1980	1990
Colorado	2,209,596	2,889,735	3,294,394
Iowa	2,825,368	2,913,808	2,776,755
Kentucky	3,220,711	3,660,324	3,685,296
Nevada	488,738	800,508	1,201,833

1 Which state had the greatest population in 1970? In 1980? In 1990?

2 Name the state or states that had a greater population in 1990 than in 1980.

3 Which state nearly doubled in population between 1970 and 1980?

4 Which state, if any, gained in population between 1970 and 1980 and lost in population between 1980 and 1990?

5 Which state had close to a million people in 1980?

Add or subtract.

6
$$
\begin{array}{r} 45 \\ + 34 \\ \hline \end{array}
$$

7
$$
\begin{array}{r} 73 \\ + 18 \\ \hline \end{array}
$$

8
$$
\begin{array}{r} 84 \\ - 54 \\ \hline \end{array}
$$

9
$$
\begin{array}{r} 50 \\ - 26 \\ \hline \end{array}
$$

10
$$
\begin{array}{r} 269 \\ + 407 \\ \hline \end{array}
$$

11
$$
\begin{array}{r} 784 \\ - 512 \\ \hline \end{array}
$$

12
$$
\begin{array}{r} 472 \\ - 385 \\ \hline \end{array}
$$

13
$$
\begin{array}{r} 8592 \\ + 3714 \\ \hline \end{array}
$$

14
$$
\begin{array}{r} 2003 \\ + 5458 \\ \hline \end{array}
$$

15
$$
\begin{array}{r} 269 \\ - 182 \\ \hline \end{array}
$$

16
$$
\begin{array}{r} 660 \\ + 299 \\ \hline \end{array}
$$

17
$$
\begin{array}{r} 750 \\ + 250 \\ \hline \end{array}
$$

18
$$
\begin{array}{r} 481 \\ - 101 \\ \hline \end{array}
$$

19
$$
\begin{array}{r} 357 \\ + 728 \\ \hline \end{array}
$$

20
$$
\begin{array}{r} 1000 \\ - 545 \\ \hline \end{array}
$$

Cumulative Review
Use after Lesson 17.

Replace ● with <, >, or = to make each statement true.

1 37 ● 29

2 71 ● 21 + 50

3 70 ● 81

4 11 ● 77 − 55

5 5 + 8 ● 8 + 5

6 54 ● 34 + 10

7 6 ● 16 − 6

8 6 + 7 ● 20 − 8

9 100 ● 84 + 20

10 50 ● 33 + 22

11 62 + 6 ● 62 + 3

12 91 − 19 ● 82 − 28

13 76 − 21 ● 15 − 4

14 21 ● 17 + 4

Solve these problems.

15 Mrs. Moran bought 11 apples, 13 oranges, 17 bananas, and 26 carrots. How many more pieces of fruit than vegetables did she buy?

16 Matt had $6.76. He bought a pen for 75¢ and a book for $2.96. How much money does he have left?

17 Karen and her family are driving to their favorite amusement park. The park is 50 kilometers from their house. So far, they have driven 13 kilometers. How much farther do they have to drive to reach the park?

Choose the correct answer.

18
$$\begin{array}{r} 70 \\ + 35 \\ \hline \end{array}$$
  a. 917   **b.** 1076   **c.** 1194

19

  a. 504   **b.** 484   **c.** 319

Solve for *n*. Watch the signs.

20 $2 + n = 11$

21 $n + 6 = 40$

22 $n − 8 = 41$

23 $25 − n = 5$

24 $n − 7 = 7$

25 $n + 10 = 17$

Cumulative Review
Use after Lesson 21.

Which statements do not make sense?

1. One half of Chan-Ho's cousins are boys and $\frac{3}{4}$ are girls.

2. Ruby took 30 foul shots and made 25 of them. She made $\frac{1}{2}$ of the foul shots.

3. There are 12 eggs in a dozen. If Robert uses six eggs for breakfast, $\frac{1}{2}$ of the dozen will remain.

4. The top half of the brick is bigger than the bottom half.

Solve these problems.

5. Kelli is in a walk-a-thon to raise money for charity. She has walked 12 of the 20 kilometers. Is she halfway there?

6. The Math Club has 24 members. Two thirds of them are boys. Are there more boys or girls in the club?

7. Skates that usually sell for $100 are on sale for $68. Is that more or less than $\frac{1}{4}$ off the regular price?

8. Rege has six dollars and eight dimes. Write the amount in dollars and cents.

9. The largest audience ever to see a circus was 52,385 people. They saw the circus inside the Superdome in New Orleans, Louisiana, in 1975. The largest audience for a circus inside a tent was 16,702 people. They saw it in Concordia, Kansas, in 1924. About how much larger was the Superdome audience than the tent audience?

   a. About 35,000   **b.** About 3500   **c.** About 350,000

Add or subtract.

10. 45,710 − 9,804

11. 465 + 9102 + 66 + 3

12. 381,840 + 77,096

13. 123,456,789 + 234,567

14. 50,000 − 41,072

15. 4307 − 906

Cumulative Review

Use after Lesson 25.

Write the amount in dollars and cents.

1 1 cent

2 4 dimes

3 5 dimes and 3 cents

4 9 dimes and 9 cents

5 1 dollar and 1 dime

6 4 dollars and 7 dimes

7 7 dollars and 3 cents

8 8 dollars, 4 dimes, and 6 cents

Replace ● with <, >, or = to make each statement true.

9 $2.00 ● $1.79

10 $0.63 ● $6.03

11 $4.77 ● $4.68

12 $0.80 ● $0.08

13 $52 ● $52.00

14 $48.92 ● $50

15 $54.39 ● $54.93

16 $4.89 ● $4.87

Add or subtract. Use shortcuts when you can.

17 $14 + $2.33

18 $20.00 − $4.75

19 $0.50 + $0.25

20 $6.48 − $1.04

21 $39.88 − $9.88

22 $4.63 + $31

Use the menu to answer the questions.

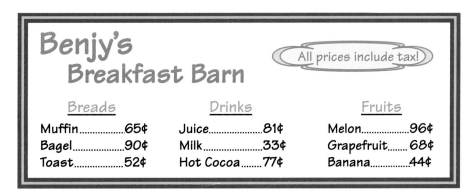

Benjy's Breakfast Barn

All prices include tax!

Breads		Drinks		Fruits	
Muffin	65¢	Juice	81¢	Melon	96¢
Bagel	90¢	Milk	33¢	Grapefruit	68¢
Toast	52¢	Hot Cocoa	77¢	Banana	44¢

23 How much will it cost for a muffin, a milk, and two bananas?

24 Tara has $1.50 to spend on breakfast. If she orders a bagel, what drink can she afford to get with it?

25 Leon orders melon, hot cocoa, and toast. How much change will he get back from $5?

Cumulative Review
Use after Lesson 27.

Use the table to choose the best answer.

Distances from Washington, D.C.	
City	Distance (in miles)
Atlanta, Georgia	632
Boise, Idaho	2397
Cleveland, Ohio	380
Houston, Texas	1414
Orlando, Florida	842
Seattle, Washington	2788

1 About how far is it from Washington, D.C., to Houston?

   a. About 2000 miles   **b.** About 1400 miles   **c.** About 140 miles

2 About how much farther is it from Washington, D.C., to Boise than from Washington, D.C., to Orlando?

   a. About 1600 miles   **b.** About 3000 miles   **c.** About 1000 miles

3 About how far is it from Cleveland to Washington, D.C., to Atlanta?

   a. About 250 miles   **b.** About 1000 miles   **c.** About 700 miles

4 About how far is it from Seattle to Washington, D.C., and back?

   a. About 2800 miles   **b.** About 4000 miles   **c.** About 5600 miles

Add or subtract.

5 $5.08 − $3.26

6 $0.75 + $2.13

7 $25.87 + $44.50

8 $5 − $0.88

9 $30.00 − $17.49

10 $1.23 + $4.56 + $7.89

Cumulative Review
Use after Lesson 32.

Multiply to solve for *n*.

1 $4 \times 0 = n$ **2** $4 \times 5 = n$ **3** $0 \times 8 = n$

4 $1 \times 7 = n$ **5** $4 \times 4 = n$ **6** $6 \times 6 = n$

7 $9 \times 6 = n$ **8** $2 \times 5 = n$ **9** $8 \times 4 = n$

10 $7 \times 3 = n$ **11** $3 \times 6 = n$ **12** $8 \times 3 = n$

Multiply.

13 $\begin{array}{r} 8 \\ \times\ 7 \\ \hline \end{array}$ **14** $\begin{array}{r} 9 \\ \times\ 4 \\ \hline \end{array}$ **15** $\begin{array}{r} 7 \\ \times\ 7 \\ \hline \end{array}$ **16** $\begin{array}{r} 6 \\ \times\ 8 \\ \hline \end{array}$ **17** $\begin{array}{r} 4 \\ \times\ 3 \\ \hline \end{array}$

18 $\begin{array}{r} 5 \\ \times\ 9 \\ \hline \end{array}$ **19** $\begin{array}{r} 4 \\ \times\ 7 \\ \hline \end{array}$ **20** $\begin{array}{r} 3 \\ \times\ 9 \\ \hline \end{array}$ **21** $\begin{array}{r} 2 \\ \times\ 4 \\ \hline \end{array}$ **22** $\begin{array}{r} 9 \\ \times\ 2 \\ \hline \end{array}$

Complete the chart.

	Length of Side	Area of Square
23	1 cm	▪
24	3 cm	▪
25	5 cm	▪
26	7 cm	▪
27	9 cm	▪

Solve for *n*.

28 $16 - n = 4$

29 $25 + n = 34$

30 $18 - n = 7$

Cumulative Review
Use after Lesson 37.

Copy and complete the price chart.

Beads at 8¢ Each

①
0	1	2	3	4	5	6	7	8	9	10
0	8	■	■	■	■	■	■	■	■	■

Use the price chart to answer these questions.

② Siri buys six beads and pays with a $1 bill. How much change should she get back?

③ The Bead Shop has a sale. For every two beads Siri buys, she gets one free. How much will she spend for six beads on sale?

What time is it?

④ 20 minutes after 4:45 P.M.?   ⑤ 45 minutes after 12:30 A.M.?

⑥ 10 minutes after 1:05 P.M.?   ⑦ 5 minutes before noon?

How long is each event?

⑧ A play that has a 55-minute first act, a 15-minute intermission, and a 50-minute second act.

⑨ A football game that has four 15-minute quarters, two 5-minute intermissions, and one 12-minute half-time.

⑩ A school day that has seven 50-minute class periods, six 10-minute breaks, and one 35-minute lunch period.

⑪ Making cookies that take 35 minutes to mix the batter, 12 minutes to bake, and 25 minutes to cool.

Multiply.

⑫ 7×8 ⑬ 7×7 ⑭ 8×9 ⑮ 9×6

Cumulative Review
Use after Lesson 42.

Solve these problems. Simplify each answer.

① 2 weeks 5 days + 4 weeks 4 days = ■

② 3 hours 50 minutes + 2 hours 45 minutes = ■

③ 6 weeks 2 days − 4 weeks 6 days = ■

④ 4 days 10 hours − 20 hours = ■

⑤ 5 days 18 hours + 1 week 9 hours = ■

⑥ 3 days 11 hours 36 minutes − 1 day 20 hours 5 minutes = ■

Use a computer or other means to copy and complete this chart about rectangular swimming pools.

	Whose Pool	Length (meters)		Width (meters)		Area (square meters)	
		At Least	No More Than	At Least	No More Than	At Least	No More Than
⑦	Ellie's	9	10	8	9	■	■
⑧	Jacob's	4	5	6	7	■	■
⑨	Nora's	5	6	5	6	■	■
⑩	Van's	7	8	9	10	■	■

Multiply to solve for *n*.

⑪ $2 \times 8 = n$ **⑫** $4 \times 9 = n$ **⑬** $6 \times 8 = n$

⑭ $3 \times 4 = n$ **⑮** $8 \times 8 = n$ **⑯** $3 \times 9 = n$

⑰ $5 \times 0 = n$ **⑱** $6 \times 4 = n$ **⑲** $2 \times 6 = n$

⑳ $6 \times 7 = n$ **㉑** $7 \times 8 = n$ **㉒** $5 \times 7 = n$

㉓ $9 \times 8 = n$ **㉔** $4 \times 4 = n$ **㉕** $1 \times 1 = n$

Cumulative Review
Use after Lesson 47.

Solve for *n*.

1. $2 \times n = 14$
2. $6 \times n = 24$
3. $3 \times n = 21$
4. $n \times 4 = 20$
5. $n \times 8 = 56$
6. $n \times 6 = 30$
7. $50 = n \times 5$
8. $45 = n \times 5$
9. $63 = n \times 9$
10. $36 = n \times 4$
11. $72 = n \times 8$
12. $42 = n \times 6$

Solve these problems.

13. Each day, Mara feeds 4 cups of dry food to her cats. A bag of cat food has 40 cups. How many days can Mara feed her cats from one bag of cat food?

14. Jess has to make 30 posters for the school fair. If he makes four posters each day, will he finish in a week?

15. Mr. Freed bought 65 new books for the library. So far he has shelved 47 of them. How many more books must be shelved?

16. Stacy has a limit of three hours a week of Internet time. If she spends 20 minutes a day on the Internet, will she be over or under her limit? By how much?

Divide. Watch for remainders.

17. $8 \div 8 = n$
18. $27 \div 9 = n$
19. $n = 16 \div 4$
20. $42 \div 7 = n$
21. $6 \div 1 = n$
22. $n = 36 \div 6$
23. $18 \div 3 = n$
24. $70 \div 10 = n$
25. $n = 28 \div 4$

26. $10\overline{)62}$
27. $6\overline{)30}$
28. $3\overline{)14}$
29. $5\overline{)40}$
30. $9\overline{)62}$

31. $8\overline{)32}$
32. $7\overline{)50}$
33. $4\overline{)28}$
34. $2\overline{)7}$
35. $1\overline{)3}$

Cumulative Review
Use after Lesson 50.

Divide. Watch for remainders.

1 $10\overline{)36}$ **2** $6\overline{)35}$ **3** $3\overline{)16}$ **4** $5\overline{)44}$ **5** $9\overline{)13}$

6 $8\overline{)30}$ **7** $7\overline{)47}$ **8** $4\overline{)28}$ **9** $2\overline{)13}$ **10** $6\overline{)40}$

11 $9\overline{)60}$ **12** $6\overline{)16}$ **13** $3\overline{)15}$ **14** $5\overline{)21}$ **15** $9\overline{)42}$

Solve.

16 Raymond baked 24 muffins. He gave the same number of muffins to each of three friends. How many muffins did each friend get? How many muffins were left over?

17 A van holds eight students. Thirty students are going on a field trip by van. How many vans are needed to carry everyone?

18 Lucy is buying party invitations. The invitations she likes come eight to a package. She needs to send 20 invitations. How many packages of invitations should she buy?

Solve for *n*. Watch the signs.

19 $27 \div (9 \div 3) = n$ **20** $11 - (4 \times 2) = n$

21 $(6 \times 5) + (21 \div 3) = n$ **22** $(32 \div 8) \times (10 - 6) = n$

23 $(3 \times 6) \div 2 = n$ **24** $15 - (5 \times 2) = n$

Solve this problem.

25 Jason bought three oranges. He cut each orange into six slices. He put half of the slices in his lunch box and the rest in his brother's lunch box. How many slices of orange did Jason take for his lunch?

Cumulative Review

Use after Lesson 54.

Use the coordinate grid.

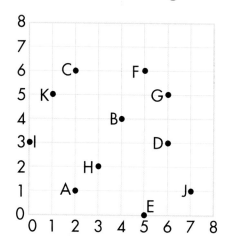

① What are the coordinates of point *H*?

② What are the coordinates of point *K*?

③ What are the coordinates of point *A*?

④ What are the coordinates of point *E*?

⑤ What are the coordinates of point *D*?

⑥ What is the letter at (5, 6)?

⑦ What is the letter at (6, 5)?

⑧ What is the letter at (0, 3)?

⑨ What is the letter at (7, 1)?

In each case, tell what *y* is.

⑩ 9 ──(+3)──▶ *y*

⑪ 9 ──(÷3)──▶ *y*

⑫ 9 ──(×3)──▶ *y*

⑬ 11 ──(−8)──▶ *y*

⑭ 35 ──(−8)──▶ *y*

⑮ 15 ──(×2)──▶ *y*

Cumulative Review
Use after Lesson 59.

Write the numbers in standard form.

1 8000 + 300 + 50 + 2

2 9000 + 20 + 6

3 30,000 + 4,000 + 8

4 10,000 + 4,000 + 500 + 70 + 1

5 400,000 + 20,000 + 8,000 + 500 + 70 + 9

6 600,000 + 80,000 + 7,000 + 900 + 30 + 1

Find the perimeter.

7
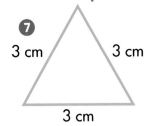
3 cm   3 cm
3 cm

8
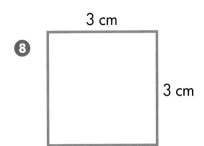
3 cm
3 cm

9
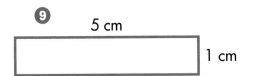
5 cm
1 cm

10
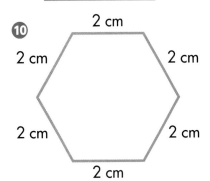
2 cm
2 cm   2 cm
2 cm   2 cm
2 cm

Add or subtract.

11 847 − 598	**12** 612 − 377	**13** 9827 + 3878	**14** 2314 + 5986	**15** 36 + 43
16 700 − 472	**17** 650 + 199	**18** 721 − 201	**19** 3000 − 875	**20** 29 − 17

Cumulative Review
Use after Lesson 63.

Write the amount in dollars and cents.

1 4 dimes and 3 cents

2 2 quarters and 6 cents

3 3 dollars, 7 dimes, and 2 cents

4 7 dollars and 3 quarters

5 8 dollars and 9 cents

6 5 dollars, 3 dimes, and 2 cents

7 5 dollars, 1 dime, and 6 cents

8 1 dollar and 3 cents

Subtract.

9
```
   508
 − 329
```

10
```
   634
 − 367
```

11
```
   320
 −  78
```

12
```
   544
 − 479
```

Copy each list of ordered pairs. Replace the *x* or *y* with the correct number.

13 *x* —(÷3)→ *y*   (6, *y*), (9, *y*), (21, *y*), (*x*, 5), (*x*, 4)

14 *x* —(×6)→ *y*   (9, *y*), (7, *y*), (5, *y*), (*x*, 24), (*x*, 42)

Copy and complete these charts.

15 *x* —(×4)→ *y*

x	y
0	▩
4	▩
▩	20
▩	32

16 *x* —(÷7)→ *y*

x	y
70	▩
56	▩
▩	7
▩	5

Multiply or divide.

17 7 × 8

18 45 ÷ 5

19 48 ÷ 6

20 4 × 9

Cumulative Review
Use after Lesson 68.

Divide. Watch for remainders.

1 $9\overline{)31}$ **2** $2\overline{)9}$ **3** $8\overline{)36}$ **4** $3\overline{)32}$

5 $4\overline{)20}$ **6** $6\overline{)46}$ **7** $5\overline{)19}$ **8** $1\overline{)8}$

Solve these problems.

9 Nia has to read 35 pages for homework. She has seven more pages to go. How many pages has she already read?

10 Andre took $53.90 from his bank account to buy a skateboard. Now his balance is $136.45. How much money did he have in the bank before he bought the skateboard?

11 In 1984, 37,290,870 American households got cable television. By 1994, 60,483,600 households had cable television. About how many more households had cable TV in 1994 than in 1984?

12 The Millers went to Ocean World. They bought two adult tickets at $7 each and three children's tickets at $4 each. They paid $3 to park their car, $10 for snacks, and $5 for a toy shark. How much did they spend at Ocean World?

13 Priscilla makes clown puppets. Each puppet needs seven buttons. If Priscilla has 32 buttons, how many clown puppets can she make?

14 Felipe bought six pairs of socks. Each pair cost $3, including tax. He gave the clerk $20. How much change should he receive?

15 Darren ordered concert tickets over the phone. Tickets cost $9 each. Darren paid a service charge of $3 to cover the cost of mailing the tickets to his home. He spent a total of $30. How many tickets did he order?

Cumulative Review
Use after Lesson 73.

Copy the list of ordered pairs, but replace each *x* or *y* with the correct number. Then graph each set of ordered pairs.

1 $x \longrightarrow \boxed{-2} \longrightarrow y$

(5, *y*), (7, *y*), (*x*, 4), (*x*, 3), (3, *y*), (*x*, 1)

2 $x \longrightarrow \boxed{\times 3} \longrightarrow y$

(2, *y*), (5, *y*), (*x*, 9), (*x*, 3), (6, *y*), (*x*, 12)

Find the value of *y* in each composite function machine.

3 $6 \longrightarrow \boxed{+2} \longrightarrow n \longrightarrow \boxed{\times 5} \longrightarrow y$

4 $27 \longrightarrow \boxed{\div 9} \longrightarrow n \longrightarrow \boxed{\times 2} \longrightarrow y$

5 $25 \longrightarrow \boxed{-10} \longrightarrow n \longrightarrow \boxed{\div 3} \longrightarrow y$

Solve these problems. Watch the signs.

6
$$\begin{array}{r} 32{,}469 \\ + \ 28{,}047 \\ \hline \end{array}$$

7
$$\begin{array}{r} 6024 \\ - \ 1296 \\ \hline \end{array}$$

8
$$\begin{array}{r} \$35.08 \\ + \ 27.55 \\ \hline \end{array}$$

9
$$\begin{array}{r} \$40.00 \\ - \ 7.88 \\ \hline \end{array}$$

10 $7\overline{)63}$

11
$$\begin{array}{r} 8 \\ \times \ 8 \\ \hline \end{array}$$

12
$$\begin{array}{r} 10 \\ \times \ 9 \\ \hline \end{array}$$

13 $6\overline{)44}$

14
$$\begin{array}{r} \$\ 4.12 \\ + \ 30.97 \\ \hline \end{array}$$

15 $4\overline{)38}$

16
$$\begin{array}{r} 156{,}033 \\ + \ 280{,}829 \\ \hline \end{array}$$

17
$$\begin{array}{r} 800 \\ - \ 257 \\ \hline \end{array}$$

18
$$\begin{array}{r} 5119 \\ - \ 4973 \\ \hline \end{array}$$

19
$$\begin{array}{r} 80{,}451 \\ + \ 39{,}859 \\ \hline \end{array}$$

20 $9\overline{)85}$

21
$$\begin{array}{r} 10 \\ \times \ 3 \\ \hline \end{array}$$

22
$$\begin{array}{r} \$\ 2.05 \\ + \ 32.83 \\ \hline \end{array}$$

23
$$\begin{array}{r} \$70.20 \\ - \ 9.43 \\ \hline \end{array}$$

24 $8\overline{)49}$

25
$$\begin{array}{r} 53{,}705 \\ + \ 27{,}486 \\ \hline \end{array}$$

Cumulative Review
Use after Lesson 77.

In each case, tell whether the lines are *parallel*, *perpendicular*, or *neither*.

1

2

3

4

5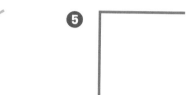

6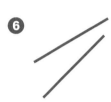

Identify and draw each polygon.

7 It has three sides and a right angle.

8 It has four equal sides but no right angles.

9 It has eight sides.

10 It is a quadrilateral with only one pair of parallel sides.

11 It is a quadrilateral with two pairs of parallel sides.

Trace each figure. Tell how many lines of symmetry it has.

12

13

14

15

Cumulative Review

Use after Lesson 82.

Tell whether the figures are *congruent*, *similar*, or *neither*.

1

2

3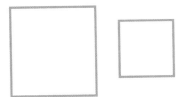

4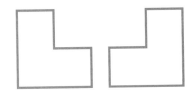

Multiply.

5 10 × 8

6 10 × 36

7 100 × 582

8 1000 × 24

9 10 × 100

10 100 × 100

11 1000 × 1000

12 10,000 × 100

13 1,000 × 100,000

14 1,000,000 × 100

15 100,000 × 10,000

16 10,000 × 10,000

17 40 × 100

18 300 × 600

19 200 × 9000

Complete each statement.

20 6 meters = ▨ centimeters

21 5 liters = ▨ milliliters

22 34 kilometers = ▨ meters

23 82 centimeters = ▨ millimeters

Solve these problems.

24 An outdoor sports stadium has 80 sections. Each section has 400 seats. How many seats are in the stadium?

25 Mr. Jenks has 70 dairy cows. Each cow gives about 10 liters of milk a week. How much milk do the cows give in a week?

Cumulative Review

Use after Lesson 88.

Multiply. Solve for *n*.

1 $800 \times 50 = n$

2 $1,000 \times 10,000 = n$

3 $300 \times 600 = n$

4 $10 \times 47 = n$

5 $90 \times 7000 = n$

6 $100 \times 5142 = n$

7 $6 \times 70,000 = n$

8 $62 \times 100 = n$

9 $2000 \times 100 = n$

10 $100 \times 449 = n$

11 $7000 \times 8000 = n$

12 $703 \times 1000 = n$

13 $10,000 \times 30 = n$

14 $123 \times 100 = n$

15 $900 \times 90,000 = n$

16 $500 \times 20,000 = n$

Round to the nearest ten.

17 71

18 36

19 55

20 322

Round to the nearest hundred.

21 739

22 260

23 1296

24 650

Round to the nearest thousand.

25 4867

26 2075

27 34,624

28 8554

Approximate to solve these problems.

29 Tariq wants to buy four blocks of modeling clay for $2.77 (277 cents) each. He has $15. Does he have enough money for the clay?

30 Drew's heart beats about 76 times every minute. He says that his heart beats over 100,000 times a day. Is he right? (There are 60 minutes in one hour and 24 hours in one day.)

Cumulative Review
Use after Lesson 91.

Approximate to choose the correct answer.

1
$$43 \\ \times\ 29$$

a. 927

b. 1657

c. 1247

2
$$84 \\ \times\ 76$$

a. 56,724

b. 6384

c. 7204

3
$$196 \\ \times\ 88$$

a. 153,618

b. 17,248

c. 1948

4
$$408 \\ \times\ 61$$

a. 24,888

b. 30,608

c. 20,758

Multiply.

5
$$33 \\ \times\ 3$$

6
$$81 \\ \times\ 3$$

7
$$17 \\ \times\ 9$$

8
$$16 \\ \times\ 8$$

9
$$52 \\ \times\ 6$$

10
$$96 \\ \times\ 4$$

11
$$77 \\ \times\ 2$$

12
$$23 \\ \times\ 7$$

13
$$68 \\ \times\ 8$$

14
$$82 \\ \times\ 7$$

15
$$60 \\ \times\ 9$$

16
$$18 \\ \times\ 4$$

17
$$43 \\ \times\ 5$$

18
$$462 \\ \times\ 4$$

19
$$751 \\ \times\ 8$$

20
$$119 \\ \times\ 8$$

21
$$309 \\ \times\ 2$$

22
$$284 \\ \times\ 5$$

23
$$518 \\ \times\ 3$$

24
$$841 \\ \times\ 5$$

25
$$676 \\ \times\ 7$$

26
$$934 \\ \times\ 9$$

27
$$604 \\ \times\ 6$$

28
$$953 \\ \times\ 3$$

Solve these problems.

29 How many pounds in 38 tons?

30 How many feet in 5 miles?

Cumulative Review

Use after Lesson 95.

Multiply.

①   53
× 36

②   81
× 93

③   57
× 42

④   29
× 15

⑤   86
× 70

⑥   44
× 54

⑦   73
× 12

⑧   85
× 31

⑨   60
× 58

⑩   48
× 67

⑪   423
× 29

⑫   621
× 14

⑬   167
× 15

⑭   218
× 50

⑮   505
× 49

⑯   209
× 12

⑰   843
× 37

⑱   600
× 89

⑲   430
× 70

⑳   891
× 15

Solve these problems.

㉑ A rectangle is 73 meters long and 51 meters wide.

  a. What is the area of the rectangle?

  b. What is the perimeter of the rectangle?

㉒ A square is 25 centimeters on a side. What is the area of the square?

㉓ A case of cat food has six rows with nine cans in each row. How many cans are in 12 cases?

㉔ A National Basketball Association (NBA) professional team has 12 players. How many players are there on the 29 teams that make up the NBA?

㉕ Fourteen buses each took 52 people to a baseball game. How many people rode the buses all together?

Cumulative Review

Use after Lesson 100.

Multiply.

1 435	**2** 618	**3** 792	**4** 636	**5** 307
× 531	× 420	× 300	× 859	× 370

6 742	**7** 210	**8** 1272	**9** 5419	**10** 54,073
× 802	× 448	× 3086	× 8672	× 209

Solve for *n*. Watch the signs.

11 $8 + 5 = n$ **12** $11 - n = 4$ **13** $7 \div 7 = n$

14 $7 + n = 15$ **15** $24 \div 3 = n$ **16** $17 - n = 9$

17 $n = 3 \times 10$ **18** $30 \div n = 5$ **19** $8 \times 0 = n$

20 $7 + n = 13$ **21** $n = 13 - 5$ **22** $48 \div 6 = n$

Use the menu to answer the questions.

The Snack Shack    (All prices include tax!)

Sandwiches	Side Orders	Drinks
Tuna..................$3.25	French Fries............$1.50	Milk..................$ .60
Turkey...............$4.50	Garden Salad........$1.75	Lemonade........$ .85
Salami..............$3.75	Cole Slaw................$ .95	Iced Tea...........$ .70
Cheese.............$2.60	Applesauce............$ .75	Soda................$1.10

---

23 What is the most money you can spend on a sandwich, a side order, and a drink?

24 What is the least money you can spend on a sandwich, a side order, and a drink?

25 RaeLynn has $4.80 to spend on lunch. If she orders a tuna sandwich, what side order and drink can she also get?

Cumulative Review
Use after Lesson 103.

Solve these problems.

On the highway, Alex travels about 60 miles in one hour. His car can go about 27 miles on 1 gallon of gasoline. The tank holds 18 gallons.

1 About how far can Alex travel on one tankful of gasoline?

2 About how far does he travel in four hours on the highway?

3 Alex is planning a trip. He estimates that it will take 18 hours of driving time. About how many miles long is the trip?

4 Can Alex make it there on two tankfuls of gasoline?

5 A gallon of paint covers about 400 square feet. Dan is going to paint a wall that is 36 feet long and 11 feet high. He wants to put on two coats. Will 1 gallon of paint be enough for the job?

6 A jar of pickles costs $2.67. How much will eight jars of pickles cost?

7 Paper comes in packs of 500 sheets. How many sheets of paper will Lina have if she buys 20 packs?

8 All 475 students from Bell Top School are going on a field trip. They are traveling by bus. Each bus can seat 45 students. It costs $98 to rent each bus for the day.

   a. Will 11 buses be too few, just enough, or too many?

   b. How many extra seats, or how many seats too few, will there be?

   c. How much will it cost to rent 11 buses for the day?

Find the area and the perimeter.

9 A rectangle has a length of 5 cm and a width of 2 cm.

10 A square has a side of 4 cm.

Cumulative Review

Use after Lesson 107.

Divide. Watch for remainders.

1 $4\overline{)35}$ **2** $7\overline{)40}$ **3** $2\overline{)15}$ **4** $9\overline{)66}$

5 $6\overline{)30}$ **6** $8\overline{)68}$ **7** $3\overline{)25}$ **8** $5\overline{)33}$

9 $4\overline{)27}$ **10** $7\overline{)49}$ **11** $2\overline{)9}$ **12** $9\overline{)56}$

13 $6\overline{)41}$ **14** $8\overline{)53}$ **15** $3\overline{)15}$ **16** $6\overline{)59}$

17 $8\overline{)15}$ **18** $5\overline{)47}$ **19** $1\overline{)4}$ **20** $9\overline{)84}$

Approximate to solve these problems.

21 Sound travels about 1100 feet in one second. At that rate, about how far does sound travel in one minute?

22 It takes one year for Earth to travel one time around the sun. This is a distance of about 965 million kilometers. About how many kilometers has Earth traveled since you were born?

Find the area and the perimeter.

23 74 mm

11 mm

24 10 mm

Solve for *n*. Watch the signs.

25 $42 \div 6 = n$ **26** $n \div 4 = 8$

27 $n = 15 - 7$ **28** $8 + n = 8$

29 $n \times 6 = 0$ **30** $64 \div 8 = n$

Cumulative Review
Use after Lesson 112.

Solve for *n*. Watch the signs.

1 $32 \div n = 8$ **2** $n \div 7 = 6$ **3** $n = 21 \div 7$

4 $63 \div 9 = n$ **5** $54 \div 6 = n$ **6** $18 \div n = 6$

7 $n \div 3 = 3$ **8** $n = 36 \div 6$ **9** $12 \div n = 3$

10 $n \div 5 = 8$ **11** $n = 5 \div 5$ **12** $16 \div 2 = n$

Add or subtract.

13	**14**	**15**	**16**	**17**
699	296	10,281	21,649	15,829
+ 431	− 154	− 8,479	+ 14,298	− 12,969

Divide. Check your answers.

18 $165 \div 5$ **19** $728 \div 7$ **20** $303 \div 4$ **21** $961 \div 6$

22 $994 \div 9$ **23** $305 \div 5$ **24** $453 \div 2$ **25** $288 \div 3$

26 $842 \div 7$ **27** $791 \div 8$ **28** $297 \div 4$ **29** $490 \div 5$

Solve these problems.

30 Six lemons cost 90¢. How much is one lemon?

31 Three stamps cost 96¢. How much is that per stamp?

32 Four jugs of cider cost $7.56 (756¢). How much is that per jug?

33 Two T-shirts cost $18. How much is one T-shirt?

34 An 8-ounce jar of olives costs $3.28 (328¢). How much is that per ounce?

35 A 5-pound bag of rice costs $1.25 (125¢). A 9-pound bag of rice costs $1.98 (198¢). Which bag is the better buy? Why?

Cumulative Review
Use after Lesson 116.

What time is it . . .

① 15 minutes after 5:50 P.M.?

② 40 minutes after 6:25 A.M.?

③ 20 minutes before 1:05 P.M.?

④ 55 minutes before 2:40 A.M.?

How much time has gone by . . .

⑤ between 3:05 P.M. and 7:30 P.M.?

⑥ between noon and 4:45 P.M.?

⑦ between 10:25 A.M. and 1:00 P.M.?

⑧ between 11:40 P.M. and 2:10 A.M.?

In each case, tell whether the lines are *parallel*, *perpendicular*, or *neither*.

⑨ **⑩**  **⑪**

Tell whether the figures are *congruent*, *similar*, or *neither*.

⑫  **⑬**  **⑭**

Divide and check.

⑮ 4)615

⑯ 5)7126

⑰ 8)2000

⑱ 1)378

⑲ 3)1296

⑳ 7)1492

Cumulative Review
Use after Lesson 122.

Look at the graph. What are the coordinates of these points?

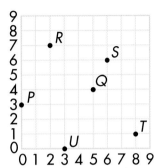

① P **②** Q **③** R **④** S **⑤** T **⑥** U

Multiply.

⑦ 100 × 7

⑧ 10 × 45

⑨ 100 × 100

⑩ 1000 × 693

⑪ 10,000 × 10,000

⑫ 3000 × 4000

⑬ 100,000 × 10,000

⑭ 50,000 × 30,000

⑮ 1,000,000 × 900

Solve these problems.

⑯ A rectangular pool is 75 feet long and 48 feet wide.

    a. What is the area of the pool?

    b. What is the perimeter of the pool?

⑰ A square table is 167 centimeters on a side.

    a. What is the area of the table?

    b. What is the perimeter of the table?

⑱ A rectangle has an area of 216 square meters. Two sides of the rectangle are 8 meters each. How long are the other two sides?

⑲ A square has a perimeter of 32 feet. How long is one side?

Divide. Use shortcuts when you can.

⑳ 6)420

㉑ 4)300

㉒ 5)715

㉓ 9)632

㉔ 3)612

㉕ 7)444

Cumulative Review

Use after Lesson 125.

Solve these problems.

1 Dana paid $2.45 (245¢) for seven postcards. How much did each postcard cost?

2 Simon bought four tortillas for 72¢. How much should six tortillas cost?

3 Adam needs 46 candles for his father's birthday cake. Candles come in packages of ten.

    a. How many packages should he buy?

    b. How many extra candles will he have?

4 Felice bowled three games. Her scores were 87, 106, and 128. What was her average score for the three games?

5 Mr. Glazer drove 310 miles in five hours. What was the average number of miles he drove each hour?

Find the mean of each set of numbers.

6 14, 16, 18, 13, 24

7 55, 66, 33, 88, 22, 77, 44

8 3253, 3542, 3425, 3244, 3526

Solve for _n_.

9 $90 \div 9 = n$ **10** $54 \div 6 = n$

11 $0 \times 1 = n$ **12** $5 + n = 13$

13 $n \times 4 = 24$ **14** $n \div 7 = 6$

15 $27 + n = 54$ **16** $18 \div n = 3$

17 $81 \div n = 9$ **18** $59 - n = 21$

19 $49 \div n = 7$ **20** $8 \times n = 64$

Cumulative Review
Use after Lesson 131.

Solve these problems without dividing. Use the information to the right to help you.

1 24)576

2 61)3965

3 150)900

4 98)8722

5 43)2365

6 34)578

7 6)900

8 89)8722

$61 \times 65 = 3965$	$89 \times 98 = 8722$
$55 \times 43 = 2365$	$24 \times 24 = 576$
$17 \times 34 = 578$	$6 \times 150 = 900$

Choose the correct answer without dividing.

9 13)65   **a.** 3   **b.** 4   **c.** 5   **d.** 6   **e.** 7

10 22)484   **a.** 10   **b.** 15   **c.** 20   **d.** 22   **e.** 25

11 250)2000   **a.** 8   **b.** 10   **c.** 12   **d.** 14   **e.** 16

12 18)288   **a.** 15   **b.** 16   **c.** 17   **d.** 18   **e.** 19

Solve.

13 List five prime numbers between 1 and 20.

14 List five composite numbers between 20 and 30.

15 List five numbers between 1 and 20 that have exactly two factors.

16 List five numbers between 20 and 30 that have more than two factors.

List all the factors of each number.

17 8   **18** 9   **19** 12   **20** 27

Cumulative Review
Use after Lesson 136.

Find the mean for each set of numbers.

1 11, 11, 11, 11, 11

2 4, 8, 12, 16, 20, 24, 28

3 100, 200, 300, 400

4 37, 44, 27, 39, 43

Complete each statement.

5 If something cannot happen, the probability is ■.

6 If something is certain to happen, the probability is ■.

7 If you flip a coin, the probability of getting heads is ■.

8 If you roll a 0–5 cube, the probability of getting a 4 is ■.

What fraction of the set is shaded?

9 ○ ○ ○ ○ ○

10 ▢ ▢ ▢ ▢ ▢ ▢ ▢

11 ▽ ▽ ▽ ▽ ▽ ▽ ▽ ▽ ▽

12 ⇨ ⇨

Solve.

13 $\frac{1}{2}$ of 14

14 $\frac{1}{3}$ of 15

15 $\frac{1}{4}$ of 28

16 $\frac{2}{3}$ of 15

17 $\frac{1}{5}$ of 50

18 $\frac{1}{8}$ of 32

19 $\frac{3}{10}$ of 50

20 $\frac{7}{8}$ of 32

Cumulative Review

Use after Lesson 140.

Complete each equivalent fraction.

1 $\dfrac{1}{2} = \dfrac{\blacksquare}{8}$

2 $\dfrac{\blacksquare}{5} = \dfrac{4}{20}$

3 $\dfrac{2}{3} = \dfrac{6}{\blacksquare}$

4 $\dfrac{5}{\blacksquare} = \dfrac{25}{35}$

5 $\dfrac{3}{10} = \dfrac{\blacksquare}{100}$

6 $\dfrac{3}{8} = \dfrac{\blacksquare}{56}$

7 $\dfrac{3}{4} = \dfrac{21}{\blacksquare}$

8 $\dfrac{4}{7} = \dfrac{400}{\blacksquare}$

Replace ● with <, >, or =.

9 $\dfrac{1}{2}$ ● $\dfrac{1}{3}$

10 $\dfrac{2}{3}$ ● $\dfrac{10}{12}$

11 $\dfrac{2}{3}$ ● $\dfrac{6}{9}$

12 $\dfrac{5}{10}$ ● $\dfrac{4}{8}$

13 $\dfrac{3}{10}$ ● $\dfrac{3}{5}$

14 $\dfrac{1}{6}$ ● $\dfrac{1}{4}$

15 $\dfrac{3}{4}$ ● $\dfrac{7}{8}$

16 $\dfrac{11}{12}$ ● $\dfrac{1}{2}$

Write a mixed number to show how many.

17

18

19

20

Rewrite each mixed number as an improper fraction.

21 $3\dfrac{1}{3}$ **22** $4\dfrac{4}{7}$ **23** $1\dfrac{5}{8}$ **24** $2\dfrac{5}{6}$ **25** $6\dfrac{7}{10}$

Rewrite each improper fraction as a mixed number.

26 $\dfrac{11}{5}$ **27** $\dfrac{17}{3}$ **28** $\dfrac{14}{9}$ **29** $\dfrac{13}{2}$ **30** $\dfrac{15}{4}$

Cumulative Review
Use after Lesson 144.

Estimate the length. Then measure to the nearest $\frac{1}{8}$ inch.

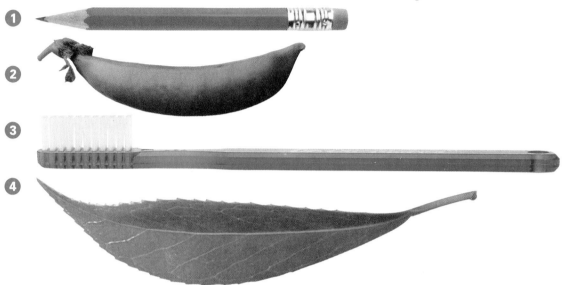

1

2

3

4

Add or subtract.

5 $\frac{1}{3} + \frac{1}{3}$

6 $\frac{3}{8} + \frac{4}{8}$

7 $\frac{3}{10} + \frac{4}{10}$

8 $\frac{9}{12} - \frac{4}{12}$

9 $\frac{7}{8} - \frac{6}{8}$

10 $\frac{9}{10} - \frac{6}{10}$

11 $\frac{3}{5} - \frac{1}{5}$

12 $\frac{4}{9} + \frac{4}{9}$

Write in standard form.

13 4 ones, 3 tenths, and 9 hundredths

14 8 tens, 2 ones, and 6 tenths

15 9 hundreds, 4 tens, 0 ones, 7 tenths, and 8 hundredths

16 7 thousands, 5 tens, 1 tenth, and 8 hundredths

Add.

17 20 + 5 + 0.3 + 0.09

18 70 + 1 + 0.6 + 0.02

19 10 + 4 + 0.6 + 0.01

20 50 + 4 + 0.9 + 0.07

Cumulative Review
Use after Lesson 148.

Write each amount as a decimal.

1 4 dimes and 5 cents

2 9 cents

3 7 dimes

4 0 dimes and 3 cents

5 60 cents

6 1 cent

Order the decimals from least to greatest.

7 0.12, 2.01, 1.02, 0.21

8 0.473, 0.309, 0.2, 0.07

9 1.083, 0.854, 0.9, 1.6, 0.44

10 0.926, 0.6, 0.29, 0.602, 0.91

Solve. Watch the signs.

11 468 + 694

12 5591 ÷ 8

13 $12.00 − $9.52

14 84 × 57

15 62,057 + 8,409

16 7124 − 5806

17 428 × 63

18 907 ÷ 4

19 40,000 × 90

Solve these problems.

20 Guy has $418.91 in his checking account. He writes a check for $39.74 to buy a telephone. How much money does he have left in his account?

21 Zola spent $30 for six pairs of tights. If she bought two more pairs of tights, how much would she spend all together?

22 Randy has 15 cousins. Two thirds of them live in Maine. How many of his cousins live in Maine?

23 A play lasts 2 hours and 55 minutes. If it begins at 2:30 P.M., what time will it end?

24 Alyssa had $1\frac{1}{2}$ pounds of clay. She used $\frac{1}{4}$ pound to make beads. How much clay is left?

25 Mrs. Bellini wants to buy three magazines for $2.50 each. How much change should she receive from a $10 bill?

Cumulative Review

Use after Lesson 153.

Copy and complete the chart.

	Item	Cents		Dollars and Cents	
		Price for 1	Price for 10	Price for 1	Price for 10
1	bolt	49¢	■	■	■
2	tack	13¢	■	■	■
3	nail	8¢	■	■	■
4	screw	24¢	■	■	■
5	hook	77¢	■	■	■
6	washer	11¢	■	■	■

Multiply.

7 10×6.7

8 100×0.45

9 10×63.08

10 100×1.085

11 10×3.27

12 1000×7.9

13 100×71

14 1000×32.61

15 100×8.4

16 1000×2.852

17 100×7.43

18 1000×0.104

Divide.

19 $34 \div 10$

20 $3.4 \div 10$

21 $0.34 \div 10$

22 $4.17 \div 10$

23 $19 \div 100$

24 $2.8 \div 100$

25 $0.56 \div 100$

26 $2065 \div 100$

27 $4 \div 1000$

28 $62 \div 1000$

29 $7.35 \div 1000$

30 $4307 \div 1000$

Rewrite each mixed number as an improper fraction.

31 $2\frac{1}{3}$

32 $3\frac{3}{5}$

33 $1\frac{4}{7}$

34 $8\frac{1}{6}$

35 $5\frac{7}{10}$

Rewrite each improper fraction as a mixed number.

36 $\frac{19}{5}$

37 $\frac{22}{3}$

38 $\frac{16}{9}$

39 $\frac{17}{2}$

40 $\frac{21}{4}$

Cumulative Review

Use after Lesson 156.

Tell the length of each object in millimeters, then in centimeters.

1

2

3

4

Add or subtract.

5 5.24
      + 69.4

6 6.7
      − 0.81

7 8.14
      − 6.932

8 21.05
      + 7.85

9 11
      − 3.4

Solve for *n*.

10 $3.15 + 8.2 = n$

11 $43.06 − 9.7 = n$

12 $0.64 + 1.7 = n$

13 $10.4 − 0.7 = n$

14 $10 − 6.254 = n$

15 $0.7 − 0.13 = n$

16 $5.48 + 23 = n$

17 $32.62 + 9.09 = n$

18 $6.8 + 4.32 = n$

Multiply or divide.

19 4.05×13

20 8.2×5.03

21 0.61×45

22 $69.2 \div 100$

23 $1.25 \div 10$

24 $17.84 \div 1000$

Complete each statement.

25 4 g = ■ kg

26 52 g = ■ kg

27 7.8 kg = ■ g

28 6 mL = ■ L

29 0.05 L = ■ mL

30 750 mL = ■ L

Metric System

Length		Weight (mass)		Liquid Volume (capacity)	
millimeter (mm)	0.001 m	milligram (mg)	0.001 g	milliliter (mL)	0.001 L
centimeter (cm)	0.01 m	centigram (cg)	0.01 g	centiliter (cL)	0.01 L
decimeter (dm)	0.1 m	decigram (dg)	0.1 g	deciliter (dL)	0.1 L
meter (m)	1 m	gram (g)	1 g	liter (L)	1 L
dekameter (dam)	10 m	dekagram (dag)	10 g	dekaliter (daL)	10 L
hectometer (hm)	100 m	hectogram (hg)	100 g	hectoliter (hL)	100 L
kilometer (km)	1000 m	kilogram (kg)	1000 g	kiloliter (kL)	1000 L

◆ **Meaning of Metric Prefixes**

milli	one thousandth	A millimeter is one thousandth of a meter.
centi	one hundredth	A centiliter is one hundredth of a liter.
deci	one tenth	A decigram is one tenth of a gram.
deka	ten	A dekaliter is ten liters.
hecto	one hundred	A hectometer is one hundred meters.
kilo	one thousand	A kilogram is one thousand grams.

◆ **Units of area are derived from units of length.**

square centimeter (cm²) $1 \text{ cm}^2 = 0.0001 \text{ m}^2$

square meter (m²) $1 \text{ m}^2 = 10,000 \text{ cm}^2$

hectare (ha) $1 \text{ ha} = 10,000 \text{ m}^2$

square kilometer (km²) $1 \text{ km}^2 = 1,000,000 \text{ m}^2$

Examples:

The area of this square is
1 square centimeter.

A square 1 meter long on a side has an area of 1 square meter.

A square 100 meters long on a side has an area of 1 hectare.

A square 1 kilometer long on a side has an area of 1 square kilometer.

◆ **Units of volume can also be derived from units of length.**

cubic centimeter (cm³)

cubic meter (m³)   1 m³ = 1,000,000 cm³

Examples:

The volume of this cube is
1 cubic centimeter.

A cube 1 meter long on a side has a volume of 1 cubic meter.

◆ **Descriptions of some common units:**

kilometer	*You can walk a kilometer in about 12 minutes.*
meter	*Most classroom doors are about 1 meter wide.*
centimeter	*This line segment is 1 centimeter long.* ———
millimeter	*This line segment is 1 millimeter long.* ▪
liter	*Four average-sized glasses hold about 1 liter of liquid all together.*
milliliter	*This cube holds about 1 milliliter of liquid.*

kilogram	*A pair of size-10 men's shoes weighs about 1 kilogram.*
gram	*A nickel weighs about 5 grams.*

Customary System

◆ Length

inch (in.)	1 in. =	$\frac{1}{12}$ ft
		$\frac{1}{36}$ yd
foot (ft)	1 ft =	12 in.
		$\frac{1}{3}$ yd
yard (yd)	1 yd =	36 in.
		3 ft
mile (mi)	1 mi =	5280 ft
		1760 yd

◆ Area

square inch (sq in. or in.²)		
square foot (sq ft or ft²)	1 ft² =	144 in.²
square yard (sq yd or yd²)	1 yd² =	9 ft²
acre (A)	1 A =	4840 yd²
square mile (sq mi or mi²)	1 mi² =	640 A

◆ Weight

ounce (oz)	1 oz =	$\frac{1}{16}$ lb
pound (lb)	1 lb =	16 oz
ton (T)	1 T =	2000 lb

◆ Volume

cubic inch (cu in. or in.³)		
cubic foot (cu ft or ft³)	1 ft³ =	1728 in.³
cubic yard (cu yd or yd³)	1 yd³ =	27 ft³

◆ Liquid Volume (capacity)

fluid ounce (fl oz)	1 fl oz =	$\frac{1}{8}$ cup	**quart** (qt)	1 qt =	32 fl oz
cup (c)	1 c =	8 fl oz			4 c
		$\frac{1}{2}$ pt			$\frac{1}{4}$ gal
pint (pt)	1 pt =	16 fl oz	**gallon** (gal)	1 gal =	128 fl oz
		2 c			16 c
		$\frac{1}{2}$ qt			8 pt
					4 qt

◆ Descriptions of some common units:

mile *You can walk a mile in about 30 minutes.*

yard *Most classroom doors are about 1 yard wide.*

foot *This book is about 1 foot long.*

inch *This line segment is 1 inch long.*

gallon  **quart**  **pint**

You can buy milk, orange juice, and other drinks in several sizes of containers.

cup *One average-sized glass holds about 1 cup of liquid.*

ton *A small car weighs about 1 ton.*

pound *Three apples weigh about 1 pound.*

ounce *A marble weighs about 1 ounce.*

A

addend A number that is added to another number to make a sum. For example:

$$35 \text{ —— addend}$$
$$+ 48 \text{ —— addend}$$
$$\overline{83} \text{ —— sum}$$

$$7 + 8 = 15 \text{ —— sum}$$
addend
addend

algorithm A step-by-step way to solve a certain type of problem.

approximation An answer to a mathematical problem that is not precise but is close enough for the purpose. Sometimes an approximate answer is more useful than a precise answer. (See *estimate*.)

area The number of square units inside a figure. The area of this rectangle is 6 square centimeters:

3 cm

2 cm

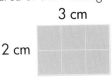

arrow operation A way to show an action of a function machine. In 7 —— ×8 —→ 56 , 7 goes in and is multiplied by 8 to give 56. The function rule in this case is ×8. In the operation 6 ←— −5 —— 11 , 11 goes in and 5 is subtracted from it to give 6. The function rule in this case is −5.

average A number that can sometimes be used to describe a group of numbers. To find the average of a set of numbers, add the numbers and divide the sum by how many numbers were added. The average of 5, 6, 6, 8, and 10 is 7 (5 + 6 + 6 + 8 + 10 = 35, and 35 ÷ 5 = 7). (Also called *mean*.)

axes (of a graph) The two zero lines of a graph that give the coordinates of points. The horizontal axis is the *x*-axis. The vertical axis is the *y*-axis.

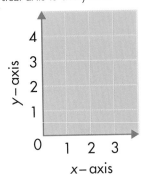

B

balance 1. The amount of money remaining in an account. 2. A double-pan balance is an instrument used to measure weight.

bound A number that an answer must be greater than or less than. For example, 36 × 21 must be less than 40 × 30, or 1200. So 1200 is an upper bound. The answer to 36 × 21 must be greater than 30 × 20, or 600. So 600 is a lower bound.

C

circle A figure (in a plane) in which all points are the same distance from a point called the *center*. In this figure, for example, points *A*, *B*, and *C* are the same distance from point *O*, the center of the circle:

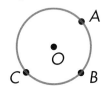

common multiple A number that is a multiple of two or more numbers.

composite function A function with two or more operations.

For example:

composite number A whole number having factors other than 1 and itself.

congruent Figures that are the same size and shape; that is, they fit perfectly when placed on top of each other. These triangles are congruent:

These triangles are not congruent:

coordinates Numbers that give the position of a point on a graph. In the figure shown, for example, the coordinates of point *A* are (2, 3). 2 is the *x*-coordinate. 3 is the *y*-coordinate.

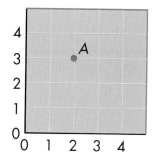

cylinder A space figure with two faces that are circles.

decimal point A dot used to separate the ones digit from the tenths digit.

denominator The part of a fraction written below the line. The part written above the line is called the *numerator*. The denominator tells how many equal parts something is divided into; the numerator tells how many of those parts are being referred to. In the fraction $\frac{3}{4}$ the denominator (4) indicates that something is divided into four equal parts. The numerator (3) says to consider three of those parts.

diameter A line segment, going through the center of a circle, that starts at one point on the circle and ends at the opposite point on the circle. (Also, the length of that line segment.) *AB* is a diameter of this circle.

difference The amount by which one number is greater or less than another. For example:

```
  43 —— minuend        10 − 7 = 3 —— difference
− 16 —— subtrahend              └──── subtrahend
  27 —— difference               └──── minuend
```

digit Any of the numbers 0, 1, 2, 3, 4, 5, 6, 7, 8, and 9. The two digits in 15 are 1 and 5.

dividend A number that is divided by a divisor. For example:

```
6 ÷ 3 = 2 —— quotient       divisor —— 8)347 —— dividend
      └——— divisor                      32
  └——————— dividend                     27
                                        24
                                         3   —— quotient
```

divisor A number that a dividend is divided by. (See *dividend*.)

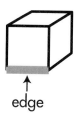

edge The segment where two faces of a space figure meet.

edge

equilateral triangle A triangle with all three sides the same length. For example:

equivalent fractions Fractions that have the same value. For example, $\frac{2}{6}$, $\frac{4}{12}$, and $\frac{1}{3}$ are equivalent fractions.

estimate A judgment about the size or quantity of something. (Also, to make such a judgment.) Sometimes it is more useful to make an estimate than to measure or count precisely. (See *approximation*.)

even number Any multiple of 2. The numbers 0, 2, 4, 6, 8, and so on are even numbers.

face A flat surface of a space figure.

factor A number that is multiplied by another number. (See *multiplicand*.)

fraction Examples of fractions are $\frac{1}{2}$, $\frac{3}{4}$, and $\frac{7}{8}$. The fraction $\frac{3}{4}$ means that something is divided into four equal parts and that we are considering three of those parts. (See *denominator* and *numerator*.)

function machine A machine (sometimes imaginary) that does the same thing to every number that is put into it. (See *arrow operation*.)

function rule See *arrow operation*.

half line See *ray*.

heptagon A polygon with seven sides.

hexagon A polygon with six sides.

hundredth If a whole is divided into 100 equal parts, each part is one hundredth of the whole.

improper fraction A fraction whose numerator is greater than or equal to its denominator.

inequality A statement that tells which of two numbers is greater. For example, 4 > 3 is read "4 is greater than 3," and 3 + 6 < 10 is read "3 plus 6 is less than 10."

intersecting lines Lines that meet. In this figure, lines *AB* and *CD* intersect at point *E*:

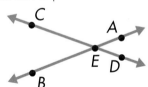

inverse operation An operation that undoes the results of another operation. Multiplication and division are inverse operations; addition and subtraction are inverse operations.

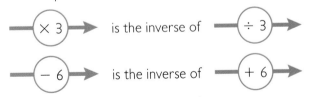

isosceles triangle A triangle with two equal sides. These are isosceles triangles:

line of symmetry A line on which a figure can be folded into two congruent parts.

line segment A part of a line with two endpoints. For example, *AB* is a line segment; points *A* and *B* are its endpoints.

mean See *average*.

median The middle number in a group of numbers when they are listed in order from least to greatest. If there are two numbers in the middle, their average is the median. The median of 2, 3, 4, 5, and 6 is 4.

minuend A number from which another number is subtracted. (See *difference*.)

mixed number A number made up of a whole number and a fraction. The numbers $1\frac{1}{2}$, $2\frac{3}{4}$, and $7\frac{7}{8}$ are mixed numbers.

mode The number that occurs most often in a set of numbers. The mode of 1, 2, 3, 1, 4, and 1 is 1.

multiple A number that is some whole number of times another number. 12 is a multiple of 3 because 3 × 4 = 12.

multiplicand A number that is multiplied by another number, the multiplier. For example:

The multiplier and multiplicand are also called the factors of the product.

multiplier See *multiplicand*.

numerator The part of a fraction written above the line. (See *denominator*.)

octagon

polygon

octagon A polygon with eight sides.

odd number A whole number that is not a multiple of 2. All whole numbers that are not even are odd. The numbers 1, 3, 5, 7, 9, 11, and so on are odd numbers.

ordered pair Two numbers written so that one is considered before the other. Coordinates of points are written as ordered pairs, with the *x*-coordinate written first, then the *y*-coordinate. For example: (3, 4). (See *coordinates*.)

parallel lines Lines in a plane that do not intersect. Lines *AB* and *CD* are parallel:

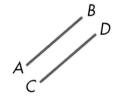

Lines *EF* and *GH* are not parallel:

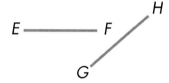

parallelogram A quadrilateral with opposite sides parallel and congruent.

parentheses A pair of symbols ( ) used to show in which order operations should be done. For example, (3 × 5) + 7 says to multiply 5 by 3 and then add 7. 3 × (5 + 7) says to add 5 and 7 and then multiply by 3.

partial product The product that comes from multiplying the multiplicand by one of the digits of the multiplier. For example:

```
    36
  × 12
  ────
    72      This partial product comes from
            multiplying 36 by 2 ones.
    36      This partial product comes from
  ────      multiplying 36 by 1 ten.
   432      The product comes from
            adding the partial products.
```

pentagon A polygon with five sides.

perimeter The distance around a figure. The perimeter of this rectangle is 6 cm:

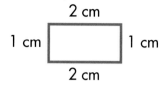

perpendicular lines Lines that intersect at right angles. These lines are perpendicular:

So are these:

But these are not:

place value The value of a digit in a number. The value of 7 in 27 is 7 ones; in 74 its value is 70, or 7 tens; and in 726 its value is 700, or 7 hundreds.

polygon A certain kind of figure with straight sides. These figures are polygons:

These are not:

Here are the names of some common polygons and the number of their sides:

Number of Sides	Name
3	triangle
4	quadrilateral
5	pentagon—a regular pentagon has five equal sides:

Glossary • **577**

6   hexagon—a regular hexagon
       has six equal sides:

8   octagon—a regular octagon
       has eight equal sides:

prime number A whole number divisible only by 1 and itself.

prism A space figure with two parallel, congruent faces, called bases. These are prisms:

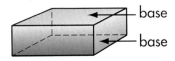

probability How likely it is that something will happen. The probability that a certain thing will happen is a fraction. The denominator is the total number of possible things that can happen, and the numerator is the number of ways this particular thing can happen. The probability that an ordinary coin will land on heads when it is flipped is about $\frac{1}{2}$.

product The result of multiplying two numbers together. (See *multiplicand*.)

profit In a business, the money that is left after all expenses have been paid.

pyramid A space figure formed by connecting points of a polygon to a point not in the plane of the polygon. These are pyramids:

quadrilateral A polygon with four sides.

quotient The result (other than the remainder) of dividing one number by another number. (See *dividend*.)

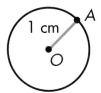

radius A line segment that goes from the center of a circle to a point on the circle. (Also, the length of such a segment.) *OA* is a radius of the circle shown here. The radius of this circle is 1 centimeter.

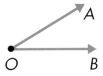

ray A set of points that has one endpoint and extends without end in one direction. In the figure below, *OA* and *OB* are rays.

rectangle A quadrilateral in which all four angles are right angles.

reflection A change in the location of a figure when it is flipped over a line.

regroup To rename a number to make adding and subtracting easier.

Example of regrouping in subtraction:

$$\begin{array}{r} \overset{1\ \ 15}{\cancel{2}\cancel{5}} \\ -\ 17 \\ \hline 8 \end{array}$$

(To subtract in the ones column, 2 tens and 5 is regrouped as 1 ten and 15.)

Example of regrouping in addition:

$$\begin{array}{r} \overset{1}{2}96 \\ +\ 442 \\ \hline 738 \end{array}$$

(After the tens column is added, 13 tens is regrouped as 1 hundred and 3 tens.)

relation signs The three basic relation signs are > (greater than), < (less than), and = (equal to). (See *inequality*.)

remainder A number less than the divisor that remains after the dividend has been divided by the divisor as many times as possible. For example, when you divide 25 by 4, the quotient is 6 with a remainder of 1:

right angle An angle that forms a square corner. These are right angles:

These are not:

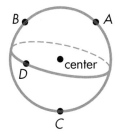

rotation A change in the location of a figure when it is turned in a circle around a point.

rounding Changing a number to another number that is easier to work with and that is close enough for the purpose. (See *approximation*.)

sphere A space figure with all points the same distance from a point called the *center*.

square A quadrilateral with four equal sides and four equal angles.

subtrahend A number that is subtracted from another number. (See *difference*.)

sum The result of adding two or more numbers. (See *addend*.)

symmetrical figure A figure that can be divided in half so that each half looks exactly like the other. (See *line of symmetry*.)

tenth If a whole is divided into ten equal parts, each part is one tenth of the whole.

translation A change in the location of a figure when it is placed on top of another figure.

trapezoid A quadrilateral with exactly one pair of parallel sides. This is a trapezoid:

triangle A polygon that has three sides.

unit cost The cost of one item or one specified amount of an item. If 20 pencils cost 40¢, then the unit cost is 2¢ for each pencil. If dog food costs $9 for 3 kilograms, then the unit cost is $3 per kilogram.

vertex 1. The point where two rays meet. 2. The point of intersection of two sides of a polygon. 3. The point of intersection of three edges of a space figure.

volume The number of cubic units that fit inside a space figure.

whole number The numbers that we use to show how many (0, 1, 2, 3, and so on). The number 3 is a whole number, but $3\frac{1}{2}$ and 4.5 are not whole numbers.

Z

zero The number that tells how many things there are when there aren't any. Any number times 0 is 0 and any number plus 0 is that number: $0 \times 3 = 0$ and $0 + 3 = 3$.

ACKNOWLEDGMENTS

Photo Credits

Unit Openers/Table of Contents
pp. 2-3, Aaron Haupt; **98-99**, Aaron Haupt; **174-175**, Super Stock; **266-267**, Super Stock; **354-355**, Gabe Palmer/The Stock Market; **430-431**, Jennifer Graylock/Photo Nats.

Unit 1
p. 12, Photo Disc, Inc.; **16**, Super Stock; **18**, Photo Disc, Inc.; **19** Super Stock; **22**, Photo Disc, Inc.; **24**, ©Fotosmith; **29**, ©Timothy Fuller; **30**, Mark E. Gibson/Visuals Unlimited; **31**, Photo Disc, Inc.; **34–35**, Photo Disc, Inc.; **38**, Photo Disc, Inc.; **43**, ©Fotosmith; **45**, ©Timothy Fuller; **48–49**, Photo Disc, Inc.; **52**, William Rosenthal; **53**, Photo Disc, Inc.; **56–57**, Photo Disc, Inc.; **58**, Aaron Haupt; **60**, Courtesy, The White House Historical Society; **61–63**, Photo Disc, Inc.; **64**, ©Timothy Fuller; **70**, FOTOfactory; **72**, FOTOfactory; **73**, ©Fotosmith; **76**, FOTOfactory; **79**, Super Stock; **82–83**, Photo Disc, Inc.; **84**, Super Stock; **93**, FOTOfactory; **97**, Photo Disc, Inc.

Unit 2
p. 100, Super Stock; **111**, ©Fotosmith; **114**, Photo Disc, Inc.; **116**, FOTOfactory; **120**, Photo Disc, Inc.; **121**, ©Fotosmith; **124**, FOTOfactory; **126**, ©Fotosmith; **127**, ©Fotosmith; **129**, FOTOfactory; **133**, ©Fotosmith; **134**, Photo Disc, Inc.; **135**, Photo Edit; **139**, Photo Disc, Inc.; **140**, Super Stock; **141**, ©Fotosmith; **142**, Super Stock; **146**, Photo Disc, Inc.; **148**, Super Stock; **149**, FOTOfactory; **150**, Super Stock; **151**, FOTOfactory; **152**, FPG; **153**, FOTOfactory; **156**, Photo Disc, Inc.; **160–162**, Super Stock; **163**, ©Fotosmith; **165**, Photo Disc, Inc.; **169**, Super Stock.

Unit 3
p. 177, NASA/FPG; **191**, Photo Disc, Inc.; **197**, Photo Disc, Inc.; **201**, Photo Disc, Inc.; **208**, Super Stock; **211**, Super Stock; **213**, Photo Disc, Inc.; **215**, Francois Gohier/Photo Researchers; **217**, Super Stock; **219**, Photo Disc, Inc.; **224**, (l) Leslye Bordem/Photo Edit, (r) Corn Growers Association/Photo Edit; **230**, Photo Disc, Inc.; **232**, (tl) Super Stock, (lc) Super Stock, (lb) Super Stock, (tc) Super Stock, (tr) Super Stock, (rc) Super Stock, (cc) Photo Disc, Inc., (bc) Photo Disc, Inc., (rb) Photo Disc, Inc.; **245**, Photo Disc, Inc.; **254**, Photo Disc, Inc.; **259**, Photo Edit; **264**, William Rosenthal; **265**, Wiliam Rosenthal.

Unit 4
pp. 270–271, Super Stock; **273**, ©Fotosmith; **275**, ©Fotosmith; **276–277**, Photo Disc, Inc.; **280**, Super Stock; **283**, Super Stock; **284**, Super Stock; **290**, Photo Disc, Inc.; **295**, Photo Disc, Inc.; **298**, ©Fotosmith; **306**, FOTOfactory; **309**, Photo Disc, Inc.; **311**, ©Fotosmith; **314**, William Rosenthal; **321**, ©Fotosmith; **324**, FOTOfactory; **329**, Photo Researches; **335**, Photo Disc, Inc.; **337**, Photo Disc, Inc.; **343**, Photo Disc, Inc.; **348**, Super Stock; **349**, Super Stock; **351**, William Rosenthal; **352**, Super Stock; **353**, David Young Wolff/Photo Edit.

Unit 5
pp. 356–357, FOTOfactory; **359**, ©Fotosmith; **361**, ©Fotosmith; **368**, Super Stock; **370**, Suzanne Arms-Wimberly/Jeroboam; **371**, Roy Saigley/Jeroboam; **372**, ©Fotosmith; **377**, Tim Davis/Photo Researchers; **379**, Photo Disc, Inc.; **380**, J. Mann/Jeroboam; **382**, Photo Disc, Inc.; **384**, FOTOfactory; **388–389**, Photo Edit; **391**, Photo Disc, Inc.; **392**, Dick Luria/FPG; **395**, (t) ©Fotosmith, (b) Photo Disc, Inc.; **398**, Jonathan Nourok/Photo Edit; **408**, Bonnie Kamin/Photo Edit; **410–411**, Photo Edit; **413**, Tom Carter/ Jeroboam; **414**, Photo Disc, Inc.; **425**, Frank Siteman/Jeroboam; **427**, Photo Disc, Inc.; **428**, D. & I. MacDonald/Jeroboam.

Unit 6
p. 433, Photo Disc, Inc.; **435**, ©Fotosmith; **438**, FOTOfactory; **444**, FOTOfactory; **446**, FOTOfactory; **447**, ©Fotosmith; **448**, (t) Photo Disc, Inc., (b) FOTOfactory; **449**, **452**, William Rosenthal; **453**, (tl) FOTOfactory; **455**, Photo Edit; **458**, ©Fotosmith; **462**, FOTOfactory; **463**, ©Fotosmith; **467**, ©Fotosmith; **473**, ©Fotosmith; **475**, ©Fotosmith; **479**, Photo Disc, Inc.; **480**, Photo Disc, Inc.; **482**, FOTOfactory; **484**, Photo Disc, Inc.; **489**, Photo Disc, Inc.; **491**, Photo Disc, Inc.; **493**, (tl)(c)William Rosenthal, (bl) Photo Disc, Inc., (tr) William Rosenthal, (rc) FOTOfactory, (br) William Rosenthal; **495**, FOTOfactory; **496**, Photo Disc, Inc.; **499**, Photo Disc, Inc.; **500**, Deborah Davis/Photo Edit; **504**, Photo Disc, Inc.; **506**, Super Stock; **507**, ©Fotosmith; **510**, Tony Freeman/Photo Edit; **512**, Photo Disc, Inc.; **514**, FOTOfactory; **515**, ©Fotosmith; **517**, Photo Edit; **518**, Tony Freeman/Photo Edit; **519**, ©Fotosmith; **522**, William Rosenthal; **524**, Photo Disc, Inc.; **528**, Michael Newman/Photo Edit.

Cumulative Review
p. 565, FOTOfactory; **566**, Photo Disc, Inc.; **569**, Photo Disc, Inc.; **573**, (t) FOTOfactory, (c) Super Stock, (b) Photo Disc, Inc.

Technical Illustration Credits
Units 1–6 Ruttle Graphics, Inc.

Illustration Credits
pp. 4-7, 520-521, Mimi Powers; **8-9, 138, 209, 303, 318-319, 446, 487, 490, 494**, Katy Farmer; **20, 228, 573**, Joel Snider; **23, 26-28, 54, 71, 115**, Jane Caminos; **52, 124**, Bill Colrus; **68, 89, 92, 95, 268, 502-503, 532-533**, John Edwards & Associates; **286**, Kate Gorman; **383**, Joseph Loughman; **478, 479, 488, 489, 505, 513** Jim Shough.

Cover Credits
Front cover photo, Timothy Fuller; **Design and Illustration front cover,** Morgan-Cain & Associates; **Back cover photo,** Timothy Fuller and Fotosmith.